International Security

To Agnès, with love

International Security

The Contemporary Agenda

Second Edition

ROLAND DANNREUTHER

polity

First published in 2013 by Polity Press

Polity Press
65 Bridge Street
Cambridge CB2 1UR, UK

Polity Press
350 Main Street
Malden, MA 02148, USA

ISBN-13: 978-0-7456-5376-1
ISBN-13: 978-0-7456-5377-8 (pb)

A catalogue record for this book is available from the British Library.

Typeset in 9.5 on 13 pt Swift Light
by Toppan Best-set Premedia Limited
Printed and bound in Great Britain by MPG Books Group Limited, Bodmin, Cornwall

The publisher has used its best endeavours to ensure that the URLs for external websites referred to in this book are correct and active at the time of going to press. However, the publisher has no responsibility for the websites and can make no guarantee that a site will remain live or that the content is or will remain appropriate.

Every effort has been made to trace all copyright holders, but if any have been inadvertently overlooked the publisher will be pleased to include any necessary credits in any subsequent reprint or edition.

For further information on Polity, visit our website: www.politybooks.com

Contents

Figures and Tables

Figures

Tables

Acknowledgements

The author would like to thank Jamie Allinson for his editorial and scholarly support for the second edition, in particular for his writing of a new chapter on 'Cyber-Warfare and the New Spaces of Security' (chapter 11) and for his updating of the section on critical security studies in chapter 2. Jamie Allinson is currently postdoctoral research and teaching fellow at the Department of Politics and International Relations, University of Westminster.

Introduction: The Challenge of the New Security Agenda

The subject of international security has been in ferment since the end of the Cold War. The concept of international security, rather than the more traditional concept of national security, is itself a product of the Cold War. It expressed the conviction that national security in the age of mutual nuclear vulnerability could only be achieved through international cooperation and a minimal degree of shared understandings. For those intellectually engaged in seeking to overcome the mutual threat of global destruction, the challenges and responsibilities were considerable. There was, though, an enviable clarity of purpose and academic endeavour. The focus for the study of international security was on clearly defined enemies, whether to the east or the west; the threat was of the use, or the threat of use, of deadly military force; the fear was of the uncontrolled escalation of military conflict to a nuclear level. The historical imagination was forged by the memory of the ideological confrontations and total wars of the twentieth century, with their untold brutalities and millions of dead, and the consequent need to avoid a third world war which could be fatal for the future of all humanity. The study of international security was effectively synonymous with military strategy and statecraft. It was the age of the intellectual dominance of 'strategic studies'.

The end of the Cold War radically undermined this clarity of purpose and unity of intellectual endeavour. The collapse of the Soviet state, and its military power, dethroned the strategic centrality of the militarized and nuclearized bipolar confrontation. As with much else in international relations, the study of international security lost its focus and many of its seemingly fixed foundations. The assumption of the identification of the state with security was assaulted from many quarters: some argued that the individual's security must be paramount and that the state is more of a threat than a guarantor of such individual security; others prioritized the security concerns of subnational communities and ethnic or identity groups or the threats posed to the global economy or the environment. The scope and subject matter of international security proliferated in a similarly expansive way. Although the fear of violent conflict never completely disappeared, there were increasingly non-military competitors for attention, such as the threat of environmental degradation, economic disparities and chronic poverty, diseases such as HIV/Aids, transnational crime and international migration.

This more diverse, seemingly chaotic and prolix subject area of 'security studies' is variously interpreted as evidence of deep intellectual confusion or as an act of intellectual liberation. Traditionalists, seeking to defend the gains of strategic studies during the Cold War period, condemn the excessive expansion of the field of security studies which threatens to 'destroy its intellectual coherence and make it difficult to devise solutions to any of these important problems' (Walt 1991: 213). Lawrence Freedman has similarly articulated the widespread concern, found not only among traditional scholars but also among many left and radical critics, about the dangers of dealing with a whole range of non-military topics in a 'conceptual framework geared toward coping with military threats' (Freedman 1998: 51; see also Deudney 1990). Wideners and other enthusiasts for a new security agenda generally reject these reservations and highlight the advantages in including and prioritizing non-military threats to international security. Richard Ullmann argued as early as 1983 that the traditional tendency to prioritize military threats 'conveys a profoundly false image of reality' which 'causes states to concentrate on military threats and to ignore other and perhaps more harmful dangers . . . and contributes to a pervasive militarization of international relations that in the long run can only increase global insecurity' (Ullmann 1983: 129; see also N. Brown 1989; Mathews 1989; Haftendorn 1991).

Aims and objectives

The debate between 'traditionalists' and 'wideners' has conventionally been framed as a debate over the meaning of the concept of security (Little 1981; Buzan 1991, 1997). But it is just as much a more parochial internal academic concern over the appropriate definition of the borders of the subdiscipline of security studies. Indeed, the claim that the concept of security is at stake in this debate is questionable. David Baldwin (1997) has convincingly argued that security as 'the absence or low level of threats to acquired values' is a relatively empty and meaningless concept unless the context of its usage is clearly specified and it is established which values are being protected, for whom, and against which threats. As such, whether something is properly a security issue, which should be included within security studies, should be determined not *a priori* but only through the empirical detail of the particular instance through which security concerns are raised. It is this more pragmatic approach which this book adopts, concentrating less on abstract theorizing, and more on engaging with the theoretically informed empirical detail of the arguments and their relative strength and cogency in promoting new priorities and perspectives in international security.

The guiding spirit of this book is to bring across some of the intellectual excitement and dynamism of the post-Cold War rethinking of international security. The key criterion for the selection of topics is the quality of the arguments and the ways in which these arguments have challenged our understanding of the outside world and of contemporary international security. This is not to eschew theoretical sophistication or to ignore the major theoretical debates, but to integrate theoretical analysis with key contemporary issues which have direct meaning for our everyday existence and for international politics more generally. There is also no cult of the 'new' in the proposed focus on the 'contemporary security agenda'. The attribution of 'newness' to certain perceived threats is not that such threats have no parallel or historical antecedents but that they have normally been obscured or ignored during the Cold War and have gained a 'new' immediacy and prominence in the changing post-Cold War international environment. Indeed, the 'newness' of the 'contemporary security agenda' is often a rediscovery of deeper historical continuities which the strategic narrowness and exceptional nature of the Cold War ignored or marginalized. In this sense, this study supports and celebrates the widening of security studies, its liberation from the more narrow existential concerns of the Cold War, and its closer intellectual engagement with other parts of international relations and with other academic disciplines.

This book has, though, no pretensions to comprehensiveness. This is probably impossible for one book, unless one is willing to sacrifice substance for scope, and certainly impossible for one author, whose intellectual range and expertise is necessarily limited. The choice of topics is my own selection, which certainly follows my particular intellectual interests and concerns. But the choice is also guided by a desire to provide a genuine overview of contemporary international security and by focusing on issues and arguments which strike me as being of enduring importance and broader intellectual interest. The aim is to provide an inevitably personal but insightful overview of a dynamic and evolving subject.

Content

There are four main parts to the book. The first part provides a general overview of the changing nature and conditions of international security since the end of the Cold War. Chapter 1 argues that there have been three major shifts in our understanding and conceptualization of international security since that time. These are:

- the significant reduction in the expectation of a major war between the great powers;
- the shift of global focus and attention from the East–West to the North–South axis, along with a growing scepticism about the state's role as the sole, or the most effective, security provider;

- the shift from a bipolar system to a more indeterminate system which has characteristics of unipolarity, with the US as the dominant power, as well as being increasingly multipolar, most notably with the rising power of China.

Chapter 2 provides an overview of how international relations (IR) theory has sought to provide conceptual and analytical insights into understanding these shifting dynamics in the field of international security. This theoretically focused chapter examines the growth in popularity of constructivist, liberal internationalist and critical approaches to the study of IR, which have in particular brought out the subjective and ideational dimensions of international security. However, it is argued that the historical sociological approach and the realist normative tradition provide a useful corrective for an overoptimistic expectation of a radically transformative shift in international behaviour.

The remaining three parts provide a more empirical and focused analysis where the themes and issues raised in the first section are directly confronted. Part II addresses the core issues of war, intervention and security alliances in the post-Cold War context. It examines the claims of the emergence of distinctively new forms of warfare – the so-called new wars (chapter 3), the proposed emergence of a norm of humanitarian intervention (chapter 4), and the changing role of key alliances and security communities in managing conflict and war (chapter 5). These are major post-Cold War themes, reflecting the concerns over the rise of ethnic and religious-inspired wars in sub-Saharan Africa and elsewhere, and the complex debates over the justification and efficacy of military interventions, such as in Somalia, Kosovo and Libya, which have involved security organizations such as NATO and the UN.

Part III covers the broad area of environmental security, which has been a particularly dynamic and innovative post-Cold War area of research and concern. Chapter 6 provides an overview of the meaning and content of the concept of environmental security. The following chapter develops these general concerns with a comparative case-study of the implications for international security of the struggle for access to water and to oil. Chapter 8 deals with one of the most controversial 'new' security issues: the security implications of international migration.

The fourth and final part of the book focuses on the implications of the terrorist attacks of 9/11 and how the issues of international terrorism (chapter 9), the proliferation of weapons of mass destruction (WMD) (chapter 10), and the fears over cyber-warfare (chapter 11) have come to dominate the contemporary security agenda. Again, none of these issues is completely novel – terrorism and WMD have been with us for a long time, and use and control of information has always been critical – but the events of 9/11 and the dynamics of post-Cold War international developments do bring out distinctively new concerns and fears.

The role of the security analyst

But, before delving into these substantive topics, there is a need for some self-reflection on the nature and limitations of the task. International security is an inherently difficult and complex phenomenon to define and comprehend. Some very basic questions necessarily raise themselves and require some sort of answer, however imperfect that might be: What sort of role can the academic security analyst play? Is the subject a science or an art? Can one hope for objectivity or are the limitations of time, place and culture such as to make all judgement inevitably subjective and culturally limited? Should the security analyst be at the service of those who wield power or is it their proper role to be a tireless critic of the powerful and a defender of the marginalized and the powerless? It is these fundamental concerns and issues which the rest of this chapter addresses.

The security analyst as scientist

During the Cold War, there was certainly a tendency for the strategic studies community to perceive themselves as scientists and as an 'epistemic community' providing impartial technical expertise (Adler and Barnett 1998). Their subject matter was the relatively fixed and unchanging threats of the period, and the intellectual challenge was how best to describe this external threat environment and promote the most effective and appropriate responses. But throughout the Cold War this claim of scientific objectivity never went unchallenged. It was most brilliantly caricatured in Stanley Kubrick's film *Dr Strangelove*, where the eponymous hero, reportedly drawn from the eminent nuclear strategist Herman Kahn, is the embodiment of the irrational and amoral logic of nuclear strategy, personal insecurities and a subordination of scientific objectivity to the interests of the military-industrial complex. Within academic studies, this scepticism of mainstream strategic studies developed into a strong alternative radical view, most notably in critical security studies, which eschewed claims of scientific objectivity and whose research agenda concentrated on exposing the underlying power structures and interests behind politically powerful constructions of international security (for example, see Booth 1991; Krause 1998; Wyn Jones 1999).

However, the radical claim that the security analyst cannot hope to make objective statements or be able to provide a rigorous understanding of external phenomena is not one that is supported in this book. This does not imply, as a result, a commitment to a crude empiricism but rather a defence of the need, following Kant, to treat the external world 'as if' it were real, for otherwise there is no alternative to relativism. The radical subjectivist approach does, though, correctly reveal that security is not just about 'threats out there', but that it is also about how such threats are also 'threats in the mind' and are subjectively interpreted and understood. As such, international security is a constructed reality, forged through a necessarily interactive process, where mutual perceptions and intersubjective understandings frame converging and competing conceptions of international behaviour. Arnold Wolfers, in his seminal article on national security, captured well these competing subjective and objective elements: 'The possible discrepancy between the objective and subjective connotation of the term is significant in international relations despite the fact that the chance of future attack never can be measured "objectively": it must always remain a matter of subjective evaluation and speculation' (Wolfers 1952: 485).

A further central insight of Wolfers is that security should not be considered an absolute value which one does or does not possess. The Soviet Union was one country which did attempt to achieve the illusory goal of 'absolute security' and where the costs in terms of repression, loss of freedom, human rights abuses and failed economic development are well known. A degree of insecurity is, therefore, a necessary precondition for other societal values to flourish. Security is best understood as a relative value where there are varying degrees of security and insecurity. The role of the security analyst is to try to find and promote the most appropriate balance between the two.

The radical critique of traditional strategic studies does, though, highlight an ingrained tendency or predilection to exaggerate or overemphasize security threats. As in military planning, there is an operational culture in security studies of focusing on the 'worst-case scenario', where a low probability but potentially catastrophic outcome becomes the centre of attention. The strategic debate during the Cold War about how to 'win' a nuclear war reflected this pessimistic and seemingly amoral mentality. The tendency towards making security studies a 'gloomy science' is also linked to the temptation for security analysts to reflect the interests of those who provide their funding, not least governments, who have a well-known proclivity to exaggerate security threats so as to distract attention from domestic problems.

The role of the security analyst as the fearless sceptic, who 'speaks truth to power' and exposes the exaggerated construction of external threats, is certainly a vital one. But there is also a danger of moving too far in the other direction and being excessively optimistic about the security environment, so underestimating potentially serious security threats. Governments often seek to highlight only security threats that they can deal with, while ignoring others which are just as serious but are more intractable and less able to be resolved. In addition, the historical lesson of appeasement, which was, it should be remembered, conceived as a *security* policy, is that wishful thinking can sometimes wilfully ignore real dangers. Liberal ideology and thought can often be complicit in this. Liberalism tends to explain societal violence and aggression as a form of irrationality, linked to outdated notions of power politics and state sovereignty, and to assume that peace will naturally flow from the progression of liberal norms and values. The prospect that some individuals or groups might have very rational reasons for engaging in violent conflict is sometimes difficult for the liberal imagination to comprehend (see Keen 1998). The wars of succession in the former Yugoslavia in the early 1990s provided the first strong antidote to an overoptimistic expectation of a conclusive post-Cold War international peace or the 'end of history' (Fukuyama 1992). The events of 9/11 have only confirmed this with greater vigour.

The security analyst as internationalist

The subject area of international security also raises the question as to how 'international' in perspective and outlook the security analyst can realistically expect to be. A self-critical security analyst has necessarily to be conscious of the possibilities of reflecting, rather than critically engaging and questioning, the prejudices and fears of his or her social grouping or cultural background. This is, to a certain extent, an unavoidable danger. The philosopher Thomas Nagel has argued that there is 'no view from nowhere' and that any attempt to define a view *ex specie aeternatis*, a view from the standpoint of eternity, is bound to fail (Nagel 1986). As social animals, we are all undeniably conditioned by our inherited cultural predispositions, traditions and particular processes of socialization. We are born into or become part of a particular community of values which helps to define the ways in which we understand and interpret reality. The fact that I am a white male from the periphery of Western Europe undeniably influences my outlook on international relations. Geography, history and culture have formed a distinctively British and European conceptualization of security which has undoubtedly influenced my own views.

Nevertheless, the ambition of the security analyst must be to transcend these limitations. In the field of international security, this is to recognize that there is no one privileged 'Western' standpoint or conception but that there are multiple conceptions, not only from the global South but from within the West as well. The related requirement is to recognize that international security, as against national security, is a necessarily multidimensional and complex phenomenon which resists simple categorization. One example of this, which is explored further in chapter 7, is the issue of energy or oil security. In the academic literature, there is almost an unquestioning assumption that energy security means the security of the Western oil importers and their concerns over the security of supply. Yet the issue of energy security has multiple other dimensions to consider as well. This includes, most notably, the security concerns of the oil exporters and the complex ways in which resource- and oil-rich countries frequently generate significant internal insecurities. It is also invidious to exclude the insecurities and concerns of the many millions of the poor in the world who simply do not have access to supplies of oil or other cheap and secure energy resources. Furthermore, a comprehensive security analysis should incorporate consideration of the global environment, as the rapid growth in demand for oil greatly increases environmental problems, most notably global warming. Even more fundamentally, the question of whether oil will eventually run out and bring to an end the era of cheap fuel, on which our modern fossil-fuel civilization is inordinately dependent, should not be ignored as a vital long-term security concern.

The security analyst needs therefore to attempt to provide a multidimensional and internationalist perspective, taking into account the security views and perceptions of others, but without dispensing with his or her own set of values and cultural predispositions. Thomas Nagel puts this challenge well as the need to 'combine the recognition of our contingency, our finitude, and our containment in the world with the ambition of transcendence, however limited may be our success in achieving it' (Nagel 1986: 9).

The security analyst as moralist

One aspect of this 'recognition of our contingency' is the understanding that international security policy, as with national or other security policies, is an inherently normative exercise. Given that, as argued above, security is a relative value, there is continually the question of exactly how much value to accord to security as against other values. This is essentially a moral or normative task. Again, Arnold Wolfers identified well this dimension: 'The policy of national security is primarily normative in character. It is supposed to indicate what the policy of a nation should be in order to be either expedient – a rational means to an accepted end – or moral, the best or least evil course of action' (1952: 483–4).

This normative dimension, viewing security as one value among other competing values, places international security firmly in the realm of the political. This goes against the grain of some contemporary accounts of security which tend to separate the realm of security from that of politics, and where security is evoked essentially to bring to an end political debate. This understanding of security is found in the concept of securitization (discussed more fully in chapter 3), where security is presented as a movement 'into the realm of "panic politics", where departures from the rules of normal politics justify secrecy, additional executive powers and activities that would otherwise be illegal' (Buzan 1997: 14; see also Waever 1995). This is, certainly, a legitimate definition in that it highlights how security policy is quintessentially about the prioritization of values and the appropriate allocation of scarce resources to secure those values. But its disadvantage is to limit the scope of security to the exceptional and existential and to restrict its use as an integral and everyday part of general political discourse. In practice, security concerns pervade the political, whether in terms of individual concerns for personal security, the security concerns faced by firms and large organizations, the security of supplies of food, energy or water, or the ensuring of the security of external borders. Many of these security concerns are dealt with in the mundane world of politics, and the fact that they do not necessarily generate exceptional responses, such as the mobilization of military forces, does not *a priori* negate their relevance as concerns over security.

The more general point is that the security analyst should constantly be aware of the essentially normative political challenge of the complex inter-relationship between security and other core values which a society deems to be critical to the 'good life'. To some extent, at least, the security analyst needs to engage as a political philosopher. This is because the value of security is in constant tension and interdependence with other values, most prominent of which are the values of freedom, prosperity and justice.

The linkages and trade-offs between security and freedom or liberty are probably the most apparently obvious. It is a legitimate concern for all concerned citizens that the values of freedom and liberty should not be sacrificed to the demands of security. It is unexceptional to note, but still of vital importance for any security analyst, that the pursuit of security has costs in terms of freedom. Civil liberties are eroded at times of heightened security and, even in peace and in liberal democratic societies, the security forces are significantly less open to demands of accountability and transparency than other government actors. Excessive security measures undermine freedom and thus, if freedom is to be defended and preserved, a significant degree of insecurity has to be accepted. Kenneth Waltz captures this well: 'states, like people, are insecure in proportion to the extent of their freedom. If freedom is wanted, insecurity must be accepted' (1979: 112). But the understanding of security as a force constantly eroding freedom is only a partial one. Political philosophers have also noted that security is itself a precondition of freedom, if one is to avoid what Hobbes described as the 'useless liberty' of the state of nature, in which conditions of anarchy lead to a generalized insecurity where all are fearful for their life and survival. The security–freedom relationship is, therefore, a complex one, and many of the substantive debates in political theory, such as the distinction between negative and positive freedom, are debates about the amount of freedom which is compatible with the security of individuals within society. The security analyst cannot help but make substantive judgements in this regard, seeking to establish the point at which security enhances the exercise of freedom rather than being an obstacle to that freedom.

The relationship between security and the pursuit of prosperity, a core value for all societies, is similarly complex and interdependent. Insecurity, conflict and war are uncontroversially destroyers of economic value, and security measures normally entail significant non-productive economic costs. But, as with preserving the value of freedom, so the prospects for economic improvement, which is itself dependent on permitting a relatively free flow of goods, services and people, require a significant degree of insecurity. The liberal doctrines of free trade, on which the dynamics of globalization depend, are themselves arguments against the security impediments constructed by states to inhibit such trade. Countries which spend too much on military preparation, such as the Soviet Union, ultimately pay a high economic cost. But it is also recognized that economic interdependence, with its modern incarnation in globalization, has ambiguous effects and that, as much as it benefits honest and productive businesses, it also strengthens the capacities and malign influence of global mafias and international terrorists. In addition, economic liberalization and deregulation periodically lead to economic crises which have negative global impacts, such as the 2008–9 financial crisis.

There is also a more fundamental interrelationship between security and global prosperity. This is the relatively uncontroversial link between conditions of global poverty and inequality, on the one hand, and insecurity, on the other. Development and security are, to a significant degree, mutually supportive processes, so that the richer a society becomes the more secure it should be. Liberal thought is again premised on the assumption that economic liberalization contributes to the process of political democratization which itself consolidates the 'liberal peace'. But these correlations are again more disputed and controversial than conventional wisdom suggests. Globalization and economic liberalization can themselves breed significant societal insecurities and potentially entrench the non-productive and illiberal powers of the army and the security forces.

The final part of the 'value jigsaw' is between security and justice. This is arguably the most critical and pressing of the normative challenges facing the security analyst, since it brings out most clearly the inherent inequalities of the global structure of international security. The tension here is between the claim that overcoming the injustices of the international system – most notably the enormous differentials in wealth and political power – is a precondition for international security and the claim that the demands of international security require subordinating the claims of justice to the exigencies of security. This tension is central to the 'English School' tradition in international relations where, for Hedley Bull and many of his followers, the need for order, and by implication international security, has a higher priority than claims for justice, which are, by their very nature, destabilizing for international security and, if pursued for their own sake, can lead to endemic conflict and instability (see Bull 1977). It is this consequentialist ethic that the great powers utilize to justify their preponderant power as a necessary precondition for assuming their responsibilities for ensuring international security. The countervailing perspective, though, is that it is the structural injustices which underpin these claims for hegemonic leadership that are the deeper sources of global insecurity. The underlying paradox is that justice is in continual tension with order and that in international politics injustice is both a source of insecurity and a necessary precondition for international security.

On to the study of international security . . .

The principal challenge for the analyst in the field of international security is, therefore, one of making critical judgements, both empirical and normative. It is a challenge to understand both the nature of the perceptions and the reality of the dominant security threats and concerns; to exercise judgement as to their significance and prioritization without falling into the trap of either exaggeration or underestimation, and with due attention to their multidimensional character; and to exercise moral judgement as to how security policies can promote the needs not only of international security but also of other critical values, such as freedom, prosperity and justice. This is a significant and demanding challenge, but it is also what makes the study of international security so rewarding and exciting.

Questions for Research and Discussion

1 Why has the end of the Cold War led to a 'widening' of the international security agenda?
2 What do you see as the key role and challenges of being a security analyst?
3 What are the potential areas of conflict between security and liberty? What examples can you provide?

WEBSITES

www.e-ir.info
The world's leading website for students of international relations and a good site for recent debates and contemporary analyses.

www.ciaonet.org
Columbia International Affairs Online – a very comprehensive source for theory and research in international relations, which has published a wide range of scholarship from 1991 onwards. This website requires an institutional subscription.

www.worldmapper.org
A useful collection of maps where territories are resized according to subjects such as population, income, wealth and violence.

PART I

Analytical Framework

CHAPTER 1

Thinking about Security after the Cold War

Certain events come to define a critical turning point in history, to punctuate the end of one era and to inaugurate a new and distinctively different age with all its unknown qualities and uncertainties. The end of the Cold War is undoubtedly one of these historical points. Its symbol-filled date is 1989, when a series of popular revolutions liberated East-Central Europe, dismantled the 'iron curtain', and so enfeebled the Soviet Union that the once all-powerful state disintegrated and collapsed two years later. With such a fundamental shift in the strategic landscape, security analysts naturally seized on the opportunity to think critically about the meaning and implications of the end of the Cold War for the study of international security. This chapter identifies three of the most radical of these questionings of Cold War working assumptions and principles. There is, first, the debate over the changing nature of contemporary war and, in particular, the argument that the threat of large-scale conflict between the great powers appears to have disappeared or greatly declined. Second, there are the implications of attention shifting from an East–West to a North–South axis, with the growing scepticism of the capacity of the 'state' to assume its traditional responsibility for the provision of security. And, third, there is the structural change from a bipolar world and the resultant implications for the relationship between power, security and legitimacy in international politics.

These concerns, and the wide-ranging debates and arguments they have generated, are clearly intimately linked to the transition from the Cold War to the post-Cold War period. The decline in the threat of large-scale warfare, the increasing focus on the South and state weakness, the problem of how to manage a single global hegemon while new great powers are emerging: these are all significant outcomes of the collapse of the Cold War structure. But the Cold War captures only one, and sometimes not the most important, dimension of the changing dynamics in international security. Two other global processes and longer-term developments need at the very least to be added: the material transformations linked to globalization; and the ideational and normative changes which contribute to longer-term processes such as the delegitimization of imperialism and other fundamental shifts in moral understandings of appropriate international behaviour. Neither of these two dynamics fits neatly on to the structure or the timing of the Cold War.

Trying to fit dates to globalization is controversial, with debates over whether it is a twentieth-century phenomenon or whether it has its roots in the nineteenth century or even earlier (see R. Jones 1995; Hirst 1997; Hobson 2004). However, in the late twentieth century, the most recent phase of globalization is generally recognized to have gained its initial momentum in the late 1950s and then, with the exception of the economic downturn of the 1970s, to have been in a fairly constant upward trajectory both during and beyond the Cold War. The result has been an exponential increase in the amount of goods and services traded internationally; a transformation in the opportunities for travel and communications; and a proliferation of regional and international regimes and institutions, many of which were created specifically to meet the demands of globalization. The end of the Cold War only encouraged and opened new opportunities for the process of globalization. Indeed, the main impact of the Cold War was to limit globalization to the West because of the Soviet-imposed economic autarky in the East. It was also, at least in part, the failure of the Soviet Union to adapt to the challenge of globalization which finally sealed its fate (see, for example, Wohlforth and Brooks 2000–1). The end of the Cold War thus only further invigorated and provided a more expansive stage for the dynamic of globalization.

The charting over time of more subtle normative transformations, such as the delegitimization of imperialism, is even more problematic. But the Cold War was distinctive in that, for the first time, the main hegemonic actors – the United States and the Soviet Union – self-consciously defined themselves as anti-imperialist and supported the national self-liberation of colonial states formerly controlled by Europe. This resulted in the number of states growing from the fifty-one original signatories of the United Nations Charter in 1945 to the current 193 member states. This, by its very nature, complicated international security arrangements and gave a 'voice' to peoples and nations formerly excluded from international debate. It also underlined a normative consensus that imperialism could no longer be recognized as a legitimate form of governance. This, in turn, has placed significant constraints on the actions and policies of the more powerful states in the international system and, in theory if not always in practice, strengthened the claims of the weak. Analysts have sought to identify similar cumulative ideational transformations, such as the expansion of the norms of human rights and democracy over the twentieth century, which have had similarly radical implications for international practice (on democracy, see Diamond and Plattner 1996; on human rights and humanitarian intervention, see Finnemore 2003; Wheeler 2000).

Debating the causes of the great power peace

The relative unimportance of the Cold War and the potential significance of other material and ideational shifts are illustrated by the debate over the causes for the perceived decline in the threat of large-scale warfare between the great powers. It is generally recognized that the end of the Cold War was itself a symptom rather than an independent cause of this. The threat of large-scale warfare has been a constant feature of the history of modern Europe, and the Cold War was 'fought' on the same basic assumption that such a devastating war was an ever present possibility. The historical unique-ness of the Cold War was not in the way it was conducted but in the manner of its conclusion. Unlike earlier hegemonic challenges to gain European supremacy, the confrontation ended peacefully and without recourse to war. This broke Churchill's cardinal rule that 'people talked a lot of nonsense when they said that nothing was ever settled by war. Nothing in history was ever settled except by war' (quoted in Gilbert 1983: 860–1). How then to explain this resolution of a major ideological confrontation, which, as Fred Halliday notes, was a comprehensive social, political and economic conflict, in essentially a peaceful manner (Halliday 1994: 170–90)? What more funda-mental lessons does this hold for understanding the prospects of war in the post-Cold War period?

It should be stated that not everyone is convinced that the ending of the Cold War signals a radical transformation in the conditions for war and peace. Some hold firm to the traditional (realist) rules of the game and argue that the decreasing expectation of war is only a temporary aberration and that traditional great power military competition will eventually return with a vengeance (see Mearsheimer 1990; Waltz 2000). Such critics would also tend to point to China and the substantive debate remaining about the potential military threat it poses (D. Roy 1996; Munro 1997; M. Brown et al. 2000). But these sceptics are a minority compared to those who do accept that at least the most economically and politically powerful states in the international system – the US, Europe and Japan – now enjoy the unprecedented historical luxury of not needing to prepare for war against one another. This is most markedly felt in Europe, where the process of European integration is gener-ally seen to have made war practically inconceivable between the formerly warring states of the region. For these analysts who see a critical transforma-tion in the structural conditions of international politics, the key question is what the underlying causes might be (see, for example, Van Evera 1990–1; Jervis 1991–2; Mandelbaum 1998–9).

Declining political instrumentality of war

A good starting point for thinking about this is to take Carl von Clausewitz's central insight that war is quintessentially a political activity and 'not merely an act of policy, but a true political instrument, a continuation of political intercourse, carried out with other means' (Clausewitz 1984 [1832]: 87). War is a purposeful activity and its rationale and logic are defined in terms of its political instrumentality. But Clausewitz was also one of the first to recognize that the attainment of political objectives becomes more difficult in an age of political revolution and mass democracy. With his own experience of fighting in the Prussian army against the mass popular armies of revolutionary France, he saw that now 'war, untrammelled by any conventional restraints, had broken loose in all its elemental fury' (ibid.: 593). Clausewitz was, in this sense, a prophet of the total wars of the twentieth century where whole societies became mobilized to fight for their country and for the goal of 'unconditional surrender'. Certain technological advances, most notably the invention of the railways and the machine gun, dramatically increased the bloodiness and brutality of war by making it possible to bring more soldiers to the battlefield and then to kill those soldiers in a more efficient manner. The sociologist Charles Tilly has made a rough calculation that battle deaths increased from 9,400 per year in the sixteenth century to 290,000 per year during the first half of the twentieth century (Tilly 1990: 74).

John Mueller argues that it is this experience of the totality and bloodiness of the two world wars which is the principal cause for the 'obsolescence of war' and the general realization that war has lost its political instrumentality in the management of great power relations (Mueller 1989, 2004). For other analysts, such as Martin Van Creveld, it is the subsequent development of nuclear weapons, and the gradual realization that there could be no conceivable political justification for an all-out nuclear war, that reduced the prospect of large-scale interstate war and dramatically reversed the earlier four-century increase in the scale of warfare (Van Creveld 1991a). As such, the critical turning point was the promotion by the Soviet leader Nikita Khrushchev of 'peaceful coexistence' and the subsequent development of détente between the superpowers. Kenneth Waltz extended the implicit logic of this contention to argue that 'the more nuclear weapons the better', on the basis that such nuclear proliferation would replicate globally the stability found in the superpower relationship (see chapter 10 below; and Waltz 1981). The uneasiness and reservations many have felt towards such nuclear optimism reflect a broader scepticism over whether possession of nuclear weapons and peace can be so easily conflated (Sagan and Waltz 2003: ch. 2). The fact that military planners on both sides of the iron curtain continued to prepare for a nuclear war similarly qualifies an unduly benign perception of the pacifying effects of nuclear weapons (Kissinger 1957; Freedman 1989: 87–114). But there is nevertheless much plausibility in the realist-informed claim that nuclear weapons do generally change the strategic advantage of those possessing them, increasing the advantages of defensive as against offensive warfare. This, in turn, discourages aggression and generally reduces the security dilemma faced by all states (Lynn-Jones 1995; Van Evera 1999).

Increasing economic benefits of peace

A logical counterpart to the argument of the declining political instrumentality of war is that the economic benefits of peace have correspondingly grown.

The argument of the pacific effects of high levels of economic interdependence is a foundational belief in liberal thought, with free trade and economic integration having been seen, from Adam Smith and David Ricardo onwards, to have political as well as economic benefits. The architects of the European integration process after the Second World War were driven by such convictions and were far from complacent that the mere memory of the horrors of two world wars would be sufficient to avoid further relapses into traditional European rivalries. They were convinced that peace needed to be physically constructed through the building of dense economic linkages and interdependencies so as to make it increasingly irrational to use force for the resolution of political conflicts (Haas 1958; Monnet 1978). Similar claims are also increasingly made about the dynamic of globalization, in that the deepening of global economic ties reduces the benefits of military prowess and territorial acquisition. Richard Rosecrance has expressed this as the rise of the 'trading world', which has finally gained supremacy over the more traditional 'military-territorial' world (Rosecrance 1986).

The assumed linkage between trade and peace is, though, controversial. The classic counter-example is the First World War where, contrary to the optimism of such contemporary liberals as Norman Angell, conflict developed between the two most interdependent trading nations of Germany and Great Britain (Angell 1912; Waltz 1988). Studies have also suggested that military occupation can pay economically and is not necessarily the economic burden often depicted by liberal critics of war (Mearsheimer 2001: 12; see also Labs 1997). Global capitalism tends to suffer from periodic crises and recessions, such as that of 2008–9, which exacerbate international tensions. More radical critics of globalization highlight the way that power relations of domination and coercion provide the underlying context for the seemingly apolitical and non-violent global processes of economic (neo-liberal) expansion. Even the case of European integration requires a critical recognition that it was a process actively supported by the United States and was dependent on US external security guarantees (Joffé 1984; Lundestad 1998). This was not just a US guarantee against Soviet attack but also a reassurance against potential revanchist German aggression. Without such extensive security guarantees, it would have been unlikely that France, in particular, would have been sufficiently confident to take the path of European integration.

Nevertheless, when the arguments for the benefits to be gained through economic interdependence are combined with the increased costs and loss of instrumentality of large-scale warfare, then a stronger cumulative case for the great power peace can be made. The shift in the overall strategic calculations of the relative costs and benefits to be gained through war has certainly contributed to the transformation of the European continent. This ultimately also extended as far as the Soviet Union, where it gradually became clear to Soviet elites that their relative power was being undermined by the failure to integrate with the wider world. The Soviet Union then followed China's earlier shift from a strategic posture based on relative war-fighting capabilities to one conditioned on export-oriented growth. The necessary precondition for this was to restructure relations with the West on the basis of inclusion and integration rather than on autarky and military confrontation. Economic processes were, therefore, significant forces for peace.

Towards the democratic peace?

Nevertheless, the continuing authoritarianism, nationalist self-assertion and evidence of regional bullying found in post-Cold War Russia and China weaken the confidence that the strategic cultures of both countries exclude the option of war, including large-scale war. This provides one supporting element in the argument that the most critical condition for pacific interstate relations is the presence of a community of democracies, which is furthermore demonstrated by the empirical claim that no democratic state has ever gone to war with another democratic state (Doyle 1983a, 1983b; Russett 1993; J. Ray 1995; Brown, Lynn-Jones and Miller 1996; Russett and Oneal 2001). The democratic peace thesis has gained much of its prominence through capturing the spirit and optimism of the post-Cold War period, ensuring a popularity not only within academia but among policy-makers and world leaders. The thesis also gained credibility with the significant expansion of the number of democracies from the 1970s, which culminated in the democratic liberation of East-Central Europe (Huntington 1991). With the end of the Cold War, the Kantian dream of realizing a 'democratic peace' has never seemed closer, particularly in traditionally war-torn Europe.

There are three broad arguments which have sought to provide fuller causal explanations for how peace develops from democracy. The first highlights the institutional constraints within liberal democracies which inhibit the initiation of large-scale conflict. Among these are the separation of powers, the checks and balances within the political system, and the need to engage public support for any war-making activity. All of this contrasts with dictators or authoritarian leaders, who can potentially initiate wars secretly and swiftly on their own personal whim (Russett 1993: 30–8; see also Lake 1992). The second focuses on the norms and values which distinguish liberal democracies from their authoritarian counterparts. Here the argument is that liberal democracies are habituated to the resolution of conflicts through compromise, negotiation and respect for the rule of law in their own domestic affairs. When such democracies engage with other democratic states, these norms and habits are externalized and a mutual respect for common political values precludes resort to the use of force (Doyle 1986). The third aspect highlights how these mutually respected common norms and values forge shared transnational identities, which consolidate a sense of community and common purpose among democratic states. Such 'communities of values', it is argued, are particularly evident within Europe and between Europe and the United States, where highly institutionalized European and transatlantic security communities can be found (Risse-Kappen 1995; Kahl 1998–9).

Democratic peace theory often also includes arguments about the pacific benefits of economic interdependence (Russett and Oneal 2001: ch. 4). But, as with the economic argument in the previous section, there remains the counter-argument that a simpler and more parsimonious explanation is that the brute realities of countering the Soviet threat, along with the disciplining power of the United States, are the main reasons for the pacific relations between the Western democracies (Layne 1994; Farber and Gowa 1995). The argument that liberal powers are inherently pacific in nature is also significantly questioned by the continuing predilection of liberal democracies to engage in regular military interventions against states in the developing world (Lake 1992; Reiter and Stamm 1998). Similarly, during the Cold War the United States and other Western countries frequently sought to subvert democracies in the developing world, such as in Chile or Iran. Viewed in this critical light, the democratic peace thesis has a less benign aspect, providing a comfortable ideological justification for the North to support its coercive subordination and disciplining of the global South (Barkawi and Laffey 1999; Duffield 2001).

Despite these criticisms, a plausible case can still be made that the consolidation of liberal democracy between the leading states has changed attitudes towards, and the justifications for, war between themselves. In part, this is driven by the sense of the declining utility of war and the increased economic benefits of peace. But the spread and consolidation of democracy have themselves promoted a more consensual and homogeneous political system, where there is a broader acceptance of the political status quo. In the West, anti-systemic threats to democratic states have declined both internally, heralded by the 'end of ideology' (Kirchheimer 1966), and externally, through greater cooperation. In contrast to earlier parts of the twentieth century, virulent nationalism has been delegitimized and the sense of the racial superiority of different nations no longer has the same resonance. In Europe in particular, territorial borders have lost their emotive power, so that the fate of Alsace-Lorraine or of the 'lost' German territories no longer preys on the minds of European leaders (Vasquez 1993; M. Anderson 1996; Huth 1996). The 'post-heroic' age has, thus, greatly reduced the earlier celebration of the cult of war and the glorification of the warrior.

Implications of the great power peace

By emphasizing the multiple causalities of the reduction of the prospect of large-scale interstate warfare, a more nuanced understanding is possible of the prospects for war and peace around the world. The conditions for an internal peace are strongest among the most economically developed liberal democracies, such as the United States, Europe and Japan, where there is a general satisfaction with the prevailing liberal order and a corresponding sense of the illegitimacy of the use of force in their mutual relations. For powerful new emerging powers, such as Russia, China and India, there is less evidence of such a normative shift, and territorial claims and dissatisfaction with their international status persist. In these countries, it is more the costs of war and the benefits from engagement with the global economy which act as the stronger constraint on the contemplation of large-scale military confrontation.

Overall, though, the general robustness of the great power peace is a significant factor in understanding contemporary international security. It does, and should, engender a degree of confidence that traditional patterns of virulently nationalistic interstate conflict have been disrupted and potentially overcome in key regions in the world. But this should not breed complacency. There is, first, the inherent problem of predicting future developments and thus the longer-term durability of any liberal or great power peace. Even optimistic advocates of the liberal peace, such as Francis Fukuyama, are troubled as to whether the rationalism and materialism of modern liberal societies might dissolve the more irrational ideals, such as national pride, which are the integral bonds of a strong community (Fukuyama 1992). Robert Cooper, in a similar spirit of liberal self-doubt, has suggested that while 'war can destroy states. It may be peace that will destroy society' (1999: 25). War is also recognized to be a double-edged sword, with the threat of war, and the promotion of the external 'other', helping to form strong and cohesive societies (Schmitt 1976; Hartmann 1982). The rise of anti-migrant sentiment and other xenophobic tensions in Europe suggests that older atavistic values and sentiments have been far from dissolved. The economic recession engendered by the global financial crisis of 2008–9 has only added to these negative global trends.

The second important qualification is that the end of the Cold War and the sense of a great power peace has not eliminated the perception of threat and fear in international politics. Prominent sociologists such as Ulrich Beck and Anthony Giddens have identified increasing levels of anxiety in individuals and communities facing a 'world risk society' or a 'runaway world' (Beck 1999; Giddens 1999). What is notable about these new threat perceptions is the multiple ways in which they are linked to the poorer countries in the South. There is a clearly discernible shift, with the East–West axis of the Cold War increasingly being displaced by a post-Cold War North–South axis. It is this shift in strategic attention both in popular perceptions and in security studies which is the second highly significant development in the contemporary study of international security.

From East–West to North–South: The state as the problem?

The great power peace thesis itself implies that it is in the South that the residual source of the threat of war is to be found. In the poorer developing world, the strategic logic and dampening influence of nuclear weapons do not apply, and it is the technologically backward but bloodily efficient Kalashnikov rifle or even the machete which does most of the killing (Institute of International Studies 2005). The economic disincentives to waging war are also less strong and, particularly when valuable natural resources can potentially be plundered, there is a strong economic rationale for engaging in violent conflict (Keen 1998; Collier 2000). Political conditions also tend towards either authoritarianism or a democracy so weakly consolidated as to exacerbate, rather than resolve, intersocietal conflict (Snyder 2000). Yet, even in the South, the incidence of classical interstate war has greatly declined. But this has been counterbalanced by the rise of complex and long-lasting civil wars which have, as in West Africa or Central Asia, led to chronic regional insecurity (Hironaka 2005). It is in regard to such regions that the notion of the 'failed state' has been evoked and the very resilience and sustainability of the modern state has been called into question (Zartman 1995; Milliken 2003).

The centrality of the North–South dimension to contemporary international security is evident in much of the rest of this book. In Part II, a central issue is contemporary war being perceived to occur almost exclusively in the South, in the 'zones of turmoil', as against the 'zones of peace' in the North (see, for example, Goldgeier and McFaul 1992; Singer and Wildavsky 1993). In the book's third part, which focuses on environmental degradation, the struggle for natural resources and differential demographic growth, it is similarly from the South that the main challenges and potential sources of threat are generally perceived, at least by those in the North, to emanate. In the final part, the concerns over international terrorism and the proliferation of weapons of mass destruction have a clearly Southern focus, particularly after 9/11. Overall, the end of the Cold War has seen an increased concern about those regions residing in what the former US Defense Secretary Zbigniew Brzezinski once called the 'arc of crisis', from East and Central Asia, through the Middle East, to sub-Saharan Africa.

However, a crude binary opposition between North and South should not be taken too far and must be qualified. These are only ever inexact and imperfect designations, and the North and the South are deeply interdependent in many ways. The fact that it was in the heart of Europe, in the former Yugoslavia, that some of the most violent post-Cold War conflict took place suggests that 'zones of turmoil' can be found in the North. Similarly, the relative stability of the interstate peace in Latin America, traditionally seen as an integral part of the South, suggests that peace extends beyond the 'democratic' North (Hurrell 1998). Furthermore, the South is clearly a highly heterogeneous grouping, representing not only very diverging cultures but also considerable differentials in wealth. The difference in the potential for growth between, for example, East Asia and sub-Saharan Africa or the Middle East is already large and growing. In the North, fundamental differences in strategic culture and outlook were highlighted in the transatlantic turmoil between the US and France and Germany over the war in Iraq in 2003 (see Kagan 2003). The North–South division is necessarily a crude and potentially misleading depiction of international relations.

Nevertheless, there remains an analytic utility to a North–South categorization as an interpretive tool for conceptualizing post-Cold War international security. There are two reasons for this: first, the North–South division exposes the main structural economic inequalities, including the continuing deprivation and poverty of many millions of people, which represent a significant root cause of global insecurity; and, second, the division identifies the significant cultural variations and differing trajectories of state formation between the Northern core and the Southern periphery.

Economic inequality and international security

During the Cold War, strategic centrality was accorded to the division between the pro-capitalist and pro-communist ideological camps. There was an alternative socio-economic map of the world divided between the rich and the poor, but its strategic significance tended to be limited to those working within a more radical and leftist tradition (see, for example, Frank 1967; Wallerstein 1974a). Figure 1.1 illustrates the ways in which the North has gained in power and wealth. In 1500, Europe and Asia were relatively similar in their wealth while the Americas were economically marginal. By 1990, the advanced industrialized states, most notably the United States, Europe and Japan, had obtained a disproportionate, some would say obscene, wealth when compared to developing states, such as those in sub-Saharan Africa or South Asia. The projected wealth distribution by 2015 highlights the economic successes of East Asia, particularly that of China, and that has, as a consequence, undermined the crude deterministic theories of Marxist dependency theory, which saw the North deliberately seeking to impoverish the South, but the continuing structural inhibitions against fully 'catching up' with the North remain powerful (Hall and Zhao 1994). It is salutary to note that, in the twentieth century, only Japan managed to move definitively from the third to the first world, and even today China remains still a largely developing country.

The inherent moral injustice of the continuing extreme disparities of wealth is difficult to deny and is intermittently recognized by the North at

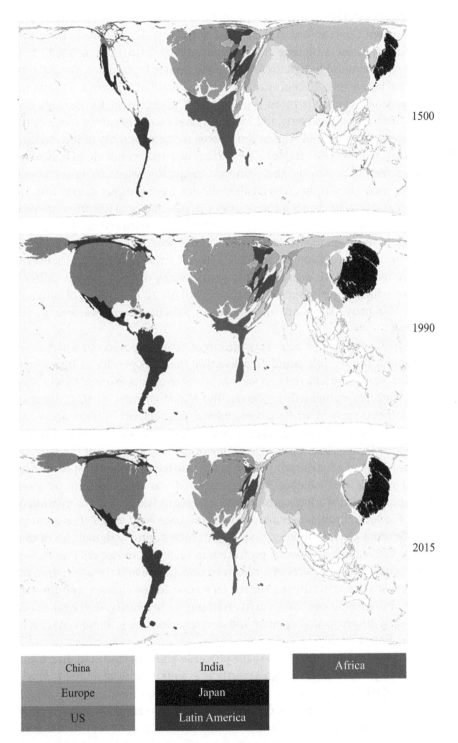

China

Europe

US

India

Japan

Latin America

Africa

Figure 1.1 Comparative wealth maps: 1500, 1990, and 2015
Source: Worldmapper: http://www.worldmapper.org/index.html.

the international level. This can be seen, for instance, in the 2000 Millennium Development Goals agreed at the United Nations, which include halving the numbers of those suffering extreme poverty by 2015 (Annan 2000). But whether such moral indignation, and the responses it generates, should also translate into a specific concern that such inequalities represent a threat to international security is more problematic. The argument for the security implications of such poverty and inequality has certainly gained in strength since the end of the Cold War, as can be seen in the popularity of the concept of human security (see chapter 2 for further discussion). But there is a counter-argument that poverty and economic inequality, while being reprehensible in their own right, nevertheless do not have a direct causal link to conflict and insecurity. For a recent example, international terrorists, as seen with the followers of al-Qaeda, are more often drawn from the more educated and Westernized middle classes than from the poor.

But while this argument qualifies a direct causal connection between poverty and conflict, it does not take away the many more subtle and indirect ways in which poverty and inequality contribute to conditions of international insecurity. There are three ways in which this can be seen to be the case.

The first relates to the actual conditions of absolute poverty in which over 1 billion of the world's population live. For these people, life is inherently insecure, since they lack the necessary protection against external shocks and suffer multiple vulnerabilities internally. Minor changes in their natural environment, such as when environmental degradation inhibits access to clean water or to primary energy resources, can be matters of life and death (see Homer-Dixon 1991; Dalby 2009). One of the major causes of the poverty and insecurity of a significant proportion of this population is the prevalence of endemic societal violence, civil conflict and war. The destitute refugee, fleeing home and work because of the ravages of war, is the international symbol of such chronic insecurity (Dowty and Loescher 1996). Refugee status also identifies the moral obligation, freely entered into by signatories of the Geneva Convention, to provide protection to such victims (see chapter 8). For these people, the prospects of a return to normal life and the alleviation of their poverty are critically dependent on a cessation of violence and the fostering of the conditions for security. Without such security, development is impossible. International security and development are, in these ways, inextricably linked.

The second dimension relates to the processes and trajectories leading from poverty to prosperity. Although security is essential for development, development does not necessarily lead to security. Indeed, as depicted in Karl Polanyi's (1944) seminal work on European industrialization, development is always a wrenching, disruptive and socially destabilizing force, which brings with it significant increases in inequality, personal alienation and societal conflict. The security and stability that development offers are prizes to be gained at the end of the process. The intermediate security risks and challenges are, though, frequently forgotten, as seen in the overly optimistic projections of modernization theories in the 1950s and the neo-liberal prescriptions of the 1980s and 1990s (So 1990: 17–87; Stiglitz 2002). The ideological battles between liberalism, Marxism and fascism of Europe's past were ultimately the quarrelling godchildren of the disruptive process of development (see Mazower 1999). It is not surprising that post-Second World War developing countries face similar challenges of managing the process of development while seeking to contain the multiple conflicts generated by this very process (Huntington 1968).

The third dimension emphasizes the security implications of the subjective, rather than the strictly objective, perceptions of poverty and inequality. One of the major insights in conflict theory is that it is relative deprivation, rather than absolute deprivation, which is the most significant determinant of conflict (Gurr 1970; Finkel and Rule 1986). In a similar way, it is those countries and societies which have embarked on the path of development which tend to be the more acutely aware of the injustices of the global distribution of wealth and political power. Countries such as China and India have the opportunity to assert themselves against the legacies of imperial domination and racial discrimination. This dynamic can be illustrated further by those post-Soviet and Middle Eastern states which are neighbours of the European Union but have no immediate prospect of joining it (see Zielonka 2001; Dannreuther 2004). These states do not generally suffer from the absolute poverty found in many sub-Saharan countries, but they are relatively poor compared to their neighbour, the European Union, with about one-tenth of the GDP per capita of the EU average. The resentments and fears this generates between the EU and its neighbours can be mutually reinforcing. For those outside its prosperity and freedoms, the Union can be perceived as an exclusionary body whose purpose is to place obstacles to migration or trade. For those within the Union, their poorer neighbours can be viewed as the principal sources of criminality, illegal migration, ethnic conflict and terrorism and thus as significant potential threats to EU security. Such fears and mutual concerns, driven by a mix of substantial inequalities and regional proximity, breed a broader regional insecurity, which contributed to the popular revolts of the so-called Arab Spring in 2011.

Cultural and political diversity and international security

As well as the North–South divide being defined in economic terms, there is a cultural dimension which has gained increasing importance since the end of the Cold War. This is partly because, with the decline of the capitalist–communist ideological division, the ethno-cultural roots of many regional and international conflicts have become more evident. The outward manifestation of the post-Cold War wars of succession in the former Yugoslavia or in the North Caucasus was more religio-national than ideological. The growing salience of culture is also connected to a widespread defensive counter-reaction to the perceived homogenizing force of globalization. This is apparent, for instance, in the rise of Islamist movements in the Middle East in the period since the Iranian revolution in 1979 introduced a consciously anti-Western indigenous Islamic order. In Asia, a similar reaction can be seen in the promotion of 'Asian values' as distinct from, and in places superior to, Western values (Mahbubani 1992). In the West, this defensiveness is also apparent, most controversially in Samuel Huntington's thesis of the upcoming 'clash of civilizations', where the North–South divide becomes conflated with a cultural struggle of the 'West vs. the Rest' (Huntington 1993).

Huntington's (1996) later more subtle development of his argument sought to demonstrate that the roots of Western culture preceded the modern era by many centuries. He argued that there is, therefore, no necessary rule that non-Western countries will become more Western as they become more modern. Indeed, he maintained that the very opposite was often actually the case and that, 'in fundamental ways, much of the world is becoming more modern and less Western'. This argument represents one side of a critical debate over the role of culture in understanding international politics. Huntington's logic conforms to what might be termed an 'essentialist' understanding of culture, where cultures represent different and incommensurate meaning systems, self-contained and unchanging in their essential characteristics. Such an approach is seen particularly among those who identify Islamic culture as the principal cause of the economic and political failings of Middle Eastern states and the pervasive strength of anti-Western sentiment in the region (see, for example, Ajami 1998; Lewis 2002). From this perspective, the 'war on terror' is a cultural war where Western values need to be protected against their anti-Western cultural enemies (Pipes 2002).

There is, though, an alternative and less bleak understanding of the role of culture in international politics. Cultures, according to this interpretation, are located within a constantly changing and evolving historical narrative, where the primary challenge common to all postcolonial developing countries, whether in the Middle East or elsewhere, is that of adapting successfully to the colonial legacies of the modern state and the Western-dominated international state system. Culture is not unimportant in this understanding, but cultures are viewed as considerably more dynamic, evolving and adaptive than in the alternative essentialist conception. This includes recognition, for instance, that there are many different forms of Islam and that most contemporary Islamist movements are more a particularist adaptation to the conditions of modernity than a genuine return to a medieval theocratic order (see Kepel 2002; O. Roy 2004). Certainly, indigenous cultures play a critical role in the articulation of distinctive responses to the demands of the modern state and the international system, but the fundamental commonalities of the nature of the challenges faced by all developing states need to be recognized over and above their cultural differences (Halliday 1996: 27–30). The North–South division has a resonance, in this context, not in how it underlines cultural or civilizational divides, but in how it recognizes the continuing legacy of European colonial rule, which imposed Western-developed conceptions of the nation, the modern state and the rules of the international system on the rest of the non-Western world. It is this legacy which continues, in multiple ways, to have a serious and lasting impact on international security (see chapter 3 for how it continues to influence the nature and course of contemporary warfare).

The 'problem' of the state

This also brings in the question of the putative role of the state, as a delineator of distinctive cultures, in ensuring security. In similar ways to those in which culture has been seen to be a significant cause of conflict, so the state has been increasingly stigmatized as itself a threat to international security. This is seen most notably in the human security and critical security approaches, discussed more fully in the next chapter, whose main target is the perceived conflation of the state with the provision of security, as set out in traditional security studies. To do this, it is argued, critically misses the point that it is the individual rather than the state whose security must be protected and safeguarded, not least from states and governments, which are habitually the principal oppressors and causes of human suffering. This scepticism towards the state is also extended to seeing a far more positive role to be played by non-state actors instead of states. The role of transnational activist groups and non-governmental organizations (NGOs) in securing the Ottawa Convention outlawing landmines is one of the most frequently cited examples of non-state actors circumventing and constraining the more conservative and conflict-inducing roles of states (Price 1998).

A historically sensitive North–South perspective suggests that there are two distinct sets of arguments underlying these critiques of a state-centric conception of security. The first relates primarily to the experience of the developed industrialized world of the North, where the ideal of the centralized, homogeneous nation-state has been progressively undermined by the forces of globalization from above and by subnational regionalism from below. This has, it is argued, increasingly removed the state from its essentially repressive and unjustified monopoly of the use of force and devolved this authority to regional and international organizations, such as the United Nations, the European Union or more diffuse transnational activist popular networks. The second has a very different Southern context. Here the problem is less of sovereignty being progressively undermined than of the failure of a number of states ever properly to exert sovereign powers and to have a genuine monopoly of the use of force in the first place. Robert Jackson (1990) has called this the 'quasi-state' phenomenon, where the colonial state, principally but not exclusively in sub-Saharan Africa, was granted formal external recognition of its sovereignty but lacked the key attributes of internal sovereignty such as territorial control. In such cases where states exist more on paper than in reality, premodern non-statist forms of political organization and communal identity fill the political vacuum. The 'state' in this context is often better described as one social force or set of marauding bandits among others but with the significant strategic advantage of having legal impunity against the repression of its own people. The concept of the 'failed' or 'collapsed' state identifies this longer-term failure of many states in the South to develop legitimate and responsive governments.

It is questionable, though, whether these two processes of putative state deconstruction mean that the state is now an outdated and anachronistic vehicle for the provision of security. The more powerful Northern states show little evidence of wishing to relinquish ultimate control to international and regional organizations, which is reflected in the operational weaknesses of the UN. The responses to 9/11 similarly suggest that, while there is recognition that a collective international response to al-Qaeda is essential, it is states, rather than non-state institutions and groups, which coordinate and oversee this response.

For the problem of the weak or failing states in the South, there has certainly been a growing recognition that there needs to be a more consistent international response to the human consequences of their failure to fulfil their 'responsibility to protect' their citizens. This has, in particular, critically formed the debate over the evolving norm of humanitarian intervention, as discussed more fully in chapter 4. There has also been a post-Cold War growth, where a state has collapsed, in the number of international administrations of territories, suggestive of the old League of Nations mandate system. However, it is notable that these administrations are always defined as 'transitional' and as seeking to construct, rather than supplant, the modern nation-state. Although dissatisfaction with the state in the South, as in the North, is widespread, practical longer-term alternatives generally do not have credibility. External controls, even if by seemingly impartial bodies such as the UN, lack legitimacy in the longer term since these forces inevitably become seen as a form of imperialism, failing to gain local legitimacy. Premodern forms of social, economic and political organization can similarly appear as an attractive part of a solution, but they also have their shortcomings and insecurities, for which the state historically provided and continues to provide the longer-term solution. Lisa Anderson captures the challenge well when she notes that 'the formation of the state was a difficult, costly and painful project in the past. The failure to form states in the future promises to be even more difficult, costly and painful' (2004: 14).

The reality is that the state is a Janus-faced entity. Through its coercive powers and ability to mobilize people and resources, it has the capacity to inflict great suffering and violence not only on foreigners but also on its own people. The state has undoubtedly been the most lethal killing force in the modern period. But the state also provides for the possibility of communal self-identification in an alienating world, the mechanisms through which the exercise of power can be domesticated and legitimated, and the most durable known framework for the promotion of stability and prosperity. There might be a juncture at which the state has fulfilled its historic function and provided such a degree of peace and stability that it can be discarded, as some argue is the case in Western Europe. But this is far from the case in most regions of the world, and the challenge remains to construct states which can overcome the insecurities of premodern political systems and the pathologies of the state formation process, and yet also foster the conditions for longer-lasting security and prosperity.

From bipolarity to empire, hegemony and multipolarity

The redirection of international security away from an East–West to a North–South focus is also a reflection of a broader shift in the global balance of power. During the Cold War, the Berlin Wall was not just a powerful symbol of inhumanity and oppression but also a symbol of the division of the world into two competing blocs – the Western bloc headed by the United States and the Eastern bloc headed by the Soviet Union. With the collapse of the Soviet-led bloc and the dissolution of the Soviet Union as a unified country, this specific bipolar structure of the global system was irrevocably destroyed.

The question of what has replaced this Cold War structure has been at the heart of much post-Cold War debate about where power and authority is now located. There are two main perspectives to this. The first is that the United States, as the sole surviving superpower, has been confirmed as the overwhelming dominant power in international politics, with no other country or region offering an effective balance to it, and that the system can be best described as unipolar or even imperial. The second is that, while the United States undoubtedly remains the most powerful actor in the international system, there are other major powers, such as the European Union, Japan, Russia, China and India, which contribute to the management of the global economic and political order and that the system is best described as multipolar. The relative weight given to these diverging views has tended to shift with broader developments in international politics. In the 1990s, there was a certain expectation, at least among a number of European capitals, that the European Union might emerge as a powerful, if differently constituted, international actor to balance the dominance of the United States (Kupchan 2002; see also Bretherton and Vogler 1999). In the aftermath of 9/11, the US appeared to assume dominance and unequivocally to assert its global leadership role, seemingly losing its inhibitions to the projection of its international power. With the failure of the intervention into Iraq, and in the aftermath of the economic crisis of 2008–9, the US, and the West more generally, appeared less dominant and to be in decline relative to the rapidly growing power of China and other emerging countries, such as India, Russia and Brazil (Pape 2005b; M. Brown et al. 2009; Mandelbaum 2010). In particular, it is the prospect of China emerging as the main challenger to the US which has increasingly appeared to be the key to the future balance of power (Mahbubani, 2008; Zakaria 2008).

For those who argue that the US, following the predictive expectations of realism, has sought to capitalize on its untrammelled primacy to assume greater powers and to assert more forcefully its privileges as the sole remaining superpower, there are divided opinions about whether this has generally been beneficial to the international order. Wohlforth, along with his colleague Brooks, is a consistent advocate not only of the fact and reality of unipolarity but also for its durability, there being no real short- to medium-term contenders, and its desirability (Wohlforth 1999; Brooks and Wohlforth 2008). Wohlforth and Brooks argue, using a mix of neo-realism and hegemonic stability theory, that the presence of one unchallengeable power in the system is beneficial as it reduces interstate competition and thus reduces the risks of great power war. Post-Cold War security based on US hegemony is thus viewed as enhancing international stability. Such a benign view of US power is reflected in the debate in the mid-2000s about whether the increasingly hegemonic US was now, in some meaningful way, ushering in a new imperial age, analogous to earlier empires such as that in Britain or Rome (see, for example, M. Cox 2004; Ferguson 2004; Johnson 2004).

For others, the assumption of US primacy has had more negative or mixed effects. It led, most notably, to hubristic overextension, resulting in key foreign policy failures, such as in Iraq and in Afghanistan. It also contributed to a growing scepticism or rejection in Washington of international regimes and institutions which were perceived as potentially constraining US autonomy and freedom of action. The United Nations, the Kyoto Protocol on Climate Change, the International Criminal Court, various arms control treaties, and the North Atlantic Treaty Organization have all, in varying degrees, suffered from the US disinclination to circumscribe its sovereign independence. As Keohane notes, there is an irony that 'the US, from which the first republican critique of the concept of sovereignty emanated, has now become one of its staunchest defenders' (2002: 743). For a number of analysts, it is this apparent arrogance of power that has been a major factor in accelerating the decline of US hegemony in the international system and the rise of credible alternative contenders, such as China (Mann 2003; Nye 2002; Calleo 2009).

An alternative view argues that the 'unilateral moment', which reached its apotheosis during the Bush administrations in the 2000s, is best viewed as an exceptional period in US history. John Ikenberry has consistently argued that the broader and more long-term context of US power, which has its foundations in the post-1945 Western order, is that it is constructed on the

liberal principles of consent rather than coercive imposition; on the construction of institutions of international cooperation rather than the military
balance of power; and on the promotion of free trade rather than mercantil-
ism (Ikenberry 2001, 2011a). This commitment to liberal internationalism,
he argues, is what defines the essential foundations and legitimacy of the US
as a global power and which both the Clinton and Obama administrations,
in contrast to those of Bush, reaffirmed as their core objectives for US foreign
policy. In this understanding of the longer-term projection of US power, the
realist concerns over whether the world is unipolar or multipolar are misplaced. What is critical is whether the world will remain wedded to the
multilateralist global order inspired and constructed by the US or whether it
will slide back into the protectionist and war-prone system of the 1930s. For
Ikenberry, the rise of China and other Asian countries should be treated as
more of an opportunity than a threat, as these countries, despite their illiberal domestic systems, are increasingly being integrated into, rather than
challenging, the Western liberal international order (Ikenberry 2011b).

A number of broader issues can be drawn from this general debate. First,
whether the system is best described as unipolar or multipolar, there is a
common understanding that the US remains an extremely powerful state,
which is seen in particular in its unprecedented military power – its military
expenditure being greater than the combined spending of the next twenty
countries, as illustrated in figure 1.2. But it is also accepted, even by the most
optimistic commentators, that such supremacy will not last forever and that
other countries, most notably the rapidly growing Asian powers, are catching

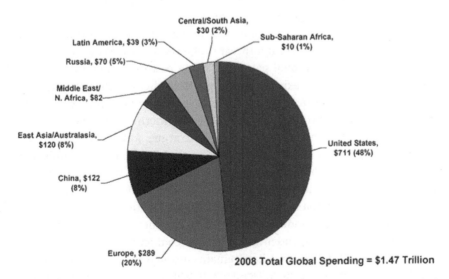

Figure 1.2 US Military spending vs. the world in 2008 (in $US billion, with % of total global
spending)
Source: Center for Arms Control and Non-Proliferation.

up. The issue is not whether but when the 'unipolar moment' will draw to an end and the US will have to share its global responsibilities with the new rising powers. There is a general recognition that the current era is experiencing what can be called a 'great convergence', where countries such as China and India will eventually regain the status of equality with the West that they last enjoyed in the premodern period (Northrup 2005; Zakaria 2008).

Second, when attempting to conceptualize how power is distributed in the international system, it is important to make a distinction between power as a set of attributes and power as a set of relations. The US might be the most powerful state in terms of strictly quantitative attributes, as defined by its cumulative military, political and economic resources, but this needs to be translated into relational terms – meaning, crudely, the ability to get others to do its will. As Ikenberry, Nye and others have convincingly argued, it is this relational power which is critical in international politics and is generally more effectively secured through the consent and mutual accommodation of others rather than through coercion and the use of force (Nye 2004, 2011; see also Baldwin 1989; M. Barnett and Duvall, 2005). The key question is whether the US failures in the 'war against terrorism', which underlined the limitations of the unilateral assertion of US power, have critically undermined American authority and legitimacy or whether the return to a more multilateralist course, as promoted by the Obama administration, can successfully restore the global reputation and trust of other states in the US.

A third issue, which has formed a growing area of debate, is how the rising power of China, which has enjoyed extremely fast growth during the 2000s, will be incorporated into the global structure of power. It is now becoming increasingly evident that China represents the most significant challenge to US hegemony. This has generated a protracted debate among Western analysts. On the one side, there are those who argue, following realist logic, that China will inevitably represent a threat to the US, and the West more generally, following the traditional pattern of rising powers seeking to challenge and radically change the existing status quo (Mearsheimer 2001: 402; Kaplan 2010). The classic historical example of this is the rise of Germany and how that contributed to two world wars in the twentieth century (Swaine and Tellis 2000). On the other, there are those who argue, following liberal internationalist logic, that China's increasing engagement and integration into the global economic and political system is gradually but inexorably promoting its socialization into Western norms and practices (Oksenberg and Economy 1999; Johnston 2003b). In an era of globalization, where China and the US are the largest trading partners to each other, the logic is towards cooperation and interdependence rather than conflict and war.

This so-called China threat debate remains inconclusive (for an overview of the debate, see Friedberg 2005; Deng 2008). Within China itself there is evidence of an increasingly open debate over the future determination of the country's rise as a great power (Shambaugh 2011). As in the West, there are 'hawks' and 'doves' who variously see the US as helping China, if reluctantly, into the global economic system and those who see the US as deliberately seeking to exclude and undermine China's rise as a great power. Again, the key issue is not whether China will assume a greatly enhanced role in international affairs but how that role will be defined and promoted. Underlying this is a major source of tension over the domestic political systems within each country, with an inherent conflict between the US ideal of promoting democracy globally and the resolve of the Chinese leadership to maintain the authoritarian centralized rule of the Communist Party.

A final dimension to this general overarching issue of the post-Cold War distribution of power in the international system is one which is often ignored. It is that the realist-inspired discussion over bipolar and multipolar systems, over hegemony and empire, is, to a significant extent, an historical anachronism. This is due to the fact, as noted earlier, that one of the key developments during the twentieth century was the normative shift which delegitimized the practice of imperialism, aided not least by the US in its support for the dismantling of the British, French and Soviet empires. As a result, the age of empires has been replaced by the age of nation-states, and attempts to reconstruct empires inevitably end up at some point being compromised by claims that the occupying force has illegitimate imperial ambitions. And, as Mann notes, the very idea of a 'new imperial age', which was widely discussed in the mid-2000s, is 'incoherent' (M. Mann 2003). The reality of the distribution of power in the contemporary international system is that it is radically diffused to an extent arguably not observed since the eighteenth century. This is seen in the fact that the number of states grew from fifty-one in 1945 to 193 in 2011, and that these states all have a certain power to resist and to challenge the more powerful state in the system. This is most clearly evident in Afghanistan, where one of the poorest countries in the world remains stubbornly unpacified despite the huge exertions of the United States and the NATO forces. This diffusion of power also extends to multiple non-state actors, such as terrorist groups and international criminal organizations, who operate outside and across the borders of states.

Given developments in Iraq and Afghanistan, it has been natural to see the problem of resistance, insurgency and imperial hubris as specific to the United States, clearly the most powerful state in the world. But the occupations of Iraq and Afghanistan should not be isolated as the only instance of a potential reinvigoration of imperialist practice. In Kosovo in 1999, in Bosnia in 1995 and in Libya in 2011 it was the US and Europe acting in close coordination which intervened in a similarly coercive manner to impose their preferred political outcomes. On a more multilateral level, the UN has assumed the responsibilities for reconstructing a number of states and of establishing often seemingly indefinite 'transitional administrations'. Some have described this as a form of 'UN imperialism'. In essence, though, the issue faced by all these actors, for which some revival of imperialism appears to be the answer, is the challenge to international security presented by those states which have simply broken apart or which deliberately refuse to abide by international norms, whether in terms of major abuse of the human rights of their citizens, through seeking illegally to gain access to weapons of mass destruction, or by deliberately supporting international terrorism. It is again a demonstration of how the apparently 'powerless' present some of the most difficult challenges for international security.

Conclusion

In many ways, this tension between the temptation of empire and the reality of an anti-imperialist age encapsulates some of the key challenges of contemporary international security. This chapter has argued that three main shifts have occurred since the end of the Cold War which have significantly revised our understanding of international security. The first is the recognition that the threat of war between great powers has greatly declined; the second is that the most critical security challenges reside in the South and in North–South interactions; and the third is the shift from a bipolar era to one where the United States remains the most powerful actor but has had difficulties in translating that power into effective policies, and where there are other countries, most notably China, challenging US hegemony.

At heart, these different dimensions of the changing nature of international security reflect an unresolved, and perhaps unresolvable, tension within the very heart of international politics. This is that the power inequalities in the international system are the source of both international security *and* global insecurity. The assertion of hegemonic leadership proclaimed by the US is a reflection of the traditional understanding that 'great powers' have a special responsibility for maintaining international order. This logic suggests that the United States, as the sole remaining superpower, has a special responsibility for the management of the international system, and that this should be recognized with an appropriate level of deference from the weaker states who collectively benefit from this US-supplied collective good. Implicit in this contention is that the power inequalities in the international system, of which the US is the major beneficiary, should be respected and preserved since it is through such inequalities that international security is maintained. But, as the less powerful states have frequently pointed out, the presumed special responsibilities of the great powers can equally be perceived as a self-righteous justification by those very same states for an indefinite prolongation of their privileges and for the maintenance of a conservative international order. It is also such systemic inequalities, and the seeming indifference of the more wealthy and powerful to the condition of their less fortunate brethren, which fuel international hostility and global insecurity. It is these fundamental questions over values, morality, legitimacy and power inequalities which are a particular concern of international relations theory, the subject of the next chapter.

FURTHER READING

A selection of some of the most influential post-Cold War reflections and projections for international politics and international security includes the liberal optimism of Francis Fukuyama, *The End of History* (1992); the cultural and political pessimism of Samuel Huntington, 'The clash of civilizations', in *Foreign Affairs* (1993), and Robert Kagan, *The Return of History and the End of Dreams* (2008); the European postmodern perspective of Robert Cooper, *The Breaking of Nations* (2003); and the sweeping historical overview of war and peace in Philip Bobbitt, *The Shield of Achilles* (2002).

On the changing nature of war, one of the most entertaining and incisive accounts is found in Martin Van Creveld, *On Future War* (1991). See also the influential analysis of Mary Kaldor, *New and Old Wars* (2012) and the excellent Herfried Münkler, *The New Wars* (2005). For a good analysis of the democratic peace theory, which includes the economic as well as the political factors, see Bruce Russett and J. R. Oneal, *Triangulating Peace* (2001), as well as Russett's earlier book *Grasping the Democratic Peace* (1993). For a wide-ranging collection of articles on the democratic peace, see Michael Brown, Sean Lynn-Jones and Steven Miller (eds), *Debating the Democratic Peace* (1996). For a good general overview of the recent literature on war and peace, see Robert Jervis, 'Theories of war in an era of leading-power peace', in *American Political Science Review* (2002).

For good general accounts of politics and security in the global South, there is no better place to start than with Christopher Clapham, *Third World Politics* (1985), and Muhammed Ayoob, *The Third World Security Predicament* (1995). For the linkages between poverty and insecurity, the works of Thomas Homer-Dixon, *Environment, Scarcity and Violence* (1999) and *The Ingenuity Gap* (2001), have proved influential, and are discussed more fully in chapter 6. The classics of Karl Polanyi, *The Great Transformation* (1944), and Samuel Huntington, *Political Order and Changing Societies* (1968), provide compelling insights into the difficulties of the transition to modernity. Fareed Zakaria, *The Future of Freedom* (2002), and Jack Snyder, *From Voting to Violence* (2000), highlight the continuing tensions and obstacles. On the issue of culture, and the purported cultural clash between the West and Islam, see the critical assessment by Fred Halliday, *Islam and the Myth of Confrontation* (1996), and the nuanced accounts by Sami Zubaida, *Islam, the People and the State* (1993), and Peter Mandaville, *Global Political Islam* (2007).

On the question of how to understand US foreign policy with the end of the Cold War, the most compelling analysis and defence of unipolarity is found in Stephen Brooks and William Wohlforth, *World out of Balance* (2008). Arguments for a more assertive and unilateral US are in Max Boot's *The Savage Wars of Peace* (2004) and Niall Ferguson's *Colossus* (2004). The defence for a historically reflective and multilateralist America is found in John Ikenberry, *After Victory* (2001) and *Liberal Leviathan* (2011), and Joseph Nye, *The Paradox of American Power* (2002) and *The Future of Power* (2011). More radical critiques are in Michael Mann, *Incoherent Empire* (2003), Chalmers Johnson, *Blowback* (2002), and David Calleo, *Follies of Power* (2009). Mick Cox provides regular updates on the US imperial debate (see Cox 2004, 2005).

On the issue of China's rise and its potential implications for the US and global order more generally, see David C. Kang, *China Rising* (2007); Fareed Zakaria, *The Post-American World* (2008); and Yong Deng, *China's Struggle for Status* (2008). For a good overview of the academic IR debates over China, see Aaron L. Friedberg, 'The future of US–China relations', in *International Security* (2005). For an overview of debates within China over its foreign policy, see David Shambaugh, 'Coping with a conflicted China', in *Washington Quarterly* (2011). For an analysis of the domestic challenges to China's rise, see Susan Shirk, *China: Fragile Superpower* (2007).

Questions for Research and Discussion

1 What are the causes of the 'great power peace'? Is it political, economic or normative factors which are more significant in explaining this phenomenon?
2 What is the relationship between global economic inequality and international insecurity?
3 How powerful is the United States and what challenge does China represent to US power?

WEBSITES

www.isn.ethz.ch/isn
The International Relations and Security Network – a worldwide network of think tanks, universities, NGOs, and international organizations. It has a large holding of research papers, policy briefs and other links.

www.foreignaffairs.com
A selection of articles from *Foreign Affairs* magazine – a good source for current debates on foreign affairs issues.

www.foreignpolicy.com
A selection of articles from *Foreign Policy* magazine – a good source for current debates on foreign policy issues.

www.cia.gov/library/publications/the-world-factbook
Information about history, people, economy, government and the military of state and non-state actors throughout the world provided by the US Central Intelligence Agency (CIA).

CHAPTER 2

Theorizing about Security after the Cold War

The argument has so far set out a challenging and demanding role for the security analyst. There is the need to sustain and balance the roles of scientist, internationalist and moralist, while at the same time the familiar security environment of the Cold War has given way to the uncertainties and unpredictable dynamics of the post-Cold War era. The contemporary security analyst does, admittedly, have the historical luxury of needing to place less strategic attention on the threat of large-scale great power war, but this is balanced by developments empowering and radicalizing the global South, where environmental and demographic pressures, civil war and resentment at the inequalities in North–South relations and the shifting distribution of power and its concentration in the United States have resulted in a new set of urgent challenges for international security. It is in this context of a radically shifting strategic landscape that the security analyst naturally turns for inspiration to the major theoretical traditions of the study of international relations (IR), whose role is to identify the regularities, continuities and longer-term dynamics behind the seeming flux and randomness of international developments.

IR theories can, however, be bewildering in their complexity and proliferation, making them often as impenetrable as the reality they seek to explain. A useful distinction to make is between two types of theoretical enquiry. The first is that of *explanatory* theory, which seeks to explain and understand why certain events and developments have taken place. At their more ambitious, such theories might also claim predictive powers. But, in practice, such expectations of being able to grasp the future have, in the realm of international relations, been compromised by failures to predict key shifts, such as the end of the Cold War and the rise of transnational terrorism (on the failure to predict the end of the Cold War, see Gaddis 1992–3). The more modest and realistic expectation is that explanatory theory should offer a sufficiently robust understanding of why events have occurred in the past to provide us with an understanding, retrospectively, of why the seemingly unexpected takes place (Krause and Williams 1996a: 243). The second category is that of *normative* theory, where the theoretical ambition moves beyond explaining how things *are* to provide a convincing case for how things *should be*, given certain moral assumptions about the proper conduct of international relations along with a realistic assessment of the possibilities for change.

This analytical distinction in the nature of theoretical enquiry can help us to have a better grasp of the major recent theoretical developments and their implications for international security. Table 2.1 provides an inevitably rough and approximate categorization of the principal IR theoretical approaches to security studies. The columns of the matrix – divided into rationalism, conventional constructivism/historical sociology and interpretivist constructivism – identify the main divisions in methodology and meta-theory on how to approach the study of IR. It is important, though, to see these not as three distinct categories but as differing positions on a spectrum from, at one end, rationalist theory, drawing from the reductionist and abstract logic of rational choice and the agency-driven dynamics of strategic interaction, to, at the other, sociologically inspired constructivist theory, with its 'thicker' idealist explanations of how reality is mutually constituted through intersubjective understandings and constructions. The rows – divided into realism, liberalism and radicalism – offer more familiar territory for IR scholars (see Doyle 1997; Walt 1998). Again, these categories should be seen not as fixed and incommensurate but as representing a spectrum from a more sceptical conception of the possibilities of normative change in international politics to a more optimistic and urgent understanding of such possibilities.

The main argument of this chapter is that there have been two significant shifts in post-Cold War theorizing about international security. The first, which is covered in the next section, represents a shift in popularity from rationalist to constructivist explanations of how to study and understand international security. The rationalist approach of neo-realism, though still a vibrant and continuing theoretical tradition, has lost some of its Cold War pre-eminence and has had to compete with constructivist accounts, where ideas, identities and norms play a more central and formative role in the dynamic reconfigurations of international security. The second shift is a move towards a less state-centric and more radical assessment of the possibilities and the need for change, where the end of the Cold War is seen to strengthen a more cosmopolitan and universalist conceptualization of international security. The popularity and prominence of the concept of human security, which is explicitly defined in contrast to state security, is reflective

Table 2.1 International relations theories and security studies

	Rationalism	*'Conventional' constructivism/ historical sociology*	*Interpretivist constructivism*
Realism	Neo-realism Offensive realism	Neo-classical realism Defensive realism	
Liberalism	Neo-liberalism	Human security	Postmodernism
Radicalism		Historical materialism	Critical security
		Marxism	Postmodernism

of this shift. Again, as with neo-realism, realism as a normative tradition, though still exercising a powerful influence, has lost ground to liberal and critical accounts.

These shifts in theoretical direction represent moves along a spectrum rather than some Kuhnian paradigm shift where the rationalist approach or realism has been terminally discredited. Overall, theoretical developments are best understood as an interactive dialogue rather than as an incommensurate clash. The central argument of the chapter is that this dialogue, where there has been a significant shift towards constructivist and cosmopolitan approaches, is beneficial and to be welcomed. Constructivism highlights the critical subjective and intersubjective dimension of security. Cosmopolitanism, as exemplified in the human security or critical security approaches, is essential for reminding us of the sufferings of the poor, the excluded and the marginalized and of the multiple ways in which state behaviour has often been a principal source of global insecurity.

But, while welcoming these shifts, three qualifications are made. The first is the danger of the constructivist critique fading into a radical relativism, where international security is understood as a mere construction and artifice, which can therefore be somehow sublimated and transcended. It is suggested that the insights of historical sociology can help to arrest such an anti-foundational and ideational tendency. Second, the commitment to cosmopolitanism has the danger of raising excessive expectations of the possibilities of international altruism and for the prospects of humanitarianism. In reality, international developments will be driven by a messy mix of altruistic humanitarianism and selfish national interests. It is argued that realism, taken as a normative theory drawing from a communitarian liberal moral tradition, provides an important check on such overly optimistic expectations.

From neo-realism to constructivism

The Cold War as an international structure appeared to conform almost perfectly to the realist and then, with the publication of Kenneth Waltz's *Theory of International Politics* (1979), to the neo-realist theoretical framework. As such, it provided an exemplary validation of the three key assumptions of neo-realism (Mearsheimer 1994–5). First, the Cold War divide reflected the realist assumption that the international system is anarchic – meaning that it contains multiple units and no overarching authority or Leviathan. The Cold War system was, in Raymond Aron's terms, heterogeneous rather than homogeneous, since there were two diametrically opposed conceptions of political order and domestic legitimacy (Aron 1966: 99–104). Significant global cooperation was rendered essentially redundant when the Soviet Union and the United States, along with their respective allies, held such divergent values and worldviews (Halliday 1994). Second, the neo-realist assumption that the key feature differentiating the units in the system is their relative power capacities, particularly their capacity to inflict damage and harm on others, was reflected in the Cold War obsession with the threat of war and the massive arms build-ups. And, third, the realist claim that states are fearful and distrustful of the intentions of others, and that the system is ultimately one of 'self-help', appeared to be amply confirmed by the enduring suspicions between East and West. Moreover, the limited attempts at cooperation, such as the period of détente in the 1970s and its subsequent collapse, appeared to confirm the realist concept of the 'security dilemma', where anarchy and distrust undermines cooperation even where the intentions of the parties concerned might initially have been benign and non-aggressive (see Jervis 1978; Glaser 1997).

In the area of security and strategic studies, neo-realism held a clear pre-eminence. Such theoretical dominance was not necessarily found in other areas of IR, such as the field of international political economy, where neo-realism had greater difficulty in explaining the dynamic of economic interdependence and globalization. Where neo-realism was dominant was in the key area where its concerns were most focused – that of international security. This had a number of implications for security studies during the Cold War. It meant that the central focus of research was on the preparation, the use, or the threat of use of military force, since force remained the *ultima ratio* of international politics, as seen daily in the nuclear stand-off between NATO and the Warsaw Pact (see Walt 1991). Non-military security issues were potentially dangerous diversions from the core concerns of the subdiscipline. Scepticism was also regularly expressed about the idea that strategic priority might be accorded to actors other than the state. Neo-realism reflected the Cold War's normative commitment to a conservative statist order which, it was argued, needed to be preserved for the sake of strategic stability and the East–West balance.

The conflation of the Cold War and neo-realism also had certain professional benefits for security analysts. It provided them with an elevated public profile and access to generous research funding, while also giving them the scientific credibility of a theoretical framework which promised predictive insights on how to identify threats and how to avoid war and preserve peace. As Waltz argued with uncharacteristic modesty, neo-realists do not pretend to know everything but they do know 'some big and important things' (1998: 384). This provided the basis for the ambition to gain cumulative knowledge on issues which had a particular urgency during the Cold War: factors governing when states balance or bandwagon against countervailing powers (Walt 1987; Schweller 1994; G. Snyder 1997; Powell 1999); questions about the forging of a credible deterrence strategy (Gray 1979; Jervis 1984; Powell 1990); and the effect on the stability of the international system if defence has the advantage over offence, or vice versa (Quester 1977; Jervis 1978; Posen 1984).

Neo-realism and the end of the Cold War

The end of the Cold War far from silenced neo-realism. Neo-realist assumptions and contributions have been central to discussions about the implications of a unipolar international system, and whether such unipolarity is sustainable or will inevitably result in multipolar counterbalancing (for unipolarity, see Wohlforth 1999; for multipolarity, see Waltz 2000; Pape 2005b). Neo-realists have also dictated much of the agenda about the future fate of Cold War alliances or regimes, such as NATO, expressing scepticism about their longer-term future and viability (Mearsheimer 1994–5; G. Snyder 1997). As argued in the previous chapter, neo-realist research on the defence–offence balance has provided a significant insight into the causes of the great power peace in the nuclear age (Lynn-Jones 1995; Van Evera 1999). Realism has also enjoyed a marked revival, especially in the United States, since the terrorist attacks of 9/11. The US National Security Strategy published in 2002 has a markedly realist flavour, with an emphasis on building a 'balance of power in favour of peace', an assertion of the legitimacy of unilateral pre-emption, and a realist-inspired scepticism about multilateralism and international institutions (White House 2002; see also Dannreuther and Peterson 2006).

Neo-realism is not, though, a monolithic or internally uncontested theoretical tradition, with competing 'offensive' and 'defensive' realisms seeking to assume the neo-realist mantle (Brooks 1997). John Mearsheimer is the most prominent advocate of the 'offensive realist' school, arguing that international relations, according to neo-realist principles, is an arena where states constantly fear one another and seek to alleviate this fear through maximizing their power and domination. The great powers, according to Mearsheimer, are inherently aggressive since 'states are disposed to think offensively toward other states even though their ultimate motive is simply to survive' (2001: 34). For Mearsheimer and others in this school, international relations is a pitiless contest where states ceaselessly seek to maximize their power and are continually ready to engage in aggression and initiate wars because this continues to provide political and economic advantage (Mearsheimer 1990; Labs 1997; Zakaria 1998).

A very different view is, though, promoted by the original founder of neo-realism, Kenneth Waltz, whose original theoretical formulation was that states were driven not solely, as Mearsheimer contends, to 'maximize power' but also to 'maintain their positions in the system' (Waltz 1979). Indeed, Waltz has consistently argued that states, once their basic survival is secured, do not engage in a ceaseless quest for power or constantly prepare for war. This position represents the alternative 'defensive realist' school, where the experience of history in consolidating stable balances of power is seen as providing a significant source for international stability. As a consequence, the defensive realist school had a considerably more benign expectation, in the immediate aftermath of the end of the Cold War, of the future of Europe compared to their offensive realist colleagues. While Mearsheimer predicted a swift return to great power competition in Europe, the defensive realist Steven Van Evera thought that Europe was now 'primed for peace' (Mearsheimer 1990; Van Evera 1990–1).

Defensive realism's gains in terms of greater empirical plausibility do, though, have some costs in terms of some of the core neo-realist assumptions. In particular, there is a tendency in such defensive realist accounts to relax the assumption that it is solely the distribution of power capabilities which determines state behaviour, and both to introduce non-material factors such as beliefs, ideas and ideologies and to include the role of domestic politics. Thus Stephen Walt's seminal analysis of alliance formation argued that states seek allies not just to balance against the countervailing power capabilities of other states but also because these states are *perceived to be threatening* (Walt 1987). On the causes of wars of expansion, Jack Snyder has argued that great powers often miscalculate the benefits of war due to powerful and unrepresentative domestic elites who perpetuate 'myths of empire' (J. Snyder 1991). For understanding post-Cold War inter-ethnic conflict, Steven Van Evera has highlighted the role of 'chauvinist mythmaking' as a key cause fuelling identity-based civil wars (Van Evera 1994). In all these accounts, beliefs, perceptions and intentions, often emanating from domestic social forces, play a central role in explaining the dynamics of power politics and conflict, which pushes defensive realism, or as it is sometimes termed neo-classical realism, more towards the constructivist end of the methodological spectrum.

A further internal critique of neo-realism can be seen to come from liberal institutionalism or neo-liberalism (see Keohane 1984; Oye 1986). Neo-liberalism sought to demonstrate that, even if one accepts the core assumptions of neo-realism and adopts the same rationalist approach, international cooperation could be generated beyond what even the most 'defensive' realists would accept. In particular, the argument was that states might be induced, over time, to seek absolute gains benefiting everyone without constantly worrying about the relative distribution of those gains, which neo-realists consistently argued impeded the prospects for institutional cooperation (Powell 1991; Snidal 1991). Neo-liberalism was always less influential in the field of international security than in international political economy, primarily because of the relative weakness of regional and international collective security regimes. But, after the end of the Cold War, NATO's perseverance even in the absence of a Soviet threat appeared as a confirmation of how institutionalized cooperation could outlast the initial realist-driven conditions for the creation of that institution (see McCalla 1996; Lepgold 1998).

The constructivist turn

However, in the late 1980s, with the dramatic events surrounding the collapsing structures of the Cold War, neo-liberalism appeared to many analysts to be as outdated and problematic as neo-realism. There was a sense that the so-called neo-neo debate (see Baldwin 1993) was an increasingly sterile intellectual terrain on which to confront the enormity of what was happening in international relations. Much as Mikhail Gorbachev promoted 'new thinking' in foreign policy, so a new generation of IR scholars saw the need for a philosophical revolution in the way that IR was theorized. This led to the rise within IR of constructivism, primarily imported from sociology, but with philosophical roots reaching back to the idealist philosophy of Kant and the Kantian-inspired linguistic philosophy of Wittgenstein and his followers John Austin and John Searle, whose principal concern was the way the structures of language construct our social reality (Wittgenstein 1953; Austin 1962; Searle 1995). The core idea of constructivism is the rejection of an unproblematized objective external reality and the need to recognize the world as a social construction, mutually constituted through shared meanings and intersubjective understandings.

The revolutionary nature of the constructivist turn in IR was in how it radically questioned the fundamental assumptions of neo-realist and rationalist IR, in particular the core assumptions of anarchy, sovereignty and the inevitability of war. In a seminal article by Alexander Wendt, the constructivist critique was applied to the concept of anarchy, seeking to undermine the idea that anarchy is an objective 'given' of international reality or a structural precondition for state interaction, and to present it as a historically contingent and socially constructed way in which states have, at times, mutually interpreted and understood their engagement and interaction with one another (Wendt 1992). The concept of sovereignty has similarly been deconstructed, with an analogous line of argument that the concept is far from a permanent feature of IR but is historically contingent on particular and frequently changing shared understandings of what count as 'national' as against 'international' spaces (see, for example, R. Walker 1993; Spruyt 1994; Bierstecker and Weber 1996; Ashley 1998). As was seen in the previous chapter, constructivists have provided accounts of the emergence of the democratic peace, linking this to European and transatlantic collective identity formations, which have overcome and sublimated conflict-inducing parochial national identities (Risse-Kappen 1995; Kahl 1998–9).

This constructivist approach, with its thicker sociological conceptualization of external reality, has proved to be highly influential for security studies since the end of the Cold War. In the first place, constructivism, with its focus on subjective ideas and intersubjective understandings, accords a greater weight to how ideas and perceptions influence and structure international reality. It was the apparent power of the ideas promoted by Gorbachev, such as the concept of 'defensive defence', a 'common European home' or the 'zero option' in nuclear arms talks, which singularly inspired an alternative constructivist interpretation of why the Cold War ended (Koslowski and Kratochwil 1995). Constructivist concerns with norms and norm creation similarly appeared to provide a more credible explanation for slowly evolving and longer-term normative transformations, such as the delegitimation of imperialism (Zacher 2001), the overthrow of apartheid (Klotz 1995), or the emergence of international human rights regimes (Finnemore 2003). Constructivism not only appeared to offer a more flexible and dynamic conceptualization of the structures of IR, it also provided a greater space for agency-driven change, where 'epistemic communities' and 'moral entrepreneurs' could directly influence international affairs, even when not directly supported by state power (Adler and Barnett 1998; Keck and Sikkink 1998). The campaign to ban landmines, where key individuals and non-governmental organizations played a central role, is often taken as a paradigmatic example of this phenomenon (Price 1998).

A second attraction of the constructivist approach is the prominence it accords to identity and culture. In post-Cold War security studies, culture and identity have become an increasingly dominant concern as the ideological confrontations of the Cold War have been displaced by identity-driven conflicts. A rationalist framework can provide an account of how conflict might emerge between competing and hostile identity-based groups (Posen 1993), but it is much less capable of explaining how these identities are formed or forged or can potentially be changed or modified. This gap in rationalist theoretical accounts of ethnic conflict has been filled by incorporating constructivist accounts of identity formation, particularly the insights of the sociology of nationalism, where figures such as Ernest Gellner (1983) and Benedict Anderson (1991) have long argued that national identities are modern constructions and do not represent some unchanging and primordial essence. Such constructivist understandings of identity-based conflicts, which recognize the critical role played by elite manipulation, and where identities are seen as being fluid and having multiple potential forms, have significantly aided analyses of multiple post-Cold War conflicts, such as in the former Yugoslavia (see Obershall 2000).

Attention to culture and cultural differentiation has also had a further significant influence on the post-Cold War study of international security. As the exigencies of the Cold War have reduced the need for anti-Soviet strategic convergence, the existence of very different national security cultures among Western states has become much more evident (see Katzenstein 1996). Constructivist scholarship has provided insights into how countries such as Germany and Japan, with their particular historical experiences and national cultures, have developed cautious, introspective and non-interventionist security norms which eschew the great power military status that their economic and political power would support (Berger 1998). The European Union's difficulties in developing an effective security and defence policy have also been directly linked to the existence of contrasting national cultures of security, from the 'extrovert' interventionist policies of the UK and France to the 'introvert' civilian policies of Germany and the non-aligned countries in Europe. Culture has been a central focus of study for understanding the severe transatlantic tensions over the war in Iraq, where some believe that the US and Europe have diverged ideologically to an extent that their basic visions of international security are essentially incommensurate (Kagan 2003).

Finally, a further attraction of the constructivist approach is the way in which it supports a shift away from identifying the state with security. This has influenced, in particular, the human security and critical security approaches, which are assessed more fully below. Constructivist scholarship has been particularly attractive for informing theoretical reflections on the European Union and the process of European integration, providing a lens to explain the transformation of this regional subsystem, and to offer insights into how sovereignty can be pooled collectively rather than concentrated nationally (see Koslowski 1999). This has, in turn, given constructivist IR theory a particularly strong base of support in Europe (Waever 2004). It is not, therefore, accidental that the most influential attempt to develop a middle-range theory for security studies, incorporating the methods and methodology of constructivism, grew from within Europe – the theory of securitization.

Securitization – its strengths and limitations

The concept of securitization, and its corollary of desecuritization, developed originally from the peace studies community in Denmark, and in particular the work of Ole Waever. The key constructivist insight of the 'Copenhagen School' is to shift attention away from an objectivist analysis of threat assessment to the multiple and complex ways in which security threats are internally generated and constructed. Waever adapted the concept of the 'speech act', drawn from the linguistic philosophy of J. L. Austin and John Searle, and applied it to the discourse of security. He argued that, when something is identified as a security issue, this constitutes a particular 'speech act' involving a process of securitization, whereby an issue is presented as 'posing an existential threat to a designated referent object' (Waever 1989). Barry Buzan has refined this definition to the assertion of an 'existential threat' which 'requires exceptional measures and/or emergency action to deal with it', meaning that it is removed from the realm of politics to the realm of security (Buzan 1997). The associated corollary of this more subjectivist conceptualization of security is the extension of security beyond the traditional politico-military sphere to what the Copenhagen School identified as the five discrete political, economic, environmental, military and societal sectors (Buzan 1991; Buzan, Waever and de Wilde 1998). The securitization approach is, therefore, closely linked to the wider post-Cold War security agenda.

The Copenhagen School's most radical impact is in the implicit democratization of the field of security studies. In place of the neo-realist scholar as elite scientist, rationally calculating the multiple security threats 'out there', the security analyst focused on securitization stands back and surveys how the general public, and their leaders, 'construct' security threats and challenges. Inspired by this more open and discursive role, the most innovative work has focused on the ways in which, since the end of the Cold War, non-traditional security threats, such as the environment, migration or transnational organized crime, have become securitized. To name one example, Didier Bigo has sought to demonstrate how the internal security forces – the police and immigration and customs officials – have successfully securitized a nexus between immigration, crime and terrorism, which has led to the popular revulsion and xenophobia concerning immigration (Bigo 1996, 2002). As discussed in chapters 6 and 8, both the environment and immigration have been critical areas where a post-Cold War process of securitization has been identified and explored by security analysts. As such, the securitization approach has provided the 'new security agenda' with a good potential theoretical base.

The concept of securitization has, in this way, provided a practical demonstration of how the constructivist approach can produce a significant research agenda. It has made clearer the ways in which security is culturally and historically influenced and how populist pressures and the manipulation of elites determine the intersubjective understandings of international security. It has also shown that security is not just a property of the state but includes other potential 'referent objects', such as identity-based social forces, regional and international institutions, and even the planet as a whole. And, critically, it has helped to provide a path to understanding the more complex and problematic security environment of the end of the Cold War, where the threat of interstate war has been displaced by more insidious fears of transnational threats to security.

There are, though, certain limitations to the constructivist-inspired approach of securitization. The first is the extent to which security is to be treated as subjectively constructed. The argument that securitization is purely a 'speech act' with no direct correspondence to any external reality posits a strong subjectivist epistemology. The logical outcome of this is a radical relativism where no one account of security is to be privileged over others. Indeed, many IR constructivist theorists adopt a radical interpretivist or postmodern stance whereby no one security discourse can be properly prioritized over another (see, for example, Der Derian 1990; Campbell 1992; R. Walker 1993). Waever, as with most 'conventional' constructivists, distances himself from such a strong interpretivism, but his argument that the Copenhagen School is committed to desecuritization is justified only by an exogenous ideological commitment to liberalism rather than as part of the theory of securitization itself (Waever 1995). Waever does, though, correctly identify the critical need to maintain some grounds for making judgements about differing security discourses, so that the dangers of the overexaggeration and underestimation of security challenges, as noted in chapter 1, can properly be addressed and identified.

A second problem with the securitization approach is the way in which it tends to isolate security as a value and separate the realm of politics from the realm of security. As argued in the first chapter, this takes away much of the complexity of the moral debate over security, where security is not necessarily always an evil to be repressed but can also be an important value for human living which needs to be balanced against other core values, such as freedom, prosperity and justice. Securitization is a valuable tool for identifying when a particular security issue is being exaggerated, but the corresponding process of desecuritization does not mean that security concerns cease to be a critical dimension of that particular issue. The problems of the concept of securitization (and desecuritization) in presenting a black and white reality – where something either is or is not a security issue – are critically addressed in chapter 8 on immigration.

There is one further problem associated with the securitization approach which is related to the more contingent factor of its European origins and roots. There is, perhaps naturally, a Eurocentric focus to much of its research agenda, reflecting concerns with the postmodern implications of the European integration process and the ways in which traditional nation-states and national identities are being displaced by Europe-wide norms and identities. The strength of the securitization approach has, admittedly, been in setting out the dangers of a European security discourse which is defined in terms of 'enemy' images of the immigrant, the Muslim world or the poor and dispossessed at Europe's gates. But its main frame of reference of a postmodern and post-sovereign Europe, involving a strictly European historical experience and conceptualization of the state and of state–society relations, has only a limited relevance elsewhere, particularly in much of the non-European global South.

Towards a via media: constructivism meets historical sociology

Some of these weaknesses in the constructivist approach can potentially be overcome or mitigated by incorporating insights from and adapting the historical sociological approach to the study of international security (see Halliday 1994; Hobden and Hobson 2002). In particular, there are significant benefits in seeking a dialogue and greater convergence between mainstream or 'conventional' IR constructivism and historical sociology (HS).

The first reason for this is the very similar concern of both conventional constructivism and HS to find a via media between warring rationalist and postmodern approaches. Within sociology, HS has consistently sought to chart a path between large-scale universalizing theory, such as that represented by rational choice theory, and anti-foundational interpretivist theory, such as postmodernism (see Dannreuther and Kennedy 2007). HS, like conventional constructivism, remains committed to causal explanation and the intellectual need to identify and explain the causal linkages which produce significant outcomes of interest. It is committed in epistemological terms to ontological realism – meaning not a commitment to a crude empiricism but rather a recognition that one has to act 'as if' there were an independent reality, for otherwise there is nothing short of relativism (M. Mann 1994: 42). But, following the main insights of constructivism, HS also recognizes that facts can only be interpreted within particular theoretical constructs and meaning systems, and that the main task of the analyst is to provide the most convincing theory to explain the facts as she or he sees them. Conventional constructivism and HS are, therefore, seeking to inhabit broadly the same centrist methodological ground, and there is considerable mutual advantage for them to join forces.

A further advantage of incorporating HS is that it acts as an antidote to the constructivist tendency to privilege ideational over material explanations of international change. Its roots in historical materialism mean that it is particularly attuned to the importance of geography and natural resource endowments, and to the multiple material sources of power, and how these translate into political gains and military conflict. At the same time, with its Weberian roots, HS is aware that power is not simply reducible to the capacity for coercion but is intimately connected to ideational factors such as the legitimacy and the presumed authority of those who seek to wield power (M. Weber 1947: 152; see also Lukes 1974). HS, therefore, provides a strong recognition that ideas, norms and ideologies matter in IR and security studies, and that one is dealing, as constructivists argue, with a socially constructed reality. But HS maintains a healthy scepticism about taking such ideas and ideologies to be purely altruistic and understands that they are more often likely to be crude exercises in manipulation to meet the material power ambitions of ambitious elites (Halliday 2005: 32–5).

Historical sociology is also notably sensitive to the historical development and evolution of the state and the complex ways in which states have formed over time in different places and regions. As is explored in more detail in the next chapter, one of the most significant contributions of HS to the understanding of international security is in its attention to how war and conflict have contributed to the formation of states. This applies particularly to the ways in which wars forged European states and how such European war-fighting capabilities led to the expansion, through imperialism, of the nation-state system to other parts of the world (Bull 1984b; Tilly 1985). In HS, the state continues to be recognized as a vital actor not only because of its powers of coercion, but also for its complex set of relations with other social forces and its varying capacity to discipline and control these forces. As an intellectual tradition, HS does not seek to reify the state or take it as a 'given', as can be found in rationalist neo-realist accounts, nor does it try somehow to sublimate or overcome the state, as in postmodern constructivist accounts.

HS thus provides a basis for recognition of the continuing vitality of the state, particularly in the area of the provision of security, but also a way to understand the very different forms of the state, and state–society relations, currently existing in different parts of the world.

Historical sociology therefore provides a critical tool for understanding the interaction of states and international security. Its sensitivity to historical processes highlights the multiple ways in which states have been formed and the continuing legacies of the experiences of state formation. It helps to break down the state into its constituent parts, particularly the varying complex ways in which it relates to and interacts with the other social forces within it. Being a catholic tradition, HS can also provide a broad and inclusive framework within which the insights of rationalist and constructivist accounts can be incorporated. One further advantage, which is particularly relevant for post-Cold War security, is that it gives a greater understanding of the roots of conflict between the North and the South. As such, HS can provide a more realistic and dispassionate theoretical voice to the South, where the Janus-faced nature of the state, as source of both security and insecurity, and its various manifestations can be most effectively understood.

From state security to human and critical security

How does all of this discussion of the varying approaches to the study of international security relate to the classical tripartite theoretical division in IR into realist, liberal and radical traditions? Part of the answer is found in the distinction between explanatory and normative theory, as described earlier in the chapter. The analysis so far, exploring the rationalist, constructivist and historical sociological theoretical approaches, has provided differing methodologies on how the security analyst might seek to *explain* the nature and development of IR and of international security. Realism, liberalism and radicalism, understood as longstanding traditions of thought in IR, certainly include explanation but also, critically, incorporate stronger ideological commitments as to how IR and international security *should* be studied and the prospects for change in the international realm. Realism, liberalism and radicalism are, in this sense, substantive IR theories, providing a more holistic and normatively charged conceptualization of the domain of international relations and of the study of international security.

There is, admittedly, much debate about how separate or distinct the realms of explanatory and normative theory are. The more one moves along the constructivist spectrum, the stronger the claim that the explanatory and normative cannot be neatly separated and that any attempt to explain the world necessarily involves certain, albeit hidden, normative assumptions. This, in part, explains how key developments in the area of substantive IR theory, as applied to international security, reflect some of the same dynamics identified above. Just as there has been a significant shift from rationalist to constructivist accounts in explanatory IR theory, so there has been a parallel shift from realist to liberal and critical normative IR theory. This is particularly evident in the critique of traditional state-centric security by the proponents of human security and the similarly anti-statist critical security approach. Such anti-realist accounts have certainly been strongly inspired by the rise of constructivism, but their deeper philosophical roots are found in the liberal and radical normative traditions, particularly liberal cosmopolitanism and neo-Marxist radicalism. It is to the concept of human security that we first turn.

Towards a human security approach

The concept of human security has arguably been the most influential post-Cold War reconceptualization of security, gaining popularity not only in academic but also in policy-making circles (see, for example, Tehranien 1999; Axworthy 2001; Commission on Human Security 2003). The concept of human security has, in particular, tapped into the widespread perception that the Cold War overemphasized state security to the clear detriment of the millions of people who suffered and died at the hands of the state. As an influential UN report stated in 1995, 'too often in the past, preserving the security of the state has been used as an excuse for policies that undermined the security of people' (UN Commission on Global Governance 1995: 81). Kofi Annan, UN Secretary-General from 1997 to 2006, similarly and consistently argued that 'states are now widely understood to be instruments at the service of their people, and not vice versa' (Annan 1999: 81). The concept of human security, therefore, resonates with the intensive post-Cold War debates over the issue of state sovereignty and intervention, and whether there has been a normative shift towards greater recognition of the international responsibility to protect those suffering from abusive states (Wheeler 2000; ICISS 2001a). The assessment of the post-Cold War dilemmas of intervention in chapter 4 of this book, which deals particularly with the debate over humanitarian intervention, is in large part a discussion about human security.

A further factor behind the popularity of the human security approach is that it offers an alternative to the pessimistic and seemingly narrow concerns of a realist conception of security. In the aftermath of the Cold War, there has been a resurgence of the more cosmopolitan and universalist tradition of liberal internationalism, to which human security is heavily indebted (Beitz 1979; Pogge 1992; O'Neill 1996). From this cosmopolitan perspective, the Cold War obsession with military interstate conflict appears not only anachronistic but also criminally complacent, ignoring the sufferings and insecurities of the millions caught in the nexus of poverty, underdevelopment and civil war. In this context, it is perhaps not unsurprising that the concept of human security was first promoted most strongly by the developmental arm of the United Nations, the UN Development Programme (UNDP), which had consistently felt itself marginalized during the Cold War. In an influential report published in 1994, the UNDP argued that the Cold War focus on state security had obscured and ignored the far more urgent security needs of the millions for whom 'security symbolized protection from the threat of disease, hunger, unemployment, crime, social conflict, political repression and environmental hazards' (UNDP 1994: 23). The UNDP's promotion of human security, in this sense, can be seen as a politically inspired attempt to broaden the concept of security, so that the narrow strategic concerns of the rich and powerful states, particularly in the less threatening post-Cold War period, appear relatively insignificant and unimportant compared to the deep insecurities of the poor and the powerless. Human security thus converts development issues and humanitarianism into explicit security priorities, representing a significant shift from the narrower Cold War conceptions of security.

Human security has certainly had its critics, not least for its purported lack of academic rigour (see Suhrke 1999; Khong 2001; Paris 2001). But its practical contribution to the study of post-Cold War contemporary security is still considerable. It has, on a broad theoretical level, demanded a shift in thinking about security priorities towards a more cosmopolitan and less narrowly state-driven approach, which produces significant new perspectives on most security issues. An instructive instance of this is examined in chapter 7, where it is argued that excessive focus on interstate geopolitical struggles over water and energy security can obscure the urgency of the human insecurity of the millions without access to clean and accessible water and cheap energy resources. Human security, in this way, highlights the often marginalized dimensions of international insecurity, in particular the insecurities tied to the global inequalities of power and wealth. The human security approach has also had a strongly practical impact through its policy-relevant and activist research agenda. This, again, has focused attention on some of the traditionally marginalized dynamics inducing violence, such as the global proliferation of small weapons, the profusion of landmines, the tragic and abusive practice of child soldiers, and the conflicts driven by competition for access to valuable resources (Krause 2004).

There are, though, some significant problems with the human security approach. As with liberal internationalism and the older concept of collective security, the human security approach has found it hard to avoid the perennial criticism that its conception of security is too broad and diffuse (Hurrell 1992; Mearsheimer 1994–5). Like collective security, which is examined more fully in chapter 5, human security has the problem that making almost everything potentially a security issue devalues the meaning of security, so that it loses its urgency, and collective responsibility for action is weakened rather than strengthened (Paris 2001: 93). The danger is that human security so expands the concept of security that it becomes conflated with a whole set of other issues, such as development, poverty, health, disease and inequality, effectively emptying the concept of substantive meaning and making it impossible to identify more or less important security challenges (see Owen 2004: 375).

An additional problem is that human security depends on isolating a cosmopolitan moral realm, where the needs of suffering individuals must be met wherever they might be, and where the particularistic and selfish strategic interests of states are excluded. In practice, this is highly idealistic. It is not just, as explored more fully in chapter 4, that human security issues like humanitarian intervention are rarely driven solely by humanitarian motives but through a complex mix of humanitarian and strategic interests. It is also that, even if human security does reflect many of the security concerns of the poorer and less powerful states and their peoples, the human security approach becomes inevitably compromised when it is used as an instrument presumptively justifying Northern foreign policy initiatives and interventions. From a Southern perspective, human security can appear, in the hands of the North, as another ideological instrument for neo-imperialism (Thomas and Tow 2002). Humanitarian agencies, development agencies and aid workers have had similar concerns. The fear here is that the promotion of human security politicizes and securitizes the provision of humanitarian assistance, making such assistance dependent on meeting certain security conditions, such as implementing anti-terrorism measures, rather than on the basis of strict need.

A further problem is that human security does not, and cannot, offer a solution to the problem of the state. This is an issue which has already been addressed in chapter 1. Suffice it to say at this point that the human security approach tends to glide over the Janus-faced nature of the state, the ways in which the state is both a source of insecurity and a provider of security to its citizens, and how the state remains, despite its abuses and murderous actions, the principal source of political legitimacy. Human security is best understood, in the context of this problematic of the state, as an unconditional indictment not of the concept of the state but rather of the abusive practices of particular states which have either collapsed or have become so perverted as to wage war against their own populations. The human security challenge is misplaced, therefore, if it seeks to replace the state by some cosmopolitan alternative rather than supporting the reconstruction of failing or failed states so that they can be minimally secure and provide for the interests of their citizenry.

The critical security alternative[1]

The 'critical security' approach shares with the human security approach the ambition to problematize the idea of the state as both provider and locus of

---

[1] I am grateful for the revisions to this section undertaken by Jamie Allinson.

security. A number of critical security theorists have sought to rework and include human security in their analysis (Dunne and Wheeler 2004), sharing much of the cosmopolitan commitment of human security and its opposition to realist and state-centric conceptualizations of security. But where there is a clear parting of the ways is in the scepticism of the critical approach about the liberal internationalism underpinning the human security agenda. This is where the intellectual roots in the radical Marxist tradition of critical security theory are most evident. Human security holds dangers in the same way that economic neo-liberalism is seen by critical theorists to be used to justify the continuing subjugation of the South by the North. Thus critical security theorists tend to highlight the ways in which human security, in the hands of the powerful, can become a tool to securitize economic and political issues and to justify pre-emptive intervention.

The IR critical security approach is broad and heterogeneous, ranging from the critical security studies school to feminist and post-structuralist contributions to security studies (for an overview, see Krause 1998; Wyn Jones 2001). What is 'critical' about this critical security theory? The unifying theme is the understanding that, in Robert Cox's words, 'theory is always for someone and some purpose' (R. Cox 1986). In this view, realism and liberalism are 'problem-solving' theories seeking technical solutions to the needs of the established political and social relations rather than questioning such relations. Critical theory, by contrast, is distinctive in its claim to challenge these relations and to identify ways in which they might be radically transformed. Critical security theory thus draws on a Marxist intellectual heritage both in its aspiration to 'ruthless criticism of all that exists' (such as the traditional notion of security embedded in the state) and in its ambition to understand this state of affairs in order to change it.

This inheritance is one more of intellectual attitude than of specific concepts. The varied body of Marxist theory in international relations has generally focused on the relationship between capitalism and the state system in two particular axes: the question of whether the tendency produced by expanding capitalist relations is towards war or a unified 'ultra-imperialism', on the one hand, and the origins and nature of the relations of subordination and domination between the North and the South, on the other. For the most part, Marxists have focused on these overarching relationships rather than on the concept of security itself – taking for granted, perhaps, that the security of the state refers to the security of the ruling class within the capitalist mode of production. This has led to the suggestion in one reading that Marxists need to incorporate a 'realist moment' into their explanations (Callinicos 2007) – a suggestion strongly resisted by those who see realism as an essentially inadequate theory of world politics (Pozo-Martin 2007: 559).

Critical security theory takes as its point of departure rather the concept of security itself and how it should be contested and problematized in order to be transformed. It thus draws heavily on the contributions of both Antonio

Gramsci and the Frankfurt School of Marxist-influenced philosophers and sociologists to understand conventional security discourses as obstacles to human emancipation. As such, the role of the critical theorist is to deconstruct these discourses in the service of a commitment to a 'freer and more self-determining society' (Booth 2007: 43). This brand of theory is particularly strongly represented at Aberystwyth and in the work of Ken Booth and Richard Wyn Jones. In this reading, presenting security as the highest value of the state therefore tends to act as an instrument of oppression rather than emancipation, since there is no neutral ground between the oppressed and the oppressor. Furthermore, the militarized nature of the traditional security discourse in fact renders many people unsafe, diverting resources away from responses to other problems or militarizing those responses themselves, as in the case in 2005 of Hurricane Katrina in the southern US (Fierke 2007: 192).

Critical security studies therefore rejects the assumption of a pact where individuals give up freedom to be protected by the state in a Hobbesian world: the resulting hierarchies that supposedly protect the weak actually reproduce the power of the strong (Fierke 2007: 190). However, it is possible for security itself to escape this bind if it is reconceived as emancipation from unchosen constraints on those individuals' lives. Such constraints include war and the threat of violence as well as poverty, environmental degradation and so forth – security and emancipation are therefore 'two sides of the same coin' (Booth 1991: 316). One way to reach this state of affairs may be through the emancipatory potential of language developed in the 'theory of communicative action' of Jürgen Habermas (Wyn Jones 2001: 18). Critical security studies thus applies the idea of emancipation to the concept of security itself.

One of the major contributions of critical security studies is thus to question hegemonic conceptions of security and to argue that these conceptions, often taken as 'given' or universal truths, frequently reflect the particular security fears and concerns of the North. Further, critical security theorists argue, such conceptions often also act as displacement mechanisms, allowing the North to blame the South for essentially Northern-generated security problems. An example of this is explored in chapter 6, where critical theorists such as Simon Dalby and Jon Barnett have argued that the concept of environmental security has been used to attempt to shift responsibility for environmental degradation from the North to the South (Dalby 1999; Barnett 2001: 86–7). Similarly there have been valuable critical security accounts of the post-Cold War linkage of security with democracy, arguing that Northern concerns are driven more by the need to subdue the security threats coming from these poorer regions than by a genuine commitment to development, which would require far more resources than the North is willing to provide (Duffield 2001). The critical security approach plays, in these and similar ways, a vital role in unmasking some of the hypocrisies and ambiguities of Northern-dominated conceptualizations of security.

Critical security studies thus retains a strong commitment to a generalized notion of human emancipation, whether in the case of North–South relations or in the concept of security itself. However, a second stream of theories looks at the traditional sphere of security through the lens of French post-structuralist (often called 'postmodern') thought such as Jacques Derrida and Julia Kristeva. These post-structuralist theorists are far more sceptical of the idea of human emancipation, identifying it with the 'classical discourse' of Marxism, Enlightenment and progress (Wyn Jones 2001: 12). Rather, these thinkers use the apparatuses of 'discourse' and 'genealogy' to analyse security, war and diplomacy. Lene Hansen, for example, argues that security is 'a particular form of identity construction . . . tied to the sovereign state . . . and a distinct rhetorical and discursive force which bestows power as well as responsibility on those speaking within it' (Hansen 2006: 34). This is similar to the Copenhagen School approach to security: however, for Hansen, threats and insecurities do not just undermine the state, they *constitute* it, for the state knows itself only through contrast with a threatening 'Other' (ibid.; see also Campbell 1992, 1998). Furthermore, this mutual constitution of Self (state) and Other (threat) occurs not in the material realm but among and between texts (Hansen 2006: 3). There are no prior, given identities that can make themselves secure in their interactions: the identity and the process are one (ibid.: 20). One example of these processes of identity construction might be the post 9/11 discursive identification of Muslims with violence, terrorism and insecurity contrasted with Western states defending democracy and freedom against that 'threat' (Fierke 2007: 89).

There is a strong crossover of approach in post-structuralist and feminist work on security (see Hansen 2000; Fierke 2007). A particular crossover is the idea that security is a *process* of discourse and practices rather than a thing (whether emancipation or deterrent capability) to be obtained or as absent (Sylvester 2002, 1994). Feminist theory has contributed to security studies in identifying the masculinized logic and grammar of security (Tickner 1992; Steans 1998). Carol Cohn's deconstruction of male sexual imagery used in Cold War nuclear discourse gives a particularly striking example of how high-level security policy is deeply embedded in conceptions of gender roles and masculinity (Cohn 1987). War and violence have perpetually relied on a distinction between male violence and female passivity, between male combatants and female non-combatants, with women's experiences being marginalized and ignored (Elshtain 1987; Enloe 1990). The binary distinctions of security studies – inside/outside, protector/protected – map closely onto gendered ideas of masculinity and femininity, so that the highest values of the state are constructed as masculine and placed above those which are positioned as feminine, with tangible effects in foreign and security policy (Hooper 2000). This is despite the fact that women are as much involved in, and victims of, armed conflict and insecurity as men (Fierke 2007: 191).

It is important to recognize, feminist theorists would add, that gender is not merely an addition to security studies and that the omission of gender in other analyses does not make them gender-neutral. Rather, to be accurate and rigorous, all scholarship must take account of the gendered nature of world politics (Sjoberg 2010: 2). Gender is not a physical fact or something that only women possess: it means 'a set of social practices and relations', intertwined with other identities, which determine what 'man' and 'woman' mean (Khalili 2011: 1476). Men are trained, not born, to fight wars, and this training centres around a discourse of toughness and violence directed either to protect the feminized sphere of the 'home front' or to humiliate the enemy by feminizing and thereby dominating them (Fierke 2007: 59). These ideas are reproduced in the discourses and practices of security studies. Even within notionally more critical approaches, women feature only as an absence. Drawing on the work of the gender theorist Judith Butler, Lene Hansen shows how the Copenhagen School is unable to recognize gender-based insecurity because women have been rendered silent and thereby invisible to the 'speech-act' methodology that underlies this approach (Hansen 2000: 300).

Feminist security studies has greatly expanded the empirical boundaries of the discipline, in particular explorations of the role women play in combat, war and conflict resolution, peacekeeping, sexual violence in war, and the securitization of gender. The last two have proven particularly important fields of research since UN Security Council Resolution 1325 of 2000, which was intended to incorporate a gender perspective into peacekeeping operations: many feminists are critical of this resolution, arguing that it has taken a largely quantitative approach to the increasing number of women, or number of times women were mentioned, when it came to peace and security resolutions, rather than looking at the way that dichotomous gender thinking operates to privilege certain policies over others (Whitworth 2004: 120). Sexual violence in war, to which men, women and children are all subject, has been shown to reflect 'sexist discourses, which arguably underpin the occurrence of rape . . . intermeshed with other power relations making up the climate of masculine violence inherent to militarization and armed conflict' (Baaz and Stern 2009: 498). In the period since 9/11, feminist security studies has looked at the 'intersectionality' of gender, race and class identity – for example, in how certain feminist rhetorics have been mobilized to support the 'war on terror' (Enloe 2004) or in the sexualized abuse of Iraqi prisoners by female US military personnel (Khalili 2011: 1482).

The post-9/11 security landscape in particular, with its diffuse sense of an enemy based on religious identity and motivated by hatred of 'our freedoms', has thus provided ample space for conceptions of security based on the construction of identity and difference. The era of the 'global war on terror' has also stimulated a stream of critical security studies importing more recent concepts from European political philosophy, especially Michel Foucault and

Giorgio Agamben, which seemed particularly apt to a situation of heightened, but dispersed, surveillance and insecurity.

Again eschewing for the most part the explicit emancipatory commitments of critical security studies, these scholars focus on security as a particular kind of 'bio-political' practice used by 'sovereign power' in the conditions of 'the state of exception' (for an overview, see Dillon and Neal 2008; Reid 2006). The term 'bio-politics' derives from Foucault's concept of 'bio-power': the disciplining practices of the modern state on human populations as a biological entity in institutions such as prisons, schools, hospitals, armies, and so on. Modern social life is thus characterized by apparatuses of security – of surveillance, punishment, regulation – in rendering the population governable both at the level of individual anatomy and at that of the 'population' in the sense of a statistical site of risk (Dillon and Lobo-Guerrero 2008: 271). However, unlike the emancipatory theorists, the Foucauldians do not posit free individuals against oppressive structures. The modern individual is in fact constituted by these processes: 'freedom is nothing but the correlative development of apparatuses of security', according to Foucault (ibid.: 265). Moreover, the key characteristic of the modern state is its sovereign power of the production of life through such practices – but also of death. In Agamben's work, sovereignty lies in the power of the state to declare a situation an 'exception' beyond the normal operation of law but without which that very operation cannot exist – an extension of its power to render certain individuals merely bodies ('bare life') rather than citizens (see Agamben 1998).

Such ideas had a powerful resonance with the idea of a 'new normal' after the 9/11 attacks in which politics would have to be reconfigured or suspended in the name of security (Agamben 2005; Butler 2004; Neal 2008; Reid 2006). Agamben argues that the 'biopolitical significance of the state of exception as the original structure in which law encompasses living beings by means of its own suspension emerges clearly' in President Bush's order establishing military commissions to try prisoners in sites such as Guantánamo Bay (Agamben 2005: 3). Indeed, the inmates of such sites represent 'bare' or 'precarious' life, reduced to bodies without citizenship (Butler 2004: 68). The state thus operates security, God-like, through the giving and taking away of life, and neither side of the equation can be ignored.

Critical security approaches, varied though they are, contribute to a different perspective towards security studies, shifting the focus away from the state, incorporating the voices of the hitherto marginalized and disenfranchised, and introducing an explicit normative commitment to emancipation. Yet critical theory itself is far from free of criticism. Perhaps the easiest criticism to be made by 'traditional' security analysts is that, even if critical security studies rejects problem-solving theory, there are still problems to solve. A more traditional security analyst might argue that, although sharply dissecting the problems of the present system, critical security studies approaches remain vague about what an emancipated world would actually look like. If critical theory judges itself by the criteria of the 'challenges that it – that we – face in the real world of world politics' (Wyn Jones 2001: 19), then, the traditional theorist might ask, is it so wrong to orient oneself towards solving those challenges through identifiable and existing means?

There is another, perhaps stronger and more radical, critique of critical security studies. This is the argument that, in identifying emancipation with security in general, critical security studies inhibits the potential for actual emancipation (see Aradau 2004; Peoples 2011). Whatever the faults of classical Marxism as a theoretical and political system, it did identify who had to emancipate themselves (the workers), from what (capitalism) and by what means (revolutionary class struggle against the capitalists). Critical security approaches seem at times to propose liberation from all threats, violence and misfortune in general. Yet this move leads critical security theorists to sidestep the question of violence committed in the name of emancipation. Columba Peoples points to the 'troubling prospect . . . that commitment to emancipatory change' may even require violence and therefore insecurity for someone (Peoples 2011: 1115). A mischievous critic might suggest, in the manner of the radical intellectual Slavoj Žižek, that, to be serious about emancipation from 'systemic violence' (Žižek 2008: 2), critical security studies should not just deconstruct security threats, but seek to become one.

Towards a realist moral critique

The inescapability of violence, even in the cause of emancipation, brings one back to more traditional concerns about the structures of power in international politics and the ways in which these might be overcome. Realism is the regular target of critical conceptualizations of security. Indeed, the common assumption is that realism, as a theory, is explicitly anti-normative and essentially amoral, given its assumption of the primacy of the state and the supremacy of selfish national interests. There is, admittedly, much justification for this view, as there is a venerable tradition within realism, following from the political philosophy of Machiavelli, Hobbes and, more recently, Carl Schmitt and John Mearsheimer, where international relations is defined exclusively as the pursuit of political and military advantage, with moral considerations playing a minimal or non-existent role.

But this does not adequately reflect the range of realist thought and thinkers (for variations in realism, see Gilpin 1984). Many realists have been deeply morally concerned citizens, not least theologians such as Reinhold Niebuhr, who was constantly aware of the 'seemingly irreconcilable conflict between the needs of society and the imperatives of a sensitive conscience' (Niebuhr 1932: 257). Hans Morgenthau, the arch-priest of modern realism, certainly criticized morality in IR, but this can be seen as a critique more of a certain type of morality – what he called moralism – than of moral considerations as a whole. A recent assessment of Morgenthau has shown him consciously seeking to offer an alternative to the bleak pessimism of Carl Schmitt and to articulate a conception of politics not purely reducible to violence (M. Williams 2004). Similarly, Henry Kissinger, the archetypical self-consciously realist foreign policy practitioner, recognizes that the moral principles underpinning American society are unavoidable and integral elements in the formulation and conduct of US foreign policy (1994: 812). More generally, realists are frequently engaged in debates about foreign policy where they advocate policies which they think will improve the conduct of international affairs (Desch 2003: 419). In this regard, E. H. Carr noted, in his famous realist critique of liberal idealism, that one of the paradoxes of political science is 'the impossibility of being a consistent and thoroughgoing realist' (1964: 89).

Carr's insight is, in large part, an implicit recognition that most realists do not see themselves as anti-liberal, even in the realm of international relations. Rather, the realist disenchantment is focused mainly on a particular form of liberalism – that of cosmopolitan liberalism. Realists have traditionally offered an alternative consequentialist ethic, incorporating a demand for prudence and pragmatism. The emphasis here is on the need to take full account of the likely intended and unintended consequences of pursuing moral goals in conditions of international anarchy where there is no global Leviathan to punish wrongdoers or reward the virtuous. Failure to take these constraints into account, according to the realist critique, tends to result in policies which not only fail to transform the world in the ways desired but also often make the situation worse than before. It is notable in this regard that realists provided some of the strongest warnings, precisely on the perceived dangers of liberal overexpansionism, against the US war in Vietnam (Morgenthau 1975) and, more recently, the US occupation of Iraq (Mearsheimer and Walt 2003).

Realism's underlying liberal normative commitment is derived, if often only implicitly, from the liberal communitarian tradition (Vincent 1986; Rawls 1993; Miller 1995). This typically includes a rejection of the Kantian universalism of liberal internationalism and the adoption of a Humean moral subjectivism, where the possibilities of moral action are facilitated or constrained by the limits of our moral sympathies. In this regard, the normative priority accorded by realists to the state in which an individual lives, rather than to foreign states, is a natural reflection of the greater sympathy and the stronger moral commitment that we have to the communities in which we live and have our meaning. One clear practical outcome of this is that inevitably the statesman is going to give greater priority to the interests of his own citizens than to foreigners. Certainly, this does exclude altruism, humanitarianism, or the prospect for improved international behaviour and international solidarity. But, as will be argued in chapter 8, when it comes to key security issues such as deciding whom the state is to welcome or reject as new citizens, the state remains an elitist and exclusivist actor. Similarly, when it comes to a decision between responding to a disaster far away in a distant land or to one just on one's doorstep, priority will almost always be given to the closer one (see chapter 4).

The realist worldview recognizes a plural rather than a monistic moral universe. It is an understanding of the world where different communities, separated however imperfectly into different states, have diverging moral conceptions and understandings as a natural consequence of their particular cultures, histories and trajectories of development. It is here that the realist outlook has some significant parallels with the insights of historical sociology. For the realist, the moral value both of the state system and of the principles of political sovereignty and territorial integrity is that they provide a minimally acceptable framework to enable differing and sometimes antagonistic moral communities to coexist. This does not mean that differing cultures are locked into incommensurate value systems, with an inevitable 'clash of civilizations' and lack of cross-cultural dialogue and agreement. But it does bring out the danger of a cosmopolitan liberal internationalism articulating universal and timeless truths which might, in practice, reflect the morality of one particular group, often the most powerful, and which can thus contribute to fatefully ignoring the reality of the moral fragmentation of international society. It is at this point that liberal internationalism can be transformed into neo-imperialism.

Conclusion

Overall, realism understood as a distinctive moral tradition plays a role similar to historical sociology in supplementing and providing additional depth to the theoretical developments in the liberal and radical traditions. Human security and the critical security approach do provide significant and important insights into contemporary security studies, often drawing on the methodological insights of constructivism, and have enriched our understanding of contemporary international security. As such, the realist and historical sociological counter-critique is not to subvert the radical conscience of critical security, particularly the reality of the deep and immoral levels of inequality in global wealth, or to deny the human security imperative to promote and defend human rights. It is also not to deny that states are often the most brutal violators of individual security and that they can use security as an instrument of oppression rather than emancipation. Instead, realism and historical sociology act as cautionary reminders of how debates and developments in international security take place in a quintessentially political framework. Security studies cannot be divorced from the international competition for material advantage and ideological supremacy, or from the political reality of a world divided culturally, developmentally and in terms of historical pasts and memories. It is also a world where neither security nor the state is likely to be transcended or sublimated, at least in the foreseeable future. It is in this messy reality that the security analyst as scientist, internationalist and moralist must seek to balance the competing needs of security over those of other core values, such as freedom, prosperity and justice. It is this task which the following more empirical chapters address.

FURTHER READING

For one of the best and most comprehensive surveys of the realist, liberal and radical traditions in IR theory, see Michael Doyle's *Ways of War and Peace* (1997). A good brief guide to more recent developments in IR theory is Jack Snyder, 'One world, rival theories', in *Foreign Policy* (2004).

In terms of the rationalist and constructivist debate within IR, the best place to start is with the key neo-realist texts by Kenneth N. Waltz, *Theory of International Politics* (1979), and John J. Mearsheimer, *The Tragedy of Great Power Politics* (2001), and the key constructivist counter-critique of Alexander Wendt, *Social Theory of International Politics* (1999). For variants in realist thought, particularly between the 'defensive' and 'offensive' schools, see Stephen Brooks, 'Duelling realisms', in *International Organization* (1997). For the so-called neo-neo debate, see David Baldwin, *Neorealism and Neoliberalism: The Contemporary Debate* (1993). For recent work in the neo-realist tradition, see Fareed Zakaria, *From Wealth to Power: The Unusual Origins of America's World Role* (1998), and, in the constructivist approach, see Margaret E. Keck and Kathryn Sikkink, *Activists beyond Borders: Advocacy Networks in International Politics* (1998).

The key text for the securitization approach is Barry Buzan, Ole Waever and Jaap de Wilde, *Security: A Framework for Analysis* (1998). A critique of the approach can be found in a special symposium in the journal *Cooperation and Conflict* (Ericksonn 1999). For an overview of the various traditions of historical sociology in IR, see Steven Hobden and John Hobson (eds), *Historical Sociology of International Relations* (2002). A more cohesive account is found in Fred Halliday, *Rethinking International Relations* (1994).

On human security and the UN, see Edward Newman and Oliver Richmond, *The United Nations and Human Security* (2001). A useful symposium on human security can be found in a special edition of the journal *Security Dialogue* (Burgess and Owen 2004). Roland Paris, 'Human security: paradigm shift or hot air?', in *International Security* (2001), provides a good, if critical, survey of the human security approach. Critical security, understood as a fairly broad and inclusive church, is covered in Keith Krause and Michael C. Williams (eds), *Critical Security Studies: Concepts and Cases* (1996), and in Karen Fierke, *Critical Approaches to International Security* (2007). The more narrowly defined Welsh School of Critical Security Studies finds its expression in Richard Wyn Jones, *Security, Strategy and Critical Theory* (1999).

Questions for Research and Discussion

1 How does social constructivism challenge realist and neo-realist understandings of international security?
2 How does securitization theory help us to understand the nature and dynamics of international security? What examples can you provide?
3 What is 'critical' about critical security studies?
4 Does human security provide a better and more moral way to understand international security?

WEBSITES

www.carnegiecouncil.org
The Carnegie Council for Ethics in International Affairs, founded by Andrew Carnegie in 1914. It aims to be the world's central resource for normative thinking and ethical decisions in international affairs.

www.hsrgroup.org
The Human Security Research Group, which seeks to track global and regional trends in human security. It produces various publications on human security, including an annual *Human Security Report*.

www.prio.no
The Peace Research Institute Oslo – a leading peace research institute which adopts a 'critical' or more radical approach to war and peace. It conducts research on the conditions for peaceful relations between states, groups and peoples.

PART II

The 'New Wars' and Intervention

CHAPTER 3

Understanding Contemporary War and Insecurity

Some of the most dynamic debates in contemporary IR theory have sought to understand and to respond to the phenomenon of the so-called new wars. As argued in chapter 1, the historical peculiarity of the post-Cold War period is in the unprecedented luxury of not expecting, at least in the near to medium term, the threat of large-scale war between the great powers. But this outwardly more benign context, where the threat of a third world war has greatly diminished, does not mean that the scourge of war has been eliminated. Rather, war has assumed new and no less brutal forms. This is evident in figure 3.1 and figure 3.2, where it can be seen that, while the incidence of wars between states has been in decline since the 1960s, this has been paralleled by a significant increase in the numbers of civil wars, peaking in the immediate post-Cold War period of the early 1990s.

These internal intrastate wars have been characterized by a seemingly new level of brutality and disregard for the basic humanitarian principles to be observed during warfare (Enzensberger 1994; Ignatieff 1998). This sense of the changing nature of contemporary warfare, where violent conflict increasingly involves brutal civil wars shorn of classical warfare's traditional Clausewitzian moorings, has led to many commentators describing these conflicts as 'new wars' (Gray 1997; Kaldor 2012; Münkler 2005). The representation of 'new wars' has also tended to posit a North–South binary opposition, between a 'zone of peace' in the developed industrialized world, where great power peace operates, and 'zones of turmoil' in the poorer developing world, where pervasive conflict and civil wars are present (see, for example, Goldgeier and McFaul 1992; Cooper 2003).

The IR theoretical response to the severity of the challenges presented by these multiple civil wars has been part of the revival of liberal internationalism and the promotion of the concept of human security as described in the previous chapter. It is the conviction of a liberal internationalist and cosmopolitan responsibility that has contributed to the emergent norm of humanitarian intervention, where the suffering of those caught up in these internecine conflicts has been seen to enjoin an obligation to intervene to end the fighting. This is discussed more fully in the next chapter. In addition, the evidence that it is civilians and non-combatants who are the principal

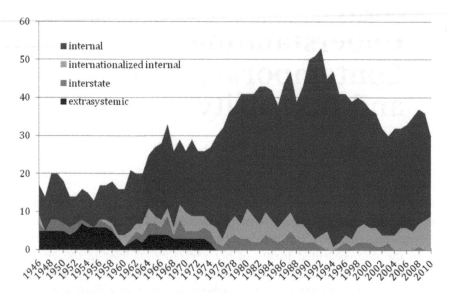

Figure 3.1 Interstate and intrastate armed conflict, 1946–2010
Source: Lotta Themnér and Peter Wallensteen, 'Armed conflict, 1946–2010', *Journal of Peace Research*, 48/4 (2011): 525–36.

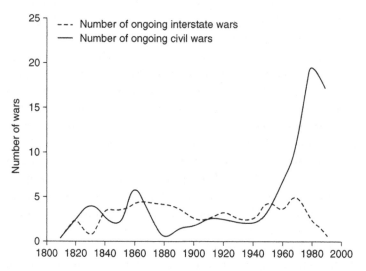

Figure 3.2 Correspondence of interstate wars and ongoing civil wars, 1816–1997
Source: Hironaka (2005: 38).

victims in these wars has promoted human security campaigns to outlaw landmines, to curtail the exploitation of child soldiers, and to stem the proliferation of small arms (UNDP 1994; Suhrke 1999; Dunne and Wheeler 2004). The evident failure of many states to provide for the security of their citizens, and often their actions as a source of violence against their own populations, has further contributed to a radical questioning of the identification of the state with security.

Such theoretical responses have been critical for framing the appropriate policy responses to the brutality of many of these civil wars. But they are less successful in providing a coherent explanation and understanding of the structural roots of the phenomenon of the 'new wars'. As argued in the previous chapter, this is where a historical sociological account is helpful, as it locates these post-Cold War developments in the broader context of the historical evolution of the insecurities of the state and of state–society relations, particularly in the South. This chapter seeks to demonstrate how the rise of these wars is one, if extreme, manifestation of a broader set of insecurities experienced by many Southern states. The main argument is that the prevalence of such insecurities, among which the 'new wars' figure, is intimately linked to the nature of the state in the South and the particular and diverse trajectories of Southern state formation.

Towards a historical sociological account

As was argued in chapter 1, the historical sociological approach is catholic in its outlook and includes, rather than excludes, alternative ways of conceptualizing contemporary international relations. This catholicity applies also to the differing interpretations of the 'new wars' phenomenon. Three of these have been most prominent in the academic literature. The first and perhaps the most influential argues that conflict is based increasingly less on ideological difference, as was the case during the Cold War, and increasingly more on issues of communal identity, whether ethnic, national, religious or even civilizational (see Huntington 1993; Brubaker and Laitin 1998; Saideman 2001). The post-Cold War wars of secession in the former Yugoslavia and the former Soviet Union have emboldened this so-called ancient hatreds explanation for the brutality of these conflicts and the replacement of communist ideology by ethnic and cultural difference (Kaplan 1994a; Kaufmann 1996).

A second popular interpretation places greater emphasis on the dynamics of globalization as the critical causal factor behind the 'new wars' and the resurgence of identity-based conflicts. On this analysis, it is primarily globalization which has led to a complementary process of fragmentation, whether of states, identities or cultures (see, for example, Duffield 1998; Kaldor 2012). At the same time, the 'negative' sides of globalization – for example, the international trade in small arms, drugs and valuable minerals such as diamonds, oil and timber – are seen to fuel civil wars and perpetuate a powerful and self-sustaining war economy (Keen 1998; Berdal and Malone 2000; Renner 2002).

A third interpretation focuses more specifically on the problems of governance and institutional capacity, highlighting the fact that the majority of these conflicts have occurred within states which have 'collapsed' or simply 'failed' to provide the institutions and practices to provide security to their citizens. The 'failed state' phenomenon has been an increasing concern of researchers and international policy-makers in seeking to understand contemporary conflict (Esty et al. 1995, 1998; Zartman 1995). This, in turn, has contributed to the oft-cited division between 'zones of peace' and 'zones of turmoil'.

All of these various explanations do have their weaknesses and problems, though, even as they help to illuminate many of the critical dimensions of contemporary warfare. At a most basic level, some commentators have challenged the claim of 'newness' for the 'new wars', arguing that historical parallels can be found with warfare in late medieval or early modern Europe or with many colonial or imperial wars (Kalyvas 2001; Münkler 2005). In addition, others have noted that many of the current civil wars actually have their root causes in the Cold War, belying a radical disjuncture between the Cold War and post-Cold War periods (Hironaka 2005: 4–5).

The claim that these conflicts should be understood in terms of 'ancient hatreds' has been challenged by analysts who argue that most of the grievances behind these wars are contingent, constructed by elites and contemporary in origin. For instance, contrary to popular perceptions, the Balkan wars were not just the resurrection of an ancient feud between Serbs and Croats, since, as Jack Snyder notes, 'Serbs and Croats never fought each other until the twentieth century' (2000: 18). Criticism has similarly been made about the idea that the 'new wars' can simply be understood as a consequence of the complex phenomenon of globalization. A purely economistic and determinist account fails, it is argued, to capture the complex historical roots and sources of many of the wars fought in sub-Saharan Africa and elsewhere (Cramer 2002; Berdal 2003). In addition, the concentration of research on 'failed states' and the implicit bifurcation between strong states in the North and weak and failing states in the South are seen by many to be too simplistic. Instead, the phenomenon of the 'new wars' needs to be placed within a broader security continuum which ranges from conditions of relative security to deeper insecurity and contestation. The reality is of much variation in both North and South, and the fact that a country in sub-Saharan Africa or the Middle East or Asia is not engaged in a civil war does not mean that it is necessarily peaceful and secure: there are often deep sources of internal and external insecurities which need to be identified and recognized.

The adoption of a distinctively historical sociological account seeks to incorporate the insights provided by these competing explanatory frameworks, while also seeking to rectify their limitations and weaknesses. The approach taken in this chapter does, though, depend on a differentiation between the experiences of state formation in the North, with roots in the European pioneers of the modern state, and those in the South, meaning those states whose state formation processes were determined by external pressures and forces, primarily those of the expansionist European imperial powers. The first section argues that the current relative stability of the North is due, in significant ways, to the legacies of earlier European wars. These wars, and the constant threat of large-scale conquest they engendered, contributed to the emergence of strong states, representative political institutions and a countervailing civil society. This experience represents the paradoxical roots of the so-called democratic peace.

The second section provides the core argument that it is the way in which the experiences and legacies of state formation in the South differ from those of the North which is a key explanatory variable in the wider condition of insecurity found in the South. Despite the manifold variations in the historical development of countries in the South, what is common is the experience of the external imposition of statehood and of the necessity to operate in a regional and international system significantly constrained and controlled by external powers. The consequence of this, it is argued, is that the South has inherited a legacy of state formation which has, at least in part, contributed to the presence of weak and often artificial states, where state–civil relations lack synergy and tend towards clientelism, and where there is only partial or limited integration into regional and global economic processes.

But this analysis does not depend on the construction of a monolithic South whose development is crudely determined by exogenous forces. State trajectories in the South differ markedly, affected by the continuing salience of premodern indigenous legacies and the differing ways in which Southern states have forged their own developmental strategies. Table 3.1 sets out the main conclusions of the chapter. The table is necessarily inexact, but it seeks to establish that it is only in the extreme category of weak and 'failed' states that the incidence of warlordism and the phenomenon of the 'new wars' are primarily located. There are, though, many states which might outwardly seem more stable, but which suffer from considerable insecurities only barely contained by severe domestic repression. This is the category of the 'praetorian' states. And there is also a third category of countries in the South which are 'globalizing', developing strong and synergistic states whose security concerns are increasingly shifting from domestic repression to external projection.

State formation and Northern security

The first part of the argument, therefore, explores the role that war has played in the European state formation process and how this has resulted in the seemingly paradoxical end-point of the European and broader Northern 'democratic' peace. It is the work of Charles Tilly and other historical sociologists, such as Michael Mann, Gianfranco Poggi and John Hall, which has brought out most clearly how the threat of war was one critical dimension in the historical roots of state formation and the emergence of the modern

Table 3.1 Typology of state types and key features

	Developed	Globalizing	Praetorian	Failed
Main features	Advanced industrialized states, i.e. US, Europe, Japan; the North or the core	Developing states which are integrating into global economy, i.e. China, India, Brazil, Russia	Developing states, normally characterized by inward-looking authoritarian regimes	Developing states where state institutions and structures have broken apart
Statehood	Strong	Strengthening	Weak	Very weak or collapsed
State–society	Synergistic	Increasingly synergistic	Repressive	Violent
Globalization	Positive and thick	Increasingly positive and thick	Thin	Thin and/or negative
Security implications	Externalized; 'democratic' or 'nuclear' peace; Southern (humanitarian) interventionism	Increasingly externalized; only partially in 'democratic peace'; opposed to humanitarian interventionism	Internalized; repression and internal conflict dominant	Warlordism, civil wars, 'new wars'; the object of most humanitarian interventions

European state (Poggi 1978; Hall 1985; Tilly 1990; M. Mann 1993). Tilly's argument that 'war makes states' asserts that the preparation and waging of wars were critical to the process of the consolidation of national states in Europe. The metaphor he uses of 'organized crime' to describe the twin processes of state-making and war-making highlights the degree of coercion and arbitrariness behind the centralization of power in the nascent state, its ambitions of territorial control and extension, and the erosion of local autonomy and difference (Tilly 1985). Moreover, it was the essentially Hobbesian war-dominated strategic environment in which these nascent states found themselves that was highly significant for this expansion of state power. It was not just a question of state-makers subduing internal challenges to state power. The process was also about state elites acting against external regional and global bids for domination and hegemony in a way that was in the interests of both state and society and thus tended to bring the two closer together.

It was this convergence of interests between state rulers and other social forces, based on a common perception of external threats and enemies, which was a central feature of the narrative of European state formation. First, the external context provided a significant contribution to defining and promoting new homogeneous national identities, which gradually supplanted the earlier overlapping subnational and supranational identities characterizing premodern and feudal societies (see Gellner 1983; B. Anderson 1991). The process was certainly slow and proved to be only partially successful, as the continuing strength of regional subnationalisms and ethnic identities in Western Europe demonstrates (A. Smith 1995). But, as Eugen Weber has highlighted, it was the construction of the threat of German hegemony, and the personal experiences of preparing for and fighting wars, which finally turned deeply provincial 'peasants into Frenchmen' (Weber 1972). Similarly, in Great Britain, it was the construction of a common Catholic enemy to the dominant Protestant inheritance that contributed most to the definition of a British national identity, and explains its limited appeal to the Irish (Colley 1992). Yet, whatever the difficulties faced in these projects of nation-state consolidation, their most significant achievement was in granting a certain legitimacy and natural givenness to states which had, in practice, often been arbitrarily forged through war and violence. The resulting concept of the nation-state was an expression of this confidence in the internal legitimacy and strength of the modern European state.

A second outcome of this competitive militaristic environment was the way in which it contributed to the development not only of consolidated national states but also of a synergistic and mutually advantageous relationship between state-makers and other groups and forces within society. One aspect of this arose because the demands of war-making in the early European period, particularly in the context of continual technological advances and changes in the scale of warfare, required the mobilization of ever increasing resources (Finer 1975; W. McNeill 1983; Parker 1988). The only way to ensure the availability of such resources was to increase levels of taxation and to develop the bureaucratic bodies necessary to administer and obtain these taxes. Over time, the military needs of the state paradoxically strengthened the civilian elements of society, since it was from these groups that the state needed to extract the resources necessary for war-making. The bankers and capitalists who were critical to the funding of wars were highly mobile and could always move their assets, relocating to places where conditions were more favourable to their profit-making activities. Overall, the effect is described by Tilly as a process whereby 'agents of states bargained with civilian groups that controlled the resources necessary for effective war-making, and in bargaining gave the civilian groups enforceable claims on the state' (Tilly 1990: 206). The resulting compact between state and civil society served to limit the despotic power of the state and to lay the foundations for increasing civil and political liberties. The state's need to engage with and to penetrate society also led to an overall increase in the power of the state, since the synergistic cooperation between state and society increased what Michael Mann has termed the 'infrastructural' power of the state (Mann 1986, 1993).

The third consequence of this competitive interstate system was its influence on economic development and capitalist expansion. There was, as has already been noted, a constant demand to increase levels of taxation to fund warring activities and to promote innovation to increase the efficiency and lethality of the projection of the use of force. Gautam Sen (1984) has illustrated how state-driven demands for war-making capabilities were critically important in the economic development of Europe and were a key factor in the process of capitalist industrialization. Even the social reforms of the nineteenth century, which contributed to the emergence of the welfare state, find their roots in Bismarck's Prussia and the perceived need for such reforms to mobilize human resources for fighting wars (M. Mann 1993; Giddens 1997). On a more global scale, it was the political and economic dynamism of the European states which led to imperial expansion and the export of the competitive inter-European economic and political systems to the rest of the world (Bull 1984b). The consequence of this was the embedding of a structural division between a rich industrialized core and a weak developing periphery, but within the context of a trading and economic system which many analysts consider to be as globalized, if not more so, than the late twentieth-century economy. Certainly, for the countries at the core, global economic interdependence has generally been perceived in a positive and beneficial light and as an integral part of the expansion of state power.

To summarize the argument so far, it is that interstate war played an important role in European state formation and was a significant influence in the emergence of well-defined and internally legitimate national states, in the formation of mutually beneficial relationships between the state and civil society, and in the evolution of a globally interconnected economy. War was certainly not the only influence or explanation for the birth of the modern state system in Europe, and various other factors – such as geography, culture and the particular form of European feudalism – all played their part in this complex historical development. But the important fact is that the ever present threat of major interstate war was itself a significant causal variable and contributed, in particular, to the conceptualization of security as being defined primarily in terms of external threats. This externalization of threat perception was itself based on the gradual development of states which were perceived to be internally legitimate, representing relatively homogeneous national societies, and where there was societal agreement over basic values and a synergistic and peaceful accommodation between the state and its citizens.

In chapter 1 a detailed assessment was provided of the various processes which ultimately transformed this history of almost constant warfare into the current internal European peace and the consolidation of the 'great power peace'. It was argued that this was due to the confluence of three factors: the declining instrumentality of war, the growth of economic interdependence, and the emergence of a normative liberal consensus associated with the 'democratic peace' thesis. But it should also be kept in mind that this progressive development was itself a fortunate and almost accidental consequence of the legacy of many centuries of bloody conflict. It is not, it should be added, a process which has produced a Northern commitment to pacifism. Although developed liberal states might have lost their appetite for fighting wars against one another, this has not affected their predilection for fighting wars with perceived dissident or abusive states in the South. The emergence of the practice of humanitarian intervention is symptomatic of this, belying the argument for the essentially pacific intentions of the liberal state (see Lake 1992; Reiter and Stamm 1998).

State formation and Southern security

The question now is why the South has generally not replicated this pattern whereby intensive interstate warfare gives rise to the conditions for a generalized peace. In part, as argued in chapter 1, some of the factors which have promoted this Northern peace – in particular, the declining instrumentality of war and the growth of economic interdependence – have affected states beyond the West. For example, a key factor behind the economic and political transitions in the former Soviet Union and China was an elite perception that their relative power was being undermined by excessive military costs and their failure to integrate with the wider world (for the case of the Soviet Union, see Wohlforth and Brooks 2000–1). This led in both cases to a fundamental shift away from defining their strategic posture in terms of military war-fighting capabilities to adopting one based on export-oriented growth.

But this still leaves open the question of why the decline in the incidence of interstate wars has been paralleled by the escalation of smaller-scale but just as brutal intrastate conflicts in the South. The argument of this section is that, again, a historically and sociologically informed understanding of the particular trajectories of state formation in the South, and how these have differed from the European or classical model, is critical to an explanation of the continued prevalence of such intrastate wars. The core of the argument is that the process of state formation in the South has contributed to security being defined primarily in terms of internal threats, where state elites are generally concerned more about the threats from within their own societies than about the threat of external aggression. In a similar fashion, social forces within the state often fear the predations of the state in which they live rather than the aggressive ambitions of neighbours. For both state elites and their citizens, the fear is of civil unrest, repression and internal threat, rather than the external threat of interstate conflict (see Buzan 1991; Migdal, Kohli and Shue 1994; Ayoob 1995).

There are two aspects of the Southern state formation process which are particularly important in this regard. The first is the simple fact that, for the majority of the states in the South, the process has been externally imposed rather than internally generated. At the extreme, the borders of many developing states were simply arbitrarily drawn by colonial diktat. For other political entities which managed to preserve a longer historical continuity, state formation was nevertheless strongly constrained by external imperial pressures. The implications were that only a limited dynamic emerged to generate processes of internal national consolidation and legitimization of the sort provided by the wars and struggles in Europe to the nascent European states. In the South, the state has often been perceived as an external given, usually coercively and arbitrarily defined, and lacking significant internal legitimacy. The process of decolonization tended to exacerbate rather than resolve this problem, since it was the colonial state, in spite of its arbitrariness and coercive origins, which was confirmed by the United Nations as the frame of reference for claims to national self-determination and political independence (Jackson 1993).

This willingness to accept the territorial status quo bequeathed by colonial administrators was driven by a second major distinguishing feature of Southern state formation – the enforced norm against territorial aggrandizement. It is a feature of a majority of Southern states that they have not generally faced the same degree of existential threats to their very survival that marked the experience of European states, and that most interstate disputes have been over more secondary and minor issues (see Herbst 1989, 1990; Wendt and Barnett 1993). There are exceptions to this, such as in Korea, Vietnam and Israel, where the East–West confrontation became superimposed on a historically defined struggle for national unification. However, the relative absence of interstate conflicts in the South can be seen in the fact that the borders of countries in Africa are generally older and more durable than those in Europe, particularly when these are compared with the continually shifting and malleable borders in East-Central Europe. Similarly, in the Middle East, when one excludes the Israel/Palestine question, the borders have remained remarkably stable. In considerable part, this reality can be linked directly to the Northern resolve to promote and enforce in the South the norm against the acquisition of territory by force.

Historically, Northern interest in upholding this norm can be seen to have gone through two stages. The first stage, principally in the nineteenth century and at the height of European imperial expansion, was when European imperial powers sought to ensure that jealousies over their respective colonial or dependent possessions should not be permitted to undermine the European balance of power. The second stage was when territorial aggrandizement was viewed, in particular after the experience of the First World War, as the principal cause of large-scale warfare and when the prohibition against the acquisition of territory by force became institutionalized as an international norm (Zacher 2001). Ian Lustick has illustrated how this norm against territorial aggrandizement, in both its nineteenth- and twentieth-century manifestations, has continually frustrated Arab regional leaders and states seeking to gain a regional hegemonic dominance. Whether it was Muhammad Ali's drive to expand Egyptian power against the Ottoman Empire, Gamal Abdel Nasser's similar ambitions in the 1950s and 1960s, or Saddam Hussein's more recent expansionist moves, these have all been thwarted by Northern intervention (Lustick 1997).

Statehood, civil society and globalization: The generation of insecurities

These two distinctive aspects of state formation in the South – the external imposition of states and the enforced norm against territorial aggrandizement – have left significant legacies for the evolution and development of most developing countries. It is these historical legacies which have made it more difficult for Southern countries to forge strong, synergistic states whose security concerns are externally rather than internally oriented. This does not, though, imply a deterministic analysis where the Southern states are passive actors under imperial or Northern hegemony or an approach which denies the existence of indigenous traditions of national identity and civil society which have successfully resisted Northern impositions. But what is argued is that the historical processes of state formation in the South, with their legacy of insecurity and conflict in many developing states, have had significant effects and consequences. Three dimensions of these are particularly salient for this analysis: the contribution to state fragility; the tendency towards weak civil societies; and the difficulties of integration into global economic processes.

Fragile states

The first general consequence or legacy of the Southern state formation processes can be seen to be the tendency towards fragile, weak and artificial states. It should be stressed that this is a tendency rather than a deterministic inevitability and that there is much variation in the South. At its extreme, though, there is the phenomenon of the so-called quasi-state – meaning a state which has been accorded judicial sovereignty but which lacks certain essential features of internal sovereignty, such as effective control of all of its territory or a centralized monopoly over the legitimate use of force (see Jackson and Rosberg 1982; Jackson 1990). Such states are principally in sub-Saharan Africa, but they are also to be found elsewhere. The sources of their problems lie frequently in the arbitrariness of their creation, cutting across ethnic, tribal and religious communities, their failure to constitute themselves as viable economic entities, and their subsequent lack of political support and legitimacy. The conservative norm of non-intervention has helped to preserve what would otherwise be considered bankrupt or failed states, such as the Congo, Lebanon and Afghanistan. The externally guaranteed stability of the territorial status quo has effectively supported the durability and even proliferation of such weak and clearly artificial states, which would probably never have survived in a European context.

The quasi-state phenomenon is, though, an extreme manifestation. For many Southern states, European imperial dominance failed to destroy a strong sense of a pre-existing national identity and a precolonial indigenous culture. However, the legacy of a colonially imposed but conservative state order has also been a major source of frustration and delegitimization. In China, the legacy of the perceived historical injustices of the European imperial powers, with the sense of territorial loss and dismemberment, has fed into a revisionist national sentiment (Johnston 1995). In the Arab and Muslim world, the perception that the existing states are artificial colonial creations, established expressly to undermine Arab and Muslim unity, has continually weakened their legitimacy, strengthened irredentist ambitions and sustained strong anti-Western sentiment. The perverse logic this has promoted among Arab leaders has been a regional competition for more extreme anti-Zionist Arab or Muslim credentials, which has arguably tended to be related less to the existential fear of Israeli aggression than to threats to regime legitimacy from internal sources of contestation (Kerr 1965; Ajami 1991).

Exceptions among states in the South, though, are those which have faced genuine existential threats to their survival – such as Israel, South Korea or China – and which have consequently also developed relatively stronger states and a greater synergy between state and society (Migdal, Kohli and Shue 1994). The developmental successes of East Asia are due at least partly to the continuing strengths and vitality of the region's traditions of statehood.

Weak civil societies

For the majority of Southern states, though, which have not been compelled by external pressure, most notably through the threat of external aggression, to foster national consolidation, the closely linked consequence has been the failure to develop a strong civil society which can curb and bring to account the despotic actions of the state. As was noted above, it was the threat of and preparation for war in early modern Europe, in the context of a highly competitive interstate system, which served as a critical factor behind the strengthening of civilian power: state-makers had to offer incentives, such as extending civil and political liberties, to ensure the timely appropriation, through taxation, of the resources required for fighting wars. In the historical evolution of the state in the South, the origins of the state as an alien and externally imposed entity have instead left a legacy of the state as an instrument of social coercion whose main purpose is to provide privileged access to the country's material resources (see Clapham 1985; Ayoob 1995).

Instead of a convergence of interests between state and society, strengthening the infrastructural and penetrative power of the state, the struggle for political power has tended to become a zero-sum conflict where differing social groups seek to gain the strategic prize of the state's coercive apparatus and the power and wealth this guarantees. Whichever social group manages to manoeuvre into a position of dominance then treats the state as an instrument both for personal and particularist enrichment and for forcibly subduing the claims of other social groups. The consequence of this is a dominant political class which is continually aware of its precarious hold on power, its lack of legitimacy in relation to other excluded and potentially powerful social groups, and its dependence on coercion for sustaining its capacity to rule. For the general population, the sense of exclusion and the perceived alien nature of the state promote various strategies to avoid or escape from its seemingly arbitrary and despotic embrace. As one commentator on Africa has argued, one of the most distinctive features of the politics of the region has been the 'art of living in a reasonably peaceful way without the state' (Lonsdale 1981).

This failure of societal integration, and the sense of alienation between state elites and other social forces, is particularly marked in those states in the South that rely primarily on external rents – whether from the export of valuable natural resources, from tourism and remittances, or from the generosity of external donors – for the financing of the activities of the state. The concept of the 'rentier' state, which is discussed further in chapter 7, was first developed in the context of the oil-wealthy Middle Eastern states, but it has been fruitfully extended to other parts of the developing world, including Africa and Russia (Mahdavy 1970; Behlawi and Luciani 1987; Yates 1996; Kim 2003). Its main utility as a model is in providing a political explanation for the seeming paradox of how the majority of resource-rich developing countries have signally failed to develop at the same rate and intensity as resource-poor countries at a similar stage of development (Ross 1999; Sachs and Warner 2000).

The rentier state is one manifestation of the alienation and weakness of a civil society, where political power, following the colonial traditions of indirect rule, is secured through a top-down cooption of local elites in complex neo-patrimonial networks of patron–client relations. The key political objective of such neo-patrimonial systems is to reward loyal elites materially rather than to secure the broader developmental interests of the country as a whole. Where resources are secured from outside the state and there is no powerful need to extract resources directly from society, there is similarly no powerful pressure to develop more democratic and accountable systems of power (Ross 2001). In such countries as well, the role of the military, generally bloated and resourced at an excessive level in relation to any potential external threat, is a vital instrument of internal control and a guarantee against internal challenges to central state power. It is not surprising that many of these states are essentially 'praetorian' or 'mukhabarat' (secret service) states, where the military and secret services are either *de facto* in control of the state or are intimately fused into the main structures of political power (Hurewitz 1969; Picard 1988; Krause 1996).

There are, though, significant variations in the nature and degree of the clientelistic political systems in the South. As in the extreme of the 'quasi-state', so also in the 'failed' or 'collapsed' state there is a severe breakdown of state–society relations. In this case, the state resembles a 'shadow state', to use William Reno's term, which is just one social force among others competing in open conflict to gain control of state resources (Reno 1998). Chris Allen has provided a highly textured analysis of how the 'new wars' in Africa, with their extremes of brutality, targeting of civilians, ethnic massacres and warlordism, are themselves part of a broader continuum in the degeneration of clientelistic and neo-patrimonial systems. He argues that 'spoils politics' defines the politics of a number of African states, where the 'primary goal of those competing for political office/power is self-enrichment' (Allen 1995, 1999; see also Chabal and Daloz 1999). Such 'spoils politics' systems, Allen argues, have internal and externally driven pressures, such as excessive corruption and economic decline, which can lead eventually to a more extreme version which he calls 'terminal politics', where there is an intensification and acceleration of violent conflict and state collapse. Terminal politics is characterized by political elites which now have the aim of retaining power 'at all costs, including the perpetuation of endemic violence and civil war, combined with an acute fear of democratic reforms, and opposition even to a sharing of power' (Allen 1999).

'Terminal politics' is, certainly, an extreme manifestation of state collapse driven by the corruption and criminalization of the neo-patrimonial state. But it is linked to broader systems of 'spoils politics' by representing the deviant case rather than the norm. A much larger category of Southern states consists of those which have developed more stable authoritarian and/or bureaucratic political systems, where a significant degree of centralization of power has occurred, and where there is some effective regulation of neo-patrimonial structures and a mitigation of the worst features of clientelistic competition. Such states can also be particularly stable, even if they lack legitimacy.

The stereotypical 'rentier' state often fits into this category, with regimes in control of oil-rich states' wealth generally demonstrating considerable durability (see B. Smith 2004). As a succession of US administrations found to their frustration, Saddam Hussein of Iraq remained firmly in power despite losing two major wars and suffering over a decade of a crippling sanctions regime, and it was only a full-scale invasion which finally dislodged him from power. The Iraqi state might have been effectively at war with its own population, as the massacres of Kurds and Shi'ites demonstrated, but its structures of power, in spite of being narrowly based and lacking in essential legitimacy, were powerfully resistant to internal subversion. The US/UK occupation of Iraq finally broke this resistance but, with the growth of the internal insurgency, the danger arose of the formerly praetorian state being transformed into a failed state. Despite their potential stability, such praetorian, rentier or bureaucratic-authoritarian regimes generally lack the mutually enforcing interactions between state and society which generate the infrastructural power necessary for broad-based state development. In practice, the political and economic rule of such states remains fragmented, indirect and beset with inefficiencies and corruption. As demonstrated by the Arab Spring in 2011, such states are not immune from the consequences of their corruption and developmental failures.

But there are also examples of Southern states where clientelist systems have been counterbalanced by the growth of an independent capitalist market, where accountability, private property and contractual rights are increasingly embedded. The most frequently cited examples are those of East and South-East Asia, such as South Korea, Singapore and Taiwan. According to one of the most authoritative accounts, provided by Peter Evans, the key factor behind the East Asian success in economic transformation is the ability to generate the requisite state–society synergy, or what Evans defines as 'embedded autonomy'. This vital quality of embedded autonomy is present, in Evans's account, when states possesses a well-developed Weberian bureaucracy that is relatively immune from manipulation by rent-seeking social forces, and where state elites are intimately enmeshed into civil society networks (Evans 1995, 1997). This reflects Ernest Gellner's insight that the best test and indicator of civil society is found in the behaviour and attitudes of state elites and the degree to which such elites have internalized values which constrain them from seeking material self-advantage and lead them to promote the broader social, economic and political goals of society as a whole (Gellner 1994).

Challenges of economic integration

The colonial legacies of fragile states and weak civil societies are, in this way, also critical factors behind the difficulties faced by Southern countries in responding to the economic and political demands of economic integration. It is not accidental that it is in East Asia, where strong states have emerged with a synergistic interaction between state and society, that the most successful engagement with the global economy is evident. In other states in the South, where neo-patrimonial and clientelistic political systems are more powerfully embedded, economic integration is seen as potentially more destabilizing, threatening to undercut the social and political bargains on which the political status quo has been constructed. The resistance to such economic integration is also driven, however, by the historical memory of Southern state formation, with the South's forcible incorporation into the European-dominated global economy and the subsequent obstacles placed in the way of autonomous Southern industrialization. It is this historically defined context which contributes to the pervasive claims that globalization is a negative force for Southern states, and that it is the unleashing of such neo-liberal global forces which has weakened the post-Cold War Southern state and provided the conditions for the emergence of the 'new wars' (Duffield 1998; Kaldor 2012).

Globalization is, though, an inherently slippery and contested concept, and such definitional and conceptual problems have tended to weaken the analytical strength of the thesis linking globalization to post-Cold War civil wars (Kalyvas 2001; Berdal 2003). Some greater clarity is possible, though, if two distinctions or disjunctures in the phenomenon of globalization are established. The first is drawn from Robert Keohane and Joseph Nye (2000), who make the distinction between 'thick' and 'thin' globalization (or globalism, as is their preferred term). Thick globalism is what most commentators mean when they refer to globalization, highlighting the intensive networks of global economic, social, political and cultural relations. A classic example of thin globalism, as cited by Keohane and Nye, is the ancient Silk Road, which provided an important but limited economic and cultural link between Europe and Asia. When examining contemporary globalization, the most intensive 'thick' globalism is found primarily inside the triad of developed, industrialized countries: the United States, Europe and Japan. A number of developing countries, such as China, or certain countries in South-East Asia and Latin America, are moving towards thickening their global economic interdependence but are still far away from matching the levels of interdependence found among the 'triad'. For other states and regions in the South, the reality is a much thinner manifestation of globalism, limited very often to the exploitation of fixed mineral resources, such as oil. In the Middle East, sub-Saharan Africa, Central Asia and Russia, foreign direct investment (FDI) is almost non-existent once investment from the oil multinationals and other international extractive firms is excluded.

The second distinction is between 'positive' and 'negative' manifestations of globalization. 'Positive' globalization refers to the production, exchange and distribution of goods and services which are legal, legitimate and part of everyday international trade. 'Negative' globalization refers to the shadow economy in the trade of prohibited or proscribed goods – such as drugs, light arms and other weapons, human trafficking, money laundering, illicit diamonds and timber – where the main actors are global networks of transnational organized criminals and terrorists (Naim 2003). As Phil Williams has argued, transnational criminal organizations often locate their operational bases in weak or failed states, where they can coopt the political leadership and be assured of a safe sanctuary from which to penetrate their target states in the developed world (Williams 1997). The same is also true for international terrorists, such as al-Qaeda. It was not accidental that it was Afghanistan, the archetypal post-Cold War failed state, that became the centre for both international drug production and international terrorism. It is particularly here, in the linkage between negative globalization and failed states, that the connection between globalization and violent civil conflict can be most clearly identified. The prevalence of resource-based conflicts is also critically dependent on the regional and global economic linkages which ensure that the warring factions can sell the resources under their control to international markets.

State formation and variations in the forms of insecurity

The argument has so far sought to demonstrate that the different legacies of state formation in the North and the South remain important for understanding contemporary international security. But, as the different forms of Southern engagement with global economic processes have shown, a simple bifurcation between North and South is unsatisfactory, and Southern states have responded in very different ways to overcome the historical legacy of Northern domination and imposed state formation. There is, in particular, considerable variation among Southern countries in their relative strength and weakness, in the degree of synergy between state and civil society, and in the ways in which these states have adapted to or resisted incorporation into global economic structures.

This recognition returns us to table 3.1 (p. 72), which attempts to provide a more schematic account of this variation in the forms of the contemporary state, their principal defining features and the associated implications for international security. The fourfold division between developed, globalizing, praetorian and failed states is by no means a rigid categorization, and individual countries may incorporate features from more than one of these categories. The range between strong statehood and very weak or collapsed states is also very much a continuum, along which individual states will be located at different points. These are 'ideal types' and help to order rather than fully to describe the conditions of contemporary states.

The first category, of developed states, refers to the industrialized countries of the North, whose state formation process resulted in strong national states, a powerful synergy between state and society, and the capacity to benefit substantially from integration into the global economy. These states have eventually come to enjoy the so-called great power or democratic peace, where war is no longer a permissible or perhaps even a conceivable policy instrument in their mutual interaction. But this peace was also constructed, as argued above, on the historical legacy of centuries of intense and increasingly violent interstate conflict. And it has not stopped these countries from fighting wars to deal with dissidence, instability and human rights abuses in the South through military or 'humanitarian' interventions.

The second category, of globalizing states, represents those Southern states which have proved capable, in varying degrees, of benefiting from the challenges of (positive) globalization. This capacity has been due in large part to the internal strength and national integration of these states and their ability to generate the state–society synergy necessary for broad developmental growth. Key examples of such states are China, the countries of South-East Asia, India, South Africa and a number of the countries in Latin America. In terms of their security conditions, these states can generally be described as moving towards a greater externalization of security threats, where the perceptions of threats to internal stability are less prominent – though not absent. Since a number of these states are not democratic, and those that are often have poorly institutionalized democratic regimes, the 'democratic peace' does not generally apply. But the perceived costs of modern warfare, and the benefits to be gained by economic integration, do help to reduce, while far from eliminating, the prospect of such conflicts. In general, these globalizing states are in a transitional phase, where security is being increasingly externalized but where their longer-term strategic ambitions are not yet clearly defined.

The case of China illustrates this well. While some see China as a rising threat and predict that 'the future of Asia will resemble Europe's past', with a real prospect of large-scale interstate war, others view China as being increasingly integrated into political and economic structures in a way which undercuts the prospect of aggression or war (D. Roy 1996; Friedberg 2005). The potential is still greater, though, for these states, compared to fully developed states, to consider engaging in larger-scale interstate warfare, particularly if their vital interests are at stake. These states also tend to be highly sensitive about the presumed right of humanitarian intervention and oppose it for fear that it implies a return to imperialist practice and an undermining of the sovereign powers they have struggled, often with great difficulty, to secure.

The third category, of praetorian states, is an inclusive category which incorporates the concepts of the rentier state, the 'mukhabarat' or secret service state, and the neo-patrimonial or prebendal state. The key security feature of the praetorian state is that state elites, the military and the security forces are concerned much more about threats emanating from within than from without the state. The praetorian state tends to be a weak state, with significant ethnic, religious or clan/tribal divisions, where state and society coexist in a mutual relationship of alienation and disaggregation. The praetorian state's incorporation into the processes of globalization tends to be of a 'thin' nature, frequently limited to the international export of valuable natural resources. These states are, in their most extreme cases, at war with their own populations, as in North Korea or in Saddam Hussein's Iraq. However, the praetorian regime is not necessarily unstable and can demonstrate considerable durability and longevity. Praetorian leaders can also, at times, export their fears of internal destabilization by engaging in external aggression – seen, for example, in Iraq's invasion of Iran in 1980, which was driven by fear of the new revolutionary state's appeal to Iraq's majority Shi'a population.

The final category, of failed states, represents those praetorian states which have fragmented and dissolved through a mix of internal and external pressures. In these cases, the weakness of the state has resulted in extensive ethnic, communal or regional fragmentation, with politics conducted as a violent 'winner takes all' pursuit of material advantage. The linkage to globalization is primarily of the thin and/or negative nature, and the export of illicit or illegal resources is a key contribution to a political economy marked by civil war and conflict. The wars that occur in these failed states tend to fit the description of 'new' wars, where central power is dissolved and replaced by competing warlords, civilians are the principal casualties, ethnic cleansing and other acts of extreme brutality are evident, and the conflict is principally intrastate rather than interstate. However, such conflicts emanating from failed states also tend to destabilize neighbouring countries and regions, resulting in a potential spread of the conflict as regional powers support different factions. These conditions can also potentially implicate Northern interests, whether strategic or humanitarian, and can result in Northern intervention.

Conclusion

The main purpose of this chapter has been to provide a broad historical and sociological framework for understanding the nature of contemporary warfare and to contribute additional insights into the current debates over the 'new wars' and the presumed bifurcation between a Northern 'zone of peace' and a Southern 'zone of instability'. In essence, the argument is that the legacy of imperialism and Northern colonial expansion continues to exert an influence on the nature and form of the Southern state, the insecurities to be found in these states, and the types of wars which are fought in the South. In particular, the sense characteristic of the Southern state of being artificial and externally imposed, together with a conservative international order which protects and sustains the territorial integrity of these states, has led to national security being conceived primarily in terms of internal rather than external threats. As a result, the main challenges to the Southern state tend to come not primarily from other states but from the internal opposition of social groups who seek to gain power through denying either the very legitimacy of the state or the legitimacy of those who act in its name.

The chapter has also sought to identify the main variations in the ways in which the Southern state has responded to the structural conditions of imperial state formation. Some countries are in the process of transcending these conditions, forging strong states with the necessary state–society synergy to integrate successfully into global economic structures. Others have succeeded only in containing these challenges, relying on indirect rule, clientelistic systems, and a resort to repression and coercion to sustain the integrity of the state and the particular regime controlling its institutions. A third category represents those states which have been overwhelmed by these internal pressures and are consequently in the process of fragmentation and internal collapse. In each of these three variations of the Southern state, the security conditions and the implications for regional and international security are significantly different. This complexity of the evolution of the Southern state, and the continuing legacy of Northern imposition and dominance, needs to be included in any substantive analysis of the nature of post-Cold War conflict. This historically informed analysis also provides a critical framework for considering the issue of intervention, particularly the post-Cold War dilemmas over humanitarian intervention, the subject of the next chapter.

FURTHER READING

For the general literature on the new wars, a good starting point is the crisp and insightful Herfried Münkler, *The New Wars* (2005), and the influential Mary Kaldor, *New and Old Wars: Organised Violence in a Global Era* (3rd edn, 2012). Other useful accounts include Ann Hironaka, *Neverending Wars* (2005),

Martin Van Creveld, *The Transformation of War* (1991), Mark Duffield, *Global Governance and the New Wars* (2001), and Stathis Kalyvas, '"New" and "old" civil wars: a valid distinction?', in *World Politics* (2001). On the political economy of the 'new wars', see David Keen, *The Economic Functions of Violence in Civil Wars* (1998), and Mats Berdal and David Malone (eds), *Greed and Grievance* (2000).

On the topic of war and European state formation, see the accounts by Charles Tilly (ed.), *The Formation of National States in Western Europe* (1975), and William McNeill, *The Pursuit of Power* (1983). For more general accounts of European state formation, see John Hall, *Powers and Liberties* (1985); Michael Mann, *The Sources of Social Power*, Volume II (1993); and Charles Tilly, *Coercion, Capital and European States, AD 990–1990* (1990). On the relationship between nationalism and state formation, see Ernest Gellner, *Nations and Nationalism* (1983), and, for an excellent case-study on the construction of the British identity, see Linda Colley, *Britons: Forging the Nation, 1707–1837* (1992). On the links between war and capitalist development, see Gautam Sen, *The Military Origins of Industrialisation and International Trade Rivalry* (1984).

On the question of state formation in the South and the generation of insecurity, a good starting point is Christopher Clapham, *Third World Politics: An Introduction* (1985). See also the important accounts provided by Robert Jackson, *Quasi-States* (1990), Mohammed Ayoob, *The Third World Security Predicament* (1995), and Joel Migdal, *Strong Societies and Weak States* (1988). On the distinctive relationship between war and state formation in various regions: for Africa, see Jeffrey Herbst, *States and Power in Africa* (2000); for Latin America, see Miguel Angel Centeno, *Blood and Debt: War and the Nation-State in Latin America* (2003); and, for the Middle East, Steven Heydemann (ed.), *War, Institutions and Social Change in the Middle East* (2000).

Questions for Research and Discussion

1 What role did war play in the process of state formation in Europe?
2 How has state formation in the South contributed to the fragility and weakness of many Southern states?
3 To what extent are post-Cold War civil and ethnic conflicts linked to the weak and failed states in the South?

WEBSITES

www.sipri.org
The Stockholm International Peace Research Institute – a leading international institute dedicated to research into conflict, armaments, arms control and disarmament. It holds extensive data on military expenditure and arms transfers.

www.pcr.uu.se/research/ucdp
The Uppsala Conflict Data Program (UCDP) collects information on a large number of aspects of armed violence since 1946.

www.humansecuritygateway.com
The Human Security Gateway is a rapidly expanding searchable online database of human security-related resources, including reports, journal articles, news items and fact sheets.

www.transparency.org
Transparency International is the leading international NGO combating corruption. It provides extensive information and undertakes research on bribery and corruption which includes a 'corruption perceptions index' for all states.

CHAPTER 4

Dilemmas and Challenges of Intervention

Intervention, meaning 'the direct and coercive application of military force in internal conflicts to affect their course and outcome', is a regular feature of international politics (MacFarlane 2002: 103). However, a novel feature of the post-Cold War security agenda is how both the issue of intervention for strictly humanitarian objectives, and the claim of an emergent norm of humanitarian intervention and a 'responsibility to protect', have gained a central place in international discourse and debate. The underlying reasons for this are not difficult to ascertain and have, to a large extent, been set out in the previous chapter. In a context where the threat of major interstate war has declined and the principal security challenges come from complex civil wars in weak or failed states, international intervention, directed primarily by the stronger developed states of the North, has increasingly been justified as a response to the humanitarian disasters created by these wars. In the face of such clear and unnecessary human suffering, the norm of humanitarian intervention is the distinctive post-Cold War answer to the moral challenge of 'what needs to be done'.

The trouble is that this claim of a new norm of humanitarian intervention remains controversial. Arguably more than any other issue, it has acted as a catalyst for forging new fissures and divisions in international and intellectual debate over contemporary international security. During the course of the 1990s, a North–South divide became increasingly apparent and only intensified in the 2000s. As indicated in the previous chapter, the idea of an emergent norm of humanitarian intervention has tended to come primarily from countries in the North, which have the capacity and military resources to intervene effectively in such conflicts and which have been released from the burden of the Cold War bipolar ideological struggle. In contrast, the states expressing the strongest criticism of the concept of humanitarian intervention have been mainly from the South, most notably from the 'globalizing' states, such as China and India, whose colonial memory of state formation makes them highly suspicious of any doctrine which would appear to legitimate renewed Northern interventionism (Gong 1984; Ayoob 2002, 2004).

On a more philosophical or theoretical level, it has been those who have interpreted the end of the Cold War as a strengthening and vindication of liberal internationalism, and the associated concept of human security, who have promoted humanitarian intervention as the key litmus test for the progressive development of an international solidarism, where the claims of humanity override the egoism and strategic amorality of state interest (Habermas 2000; Wheeler 2000; Finnemore 2003; Evans 2009). This view has, though, been opposed by many in critical security studies, following the more radical Western criticisms such as those of John Pilger and Noam Chomsky, who have condemned the practice of humanitarian intervention as a smoke-screen for traditional imperialist and Western geostrategic objectives (Pilger 1999; Chomsky 2000: 124–55). On different grounds, realists have challenged the degree to which state interests have been sacrificed to humanitarian norms and have cautioned against promoting interventionist doctrines which can lead to imperial overextension and failure (Luttwak 1999; Mandelbaum 1999; MacFarlane 2002).

The NATO-led intervention into Kosovo in 1999, which sought to stem the repressive actions of the Serb central authorities against the Kosovar Albanian population, brought these divisions to the forefront of international debate. Although heralded by many as the most striking and significant extension of the norm of humanitarian intervention, even its most ardent advocates could not disguise the moral ambiguities of such an intervention: it lacked the sanction of the UN because of the vociferous opposition of Russia and China; and the NATO aerial bombardment of Belgrade exposed the euphemism of describing the use of military force as in some substantive moral sense 'humanitarian' (Roberts 1999). The description of the Kosovo intervention as 'illegal but legitimate' only added to this sense of generalized unease and moral ambiguity (International Commission on Intervention in Kosovo 2000: 4).

Indeed, it can now be seen that Kosovo initiated a partial shift away from the discourse of humanitarian intervention in the light of its increasing tendency to generate international distrust rather than cooperation. The events of 9/11, and the articulation of a new strategic focus on international terrorism, added to this marginalization. In the aftermath of 9/11, humanitarian intervention appeared either as parochial in the new strategic environment or as a potentially dangerous means of legitimating interventions for other non-humanitarian purposes. For those with high hopes for the transformative potential of the norm, the war in Iraq in 2003, unilaterally promoted by the US and retrospectively justified on humanitarian grounds, produced a deep sense of pessimism and gloom (Minnear 2002; Rieff 2002; Terry 2002). As one engaged humanitarian scholar noted wistfully at this time, the 'sun of humanitarian intervention has set for now' (Weiss 2004: 149). However, this pessimism was premature, as the issue of intervention arose again with an uprising in Libya against the longstanding dictator Muammar Gaddafi in 2011, leading to a UN-mandated mission to intervene to protect the local civilian population. But, as in Kosovo, this intervention was far from uncontroversial with five members of the Security Council, including India, China, Russia and Germany abstaining from the critical UN vote (Jones 2011).

The objective of this chapter is not to engage directly with the complex legal and moral arguments related to humanitarian intervention (for a fuller discussion of these dimensions, see S. Hoffmann 1996; Ramsbotham and Woodhouse 1996; Holzgrefe and Keohane 2003). Indeed, a central argument of this chapter is that a more pragmatic and prudential approach, drawing from the normative realist tradition discussed in chapter 2, is required if the issues raised by humanitarian intervention are to be effectively addressed. This shift away from a more abstract legal and moral debate over the legitimacy of intervention on humanitarian grounds helps to redirect focus to the fact that all intervention, as with all uses of military force, is an inescapably political act. As such, it is the political consequences of the intervention rather than the legitimacy of the initial decision to intervene which is ultimately more critical. Humanitarian intervention cannot be divorced from the longer-term question of the sustainability of the intervention and whether or not it brings a durable longer-term solution.

More broadly, a significant problem with the liberal internationalist concept of humanitarian intervention is that it promotes an essentially false dichotomy between the amoral world of politics and the apolitical world of humanitarianism. In practice, the two are inevitably intertwined, and strategic and political considerations will always be critical drivers of policy- and decision-making. This does not exclude humanitarian intentions and outcomes from being part of political decisions and military results. The key question is, thus, not whether a new distinctively apolitical norm for humanitarian intervention has emerged but, rather, whether international state practice and politics since the end of the Cold War have opened up a greater space for military intervention to promote humanitarian ends.

This chapter argues that the empirical evidence is decidedly mixed in this regard but that neither the excessive optimism nor the extreme pessimism which have tended to characterize the general debate over humanitarian intervention is justified. The first section seeks to provide a broader historical perspective which examines both the general nature and context of contemporary international intervention and the elements of change and continuity from the Cold War to post-Cold War period. The second section gives an overview of the changing norms and patterns of intervention from 1989 onwards, which can be seen as part of a 'learning process' through which international actors have better understood the opportunities, limits and constraints of military intervention. The third section focuses on one of the most significant of these lessons: the importance of seeing beyond the specific military action of intervention to the longer-term obligations and difficulties of 'nation-building' for the normally weak and fragile states in which the intervention has taken place.

The strategic context: From the Cold War to post-Cold War

One way to examine the context for the politics and norms of intervention is to identify the structural conditions, including both material and ideational factors, which permit and constrain the actual practice of intervention. These structural conditions provide the political incentives and constraints for either engaging in or refraining from intervention. The Cold War yielded one such distinctive structure, and the shift to the post-Cold War structure has changed the political and normative context for intervention. Although the latter has certainly presented a more permissive context for intervention on humanitarian grounds, this needs also to be balanced by a recognition of the constraints against such action, which reflect elements of both continuity and discontinuity from the Cold War period. As such, a comparison examining the structural preconditions for intervention between the Cold War and the post-Cold War period, focusing on factors of permissiveness and constraint, provides essential insights into the contemporary dilemmas and challenges of intervention.

The Cold War context

The Cold War context for intervention involved a mix of permissive and constraining factors distinctively different from those of the post-Cold War period. The permissive factors were driven primarily by the all-encompassing bipolar structure of Cold War politics, which involved a comprehensive competition and struggle between two contrasting ideological models of economic, social and political organization. In Raymond Aron's useful distinction, the international system of the Cold War was 'heterogeneous' rather than 'homogeneous', meaning that there was more than one principle for domestic legitimacy (Aron 1966: 99–104). This was particularly the case for the developing and newly independent states of the South, which confronted a choice between two opposing models for socio-economic and political development: the capitalist pro-Western model, linking capitalism with the development of democratic forms of government; and an opposing socialist critique which promoted inward-oriented economic policies and strong state-directed political control in order to overcome the structural injustices of the international capitalist system (Hunt 1989; Dannreuther 1999). For the superpower guardians of these two opposing models of domestic legitimacy, any state indicating that it was contemplating the alternative model, or was internally threatened by forces promoting such a model, became a legitimate target for intervention. The fear that any one successful transition would trigger a 'domino' effect on neighbouring states promoted a regularized pattern of superpower intervention into practically every corner of the world

(MacFarlane 1985). As a consequence, seemingly insignificant conflicts in distant parts of the world became potentially intertwined with the 'high politics' of superpower relations. As Zbigniew Brzezinski notably commented, 'SALT was buried in the sands of Ogaden', referring to the way the high-level negotiations over arms control in the 1970s were perceived to have been undermined by Soviet intervention into the Somali–Ethiopian war in the Horn of Africa (Garthoff 1985: 651).

The bipolar Cold War structure, which provided such a dynamic and permissive context for superpower intervention, had the effect of marginalizing the interventionist role of other international actors, such as the United Nations and humanitarian relief agencies. In relation to the UN, the Cold War essentially paralysed the collective security mandate which had been set out in the UN Charter, with the ideological divisions between East and West making it impossible to implement the Chapter VII provisions for collective intervention. It was due to this paralysis that the concept of UN peace-keeping, which is not found in the Charter, was developed to provide an ad hoc and strictly limited role for UN intervention in those relatively few post-conflict situations where the superpowers could agree that it was in their mutual interest to introduce an impartial and multilateral external force (James 1990; Durch 1993). In the context of the Cold War, the UN's room for action was essentially circumscribed and limited to the margins of international politics, and superpower forbearance of the UN's activities was dependent on its strict observance of the traditional peacekeeping mandate of 'consent, impartiality and the minimum use of force' (Bellamy, Williams and Griffin 2010: 96). Humanitarian organizations, such as the International Committee of the Red Cross (ICRC) or Médecins Sans Frontières (MSF), whose fields of operations covered the many superpower-supported armed conflicts, developed their own rather similar conception of an impartial and consent-driven humanitarianism which was apolitical in its scope and application. The conceptualization of humanitarianism as being a separate category from politics was, to a considerable extent, a Cold War product, not dissimilar to the 'non-alignment' and 'neutrality' of those countries seeking some limited margin for action independent from the all-encompassing East–West confrontation.

It would, though, be a mistake to see the Cold War structure as providing an unlicensed invitation for unrestrained superpower intervention. In reality, there were also powerful forces which limited and acted as constraints on such intervention. One such constraint was the endemic fear that a relatively minor conflict would escalate into a superpower confrontation, with the attendant danger of nuclear brinkmanship. It was in the Middle East that this threat was strongest, particularly during the 1967 and 1973 wars, and it led to the first limited, if ultimately unsuccessful, attempts at superpower collaboration to resolve the Arab–Israeli conflict. In practice, competitive superpower intervention was limited to the less developed countries where, unlike in Europe, the East–West ideological division was still in flux and where both the US and the USSR were willing to provide limited support to their proxy allies. Such intervention was, though, carefully calibrated not to undermine the broader strategic balance in US–Soviet relations.

A further constraint was driven by the formal anti-imperialist ideologies to which both the United States and the Soviet Union subscribed. Although both superpowers certainly asserted various forms of imperial control, where they did converge ideologically was in directly encouraging the dismantling of the European empires and the formal recognition of the principle of self-determination and independent sovereignty in the territories formerly under European colonial rule. This normative anti-imperialist stance, however much breached in practice, itself acted as a constraint on the interventionist impulses of the superpowers. It set limits to the degree of formal control the superpowers felt legitimately able to assert over nominally independent countries, except where these were mutually recognized as part of their 'vital interests', such as the countries of Eastern Europe for the Soviet Union. For the rest of the world, the superpowers generally acted as conservative status quo powers, seeking to preserve rather than radically change the postcolonial territorial disposition. When they did act, it was often through 'covert' intervention which sought to change the political situation without full recourse to military intervention. As argued in the previous chapter, the Cold War period strengthened rather than weakened the norm against territorial aggrandizement, and this contributed to the difficult legacies of Southern state formation.

The post-Cold War context

Understanding the structural conditions for the Cold War practice of intervention provides an essential prism for examining the changed strategic environment for intervention in the post-Cold War period. Much has undeniably changed, most importantly in the nature and scope of the permissive and constraining factors which promote and restrain intervention. But, at the same time, this has not made the political and moral dilemmas concerning intervention substantially easier to resolve. Indeed, they have arguably become even more complex and controversial than before.

In terms of the permissive factors, there are two interlinked post-Cold War developments which can be seen to have contributed to providing greater opportunities for intervention and the prospect of a greater international consensus for the legitimation of such interventions. The first is the fact, as set out in chapter 2, that the threat of great power war has substantially diminished. This has weakened one of the main Cold War constraints: the fear that intervention in far distant conflicts could potentially escalate to threaten broader international strategic stability. This can be seen in the concerted great power intervention in the conflicts in the former Yugoslavia during the

1990s, which would have been literally unthinkable during the Cold War, when Yugoslavia was a pivotal state in the East–West strategic balance. Similarly, there was no fear that the intervention into Somalia in 1993–4 would materially damage higher-order international interests in the way the superpower interventions into the wars in the Horn of Africa in the 1970s undermined détente. There are exceptions to this more permissive environment, most notably regarding those conflicts which directly impinge on the interests of powerful regional states, such as Russia, China and India, which jealously guard their assumed prerogative to determine the modalities of external intervention in their neighbouring regions. For conflicts such as those in Chechnya, Tibet or Kashmir, higher-order strategic concerns for stability dramatically reduce the prospects for multilateral international intervention.

The second and interconnected permissive factor is the ending of the rigid Cold War ideological division. To return to Aron's distinction, the international system has turned from being 'heterogeneous' to being 'homogeneous'. In the post-Cold War era, there are only very few countries, such as North Korea and Cuba, which do not recognize that capitalism is the most effective form of economic organization (Sachs 1999). The end of the Cold War also significantly accelerated the expansion in the number of countries adopting liberal democracy for their political system (Huntington 1991; Diamond and Plattner 1996). Although there remain rather more countries which continue to be illiberal and undemocratic, what is striking is that there is now much less disagreement than in the Cold War period as to the definition and 'desirability' of democracy (Paris 2004: 21). A similar ideological convergence can also be seen in relation to the concept of human rights, which during the Cold War was severely contested between liberal, Marxist and Third World interpretations (Vincent 1986; Forsythe 1989). In the post-Cold War period, the severity of these disagreements has substantially diminished, and this has underpinned the sense of a progressive evolution in universalistic humanitarian norms and standards (see M. Barnett 1997; Barkin 1998).

The implications of these new post-Cold War permissive factors have had the most dramatic impact on those international actors most significantly marginalized during the Cold War: the United Nations and the humanitarian agencies dealing with armed conflict. The end of the Cold War liberated the UN from its straitjacket and led to an explosion in the number of UN-mandated peacekeeping operations. From 1988 to 1993, the UN established twenty new peacekeeping missions, more than it had undertaken in its previous forty-year history, and assumed a set of new and far more complex tasks, such as providing humanitarian aid, decommissioning arms and demobilizing combatants, monitoring elections and supporting democratization, and undertaking elements of peace enforcement (for overviews, see Berdal 1993; A. Roberts 1993; Tharoor 1996). For the humanitarian agencies, the end of the Cold War had a similarly liberating effect, reducing their need to defend their apolitical and independent status, since there was now a greater potential for humanitarian objectives to find international political support. This has led, in turn, to an expansion of their tasks and mandates and to much bolder political engagement and advocacy, notably seen in the transnational campaign for the international ban on landmines (Price 1998). More generally, this more permissive environment provides the context for the promotion of a new or enhanced norm of intervention. The most ambitious and coherent attempt to codify such a norm is that provided in 2001 by the report of the International Commission on Intervention and State Sovereignty (ICISS), which argued that sovereignty needed to be qualified as a conditional right dependent on a state's respect for a minimum standard of human rights and that, where this was absent, there should be a humanitarian imperative for intervention (ICISS 2001a). This report coined the phrase 'responsibility to protect' (R2P), which led to an international agreement to institutionalize and incorporate this concept into international practice at the World Summit in 2005 (Bellamy 2008).

It is vitally important, though, to counterbalance these more permissive factors, potentially transforming the context for intervention, with some countervailing constraining factors. The most significant of these is that the end of the Cold War, and of a global ideological struggle, has substantially reduced the strategic rationale for intervening in far distant conflicts. It is here that the post-Cold War attraction of a Kantian-inspired cosmopolitan liberalism comes up against the normative realist tradition and the associated moral scepticism of David Hume and questions about the limits of human sympathy, as discussed in chapter 2. In the post-Cold War period, the humanitarian arguments for intervention need to convince generally inattentive, fickle and domestically oriented Western publics, whose sense of moral outrage does not always translate into acceptance of serious costs and sacrifices. It is this lack of confidence in the public appetite for costly interventions which has led governments to prioritize strategies of aerial bombardment or, failing that, blitzkrieg ground campaigns, where Western military superiority can ensure victories with minimal casualties (Münkler 2005: 120–5). As some commentators have noted, wars of this nature have a surreal or even virtual appearance (Ignatieff 2000; Coker 2001; McInnes 2002). Interventions which might involve genuine fighting, even with the essentially amateur armed bandits found in many African countries, have been made only very reluctantly in the absence of a strong strategic imperative. The swift withdrawal of US troops from the peacekeeping mission in Somalia in 1994 after the loss of eighteen of its soldiers exemplified this reluctance. The refusal to consider any sending of large-scale ground troops into Kosovo in 1999 and Libya in 2011 is further illustration of this.

In the study of the European Union, the gap between normative ambition and actual implementation has been described as the 'expectations–capabilities gap' (Hill 1993). Such a gap is also evident for multilateral international intervention, where expansive normative expectations have been consistently constrained by the limited supply of capable military forces to engage in such interventions. Western militaries, particularly in Europe, have been notoriously slow in changing the structure of their armed forces from the Cold War defensive posture to the new expeditionary force structure required for global intervention. As Michael O'Hanlon points out, there are only 100,000 troops (out of the 22 million under arms in the world) potentially available for military humanitarian interventions, far short of the 200,000 he projects as minimally required (O'Hanlon 2003). These weaknesses in national troop contributions necessarily limit the potential for action of the United Nations, which is critically dependent on these contributions, given that it has been denied significant capabilities of its own. UN-directed operations have consistently struggled to find the necessary material resources to implement the mandates they have been given.

In addition to these constraints related to material resources, there are some constraints that are more ideational or normative. First, as noted above, there are limits to normative convergence among countries on reconceptualizing sovereignty to sanction intervention on humanitarian grounds. It was notable that the ICISS and its promotion of R2P found the strongest resistance in Asia and Latin America, where there remained a strong suspicion of the potential neo-imperialist implications of qualifying the principle of non-intervention (ICISS 2001b: 392; see also Yunling 2000). In the Middle East, there was additional frustration at the perceived 'double standards' of the Western-driven interventionist impulse, which was felt to ignore the human rights abuses inflicted on the Palestinians under Israeli occupation and to provide unconditional support to repressive Arab authoritarian regimes (Ayoob 2004: 110–14). There was, to be fair, a more positive response to the ICISS from African contributors and analysts, but they also expressed their frustration with how Africa, as compared to the Balkans, had been ignored. From this perspective, the problem is seen as too little rather than too much humanitarian intervention in sub-Saharan Africa (ICISS 2001b: 389–90).

In addition, the Cold War constraint of a normative anti-imperialism, with its defence of the postcolonial territorial disposition, has been only partially modified in the post-Cold War period. There was certainly an acceptance, driven more by necessity than choice, of the secession of the constituent republics of the Soviet Union and Yugoslavia. But this has been balanced by a strong determination to foreclose further secessionism, such as by Chechnya or Tibet. In Africa, while there has been more open discussion of the advantages of redrawing some of the dysfunctional borders of the states in the region, practical moves in this direction, such as the recognition of Eritrea's split from Ethiopia, remain the exception rather than the rule. More common is the tragedy of the Democratic Republic of Congo, where, despite limited UN-mandated international interventions, an estimated 5.4 million people have lost their lives in multiple civil and transnational wars in what is generally recognized to be a dysfunctional 'failed' state (International Rescue Committee 2008).

Admittedly, the proliferation of 'international administrations' being set up in the aftermath of a number of interventions into war-torn societies has raised claims of a new age of imperialism which appears to have a striking similarity to the 'mandate' or 'trusteeship' arrangements of earlier in the twentieth century. This is certainly one of the most interesting and controversial developments in the post-Cold War period, and it is discussed in further detail below. But what can be noted here is a general reluctance to codify or institutionalize such arrangements. As one commentator has noted, the 'idea that it might become a permanent or recurrent feature of international life is instinctively felt to be dangerous, since it undermines the principle of sovereign equality on which the current order is built' (Mortimer 2004: 12–13). Thus normative anti-imperialism remains a powerful ideational constraint against a radical restructuring of the international system, with its horizontal division into territorially defined and self-defining nation-states.

Post-Cold War record of intervention

Overall, the end of the Cold War opened up a space for humanitarian intervention which had been severely limited or even absent during the Cold War. The debate over humanitarian intervention reflects this new permissive environment. But the post-Cold War experience also involved coming to terms with some hard 'realist' lessons about the limits of altruistic state behaviour in the face even of horrendous human suffering. This has involved a recognition of those constraining factors which continue to limit and complicate the practice of intervention. The post-Cold War period can, in this sense, be viewed as a 'learning process' about the possibilities and limitations of intervention. This 'learning process' can be divided further into three main phases. First, the period from 1988 to 1994, when there was initially considerable optimism for the prospects for multilateral intervention, which was then followed by a number of failures and disillusionment. Second, the period from 1995 to 2001, when a more pragmatic approach emerged which significantly reduced the role of the UN. And, finally, the period since 2001, through the events of 9/11, to the intervention into Libya in 2011, during which the strategic context for intervention has been significantly transformed.

From expansion to disillusion: 1988–1994

Starting with the period of 'new thinking' in Soviet foreign policy in the late 1980s, the prospects for multilateral intervention radically changed. The then Soviet leader, Mikhail Gorbachev, emphasized that the UN could finally assume its responsibilities for maintaining international peace in the new era of superpower cooperation. From the late 1980s, the UN did prove itself capable of rising to this challenge by overseeing the resolution of a number of conflicts which had festered during the Cold War. In the late 1980s, the UN oversaw the withdrawal of Soviet troops from Afghanistan and of South African forces from Namibia. It then took responsibility for the successful transition of Namibia to full independence. In Central America, the UN played a similar role in successfully overseeing the implementation of the 1987 Esquipulas peace plan, which finally brought to an end the chronic civil wars in Nicaragua (1989), El Salvador (1992) and, eventually, Guatemala (1996) (Child 1992: 112–34; see also Paris 2004).

It was, though, the Gulf War of 1990–1 which most significantly revitalized the UN and brought it back onto the centre-stage of international politics. It was not a foregone conclusion that it would be accorded this role: the British Prime Minister Margaret Thatcher initially argued for a more unilateral intervention which would have marginalized the UN (Dannreuther 1992). But US President George H. W. Bush ignored this advice, utilizing the UN to construct a broad anti-Iraq coalition and to gain international legitimation for a diplomatic and military strategy. This eventually resulted in the successful passage of UN Resolution 678 (1990), authorizing the use of force to liberate Kuwait. In the immediate aftermath of the war, the UN Security Council set a further precedent through Resolution 688 (1991), which identified the repression of the civilian population of Iraq, particularly the Kurds in the North, as itself representing a threat to peace and international security. Although this resolution did not explicitly sanction armed intervention to relieve the suffering of the Iraqi population, it did provide a critical opening for including humanitarian concerns in the international legitimation for intervention (Greenwood 1993: 35–7; Teson 1997).

The centrality accorded to the UN during the Gulf War deliberations, along with the renewed sense of the post-Cold War potential for multilateral cooperation, heralded a period of considerable optimism for UN interventionism. George Bush proclaimed that there was now a 'New World Order', with the UN as its central pillar, and the UN Secretary-General Boutros Boutros-Ghali published a report entitled *An Agenda for Peace* which provided a new and highly ambitious agenda for the scope and complexity of UN peacekeeping operations (see Bush 1991; Boutros-Ghali 1992). In retrospect, it is easy to dismiss such statements as evidence of a naive utopianism which ultimately found its hubris later in the decade. But, to a certain extent, this would be unfair, ignoring the evidence of success of the UN's more ambitious role during this period. For example, in Mozambique operation ONAMUZ oversaw the demobilization of the warring groups, the resettlement of over 2 million displaced citizens, the holding of national elections in 1994, and a generally peaceful process of democratization and economic liberalization (Reed 1996). In Cambodia, operation UNTAC had admittedly less success in the longer term in bringing a democratic culture to the politics of the country, but it was nonetheless successful in overseeing a peace settlement which brought an end to a period of chronic instability and brutality (Berdal and Leifer 1996).

Nevertheless, there were four major failures in peacekeeping operations in the mid-1990s which undoubtedly severely damaged the credibility of the UN as a whole. These were in Angola (UNAVEM II), Somalia (UNASOM II), Bosnia (UNPROFOR) and Rwanda (UNAMIR) (Mayall 1996; Shawcross 2000). What links these four very different operations is that, in all of them, the UN faced far more complex and shifting conflicts than was the case for the other more successful operations. The basic context was the changing nature of war, as described in the previous chapter, which had become increasingly linked to weak and failing states where a proliferation of armed factions were often engaged in conflict with little or no regard for humanitarian principles. The hope was that the UN would need to modify its traditional practices of peace-keeping only marginally to be capable of dealing with these more complex conflicts. The concept of 'wider peacekeeping' or 'second generation peace-keeping' was developed in this regard, aiming to incorporate elements of peace enforcement while preserving the UN's traditional dependence on consent and impartiality (Mackinlay and Chopra 1992; Ministry of Defence 1995; Ginifer 1996).

In reality, this mix of rhetorical ambition and only marginal changes in the UN's traditional practices proved vulnerable to a determined opposition. In Angola, the UN-supervised electoral process came to an abrupt halt when Jonas Savimbi, the longstanding leader of the rebel UNITA forces, simply refused to accept the results of the national elections. The UN was subse-quently powerless to stop the resumption of hostilities in late 1992. A signifi-cant factor behind Savimbi's decision to ignore the UN was that he (as well as his opponents) could finance their war independently of their former superpower patrons, relying on Angola's ample natural resources, such as diamonds and oil (Le Billon 2001a). In Bosnia, the power of the war economy was also a significant factor in the UN's marginalization, but this war economy was also superimposed on deep and unresolved ethnic and communal divi-sions which fed the brutality and intensity of the conflict. In Bosnia, the UN found that its traditional peacekeeping operational norms, however modi-fied, were of little use when there was 'no peace to keep'. The nemesis of the UN Bosnian operation (UNPROFOR) came when Srebrenica, which had been designated a 'safe haven' under UN protection, fell to Serb forces in 1995, resulting in the massacre of over 5,000 Muslim men (Gow 1997).

In Somalia, as mentioned earlier, the humanitarian objectives of the UN mission were fatally compromised by the internal anarchy in the country and the ability of warlords to raise the political stakes against outside forces caught in the conflict. When it came to the US seeking to take the initiative to counter the spoiling tactics of one of these warlords, Muhammad Aideed, the political commitment of Washington was undermined by the death of eighteen marines. This, in turn, led to a marked US disillusionment with the UN, and with intervention more broadly, which resulted in Presidential Decision Directive 25 (PDD-25) setting much more stringent conditions for US participation (Berdal 1994; Weiss and Collins 2000: 103). This US resistance to multilateral peace enforcement contributed, at least in part, to the failure of the UN mission in Rwanda (UNAMIR) to act more effectively to stop the 1994 genocide which resulted in over 800,000 civilians being killed. However, the failure arose not just from a lack of political will among the main contributor states but also, as Michael Barnett has documented, from the political culture within the UN itself (Barnett 2002). In January 1994, the commander of the UN mission had warned the Secretariat of the possibility of genocide but, as the crisis developed, the UN decided to reduce rather than expand the force (see Feil 1998).

The UN was not alone in finding it difficult to adapt to this new strategic context. Humanitarian relief agencies and aid workers had their own crisis of confidence during this period. Like the UN, they found that the post-Cold War period offered them expanded opportunities for engagement, but these were in internal conflicts which were generally more complex and dangerous. They also became sensitive to the suspicion that the new support for their operations provided by states was actually a less costly alternative to military intervention to stop the fighting and human suffering. But for humanitarian actors to follow this logic and purposefully advocate military intervention appeared to be a violation of the basic principles of humanitarianism (see Minnear 2002; Rieff 2002). Even more insidious was the realization that the tradition of selfless provision of humanitarian assistance, regardless of political or ideological creed, could itself perpetuate conflict and exacerbate a humanitarian crisis (M. B. Anderson 1999; Barnett and Weiss 2008). It was again in the Rwandan conflict that aid organizations lost 'their near religious conviction that they could do no wrong' (M. Barnett 2003: 406–7). In late 1994, aid workers from Médecins Sans Frontières found themselves providing assistance to Rwandan refugee camps which were controlled by those who had just committed the genocide. In the thoughtful commentary provided by one of these aid workers, the decision by MSF to withdraw from East Zaire was driven by the realization that humanitarian action could, at a certain point, 'become a technical function in the service of evil' (Terry 2002: 2).

Retrenchment and reinvigoration: 1995–2001

The year 1994 was when the fortunes of the UN and the humanitarian impulse reached their nadir. The success in 1995 of ending the fighting in Bosnia and in enforcing a peace settlement provided the first indication of a way out of this crisis. It involved two significant modifications in earlier thinking. The first was the recognition that the UN was not an appropriate or effective organization for peacemaking or peace enforcement. In Bosnia, as a more forceful international response was considered, the UN's authority was delegated to NATO as a regional organization with the capacity to plan and execute complex military operations (discussed further in the next chapter). The second shift was the recognition that the civil wars in the former Yugoslavia represented not just a humanitarian disaster but also a politico-strategic threat to regional and international security. By 1994–5, the US and the main European states realized that significant strategic interests were under threat. The concerns included the refugee crisis in Europe, which resulted in a strong European political commitment to promote the conditions for a return of these refugees. There was also a fear that the cycle of ethnic cleansing and communal violence could extend to other parts of the Balkans. But, perhaps most importantly, there was a sense that the conflict was causing more wide-ranging damage to US–European relations, since tensions about how to resolve the conflict were in danger of tearing apart the transatlantic alliance. As a result, the prestige of the transatlantic alliance and the post-Cold War relevance of NATO were threatened.

This new conviction of the strategic as well as the humanitarian imperative for forceful intervention provided the essential precondition for an enforced resolution of the Bosnian conflict. Richard Holbrooke, the US envoy, provided the overarching strategy, which identified the Serbs as the main aggressors, offered material support for the Croat and Muslim offensive, and authorized NATO aerial bombardments to bring pressure on the Serbs to submit to an end to the conflict (Holbrooke 1999). The resulting Dayton Peace Accords were in themselves an act of pragmatic realpolitik which formally preserved the territorial unity of the state of Bosnia-Herzegovina but also involved a *de facto* partition between a Serb-controlled territory and a Croat-Bosnian Federation (Bildt 1998). However imperfect the accords were, they did at least stop the fighting (McMahon 2004–5).

The significance of the NATO-led Bosnian operation was that it set a new template for post-Cold War multilateral intervention. In part, this involved a marginalization of the role of the UN, with the number of UN peacekeepers being deployed around the world reduced from 70,000 in 1993 to fewer than 20,000 in 1996 (Bellamy, Williams and Griffin 2010: 109). It also involved a broader retreat from the sanctioning of peacekeeping and peace enforcement missions from 1994 to 1997. The new rule was that forceful intervention for humanitarian purposes would take place only when there was also a clear strategic and political rationale for such intervention and where regional hegemons or organizations, rather than the UN, would be given priority in assuring responsibility for such actions. Thus the Nigerian-dominated West African organization ECOWAS assumed responsibility for intervention into Liberia and Sierra Leone (Adebajo 2002). In East Timor in 1999, it was the forceful lead taken by Australia, the only capable military power willing to confront the pro-integration militias and Indonesian armed forces, which assured eventual East Timorese independence. However, it was in Kosovo that the Bosnian template was most evident: European and US leaders decided to act forcefully, through NATO, both to ensure an end to the suffering of the Kosovar Albanians and to prevent the conflict from escalating in ways damaging to their broader strategic interests, as had happened in Bosnia (Dannreuther 2001). The problem was that this mingling of strategic and humanitarian objectives, with humanitarianism subordinated to political strategy, could appear as self-interested and implicitly threatening to those countries, such as China and Russia, which were in any case inclined to be suspicious of Western intentions (Yunling 2000; Buckley 2001).

It is at least partly for this reason that the Kosovo crisis, which appeared dramatically to sideline the UN, paradoxically coincided with a significant rejuvenation of UN peacekeeping. In 1999, four new missions were authorized: in Kosovo itself (UNMIK), in East Timor (UNTAET), in Sierra Leone (UNAMSIL) and in the Democratic Republic of Congo (MONUC). This rejuvenation reflected a belated recognition that the UN has certain normative advantages, most notably an ability to bestow international legitimation, which more ad hoc arrangements, including the use of regional organizations, lack. It also involved a sanguine acceptance that the UN had gained certain operational capacities, developed from its experience in places such as Mozambique and Cambodia, for managing processes of transition and post-conflict peacebuilding. There was therefore a clear practical rationale, once the fighting had ended, for the UN to assume overall responsibility for the difficult processes of transition and state-building in Kosovo and in East Timor.

The establishment of the two operations in Africa – in Sierra Leone and the Congo – was driven by a further set of considerations, which in a sense reflected the moral limits of Western strategic disengagement. The lesson from Rwanda was that the UN could not afford to be tainted again by such a seemingly grotesque dereliction of its international responsibilities. Africa also lacked the same degree of cohesive and militarily capable regional organizations as existed in Europe, or even in Asia and Latin America, though efforts have been made to develop such indigenous African capacities (Boulden 2004). Furthermore, Africa was the site of a large number of the most deadly and virulent of the post-Cold War conflicts. The problem was, as the lessons of Rwanda and Somalia also demonstrated, that the continent did not normally engage the strategic interests of the West to the extent that forceful intervention, along the lines of Bosnia or Kosovo, would be a viable option. The result was that the UN Secretariat faced an invidious task: to recommend to the Security Council enough interventions to ensure that the UN could be seen to be discharging its responsibilities, while also minimizing the risks of failure from insufficient political support and military capacity.

The result was that the Security Council did authorize a return of UN peacekeeping to Africa, but there was always going to be a delicate balance in the relative prospects for success or failure. This was illustrated in Sierra Leone, where the operation verged on the brink of failure in 2000 until a contingent of British forces unilaterally intervened. In the Democratic Republic of Congo, the UN operation found itself incapable of greatly influencing the multiple conflicts which were tearing the country apart and which have resulted in the loss of over 5 million lives since 1998, the deadliest conflict since the Second World War. The record of the UN's return to Africa has been further compromised by the numbers of conflicts with which it decided not to become engaged. This includes Sudan, where the civil war over the last decade has cost over 2 million lives, and where it was only in 2005 that a UN peacekeeping operation (UNMIS) was finally approved.

From 9/11 to Libya and Syria: the new context for intervention

The terrorist attacks on the United States in 2001 undoubtedly changed significantly the context for international intervention. The nature, causes and implications of this shift are discussed more fully in chapter 9. For the purposes of this chapter, the key issue is the strong sense among many commentators, as noted above, that the post-9/11 security environment has radically changed the balance from the humanitarian to the strategic imperatives for intervention (Weiss 2004; Farer et al. 2005). But when one takes into consideration the central argument of this chapter that no easy separation can be made between politico-strategic interest and humanitarianism, the overall picture can look rather more ambiguous. The seemingly successful intervention into Libya in 2011 on predominantly humanitarian grounds, on the one hand, and the vacillations and inaction of the international community towards Syria with a similar authoritarian regime engaging in systematic human rights abuses, on the other, illustrate that the core dilemmas of intervention have been far from resolved.

On the negative side, the events of 9/11 certainly accelerated the predilection for unilateral intervention, already partially prefigured in Kosovo, with the United States in particular assuming new prerogatives, as set out in the 2002 US National Security Strategy (NSS), 'to exercise our right of self-defence by acting pre-emptively' (White House 2002: 6). The US also made it clear that the strategic context for intervention had been extended to wherever in the world there existed a potential threat of international terrorism, or where there were 'rogue states' aiming to acquire weapons of mass destruction (WMD). This, in turn, tended to deflect attention away from Africa, where most of the war-engendered humanitarian disasters take place, and towards the Middle East and Asia, where the threat of international terrorism and potential WMD proliferation are primarily to be found. The war in Iraq in 2003 also appeared fatally to compromise the norm of humanitarian intervention, where the *post facto* humanitarian justifications for the war have generally failed to be convincing.

In practice, the conviction that the events of 9/11 had transformed international relations and that the US could now engage in a transformational strategy of military intervention did not last long. The failure to bring stability and prosperity in Iraq and Afghanistan sapped US and European political will and led to the process, accelerated under President Obama, of a strategic disengagement from these two theatres of action. The Arab Spring which started in Tunisia in late 2010 illustrated that political change and revolutions could be internally generated even in regions which appeared fossilized due to political stagnation and corrupt authoritarian regimes. The threat that the universally despised dictator of Libya, Muammar Gaddafi, might crush the emergent opposition in a potential bloodbath led to a UN resolution permitting military intervention by NATO to stop civilian casualties. During 2011, NATO contributed to the success of the rebels in overthrowing the Gaddafi regime. After many years of scepticism over the prospects for humanitarian intervention, this appeared to be a vindication of its basic logic. But this muted optimism has subsequently been undermined by the divisions among the international community over Syria, with Russia and China opposing any comparable action to be taken against the similarly murderous Assad regime during 2011 and 2012.

Another post-9/11 development has been the way that weak or 'failed' states have been increasingly viewed as a strategic as well as a humanitarian challenge. This is an area where there is a consensus between the US and Europe, as expressed in both the NSS and the 2003 European Security Strategy (White House 2002: 1; EU 2003: 4). This has given a new strategic rationale for intervening in such states where previously conflicts were considered to be 'far distant', of little or no strategic interest. This can be seen most strikingly in Afghanistan, where the 2002 intervention came after more than fifteen years during which Afghanistan had fallen off the strategic map and had been left to a debilitating condition of anarchy and bloody conflict. As a result, the post-9/11 period has opened up a wider strategic context for intervention where positive humanitarian outcomes are conceivable, including in Africa, where there are concerns about the penetration of terrorist networks. In general, the post-9/11 context has also failed to marginalize the UN as much as its impotence during the war in Iraq might have suggested. As of early 2012, there were over 120,000 UN peacekeepers deployed globally, the large majority in a few relatively large-scale operations in Africa. This is higher than even the historic highs of the early 1990s. Certainly, the UN's record in peacekeeping might not have greatly improved, but its continuing relevance in international affairs, particularly for dealing with the continuing wars and crises in Africa, remains unchecked.

Post-intervention: The challenges of state reconstruction

The renewed concern post-9/11 about the security challenges presented by weak or failing states also links to another critical shift in the debate over intervention. During the 1990s, this was focused primarily on the rights and wrongs of the specific decisions leading to intervention; increasingly the issue, particularly after the war in Iraq, is about what happens after the intervention and how to meet the challenges of state reconstruction. For the US, in particular, this represents a significant policy reorientation in which, as a number of commentators have noted, the long-neglected issue of '"postconflict reconstruction" has become the foreign policy issue du jour in Washington' (Eizenstat, Porter and Weinstein 2005: 134). Certainly, much of this renewed interest comes from the poor planning for post-intervention state-building in Afghanistan and Iraq. But it also reflects a more fundamental rethinking of the dilemmas and core challenges of humanitarian intervention.

To a certain extent, the lack of attention to the issue of post-intervention reconstruction or peace-building has been linked to the relatively narrow scope of the normative debate over humanitarian intervention. This can be explained partially by the grounding of the philosophical roots of the debate in the 'just war' tradition, in which significant attention is given to the precondition of 'right intention', so that the key test is whether the intentions of the intervening forces can be characterized as 'humanitarian' (Farer et al. 2005: 226). As argued earlier, this has tended artificially to limit humanitarian interventions to those instances where humanitarian, rather than strategic, considerations predominate, thus excluding the potential for humanitarian outcomes emerging from 'impure' strategic motivations. This, in turn, has narrowed the moral determination of the justice of intervention to the moment of the decision to intervene, rather than resting on the broader longer-term outcomes and consequences of that intervention. It is here that realist critiques of humanitarian intervention, utilizing a prudential and consequentialist ethic, have their philosophical focus, arguing that such interventions, however seemingly justified in their particular instances, ultimately have a negative overall effect on the stability of the international order.

This realist application of a consequentialist ethic does not, though, provide a definitive resolution of the debate over humanitarian intervention. The problem is in plausibly positing the counterfactual of what would have happened if the intervention had never taken place. Was the intervention in Kosovo justified, for instance, because it saved the Kosovar Albanian population from the threat of genocide? Or has it proved to be a failure because of the subsequent forced emigration of the larger part of the Serb minority and the failure to develop sustainable state institutions in the province? There are no easy answers to these questions, since it is impossible to repeat history with a non-intervention scenario and have a better sense of what the future would have held. Nevertheless, what the consequentialist ethic does highlight is that those who intervene necessarily assume responsibility for what happens after the intervention. This is what US Secretary of State Colin

Powell tried, in vain, to impress on George W. Bush in the approach to war in Iraq in 2003 when he warned that, 'once you go into Iraq, you own Iraq' (Woodward 2003). In the longer run, consequences do matter because, taking the case of Iraq, if the intervention ultimately results in a bloody civil war, similar to what happened in Lebanon's civil war, it will critically undercut the earlier justifications for intervention. On the other hand, a successful transition to democracy in Iraq would *post facto* do much to justify the intervention. In Libya, the calculation that a limited intervention to support the rebel forces would be sufficient to overthrow the Gaddafi regime was ultimately justified, though the question of whether a stable and prosperous Libya will develop in the future is still an open one.

The rights and wrongs of humanitarian intervention have therefore increasingly been contextualized with the longer-term demands of 'peace-building' and the growing phenomenon of international 'transitional administrations'. Table 4.1 provides a list of these transitional administrations and highlights

Table 4.1 Transitional administrations[1]

Location	Duration
Namibia (UNTAG)	1989–90
Western Sahara (MINURSO)	1991–
Cambodia (UNTAC)	1992–3
Mozambique (ONUMOZ)	1992–4
Somalia (UNOSOM II)	1993–5
Bosnia and Herzegovina (UNPROFOR)	1995
Angola (UNAVEM III)	1995–7
Eastern Slavonia (UNTAES)	1996–8
Central African Republic (MINURCA)	1998–2000
Kosovo (UNMIK)	1999–
East Timor (UNAMET)	1999–2002
(UNMISET)	2002–
Sierra Leone (UNAMSIL)	1999–2005
(UNIOSIL)	2005–
Democratic Republic of Congo (MONUC)	1999–
(MONUSCO)	2010–
Afghanistan (UNAMA)	1999–
Liberia (UNMIL)	2003–
Iraq (UNAMI)	2003–
Bougainville (Papua New Guinea) (UNOMB)	2004–5
Côte d'Ivoire (MINUCI)	2004
(UNOCI)	2004–
Haiti (UNTMIH)	1997
(MINUSTAH)	2004–
Burundi (ONUB)	2004–6
Solomon Islands (UN EOCT)	2010
South Sudan (UNMISS)	2011–

[1] I would like to thank Elisa Randazzo for help in constructing this table.

the clear trend towards a resurrection of the quasi-imperial practice of trusteeship, where external powers (the 'international community') assume effective sovereignty over a territory or state until such time as the conditions for sustainable sovereign autonomy are present. It is in this policy area that the agendas of security and development studies have increasingly converged, and where a consensus has emerged that an essential precondition for development is the termination of civil conflicts and the reconstruction of security-providing states (Duffield 2001). The logical implication is that, where such security-providing states are simply not present, it is the responsibility of external actors to assume temporary responsibilities in these areas until such time as a viable state can be reconstructed. The closeness and interlinkages between the concepts of human security and sustainable development are symptomatic of this security–development convergence.

There is, though, little consensus about the longer-term implications of this shift towards a *de facto* international practice of trusteeship. The results so far, much like those of peacekeeping more generally, are mixed. The largest and most expensive interventions – in Bosnia, Kosovo and East Timor – have certainly stopped the fighting and involved sustained state-building exercises, but the relative success in East Timor has not been matched in Bosnia and Kosovo, where, despite the large sums spent, the root causes of the conflict have still to be resolved. The various operations in Africa have been much less generously financed, and thus the dangers of reversion and backsliding are an ever present possibility. It is notable, in this regard, that a number of the operations initiated after 2000 were set up in countries, such as Liberia, Burundi and Sierra Leone, from which the UN had earlier departed. Similarly, in Afghanistan and Iraq, the prospects of a successful process of state reconstruction remain highly vulnerable to internal sources of opposition and violent conflict.

For some commentators, this mixed record counsels caution and a reining in of the ambitions for nation-building. Amitai Etzioni provides an overview of the historical record of nation-building by foreign powers and urges a 'self-restrained' approach which recognizes that the few examples of clear success – most notably Germany and Japan after the Second World War – are the exceptions to the rule that 'over-ambitious societal engineering which seeks to overcome prevailing social forces and long-established societal structures and traditions' are generally bound to fail (2004: 15). In a similar vein, Kimberly Zisk Marten argues that the idea of international administrators transporting liberal democracy is an illusion and that international missions should limit themselves to providing security, allowing local actors to devise their own political and economic systems (Marten 2004; see also Mueller 2004). Other commentators, though, such as Simon Chesterman, maintain that the problem 'is not that transitional administration is colonial in character' but 'that sometimes it is not colonial enough' (Chesterman 2004: 12). In a similar vein, Roland Paris argues that what is required is more rather than less international engagement, with a commensurate increase in political will, financial resources and long-term commitment to state reconstruction (Paris 2004). He certainly recognizes, along with Etzioni and Marten, that most of the international nation-building exercises were excessively optimistic about the prospects for a swift transition towards liberal democracy and free market economies, reproducing the errors of the modernization theory of the 1950s. But he continues by arguing that these failures can be overcome if greater attention is given to building effective political institutions before engaging in liberalization (ibid.: 179–211).

There is not the space here to assess this debate in fuller detail. But what can be said is that this shift towards a *de facto* practice of trusteeship arguably represents the most significant development regarding the question of intervention. There are few who openly welcome or proclaim a new era of colonialism and imperialism. But a willingness to override formal state sovereignty and to intervene with a long-term agenda of state reconstruction has certainly become more urgent and more acceptable in the post-9/11 environment. In practice, this has a principal focus on sub-Saharan Africa, where there has been a recognition by 'the international community . . . that if it is to be a force for peace and democracy in Africa's weakest states, it has to engage in state building' (Lawson and Rothchild 2005: 235).

But linking these developments with the earlier discussion on the possibilities of and constraints on intervention, this view of a more permissive proto-imperial environment needs to be balanced by recognition of the countervailing restraining factors. This, first of all, means acknowledging the variation, the complexity and the inherited difficulties of state formation in the South, where, as seen in the previous chapter, the legacies of the past have resulted in states which are often fragile, where there is a lack of synergy between states and their societies, and where there is only limited integration into global economic processes. The lessons of over five decades of development assistance and ambitious state-building exercises are that we do not have ready answers to the more difficult cases of state weakness, particularly in sub-Saharan Africa (Fukuyama 2004; Lancaster 2005). When these essential difficulties are combined with the strategic inattention and impatience of most wealthy democratic states, limits are set to the willingness of the rich North to expend large-scale resources on problems in far distant countries which might bring no immediate political dividends. The second constraining factor is that anti-imperialism, despite all the discussion of humanitarian intervention, remains the overarching and dominant international norm. The constant danger for intervening forces, even when protected by the aura of international legitimacy provided by the UN, is that they are considered as alien imperial invaders, particularly by those elites and social groups who are destined to lose some or all of their privileges. The case of Iraq, where the UN headquarters was deliberately targeted by the insurgent forces, illustrates this well.

Conclusion

This chapter has sought to provide an overview of the principal dilemmas and challenges of intervention in the post-Cold War period, with particular attention to the vibrant but internationally contentious debate over humanitarian intervention. The previous chapter provided the background context for this analysis, setting out the deeper historical roots of the proliferation of complex civil wars in weak or failing states, together with the corresponding increase in demands for external intervention to deal with the resulting humanitarian crises.

The chapter recognizes that the context for intervention changed after the Cold War. But it also argues that a proper understanding of the nature of this change has been complicated by the disjuncture between the normatively charged discourse over humanitarian intervention and the far messier empirical reality of partial and selective interventions which have had a mixed record in resolving the multiple humanitarian crises. This messier reality highlights the way the more permissive post-Cold War environment for intervention, which has certainly strengthened the humanitarian impulse, has been balanced both by the constraining anti-interventionist pressures of a decline in the global strategic interest of many parts of the world where such humanitarian crises are to be found and by the continuing strength of anti-imperialist norms in international relations. Intervention is thus best analytically separated from the apolitical realm of humanitarianism and placed in the more traditional realm of politics, where decisions over military intervention have to be constantly interpreted as essentially political acts and where strategic and humanitarian motives are inescapably interlinked.

The key question is, therefore, not whether an apolitical norm of humanitarian intervention has emerged, but whether international practice since the end of the Cold War has opened up a greater space for humanitarian outcomes alongside the continuing strategic rationales for such intervention. The chapter provides evidence to suggest that the empirical record is mixed, with successes and failures fairly equally distributed, and that the most one can say is that the 'jury is out'. Furthermore, definitive judgements are complicated by a recognition that the criterion for success cannot be limited to the immediate military act; it is dependent on the longer-term developmental challenge of reconstructing states where the breakdown of societal order and state fragmentation are normally the principal causes for the intervention in the first place. The increasing acknowledgement that state weakness is itself a factor contributing to international security is suggestive that this longer-term and more realistic perspective is becoming more prevalent. But the difficulties of making these ambitious goals of state reconstruction effective in spite of the constraints of Northern strategic inattention and the continuing strength of anti-imperialist norms also indicate that the dilemmas and ambiguities of intervention will not disappear.

FURTHER READING

For a short but good overview of the issue of intervention, see Neil MacFarlane, *Intervention in Contemporary World Politics* (2002), and, of humanitarian intervention, Thomas Weiss, *Humanitarian Intervention* (2007). For classic analyses of the associated norm of non-intervention and the concept of sovereignty, see John Vincent, *Nonintervention and International Order* (1974), and Steven Krasner, *Sovereignty: Organized Hypocrisy* (1995). Hedley Bull's edited collection *Intervention in World Politics* (1984) remains well worth reading.

On the contemporary debate over the norm of humanitarian intervention a good contrast can be found between Simon Chesterman's critique in *Just War or Just Peace?* (2001) and Nicholas Wheeler's strong promotion of the norm in *Saving Strangers* (2000). Martha Finnemore provides a supportive historical account of the emergence of the norm in *The Purpose of Intervention: Changing Beliefs about the Use of Force* (2003), while Mohammed Ayoob defines and defends the Third World resistance to the norm in an article in *Global Governance* (2004). The report of the International Commission on Intervention and State Sovereignty, *The Responsibility to Protect* (ICISS 2001), is the most important and influential public contribution to this debate. Gareth Evans, the intellectual inspiration behind R2P, reflects in *Responsibility to Protect* (2009). Alex Bellamy, in *Responsibility to Protect* (2008), provides an overview of the development and implementation of the concept.

On the empirical record of UN peacekeeping after the Cold War, William Shawcross has produced a highly readable account in *Deliver Us from Evil: Warlords and Peacekeepers in a World of Endless Conflict* (2000). A more academic overview is provided by Alex Bellamy, Paul Williams and Stuart Griffin in *Understanding Peacekeeping* (2010). An insightful analysis of the changing norms after the Cold War and the implications for the UN is articulated by Michael Barnett in a *World Politics* article, 'Bringing in the New World Order: liberalism, legitimacy and the United Nations' (1997). An edited collection by James Mayall, *The New Interventionism, 1991–1994* (1996), offers a good overview of the successes and failures of this critical period. Fiona Terry, *Condemned to Repeat? The Paradox of Humanitarian Action* (2002), and Larry Minnear, *The Humanitarian Enterprise: Dilemmas and Discoveries* (2002), give compelling accounts of the similar challenges and dilemmas of intervention faced by humanitarian actors. Michael Barnett and Thomas Weiss provide an excellent overview in *Humanitarianism in Question* (2008).

The growing interest in the issues of post-conflict peace-building and in international transitional administrations is reflected in three recent books: Roland Paris, *At War's End: Building Peace after Civil Conflict* (2004); Robert Caplan, *International Governance of War-Torn Territories* (2005); and Simon Chesterman,

You, the People: The United Nations, Transitional Administration, and State Building (2004). A radical critique of the aims and intentions of the interventionism of the international community can be found in Mark Duffield, *Development, Security and Unending War* (2007).

Questions for Research and Discussion

1 Why has there been a revival of UN peacekeeping since the end of the Cold War?
2 Why did earlier optimism about the post-Cold War prospects for UN peace-keeping result in disillusionment by the end of the 1990s?
3 In what circumstances is it justified to intervene militarily on humanitarian grounds?
4 What are the major challenges of post-conflict state-building and how successful has the international community been in meeting these challenges?

WEBSITES

www.crisisgroup.org
The International Crisis Group – widely recognized as the world's leading independent organization dedicated to the prevention and resolution of deadly conflict. It produces a wide array of influential reports and publishes the monthly *CrisisWatch*.

www.un.org/en/peacekeeping
The UN Department of Peacekeeping Operations, providing information on past and current peacekeeping operations, with statistics, reports and other publications.

www.responsibilitytoprotect.org
A collection of NGOs which support and seek to advance the Responsibility to Protect (R2P) principle.

www.icrc.org/eng
The International Committee of the Red Cross, which offers extensive information on war and law, including the treaties and contemporary challenges of international humanitarian law.

CHAPTER 5

Collective Security, Alliances and Security Cooperation

The previous chapter highlighted that the post-Cold War debate over intervention has also been a debate about the most appropriate, effective and legitimate forms of security cooperation. In the immediate aftermath of the collapse of the Soviet Union and the liberation of Kuwait, many hoped and expected that the United Nations and the ideal of collective security would be resurrected. By the mid-1990s, and the perceived failure of the UN to intervene effectively in the Balkans, the Cold War alliance of NATO engaged militarily for the first time in its history and proclaimed its relevance even in the absence of the Soviet threat. In Europe, NATO jostled with various other security institutions, most notably the expanded ambitions of the EU to have a Common Foreign and Security Policy (CFSP) and a European Security and Defence Policy (ESDP). A similarly complex set of security arrangements developed in Asia, where traditional bilateral arrangements between the US and its key allies coexist with regional multilateral bodies such as the Association of South-East Asian Nations (ASEAN) and Chinese-supported security initiatives such as the Shanghai Cooperation Organization (SCO). During the 2000s, the United States appeared to lose faith altogether in international security institutions in its 'war on terror', preferring to engage either unilaterally or through more limited and ad hoc 'coalitions of the willing'.

This example of the privileging of unilateral action demonstrates that states do not always decide to cooperate with other states for security purposes. They can decide either that the stakes are too high or that the costs of collaboration outweigh the benefits, and thus resolve to act alone or with a few trusted allies. The US–UK intervention into Iraq in 2003 is an example of this, as was the UK's reclaiming of the Falkland Islands in its war against Argentina in 1982. States can also make the decision that they simply do not wish to engage with security collaboration as a national security policy. Switzerland's longstanding policy of neutralism meant that, for a long time, it was not even a full member of the UN (Belin 1956: 80–1). The United States has a tradition of isolationism, evident in the interwar period, seeking to avoid involvement in the conflicts and political machinations of the 'old' world. But it has also come to recognize that the costs of such disengagement can be great. As Brooks and Wohlforth argue, even the most hard-nosed realists acknowledge the value of security institutions, and even the most powerful state in the international system, such as the US, finds it 'harder to advance its national interests if it does not invest in [these institutions]' (Brooks and Wohlforth 2008: 54).

The key question, though, is which institutions to invest in, how much to invest, and how to discriminate between security institutions. The first section of this chapter addresses this from a theoretical and conceptual framework, drawing from the longstanding and contested debates over the relative merits of a collective defence as against a collective security system. Collective defence systems, usually formalized through treaty and alliances, involve military and security cooperation between a set of states against attack on any of its members by a clearly identified external threat. NATO is generally taken to be a model of a collective defence organization and alliance. Collective security systems are more inclusive, either on a global or a regional level, and involve commitments of collective and mutual support of all member states against acts of aggression or breaches of the peace wherever these might come from. The United Nations is the clearest example of a global collective security organization.

The second and third sections then assess these broader theoretical issues in the context of the various security institutions in Europe and Asia respectively. The main argument is that, in both Europe and Asia, there are multiple interlocking security institutions which incorporate traditional collective defence alliance structures but also elements of collective security. As such, it is a mistake to see alliances and collective security as mutually exclusive. NATO's post-Cold War transformation is the most notable European example of a shift from a posture of collective defence to one that is increasingly closer to collective security. In Asia, the coexistence of traditional bilateral alliances between the US and its allies with new forms of security cooperation, such as the ASEAN Regional Forum (ARF) and the SCO, is evidence of this complex blending of alliance and a nascent security community.

From collective defence to collective security?

Traditionally, security collaboration has been viewed as a function of the operation of the balance of power. But it is a mistake to view the balance of power as a formalistic concept. Hedley Bull correctly identified the balance of power as a vital institution of the international system which is not just a mechanical agglomeration of power but also expresses a moral and normative purpose (Bull 1977: 101–26). Historically, the balance of power as an institution represented an advance on the religious wars which had ravaged Europe in the late medieval period (Maurseth 1964). The concept of the balance of power was based on the fundamental rejection of a single hierarchical order and the imposition of religious and political conformity. It involved a recognition that the post-reformation European order had to be anarchical rather than hierarchical and that states were to be sovereign and independent in the determination of their domestic political, religious and social arrangements. As such, the balance of power was a system which sought to prevent the return to an imperial order and to resist claims of moral and ideological supremacy by any one state or group of states within the system. Its aim was to prevent the concentration of power which might tempt a state or group of states to seek to re-create an imperial system. This understanding of the role of the balance of power remains influential. The idea, promoted by Robert Pape, that countries are currently seeking to 'soft balance' against the perceived expansionist and imperialist ambitions of a 'unipolar' United States is a contemporary expression of this traditional concept (Pape 2005b).

Balance of power is at the heart of realist and neo-realist approaches to international relations. Waltz claims that, 'if there is any distinctively political theory of international politics, balance-of-power theory is it' (Waltz 1979: 117). Balances of power are necessary because, following realist assumptions, the international system is anarchical, founded on the principle of self-help, where no state can truly trust the intentions of other states and where the primary responsibility of states is to ensure their survival. In an international system where the main source of differentiation of the units of the system is, according to Waltz, the relative distribution of power, a sustainable balance of power is one which best ensures international stability and minimizes the prospects of war. Much realist thinking focuses on the options available to states – whether they best secure their national interests through balancing against or through bandwagoning with preponderant power (Christensen and Snyder 1990; Schweller 1994). And there is a similar debate about which particular balance of power is more durable and stable – whether the system is more stable in a bipolar, a multipolar or a unipolar system (see chapter 1).

For realists, alliances are the institutional expressions of the balance of power for the purposes of international security cooperation (Morgenthau 1993 [1948]: 197). It is this matching of alliances with the balance of power which makes such institutions popular with realists, despite their general scepticism towards the efficacy of international institutions. For realists, alliances are effective when formed in opposition to clearly defined external threats or concentrations of power and, as such, provide a strong common purpose for the member states to coordinate their military and defence capabilities (Wolfers 1959; Walt 1987). As demonstrated most notably by NATO during the Cold War, this can lead to a degree of military integration and interoperability which no other security institutions can hope to match. For realists, the general effectiveness of alliances is also due to their internal composition tending to reflect the intra-alliance distribution of power. This can again be seen with NATO, where the hegemonic power of the United States is materially recognized by the other member states through their acceptance that NATO's supreme allied commander in Europe (SACEUR) is a post perpetually reserved for an American general.

Realists are not, though, under any illusion that alliances are cost-free for the states that join them. Glenn Snyder notes that the security dilemma is not overcome through alliance membership but expressed in new and more subtle forms. On the one hand, alliance commitments lead to the 'fear of entrapment', where states might be forced to engage in military operations which are not in their national interests; on the other, there is the counter-vailing 'fear of abandonment', where there are concerns that other states will not, when it comes to the crunch, fulfil their treaty obligations to come to your assistance when your national interests are directly threatened (Snyder 1984, 1997). The history of NATO during the Cold War is littered with such fears and concerns. For example, the United States continually expressed exasperation at Europe's 'free-riding' on American military and security com-mitments, failing to 'share the burden' of defence and military expenditure (Olson and Zeckhauser 1966). For countries such as France the concern was more that US hegemony meant that the alliance was structured to meet the needs of the United States and not those of Europe and undermined European independence and autonomy (Kissinger 1965).

According to realism, alliances are essentially ephemeral and temporary phenomena. They wax and wane with the shifting distribution of power in the international system. During the Cold War, NATO and the Warsaw Pact Organization appeared particularly durable and impressive because of the seemingly fixed bipolar distribution of power. But, with the end of the Cold War, not only did the Warsaw Pact disappear but the general realist expecta-tion was that NATO would also eventually disintegrate due to the absence of a clear external threat to ensure alliance solidarity (Mearsheimer 1990; Waltz 1993; Walt 1997). In a multipolar system, alliances are inevitably less formal-ized and institutionalized as the balance of power is less stable. It is for this reason that Waltz argued that multipolar systems are generally less stable and more conflict-prone than bipolar systems. A unipolar system is also, according to orthodox realist thinking, bound to be temporary as other powers will inevitably, given the operation of the balance of power, seek to balance against such a concentration of power. As such, the prospect for a post-Cold war stability based on a stable balance of power, and alliance structures to match this, appear bleak.

The collective security alternative

But these realist assumptions, including the idea that alliances are the most effective and expedient forms of security collaboration, are far from univer-sally accepted. A common critique argues that alliances, as an expression of power politics or realpolitik, are in reality more a cause than a remedy for war. This was at the heart of the liberal internationalist understanding of the causes of the First World War. It was, according to this analysis, the unhealthy obsession of European elites with the 'balance of power' and the creation of ever more complex alliance commitments which triggered a war that none of the European states actually wanted. As Ernst Haas has cogently argued, the concept of the balance of power is ambiguous, and multiple different meanings can be potentially attached to the concept (Haas 1953; see also Claude 1962: 11–88; Little 2007). It is this conceptual imprecision, and the differing ways that political leaders interpret the nature and demands of the balance of power, which feeds insecurity and distrust. In addition, the pursuit of the balance of power does not in itself exclude the need for war; indeed, it might demand war so as best to preserve the balance of power (Bull 1977: 107–8). Historically, a regular victim of this has been Poland, which has suffered a succession of partitions so as to preserve the 'balance of power' between the European great powers. Overall, the liberal critique of the politics of the balance of power is that it perpetuates the dominance of the more powerful states in the system, represses smaller states, and legitimates wars to preserve the status quo.

It is this sense of disillusion with such traditional power politics, and the whole complex system of alliances and balances of power, which has provided the dynamic and inspiration for promoting a radically different form of security collaboration – collective security (for a historical overview, see Finkelstein and Finkelstein 1966). Unlike an alliance, a collective security institution is as inclusive as possible and its membership is open to all (see table 5.1 for the contrast with alliance systems). Its operation is not dependent on the identification of predetermined enemies and threats; rather, every state can potentially be an aggressor. Collective security is a form of collective insurance against the occurrence of a violent attack on the system and the core principles underpinning the system. The most important of these is the notion of 'peaceful change', meaning the commitment to resolve disputes without recourse to force. As such, collective security does not, like

Table 5.1 Collective security vs. collective defence

	Objectives	*Membership*	*Threat*	*Preferred instrument*	*Durability*	*Internal structure*
Collective defence (alliance)	Preserve the balance of power	Limited and exclusive	External and identified	Military	Temporary	Hegemonic
Collective security	Overcome the balance of power and forge a security community	Open and inclusive	Internal and not identified	Diplomatic and military as last resort	Permanent	Equality

balance of power politics, seek to preserve the institution of war but to over-come it. The use of force within a collective security system is required only when the institutions of peaceful change, such as legal arbitration, arms control and diplomacy, break down and an act of aggression takes place. In that context, the collective security system obligates all members to come to the aid of the aggressed state and to act collectively against the aggressor. This collective obligation is based on the assumption of the indivisibility of peace; that any threat to the peace is a threat to the system as a whole. It thus requires the collective response of the international community acting in concert together. It is the automaticity of this response, and the overwhelm-ing power brought to bear against any serious challenge to the system, which is expected to embed and institutionalize the preference for the resolution of disputes by peaceful means (Claude 1956: 223–60; Wolfers 1959; Kupchan and Kupchan 1991).

The ideal of collective security, of a radically new system of managing war and peace, has tended to emerge after periods of intense conflict and war. The creation of the League of Nations after the First World War and the United Nations after the Second World War were inspired by the perceived failures of existing security arrangements and the desire to institutionalize the ideal of collective security (Northedge 1986). After the end of the Cold War, there was a similar hope that a collective security system would be a logical culmination of the ending of the conflict between East and West. But, after the initial optimism, the subsequent failure of institutions such as the League and the UN to realize their ambitions has led to a broader disillusion-ment and questioning of the effectiveness of collective security. The previous chapter addressed this in relation to the UN after the Cold War and the disil-lusionment after the failure of a number of key UN peacekeeping operations in the mid-1990s.

The concept of collective security has also been regularly criticized on more theoretical grounds, particularly by realists. Mearsheimer has been a recent influential proponent of the 'false promise' of collective security, though his analysis has much in common with the critiques offered by earlier realists such as Morgenthau and Carr (Mearsheimer 1990; Morgenthau 1993 [1948]; Carr 1964). These critiques generally have three main components. The first is that the concept of collective security is an 'idealist' construction, depend-ing on a false understanding of the operation of the international system. From the realist perspective, the problem of collective security is that it pre-supposes a world where there is an essential harmony rather than conflict of interests; where states are willing to trust rather than distrust each other; and where collective responsibilities and obligations supersede and have a priority over national interests and concerns. In the world according to realism, these conditions are rarely, if ever, fulfilled, which leads to the inevi-table failure of security schemes based on the assumption of collective secu-rity. A second flaw is that the principle of collective security tends to increase rather than decrease the prospects for intervention and war. This is on account of the liberal idea of the indivisibility of security inevitably meaning that a minor conflict in a far-distant corner of the world is formally as important as any other conflict and demands the same collective response. The consequence is that every local dispute can potentially be internationalized, which results in the proliferation of incidents calling for international intervention. The third flaw is that collective security, through its unwillingness to identify predetermined threats, tends to lead to states being under-prepared for when these threats become real and actual. The classic historical case is the failure of the democratic states to act swiftly enough against Nazi Germany's expansionist ambitions. As Mearsheimer notes, the danger is that 'if security is the responsibility of everyone it is the responsibility of no-one' (Mearsheimer 1990: 36).

Such realist critiques of collective security appear to many as compelling and have contributed to a general scepticism about its practicality. Certainly, realism highlights the dangers of what Inis Claude, who is generally sympathetic to collective security, calls an 'essentially doctrinaire theoretical system' and emphasizes that a 'more pragmatic approach' is required to deal with the 'infinite variety of circumstances, the flux of contingency, the mutuality of situations' that characterize the international system (Claude 1956: 254). But, as Claude goes on to argue, the fact that the intellectual construct of collective security has clear flaws does not mean that the concept has had no substantive impact on the nature and forms of international security collaboration. In reality, it has been a source of inspiration of thinking radically about institutionalizing security cooperation, even if this has inevitably failed to meet the full ideal of collective security. Similarly, the realist critique does not itself prove the validity of the realist alternative of the eternal dominance of power politics and that the most that can be expected is the rise and fall of competing alliance systems.

An example of the continuing inspiration of collective security thinking is the identification by a number of analysts of 'security communities' in various parts of the world that have, in varying degrees, transcended the traditional logic of the balance of power. The definition of a 'security community' is a community of states that has essentially agreed to resolve their differences through non-violent means (Adler and Barnett 1998: 30). The emergence of such communities represents a historical progression where socialization into shared norms and identities has led to a strong predisposition to resolve disputes through peaceful means. The original idea of 'security community' came with the work of Karl Deutsch on NATO in the 1950s and 1960s and the perceived emergence of a transatlantic security community which had moved beyond being a traditional ad hoc alliance to becoming an institutionalized 'community of values' (Deutsch et al. 1957). Similarly, the European integration process has been interpreted by a number of analysts as a radical reconfiguring of the traditional war-prone European balance of power system into a 'security community' where war has becomes literally unthinkable among the member states of the EU (Waever 2006: Adler and Greve 2009). In Asia, some scholars have seen the emergence of a nascent Asian security community in the development of ASEAN (Acharya 2001).

(The concept of a security community is less demanding and radical than the ideal of a collective security. It articulates a world where security communities coexist with other forms of security cooperation and where, in general, a clear-cut separation between the logics of collective defence and collective security is not easily made)(Adler and Greve 2009; Buzan and Waever 2003). As such, there is a recognition that, as realists persuasively argue, the balance of power cannot simply be dismissed as outdated and backward; that to ensure peace you have to some extent to prepare for war; and that the world has not yet progressed to the point where the reflexive norm is the resolution of disputes by non-violent means. But it is also a recognition that, contrary to realist thought, there is a genuine desire to construct an international system which seeks to be more inclusive and breaks down the friend–enemy distinction; which recognizes our humanitarian conscience and the need to treat suffering around the world with equal seriousness; and within which system aggression and the recourse to war should progressively be replaced by the peaceful resolution of disputes (Kupchan and Kupchan 1995). In the next two sections, this overlapping of the reality of the need for collective defence and the hopes and expectations of collective security is studied in the European and Asian regional contexts.

Europe and the survival of NATO

The termination of periods of intensive warfare in Europe has frequently acted to catalyse new thinking and innovations for security collaboration and cooperation. As noted earlier, the balance of power as an institution emerged after the late medieval religious wars. With the conclusion of the Napoleonic wars in 1815, the balance of power system was semi-formalized and institutionalized in the 'Concert of Europe', where the major European great powers sought to resolve disputes and avoid war through diplomatic engagement and negotiation. It was the later breakdown of this system and the brutal destruction of the First World War which inspired the ideal of collective security and its institutionalization in the League of Nations and, after the Second World War, the United Nations. It was the onset of the Cold War which saw the return to more traditional balance of power politics and the formation of a counterbalancing alliance system and a complex nuclear-based deterrent system.

The end of the Cold War potentially provided a new 'critical juncture' where there were possibilities to construct new and innovative frameworks for European security collaboration. The last Soviet leader, Mikhail

Gorbachev, sought to promote a pan-European security structure to replace NATO and the Warsaw Pact which would extend from Vladivostok to Vancouver and build on the experience of the Conference for Security and Cooperation in Europe (CSCE). Others argued for a collective security arrangement which would replicate some of the features of the nineteenth-century European Concert (Kupchan and Kupchan 1991). Yet others saw the opportunity for the European Community to make the next critical step and assume political and military-security responsibilities for the management of European affairs.

In all these cases, while there was no immediate talk of winding up or dismantling NATO, there was a general expectation that NATO's future role was likely to be both radically different and significantly diminished. In the absence of a clear external threat, alliances are expected to be become redundant, according to realist logic (Walt 1997). Waltz (1993) and Mearsheimer (1990) both predicted the gradual demise of NATO. In practice, NATO has proved to be considerably more resilient than expected and, more than twenty years after the end of the Cold War, is generally recognized to be the most effective multilateral military force not only in Europe but also globally. It is, for example, NATO which spearheaded the post-9/11 intervention force in Afghanistan and the intervention into Libya in 2011. Its survival and persistence, seemingly contradicting realist assumptions, is therefore a puzzle which requires an explanation.

Two key factors provide a good part of the explanation. The first relates to the critical period between 1989 and 1991, when complex negotiations were being conducted between the West and the Soviet Union to end the Cold War and to secure the reunification of Germany. A key factor behind the survival of NATO was the absolute determination of the United States and key allies, including Germany, to ensure its continued pre-eminence. As noted earlier, Gorbachev's preference was for a pan-European security structure which would supersede and assume primacy over NATO. The West German government, with its higher-order strategic objective of the reunification of Germany, was vulnerable to agreeing to conditions which would diminish NATO's role. However, the United States, under the leadership of President George H. W. Bush, supported by German Chancellor Helmut Kohl, was absolutely determined to ensure that NATO remained the unchallenged cornerstone of Western security and stability (Sarotte 2011). As Hubert Védrine, a French foreign policy adviser, noted, the transatlantic alliance's future was the 'only issue' that truly concerned Bush at the end of the Cold War (quoted in Sarotte 2010: 113). It is a continuing source of frustration in post-Soviet Russia that the then Soviet leadership were misled by, or more probably misunderstood, the Western determination in this regard (Dannreuther 1999–2000; Kramer 2009)

This initial Western resolve ensured that NATO retained its strategic primacy and that no radically new institutional structure for European security was created. But this did not in itself ensure that NATO would retain its privileged status unless it could define a role and function which responded to post-Cold War security threats. The second critical factor behind the post-Cold War resurrection of NATO was the identification of a new set of roles and functions which went beyond the limited Cold War objective of territorial defence. This included most critically the use of military force for purposes of conflict termination beyond the territory of NATO member states, acting as a body capable of providing the peace enforcement measures which, as the previous chapter outlined, the UN finds difficult to implement. This was first demonstrated by NATO's interventions into the wars of succession in the former Yugoslavia. The military interventions into these civil wars, first in Bosnia in 1995 and then in Kosovo in 1999, represented radical departures for NATO, which, up to this point, had never fought a war. They were also not taken on lightly, and were driven more by the lack of a credible alternative rather than a predetermined NATO decision. The CSCE and the EU found early on that they simply lacked the military instruments to stop the fighting, and, as described in the previous chapter, the UN similarly failed to find the will and military means to enforce a peace on the combatants. It was at this moment in the mid-1990s that the comparative advantage of NATO's experience of integrated military planning and deployment was used decisively to enforce a ceasefire and to bring the parties in dispute to the negotiating table. But it also involved a certain transformation of NATO from a body dedicated to defence of territory to one seeking to promote and export common values and interests.

The logical consequence of NATO's intervention into the Balkans was that it had, at least in part, transformed itself from its Cold War incarnation as a strictly collective defence organization, focused solely on defence against Soviet aggression, into an increasingly collective security organization, seeking to promote security in a more expansively defined European and Euro-Atlantic region (Duffield 1994–5; McCalla 1996: Wallander 2000). This hybrid form of security institution involves a complex and sensitive balancing act. There is the need to preserve the historic benefits of collective defence within NATO, which include the legacies of military integration, interoperability, and the capacity for the collective use of military force. But this needs to be done without identifying a clearly defined enemy. Similarly, NATO needs to promote security in a more expansive and inclusive manner, which reflects the radically changed security environment in Europe. But it needs to do this without succumbing to the organizational and decision-making weaknesses of existing collective security institutions, such as the OSCE and the UN.

This complex balancing act has led to a number of difficult challenges for NATO. The first is that of membership. With the collapse of the Soviet Union and the liberation of East and Central Europe, the case for limiting membership to the original Cold War bloc was difficult to sustain, particularly when ECE countries made strong representations to join NATO as a symbol of their 'return to the West'. NATO enlargement, which has seen NATO grow from fifteen to twenty-eight members since the end of the Cold War, has been justified in terms of consolidating peace and security in Europe and in expanding the Euro-Atlantic security community (Talbot 1995). It acted, in practice, as a precursor to the process of EU enlargement, which has broadly followed the same contours of the expanded NATO. But NATO enlargement has been only partial, excluding most notably Russia, along with all the other countries of the former Soviet Union excepting the three Baltic states. Figure 5.1 identifies the current twenty-eight members of NATO as well as the states, such as Ukraine and Georgia, which have expressed interests in joining in the future.

Not unexpectedly, Russia has looked unfavourably on the survival of NATO and its gradual encroachment on Russia's borders, having never accepted the idea that it has transformed itself into a collective security organization. From Moscow's perspective, the continued existence of NATO promotes and perpetuates the perception of Russia as a threat and, instead of reconciliation and the transcendence of the Cold War divisions, its enlargement creates new divisions, now admittedly further east, between those within and those without NATO's orbit (M. Brown 1995; Dannreuther 1999–2000). This Russian stance is also implicitly supported by many of the new ECE members of NATO, whose historical experience of Soviet aggression mean that they still see a

Figure 5.1 NATO members at 2012
Source: UK Parliament.

core function for the organization to guard against Russian expansionism. For the older NATO member states, there is a studied ambiguity between recognizing the prospect that Russia, if it truly made the transformation to a consolidated democracy, could eventually join and an underlying fear that any such enlargement would condemn NATO to being an ineffective 'talking shop' like the CSCE. These diplomatic disputes over the meaning and purpose of NATO have not been limited to the chancelleries and conference rooms. A significant factor behind the Russian intervention into Georgia in 2008, which resulted in the annexation of parts of Georgian territory, was its resolve to draw a 'red line' over the enlargement of NATO and forcibly to deter Georgia's desire to join the alliance (Asmus 2010). As such, balance of power politics came back as a force in Russia–NATO relations.

Another problem, more internal, but just as complex, facing post-Cold War NATO has been the issue of the distribution of costs and responsibilities within the alliance. There has been a general recognition that Europe's shift from its position as the epicentre of a global East–West confrontation to being a more stable security region requires European states to take a greater role and responsibility for managing their own security than was the case during the Cold War, when US hegemony was essential credibly to counter the Soviet threat. This desire for a devolution of costs and responsibilities has not just been driven by the United States, whose global security concerns are now more focused on non-European regions, such as Asia and the Middle East. It is also something willed by the European states, which have sought to promote political and military as well economic integration, institutional-ized in the CFSP and ESDP (Howorth 2007). Initially, there was much debate and concern over whether NATO and the ESDP could coexist and how to ensure that the institutions complemented rather than undermined each other. Many in the US, as well as in some European countries such as the UK, feared that the ESDP could challenge the primacy of NATO and weaken trans-atlantic solidarity (Kagan 2003; Sangiovanni 2003). In practice, the fear that NATO might be undermined by the CFSP/ESDP has not been the main issue. Rather, the problem is that, despite a number of quite successful if relatively small-scale operations, the latter have not led to the rebalancing of burdens and responsibilities which would ensure a fair and equitable division of labour between the European and American pillars of the alliance (Anand 2010). The fact that it was NATO that intervened in Libya in 2011, and there was almost no discussion of the prospects for the EU to intervene, is illustra-tive of this (Anand 2011).

These internal tensions have also been reflected in controversies and chal-lenges in terms of external action. The 1995 decision to intervene in Bosnia meant that NATO had crossed the Rubicon of acting beyond the borders of its member states – what in NATO terminology is called 'out-of-area' action. The issue has then been how expansive are NATO's collective security respon-sibilities, particularly in terms of its geographical reach. The problem is that the member states within the alliance are deeply divided over this. Three different camps, among others, can be identified (Noetzel and Schreer 2009: 215–16). There are the countries such as the US, the UK and, at times, France, which seek to reform NATO to take on a more global and expeditionary form. There is, though, a second group, of which Germany is the most important state, which are far less inclined towards external intervention and see NATO remaining limited to Europe. A third group wants, as mentioned earlier, to focus the role of NATO back to the threat posed by Russia. These significant differences in national interests and security cultures among NATO member states create great difficulties in gaining consensus and concerted action. There have been serious difficulties with the NATO operation in Afghanistan, where it was only the Anglo-Saxon allies – the US, the UK and Canada – which were willing to deploy in regions where the Taliban were engaged in an active insurgency. Over Libya, France and the UK spearheaded the operation, but Germany, with a number of other states, refused to become involved. Most notoriously, the United States after 9/11 received the unanimous support of NATO but then decided to fight the 'war on terrorism' without reliance on NATO. The result of all this is the generation of considerable frustration and partial paralysis of the organization.

While highlighting these various tensions and challenges facing NATO, it is important not to be unduly pessimistic. As argued earlier, there is no compulsion for states to cooperate through global or regional security institutions, and all such institutions, where national sovereignty is so critically involved, suffer from conflicting national interests, failures of collective action and sub-optimal responses, particularly when the situation is not one of utmost urgency or does not represent an immediate and visible threat. NATO has managed to survive and, to some degree, flourish in the post-Cold War environment. And, to a significant extent, this is because it does represent a marriage of collective defence and collective security capacities which has given it a unique role in a new regional and global security system that is completely different from the Cold War period.

Asia as a nascent security community?

Moving from Europe to East Asia represents a significant shift in security cultures and in the level and intensity of security cooperation. NATO is a unique security organization in its degree of institutionalization, its military integration, and its effectiveness as an expeditionary military force. The Atlantic alliance is complemented at an economic and political level by the European integration process, which has involved the states of the region engaging in a substantive pooling of sovereignty and the creation of a powerful set of supranational institutions within the European Union. Nation-states in Europe have certainly not disappeared and traditional balance of power considerations have not been eliminated completely (Milward 2000). But there has nevertheless emerged a cohesive and dynamic security community with deeply rooted practices of multilateral cooperation in the economic, political and military spheres. As such, war between the states of Europe and North America has become increasingly inconceivable. This is a radical transformation in the historical evolution of Europe, which has traditionally been the site of almost continual warfare and which resulted in two wars in the twentieth century which almost led to the destruction of European civilization.

No such radical and fundamental transformation has occurred in East Asia. Territorial disputes, ideological confrontations, and traditional enmities between the states of the region remain salient features of the regional security complex. For many analysts, the prospects for security cooperation in the region are correspondingly bleak. For Cooper (2003), East Asia is not part of the postmodern and post-sovereign world most evident in Europe but is wedded to the traditional 'modern' world of the Westphalian state system, where the prospect for war is an ever present possibility. For realists, the post-Cold War Asian context is closer to the realities of nineteenth-century rather than twenty-first-century Europe, and the region is thus 'ripe for rivalry' (Friedberg 1993–4; Zakaria 1998). The rapid rise of China adds to the general insecurities of the region. According to Mearsheimer, the historical record of rising great powers is that they inevitably challenge the existing status quo, which inexorably leads to political and military competition and conflict (Mearsheimer 2001: 402; Swaine and Tellis 2000). All these regional insecurities are reflected, according to realists, in the relative weakness of regional security institutions in Asia as compared to Europe. Friedberg notes that, compared to the 'alphabet soup' of regional institutions in Europe, Asia offers only an institutional diet of 'thin gruel' (Friedberg 1993–4: 22).

Although there is much which is undoubtedly valid in these pessimistic analyses, they do not do justice to the complexity of the developments in security cooperation in East Asia. While the balance of power and the logic of realpolitik are critical elements in the politics of the region, and are certainly stronger than in the European context, there have also been concerted and ambitious attempts to construct institutionalized security cooperation which explicitly reject realist logic and seek to promote integration, interdependence and cooperative security. Regional leaders from South-East Asia have heralded the so-called ASEAN way as a model of regional cooperation which involves the development and entrenchment of norms of cooperation, non-intervention and the non-use of force, but without the complex legal frameworks and institutions common in Europe (Acharya 2001: 64; Stubbs 2008). China has adopted a similar language and rhetoric in its security doctrines. China's justification for the development of the Shanghai Cooperation Organization (SCO), for which it has exerted considerable political and diplomatic efforts with Russia and the Central Asian states, is that the body represents the antithesis of a traditional alliance and that it conforms more to a collective security institution to meet non-traditional security challenges in Central Asia (Aris 2009b). The resulting institutional map of Asian political and security organizations, as set out in figure 5.2, is actually quite complex, but its most important foundation is ASEAN.

There is a vibrant debate among academic scholars about how seriously to take these regional claims of the development of a non-realist security community within Asia. A number of constructivist IR scholars, of whom Amitav Acharya is the most prominent, have argued that this represents a genuine transformation of security practices and norms which have had a real and lasting impact on the security culture of the region (Acharya 2001, 2003–4, 2004; Johnston 2003b). Constructivist and liberal scholars have also argued that this has not just been limited to ASEAN member states but has changed the security outlook and approaches of China, which has increasingly become socialized into the norms of security cooperation and has evolved, in terms used by US Under-Secretary of State Robert Zoellick, into a 'responsible stakeholder' in regional and international affairs (Johnston and Evans 1999; Johnston 2003a). Other scholars have been considerably more sceptical, arguing that ASEAN has been nothing more than a glorified 'talking shop', interested more in 'process' than in 'progress', and that any notion of a nascent security community obscures the realities of endemic distrust, the limits of coopera-

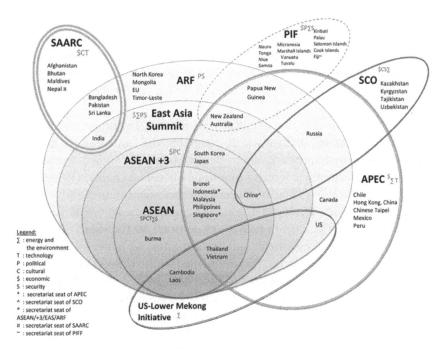

Figure 5.2 Asian security communities
Source: US Department of State.

tion, and the fact that regional stability is dependent on a political and military balance of power structure provided by the United States (Liefer 1989; Jones and Smith 2007). A similar scepticism is expressed towards China, where its rhetoric of regional cooperation is contrasted with its continuing revisionist territorial claims and its ambition to displace the United States as the regional hegemon (Gries 2004).

To begin to try and adjudicate between these two contrasting positions, it is first necessary to highlight the significant differences in the historical, geopolitical and cultural context of Asia in contrast to Europe. There are three key elements in this. The first is that, while East Asia was an integral part of the global Cold War structure, its experience of the Cold War was very different to that of Europe. The Cold War was considerably 'hotter' in Asia than in Europe, with major regional wars directly involving the superpowers taking place, most notably in Korea and Vietnam. The structure of the Cold War in Asia also did not conform to the simple East–West bipolarity, since there was not just the conflict between the Soviet Union and the United States but also the added complication of China. In addition, the end of the Cold War has been differently experienced in Asia. The dissolution of the Soviet Union led to the strengthening rather than weakening of communist power in China, with the successful marrying of political authoritarianism and market-led economic growth. The Cold War conflict between North and South Korea remains a major source of regional insecurity. As such, the structure of the network of bilateral military alliances between the United States and various states of the region (Japan, South Korea, Australia, Thailand and the Philippines) has not faced the sort of existential crisis experienced by NATO at the end of the Cold War. It has remained apparent to these states that US security engagement, particularly with a rising China, is an important and integral element in the strategic stability of the region (Ikenberry and Tsuchiyama 2002).

A second difference is that of culture and identity. In Europe, the development of NATO as an alliance which integrated the United States into the European security framework was, as Deutsch originally argued, a process of constructing a pluralistic security community based on common values and, to a degree, a common identity. The fact that no such comprehensive multilateral security body developed in Asia, as a result of the failure of the South-East Asia Treaty Organization (SEATO) to replicate NATO, reflected the lack of a similar sense of historical and cultural affinities between the United States and the Asian countries. There remained within the region a sense that there were significant differences between 'Western' and 'Asian' values, even if, for political, economic and security reasons, a strong relationship with the United States was a strategic necessity. There was also the fear that too strong an identification with the United States would alienate and increase tensions with China and undermine the historical and cultural links between China and the rest of the region.

These cultural differences are linked to the third major difference between Europe and East Asia which is more developmental in nature. This is the fact that, while the West European states are developed and advanced industrial democracies, the majority of the Asian states are in the process of development. They have a common history of imperial subordination and subjugation, are struggling to develop strong national states and identities, and face the enormous challenges of rapid economic development. In this context, the principal objectives of the governments and regimes of the region have been to enhance their national sovereignty and political independence and to limit the intervention of outside powers. There is very limited desire, as in Europe, to erode national borders and identities and to construct a supranational economic and political union (Narine 2008: 424–6).

All these different factors have meant that the extent of security collaboration in the Asian region is considerably less developed than in Europe. The underlying security structure depends on the United States providing a strategic balance through its hub-and-spoke network of alliances. China continues to be perceived as a threat by other states of the region, even if this is rarely explicitly acknowledged. There remain unresolved territorial and ideological disputes – for example, over Taiwan – which could easily escalate into a military conflict. However, this has not led to the region adopting a fatalistic realist pessimism. As noted above, ASEAN has been the rather unlikely institution through which the hopes of an alternative more cooperative regional security framework have been vested (Stubbs 2008). In traditional balance of power terms, ASEAN is an intrinsically weak organization of small to medium-sized states which has little capacity to match the larger powers of the region, such as China, Japan, Russia or the United States. ASEAN has also remained deliberately weakly institutionalized and firmly wedded to the principle of sovereign equality and the norm of non-intervention. Its proclaimed power has been in the non-material and normative claim that it has developed an institutional framework through which cooperation between states can be enhanced but without the legalism and institution-building as found in Europe. The 'ASEAN way' promotes informal, consensual and incremental decision-making and a focus on confidence-building measures as the distinctive non-realist Asian approach to building a nascent security community.

One similarity between ASEAN and NATO is that, in the aftermath of the end of the Cold War, there was a real question what role ASEAN would play in the changed global context. As with NATO, the ASEAN countries decided that enlargement and expansion of the organization's activities was the best way to ensure its survival. In 1994, there was established the ASEAN Regional Forum (ARF), which became the first regional security forum through which China, India, Japan, Russia and the United States engaged in regional dialogue with ASEAN. This was followed by the ASEAN Plus Three (APT) dialogue process, which sought similarly to tie China, Japan and South Korea more tightly into exchanges with ASEAN. The overarching aim of these initiatives was to promote strategic interdependence between the larger powers of the region so that they increasingly become committed to the core principles of ASEAN –the norms of sovereignty, non-intervention in domestic affairs, and the peaceful resolution of disputes (Goh 2007–8).

A key apparent success of this strategy has been the discernible shift in attitude and behaviour of China. During much of the 1990s, China was highly sceptical of ASEAN, seeing it as a probable American front, and engaged in a number of diplomatic and military interventions in the South China Seas which were perceived to be provocative to other states of the region. However, in the period from 1997 to 2001, the Chinese government increasingly saw this strategic approach as counterproductive and that a more fruitful policy would be to engage with regional and multilateral institutions such as ASEAN. By so doing, Beijing hoped to allay fears of its growing power through an intentional demonstration of its socialization into the norms and principles required by such multilateral engagement. Since then, China has been one of the strongest advocates of ASEAN and was actually the first of the large outside powers to sign up to the ASEAN Treaty of Amity and Cooperation in 2003 (Medeiros 2009: 130–1). The influence of the 'ASEAN way' is also reflected in the role played by China in creating the SCO with Russia and the Central Asian states, where it is regularly affirmed that this is not a traditional alliance posited against an external threat but a collective security arrangement to deal with the three so-called evils of terrorism, extremism and separatism (Aris 2009a).

All of these outwardly positive developments, and the claims of positive-sum regional security cooperation, do need to be treated with a degree of care and scepticism. ASEAN is itself about strengthening the collective power of the small South-East Asian states so as to project a greater power towards its larger regional powers (Katsumata 2006). The SCO undoubtedly also seeks to exclude the United States and, like the APT, to promote a regional Asian order where China rather than the US is the major regional hegemon. The weak legal institutionalization of ASEAN and other regional multilateral bodies also limits their effectiveness (Ravenhill 2009). In Asia, there is a complex balance of power which underpins the regional security order, and traditional realist concerns over the distribution of power and continuing territorial and ideological tensions are much more apparent than in Europe. But this strategically more complex and unstable setting does not mean that elements of a more liberal security framework are absent or that, as in Europe, there is not a complex overlay of collective defence and collective security arrangements. As in Europe, there are real attempts in Asia to seek to mitigate the dangers of realpolitik and the operation of the balance of power, to promote complex interdependence in the economic and political fields, and to socialize countries in the region into the norms of international responsibility.

Conclusion

This chapter has sought to identify the multiple and complex ways in which states engage, or decide not to engage, in multilateral security cooperation. In the theoretical debate, the main divide has historically been between those following the realist paradigm of the balance of power, where alliances play a key role in maintaining international order, and those promoting the liberal ideal of collective security, where a global system of security cooperation is the prerequisite for international peace and security. Constructivist scholars have contributed to the debate through the idea of 'security communities' which provide regional examples of security arrangements that transcend traditional balance of power politics.

This chapter has shown that the actual practice of security cooperation is more complex and messy than the theoretical debate would suggest. In Europe, the key security institution of NATO conformed outwardly to the traditional alliance structure, particularly during the Cold War, when its principal task was to counter the Soviet threat. But, even during the Cold War, NATO had other functions such as integrating Germany into Europe and in promoting a common Western 'community of values'. In the post-Cold War period, the collective security functions of NATO have become considerably more prominent, as the alliance has intervened in the Balkans, in Afghanistan and, most recently, in Libya. Even in the current period, NATO continues to play a residual balancing role against Russia, whose political orientation remains undetermined. In Asia, balance of power politics certainly plays a more critical and central role in the management of security in the region, and the network of US bilateral alliances is an integral part of the Asian security architecture. But in Asia as well, ideas of liberal cooperative security are promoted and incorporated into institutions such as ASEAN, ARF and SCO.

The important point is that the types and forms of security cooperation in which states engage are driven by the choices and decisions of those states. Even if there is a strong tendency to follow the realist logic of the balance of power, the liberal ideal of collective security has a powerful normative force which states find difficult to ignore. Beyond that, it is the specificities of history, geography and culture which provide the specific regional contexts for understanding the particular forms and extent of security cooperation that takes place.

FURTHER READING

The concept of the balance of power is so central to international relations that it is covered in most classic texts, such as Hans Morgenthau, *Politics among Nations* (1993 [1948]); Inis Claude, *Power and International Relations* (1962); Kenneth Waltz, *Theory of International Politics* (1979); and Hedley Bull, *The*

Anarchical Society (1977). Recent innovative research includes Richard Little, *The Balance of Power in International Relations* (2007), and Stuart Kaufman et al., *The Balance of Power in World History* (2007).

On the concept of collective security, a highly influential and subtle account can be found in Inis Claude, *Swords into Ploughshares* (1956). The historical evolution of collective security is outlined in Mariana and Lawrence Finkelstein (eds), *Collective Security* (1966). Debates over collective in the post-Cold War period are in George W. Downs (ed.), *Collective Security beyond the Cold War* (1994). John Mearsheimer, 'The false promise of international institutions', in *International Security* (1994–5), is a now classic realist rebuttal of the concept of collective security. Charles and Clifford Kupchan provide an influential defence of the post-Cold War relevance of collective security in 'Concerts, collective security and the future of Europe', in *International Security* (1991).

On alliances, key texts include Glenn Snyder, *Alliance Politics* (1997), and Stephen Walt, *The Origins of Alliances* (1987). The history of NATO is covered in Stanley S. Sloan, *Permanent Alliance?* (2010). For a good overview of the factors explaining the endurance of NATO since the end of the Cold War, see Wallace J. Thies, *Why NATO Endures* (2009). On the evolution and development of the EU's ESDP, there is Jolyon Howorth, *Security and Defence Policy in the European Union* (2007). Robert Kagan provides a provocative account of the increasing tensions within the transatlantic relationship in *Of Paradise and Power* (2003). On ASEAN and Asian regionalism, the key works are those of Amitav Acharya, with *Constructing a Security Community in Southeast Asia* (2001) and *Whose Ideas Matter? Agency and Power in Asian Regionalism* (2009). Yong Deng provides a good overview of China's shifting foreign policy in *China's Struggle for Status* (2008). Evelyn Goh has written an excellent article which highlights the complexities of balancing, integration and socialization: 'Great powers and hierarchical order in Southeast Asia', in *International Security* (2007–8).

Questions for Research and Discussion

1 Why does realism view the balance of power as a key feature of the international system?
2 To what extent does collective security provide a coherent and effective alternative to reliance on the balance of power and alliance systems?
3 According to realist theory, NATO should have disintegrated as an alliance after the end of the Cold War. What explains its survival?
4 What are the main differences and similarities between Asian and European security institutions?

WEBSITES

www.nato.int
The offical website of the North Atlantic Treaty Organization (NATO).

www.nato.int/strategic-concept/index.html
Debates and information on NATO's 2010 New Strategic Concept.

www.iss.europa.eu
The European Union Institute for Security Studies – the main think tank for research on security issues relevant for the EU, for developing a European security culture, and for enhancing the Common Foreign and Security Policy.

www.asean.org
The official website of the Association of South-East Asian Nations (ASEAN).

PART III

Environment, Resources and Migration

PART II

Environmental Resources
and Migration

CHAPTER 6
Environmental Security

The concept of environmental security is one distinctively associated with the end of the Cold War. The idea of linking the environment with insecurity was one of the first major attempts at the securitization of a non-military security issue, thereby promoting an agenda which moved away from the Cold War fixation with military state-focused security. At the height of the Cold War, the notion of the environment as a significant source of insecurity was simply not on the radar screen. The threat of nuclear confrontation dominated substantive debate about international security. The advent of the nuclear age was also a child of the Enlightenment tradition where man's mastery over nature, which the nuclear bomb expressed in its most stark and morally ambiguous manner, was evidence of heroic technological progress. In contrast to the elemental struggles of the past, the environment was no longer something that controlled and constrained man's activities. Insecurity was now limited to 'social–social' interaction, the threat of violence from one social group to another, rather than 'natural–social' interaction, with the environment threatening social existence.

This sense of triumph at the subjection of the forces of nature was first most seriously questioned in the 1960s and 1970s. The emergence of the international environmental movement popularized the sense that there was an imminent 'environmental crisis', linked to unrestrained population growth, growing resource scarcities, and the weakness of existing social and political institutions (see, for example, Ehrlich 1968; Meadows et al. 1972; Hardin 1998 [1968]). Another landmark development was the United Nations Conference on the Environment which was held in Stockholm in 1972. It provided the first formal recognition of the international importance of environmental issues and established the United Nations Environment Programme. Over time, this greater environmental awareness and concern led to the first demands for a rethinking of traditional understandings of security, in which the Cold War obsession with interstate military conflict neglected potentially more menacing, transnational environmental dangers (for early expressions, see Falk 1971; L. Brown 1977; Ullmann 1983).

However, these views remained marginal until the bipolar militarized structure of the Cold War finally disintegrated. In the aftermath of the Cold War, the call for a broader and more inclusive security agenda became more urgent (Mathews 1989; Prins 1990; Myers 1993; Renner 1996). Influential leaders of research funding bodies, such as Jessica Mathews, argued explicitly both for redefining security in broader terms that included attention to environmental variables and for developing research in this area. A number of political leaders in the 1990s, most notably Al Gore, then US Vice President, also endorsed the concept of environmental security and sought its inclusion in US defence planning and policy-making (Gore 1992; see also Butts 1999). The end result was that, from the early 1990s, there emerged a sustained intellectual and academic endeavour to identify and substantiate the meaning and implications of environmental security and to incorporate these findings into the policy-making of Western foreign, security and defence institutions (for reviews, see Dabelko, Lonergan and Matthew 1999; Matthew 2002; Brauch 2005; Chalecki 2012).

The concept of environmental security has, though, always been highly debated and contested. There are those who have consistently argued that the environment is not a proper object of security studies. Traditionalists have asserted that disciplinary attention should remain focused on intentional social violence and that the inclusion of environmental security is a fashionable but ultimately irrelevant diversion. More insidiously, they have argued that applying the concept of national security to the environment is a potentially dangerous development since it could lead to the inappropriate militarization of environmental issues, which are more properly dealt with by political and economic, rather than security, institutions (Deudney 1990; Levy 1995). A similar criticism, though coming from the more radical critical theory tradition, is that the concept of environmental security has been cynically used to legitimate Northern intervention into the South and to obscure the structural injustices which are the root causes of environmental insecurity (see Dalby 1999, 2002, 2009; Peluso and Watts 2001).

This broader debate over environmental security has two major aspects. The first, which is covered in the first part of this chapter, is over the very nature and extent of the threat of environmental degradation to human well-being and security. There are two extremes to this debate: a pessimistic view of the environment as being on the 'threshold' of calamitous collapse; and a more sanguine and optimistic view that human ingenuity and innovation will ensure the control and resolution of environmental threats. The relative salience of the concept of environmental security is clearly closely linked to which side of this debate is considered to be more or less convincing. This poses a particular challenge to the security analyst as a scientist, as the evidence of environmental insecurity is very different in nature from the more traditional threat of armies amassing on borders. It is also inevitably highly political, as the conceptualizations of the threat can potentially be constructed or securitized with other purposes in mind.

The second aspect of the debate, which is covered in the second part of the chapter, is on the more specific claim that environmental degradation is a direct cause of violent conflict, particularly of many of the complex civil wars or so-called new wars found in less developed parts of the world, such as sub-

Saharan Africa. This brings in a 'human security' and North–South dimension to environmental security. In addition, it raises complex questions about the causes of violent conflict and how to disentangle the environmental from the socio-political sources of such conflict.

The main argument of the chapter is that the concept of environmental security is valid and useful, not least for reminding one of the critical and fragile relationship between human beings and nature. But this needs also to be qualified by a recognition that the more pessimistic estimations of the potential threats should be put into proportion. There is a danger of overemphasizing or oversecuritizing the dangers and threats involved and underestimating the human capacity for adaptation and innovation to overcome them. But, having said that, there are three specific areas where such adaptability and innovative capacities are clearly stretched and potentially insufficient; first, where the emerging threat is truly global and the social, economic and political institutions struggle to establish an effective international response; second, where the environmental problems are rooted in conditions of poverty and structural injustice; and, third, where the struggle for resources includes a clear economic incentive which encourages competing elites and social groups to use violence to secure access to those resources.

Are we 'on the threshold' of an environmental crisis?

The first issue which needs to be addressed is how to make a properly judged and evidence-based assessment of the extent of environmental insecurity. One of the most powerful environmentalist images is that of humankind being 'on the threshold' of an environmental crisis, where continued unrestrained human activity will inevitably lead to a severe deterioration in the environment, with disastrous implications for human welfare (see Homer-Dixon 1991; Meadows, Meadows and Randers 1992). The idea that the 'carrying capacity' of the earth is in danger of being breached provides a similar image of impending crisis (Brown and Kane 1994; Rees and Wackernagel 1994). Overall, such images and concepts conform to a pessimistic view of the current environmental condition which is popularly characterized, and caricatured, as 'neo-Malthusian', in deference to Thomas Malthus, the economist and demographer of the late eighteenth century who was one of the first to highlight the dangers of population growth outstripping food production. The pessimistic stance is, though, contested by a more sanguine assessment, itself often characterized as 'Cornucopian' or even 'Promethean' in its faith in the capacity of human beings to devise solutions to environmental challenges. Although the so-called neo-Malthusian–Cornucopian debate has been criticized for its high level of generality, and even sterility, it does encapsulate the key diverging paradigms which critically influence attitudes and policies towards the environment (for this debate, see Myers and Simon 1994; see also Simon and Kahn 1984; Myers 1993).

The pessimists' outlook

The pessimistic 'neo-Malthusian' approach clearly provides the stronger support for the idea that environmental change should legitimately be considered a security threat. The basic argument of this approach is quite simple and was initially set out by Malthus when he argued that human misery and hardship were unavoidable, since the human population was growing exponentially while food production grew only linearly. This notion of exponential growth was popularized for the modern era in the Club of Rome's classic *Limits of Growth* (Meadows et al. 1972). The report argued that in five key areas – population, food production, industrialization, pollution, and consumption of non-renewable resources – there was clear evidence of exponential growth from one year to the next, which could be understood metaphorically as a process of 'doubling time'.

The fear that population growth is spiralling out of control is one of the most constant features of this more pessimistic strand of environmental thought – a fear accentuated in the twentieth century by a dramatic fall in death rates which coincided with birth rates continuing to be high (Ehrlich and Ehrlich 1991; Brown and Kane 1994). The result was a huge jump in the world's population, from 2 billion in 1950 to 7 billion in 2011, projected to rise to just under 9 billion by 2050. This has fed the popular fear that the world is becoming chronically overpopulated, vividly highlighted by Paul Ehrlich's 1960s bestseller on the population bomb:

> Psychologically, the population explosion sunk in on a stinking hot night in Delhi. The streets were alive with people. People eating, people washing themselves, people sleeping, people working, arguing and screaming. People reaching their hands in through taxi windows to beg. People shitting, people pissing. People hanging off buses. People driving animals through the street. People, people, people. (Ehrlich 1968: 16)

The associated fear is that, with this rise in population and in environmentally damaging human activity, the available natural resources will be so strained that it will eventually be impossible to meet increasing demand. In 1965, Lester Brown argued that 'the food problem emerging in the less-developed regions may be one of the most insoluble problems facing man over the next few decades' (1965: 34). As president of the influential World-watch Institute, Brown has continued to be exercised by the seemingly insuperable difficulties of ensuring that fast developing countries such as China will be able to feed themselves (Brown 1995). The processes of industrialization, urbanization and deforestation are all seen as contributing to the loss of croplands, to soil erosion and to potential threats to food production. Such fears have also been extended to non-renewable resources, most notably to the vital energy resource of oil, which experienced sharp price rises and caused political turmoil in the 1970s. Since that time, the fear that 'oil is now running out' has continued to excite popular fears (Gever 1986; P. Roberts 2004; Homer-Dixon 2009). It was similarly expected that other precious metals, such as copper, zinc and gold, would become more scarce.

The more pessimistic security-conscious approach also highlights the ways in which population growth and uneven economic growth accentuate the divide between rich and poor, entrenching ever greater global inequalities. The concern is not only the clear evidence of vast global wealth inequalities but also that, as the UN Development Programme noted, the 'global chasm between rich and poor widens day by day' (UNDP 1999: 38). While in the 1960s the richest 20 per cent of all nations earned thirty times more than the poorest 20 per cent, the ratio increased to sixty-one times in 1991 and seventy-eight times in 2004. The ultimate unsustainability, not just morally but also environmentally, of such global inequalities has led many environmental pessimists to treat liberal market-driven solutions with suspicion. Garrett Hardin famously argued that it was just such laissez-faire policies which had led to the current overpopulation, and that this 'tragedy of the commons' could only be overcome through highly coercive measures and greater state intervention (Hardin 1998 [1968]). Advocates of environmental security have often presented the advantages of this concept as precisely strengthening the necessity for such state-directed environmental activism (J. Barnett 2001: ch.10; Dalby 2002).

The optimists' response: abundance and innovation

However, this pessimistic strain of environmentalism, with its gloomy vision of the future, has its problems. Probably the most significant of these is that most of the alarming projections for future scarcities and other feared developments have, as a general rule, failed to materialize. Julian Simon, who is the doyen of the more optimistic 'Cornucopian' approach, has regularly seized on this, at one point in 1980 wagering a bet of $10,000 that, for any given raw material – chosen by his opponents – the price would have dropped after at least a year. A group of environmentalists from Stanford University, including Paul Ehrlich, took up the challenge and staked their bets on chromium, copper, nickel, tin and tungsten, selecting a time-frame of ten years. Ten years later, though, Simon won the bet, with each individual raw material having dropped in price (Myers and Simon 1994). Overall, despite temporary price hikes, it is this general pattern of critical raw materials becoming generally cheaper over time which negates the projection of greater scarcity and weakens and undermines some of the more alarmist neo-Malthusian scenarios (Lomborg 2001: 137–48). An example of this can be seen in figure 6.1, which shows a general decline in food prices from 1958 to 2000, though there is a period of rising prices during the oil crises in the 1970s. During the 2000s, with a similar increase in oil prices, food prices have again increased,

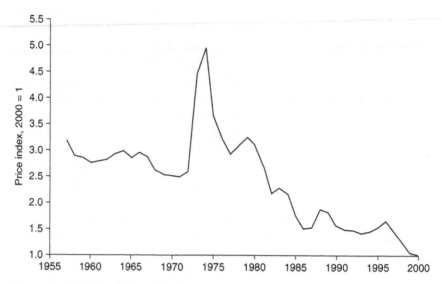

Figure 6.1 World Bank index of food prices, 1958–2000
Source: Lomborg (2001: 62).

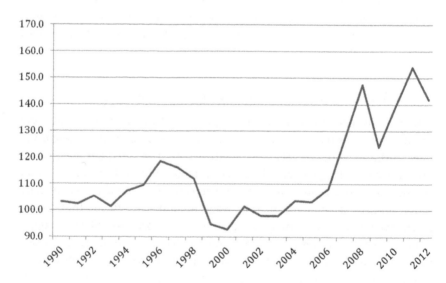

Figure 6.2 Food price index, 1990–2012
Source: Food and Agriculture Organization of the United Nations (FAO).

as seen in figure 6.2, though once more optimists will be expecting that these latest price rises will be temporary, as was the case in the 1970s.

But the more substantive critique of the pessimistic environmentalist approach is its tendency to exaggerate the implications of environmental change and to underestimate the capacity of human beings to overcome the constraints of the physical environment. A good example of this is population growth. As discussed in more detail in chapter 8, the world's population is not growing exponentially and uncontrollably but is projected to reach just under 9 billion in 2050 (a much lower level than previous estimates). It is not self-evident, as most pessimistic commentators tend to assert, that the world, even with this population density, will be 'overcrowded' (Eberstadt 1998: 35–6). Currently, the most overcrowded country in the world is the Netherlands, but it is rarely claimed that it is overpopulated. Developing countries, such as China or India, certainly have fast-growing populations, but the population problem is better characterized as one of too many poor people rather than too many people overall.

The more pessimistic approach also tends to ignore the evidence of the various technological advances, greater efficiencies, and successes in substitution that have regularly helped to overcome potential scarcities of natural resources (see H. Barnett and Morse 1963; Ausubel 1996). Humans innovate to use resources in a more efficient and intensive way and, where a resource is clearly being depleted, to discover and utilize supplies of other resources which can offer the same services. It is this capacity for resource substitution which led Julian Simon to argue provocatively that there is an 'infinite supply of natural resources' (Simon 1981: 42–50). What he meant by this is that, even if, for example, oil were to begin to run out, there would then be an incentive, through rising prices, to search out and convert other energy sources, such as wind power or shale gas. The history of human progress is one of constant innovation and the utilization and substitution of natural resources.

The more optimistic environmentalist stance is also linked to evidence, particularly in the advanced developed countries, of significant progress in terms of environmental protection. Cities which were earlier in the century renowned for their extensive pollution, such as London or Pittsburgh, are now far cleaner. Industrial regions, such as around the Ruhr valley in Germany, which suffered unbridled air pollution until the 1960s, have similarly been transformed. Environmental advances have also been made in the former communist countries of East-Central Europe with the demise of the command economy's obsession with highly polluting heavy industry. Overall, the mid-1970s can be seen as representing a fundamental shift towards environmental action in the historic heartland of pollution – North America, Europe and Japan.

This progress is indicative of a more general pattern according to which environmental degradation is most acute during the process of industrialization, but then can be expected to be reduced, and even reversed, in more developed and post-industrial societies. On this basis, the key mechanism for promoting environmental protection is not heavy-handed governmental intervention but the successful operation of the market, which can provide the appropriate price signals and incentives for innovation and technological advance (Anderson and Leal 1991; D. Ray 1993; Beckerman 1995). For poor countries facing these types of environmental constraints, the Cornucopian approach addresses the problem in terms more of development than of an insecurity driven by strict physical limitations. As a consequence, the longer-term solution generally proposed is liberal market-based practices and institutions which can generate the necessary economic growth and technological ingenuity to resolve the environmental consequences of increased prosperity.

Assessing the debate

The more optimistic approach does serve an important function in highlighting the tendency to excessive alarmism among many environmentalists. The extent to which the concept of environmental security is conceived to be dependent on such bleak projections makes it vulnerable to similar criticisms. For example, the eminent biologist Vaclav Smil has criticized the 'ahistorical and unbalanced' views behind the 'catastrophist paradigm' of the concept of environmental security (1994: 85). Smil noted that, if one had extrapolated the trends prevailing in North America and Europe in 1900, the projection would have been for mass starvation, farmland shortages, virtually complete deforestation, and unbearable air pollution from rising coal combustion. Even in the last twenty years, completely unexpected political and socio-economic changes, such as the agricultural reform process in China and the collapse of European communism, have dramatically improved environmental conditions in these countries. Thus, if the concept of environmental security is to have a significant intellectual purchase, it needs to recognize that human societies have consistently demonstrated ingenuity in finding adaptive solutions to their environmental problems.

However, this does not mean that an unqualified Cornucopian optimism is justified or that it is illegitimate to assert that processes of environmental change have a significant security dimension. Environmental security can still be a useful and insightful concept if it focuses its attention more narrowly on those areas where the evidence of the human capacity to deal with environmental change is clearly limited or constrained. There are two areas where this is particularly the case.

First, environmental security remains a critical concern for poorer developing countries and their citizens. Exhortations that the problem is merely one of development and that all that is needed is economic reform and the implementation of neo-liberal policies are simplistic. The more fundamental underlying problem is that in most poorer countries there is an absence of the skills and capacities required to resolve their most pressing environmental problems. Thomas Homer-Dixon has illustrated this well by making a distinction between the 'technical' and the 'social' ingenuity required for overcoming environmental challenges (1999: ch. 6; 2001). The problem is that many countries lack precisely those features – efficient markets, productive research centres and strong and capable state institutions – which nurture 'social' ingenuity and are a precondition for technological innovation. This absence is most evident in those collapsing or failed states where the indigenous populations face not only communal and social threats but also a rapidly changing and hostile physical environment. Leaving aside whether or not these environmental factors might be an independent cause of violent conflict – an issue covered in the next section – the security of the peoples in these states is still critically related to their capacity to prosper in a sharply deteriorating physical environment.

Even in states which have a far greater capacity to seek solutions to such environmental problems, there is no certainty that they will have the social ingenuity to combine fast economic growth with environmental protection. For example, China's economic reforms have led to a breakneck speed of economic development over the last twenty years, with inevitable consequences in terms of environmental degradation. But the lack of political reform is widely understood as inhibiting more effective and sustained action to deal with this environmental crisis (Smil 1997; Kynge 2004; Economy 2010). For China, as for most developing countries, environmental security is a highly meaningful concept.

The second area where environmental security presents some demanding challenges is in relation to those environmental problems which have a truly global dimension. At a local or regional level, there is justification, as the more optimistic approach suggests, to hope that the collective will to overcome the consequences of human-induced environmental degradation will emerge. As noted above, the success of the old industrial centres – in North America, Europe and Japan – in reversing local and regional air pollution is a striking and historic shift. The same could be said for the cleaning of the formerly highly polluted European rivers and the successful coalition which contributed to the environmental protection of the Mediterranean (see Haas 1990). But there is also evidence that, when an environmental problem goes beyond the local or regional and becomes truly global in its dimensions, the task of forging a collective will to resolve it becomes much harder. A good example to illustrate this is the challenge of water pollution. It was fairly simple to clean up the Rhine so that fish could return because the river gets new water all the time and only a few countries are involved. It was considerably harder in the case of the whole Mediterranean, and decades were required for the sea to be flushed out. If the oceans were to be polluted, all the human ingenuity and collective cooperation that could be generated would hardly be sufficient to clean them up (J. McNeill 2000: 148).

The challenge of climate change

The global environmental problem of climate change is analogous to this. While local and regional air pollution can be reversed relatively easily where the political will to do so exists, the problem is much more difficult when the damage is being inflicted on the atmosphere as a whole. There is now a general scientific consensus that human activity, through the burning of fossil fuels and the release mainly of carbon dioxide gases, has been altering the atmosphere by increasing the absorption of solar heat energy (see IPCC 2007; Dessler and Parson 2010; Dessler 2012). This is contributing to the warming of the planet, which is expected to have significant effects on the weather, food production, sea levels and the spread of diseases as well as potentially contributing to violent conflict (Barnett and Adger 2007; Brown, Hammill and McLeman 2007; Welzer 2012).

But this general consensus on the overall seriousness of the problem has proved to be extremely difficult to translate into effective action. One reason is the difficulty of specifying the nature and magnitude of the potential threat. In reality, there remain significant gaps in our scientific understanding of the planet and the interaction of its complex eco-systems (for an excellent overview, see Smil 2002). This is particularly the case as we enter what some scientists have called the Anthropocene epoch, where humans have come to rival nature in their impact on the global environment and where we must consequently expect greater instability in the future compared with the past (Steffen, Crutzen and McNeill 2007; Dalby 2009). Although there is a consensus that climate change is taking place, there are few reliable predictions of what the exact implications will be and the extent and magnitude of the losses countries or peoples will suffer (or even of the potential benefits for some). In reality, climate change is but one of a complex range of man-made effects that are changing the physics, chemistry and biology of the planet. In terms of practical politics, this scientific uncertainty makes it difficult for a clear risk or threat assessment which can provide a precise indication of how the economic costs in the short to medium term of stemming carbon dioxide emissions will translate into longer-term environmental benefits. In the United States, in particular, this scientific imprecision contributed to a strong and ultimately successful campaign against implementation of the cuts demanded by the 1997 Kyoto Protocol on the basis that the economic costs were disproportionate to the environmental benefits.

A second major factor which has constrained effective cooperation and global action over climate change is the problem of global equity. The 1997 Kyoto Protocol recognized that the Northern industrialized countries, which still have much higher CO_2 emissions per capita of the population than any of the developing countries, must assume the historical responsibility for climate change. The protocol thus specified mandatory reductions in CO_2 production only from the developed countries and left open what the actions of developing countries would be. However, the problem is that countries such as China and India, which have very large populations and are engaged in fast economic growth, are bound to increase their CO_2 emissions to an extent that would effectively cancel out any of the gains made in cuts from Northern emissions. This has made it more difficult to convince all Northern countries, most notably the United States, to ratify the protocol without stronger commitments from those key countries in the South. However, developing countries in the South feel no compunction to make commitments to problems historically caused by Northern countries, especially since they would, in any case, potentially undermine their progress towards industrialization. These problems of global equity continue to make it difficult to forge an agreement on global action towards climate change when the Kyoto Protocol expires at the end of 2012 (Helm and Hepburn 2009).

To be fair, collective political action at this global level is not impossible, as was demonstrated by the Montreal Protocol of 1987 leading to global action to reduce the production of ozone-depleting gases. In this case, the scientific evidence was more clear-cut and there were not the same troublesome economic calculations and global equity issues as are at stake over climate change. But the failure of the international community to come to an effective agreement to preserve species diversity is indicative that climate change is not an isolated example. The issue of biodiversity brings up similar problems – of scientific uncertainty, difficulties in balancing short-term economic costs against longer-term environmental benefits, and historic equity issues between North and South – to those constraining the prospects for global cooperation over climate change (UNEP 2007).

In general, the utility of the concept of environmental security in relation to global environmental challenges such as climate change and biodiversity is a precautionary one. As John McNeill (2000) has argued, modern human society has taken a calculated gamble that its commitment to exponential economic growth, and the unprecedented gains in human prosperity this has provided, will not ultimately damage the complex global eco-systems on which our highly specialized fossil fuel-based civilization is dependent. The problem is that, as McNeill states, 'the human race, while not intending anything of the sort, has undertaken a gigantic uncontrolled experiment on earth' (ibid.: 4) and that, while none of the processes are new, a change in scale and intensity has occurred where the requisite social ingenuity to rectify the environmental damage is truly stretched, as the problems of climate change and a reduction in species diversity illustrate. In this broad holistic sense, environmental security represents the archetypal non-traditional security threat, certainly requiring a degree of conceptual stretching, but mainly serving as a warning that human resourcefulness is not without its limits and that we should take seriously the security implications of this human planetary gamble.

Is environmental degradation a cause of violent conflict?

Advocates of environmental security have not, though, generally been content to limit the concept to these global, rather indeterminate, and resolutely non-military challenges. To give greater substance to the concept, and to reconnect it more fully to traditional security concerns, attempts have been made to demonstrate a clear linkage between environmental change and the anarchy, multiple civil wars and violent conflicts which have characterized many of the poorest regions of the world since the end of the Cold War. The journalist and polemicist Robert Kaplan has been one of the most effective popularizers of the notion that 'the environment' should be treated as 'the national security interest of the early twenty-first century', and that such factors as 'surging populations, spreading disease, deforestation and soil erosion, water depletion and air pollution' will 'prompt mass migrations and, in turn, incite group conflict' from which not even the richest states will be immune (1994b: 45). Kaplan's analysis was very much focused on West Africa, but he also argued that this bleak, environmentally stressed and violently conflictual picture prefigured the global future (Kaplan 1996). Jared Diamond's *Collapse* (2006) has provided further alarming global projections and offered historical analogies with past civilizations which have collapsed due to environmental pressures.

Kaplan admitted that the inspiration for his primarily journalistic and impressionistic accounts was the more rigorous academic work undertaken by Thomas Homer-Dixon (1991, 1994, 1999; Homer-Dixon and Blitt 1998). In the culmination of his decade-long research effort examining the linkage between environmental scarcity and violent conflict, Homer-Dixon reached conclusions which clearly resonate with those of Kaplan:

> Environmental scarcity . . . can contribute to civil violence, including insurgencies and ethnic clashes . . . The incidence of such violence will probably increase as scarcities of cropland, freshwater and forest worsen in many parts of the developing world. Scarcity's role in such violence is often obscure and indirect. It interacts with political, economic, and other factors to generate harsh social effects that in turn produce violence. (Homer-Dixon 1999: 177)

The environmental degradation–violent conflict thesis

The argument that leads to this conclusion is relatively straightforward (see figure 6.3). Homer-Dixon defines environmental scarcity as being comprised of three elements: supply-induced scarcity, which is caused by renewable resource depletion and degradation, such as the erosion of croplands or the declining supplies of fresh water; demand-induced scarcity, which results from population growth and increased per capita consumption of a resource; and structural scarcity, which generally arises from an unequal social distri-bution of a resource and its concentration in the hands of the relatively few at the expense of the many. These three sources of environmental scarcity interact in complex and shifting ways, but declining supplies lead eventually to more powerful groups seeking to control and monopolize the resource in question and weaker groups being forced to move on to ecologically more

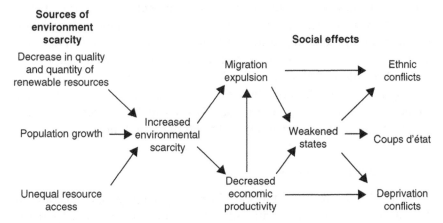

Figure 6.3 Some sources and consequences of environmental scarcity
Source: Homer-Dixon (1994: 31).

marginal lands (Homer-Dixon 1991: 97). Environmental scarcity contributes to declining agricultural production, health problems, social segmentation and weakened political institutions. People who are forced to move often intensify ethnic and group-identity tensions in the receiving areas. Moreover, the weakened capacity of the state, and its declining ability to increase taxes to respond to the deteriorating situation, undermines its legitimacy and increases its vulnerability. In such contexts, violent conflict, Homer-Dixon argues, may emerge or, if already present, worsen.

It is important to emphasize that Homer-Dixon's conclusions are rather more cautious and qualified than some of his critics might suggest (see, for example, Peluso and Watts 2001: 26). He does not claim that environmental scarcity is a direct cause of interstate conflict but only of conflict within states. Homer-Dixon also stresses that scarcity is unlikely to be a necessary or sufficient cause of violent conflict but that its contribution to such conflicts is growing. For Homer-Dixon, environmental scarcity is something which, in combination with other variables, may contribute to some conflicts (Matthew 2002: 112). He is, therefore, careful to distance himself from the alarmist neo-Malthusian tradition. But his argument that scarcity-induced conflict is growing challenges more optimistic accounts, relating back to his argument that many developing countries suffer from an 'ingenuity gap' which makes them incapable of responding effectively to growing environmental scarcity. Indeed, he maintains that the real problem is that many developing countries are increasingly caught in a vicious circle where environmental scarcities reduce state and societal capacities and so the negative consequences of environmental change are intensified rather than resolved. It is in these specific cases, where environmental degradation and poverty are closely interlinked, that violent conflict is a potential outcome.

Homer-Dixon's work has undoubtedly been influential. It has generated his own extensive research programme in Canada and similar research pro-grammes in Switzerland, Norway and even at NATO (Baechler 1999; NATO 1999). There is also evidence that the Kaplan and Homer-Dixon analyses con-tributed to policy-making, most notably in the US approach towards Africa during the Clinton administration (Matthew 2002: 111). The prominence of Homer-Dixon's research project is such that, for many, the concept of envi-ronmental security is inextricably tied to his name and thesis.

Assessing the thesis

However, the arguments put forward by Homer-Dixon are open to criticism. One of the most prominent criticisms is the overall complexity of the thesis. Particularly when he and his colleagues come to apply the model to particu-lar cases, such as rebellion in Chiapas (Howard and Homer-Dixon 1998) or violence in Gaza (Kelly and Homer-Dixon 1998), the argument tends to become extremely complicated, with such a large number of intervening variables that it is almost impossible to isolate the causal role of specifically environmental factors (Deudney 1990; Levy 1995). This is something of which, admittedly, Homer-Dixon is aware, and it is reflected in the caution with which he presents his results.

But there is also a more fundamental problem. One of the key weaknesses in the model is that no clear separation is made between the strictly environ-mental and physical as against the social and political causes of environmen-tally induced conflict. It is a problem which is built into the initial design because Homer-Dixon incorporates a socio-political factor into the original definition of environmental scarcity. This is in adding the term 'structural scarcity' – meaning the unequal distribution of wealth – to the specifically environmental factors of the increasing demand and declining supply of renewable natural resources. The challenge here is that it becomes particu-larly difficult to determine whether any particular conflict where environ-mental factors are present is actually caused by environmental scarcities or by the socio-political 'structural scarcities'.

The methodology followed by Homer-Dixon in his selection of case-studies is also open to criticism. The problem here is that, in all the cases chosen, environmental scarcity and violent conflict are already evident. None of the case-studies includes substantial variation in either of the variables – envi-ronmental scarcity existing in the absence of violent conflict or violent con-flict taking place without a significant problem of environmental scarcity. The failure to engage in such comparative research inevitably limits the sig-nificance of the findings. What Homer-Dixon's research programme can legitimately be said to have shown is that environmental scarcity does con-tribute to violent conflict in certain circumstances. What is much less clear is whether this causal relationship is found generally among all cases, and what the relative weight is that should be accorded to environmental as compared to other factors, such as regime type or poverty, which have traditionally been seen to be highly salient causes of conflict.

Where larger-scale, quantitative and cross-national studies have attempted to test a wider range of variables and contexts, the significance accorded by Homer-Dixon to environmental factors has tended not to be confirmed. Wenche Hauge and Tanja Ellingsen completed the most comprehensive test of the environmental change–violent conflict hypothesis and did admittedly find some positive correlation between environmental degradation (defined as deforestation, land degradation and low availability of fresh water) and the incidence of civil war. But they also concluded that the magnitude of these effects was small and relatively insignificant in comparison to traditional risk factors such as regime type, poverty and ethnic or religious fragmentation (Hauge and Ellingsen 2001). The State Failure Task Force commissioned by the US government in the late 1990s, which was asked to isolate the key factors behind global state failure, arrived at a strong finding of no direct measurable correlation between environmental degradation and state failure. They concluded that the best and most efficient way to differentiate between stable and failed states was to focus on three factors: the level of material living standards (measured by infant mortality), the level of trade openness, and the level of democracy. Environmental change was significant only as an indirect cause in conditions where its impact significantly influenced overall living standards and trade (Esty et al. 1995, 1998).

Moving beyond Homer-Dixon

Some have concluded from these critiques of Homer Dixon that research into the link between environmental change and conflict is fruitless and misconceived (Gleditsch 2001). But this would be an unfortunate conclusion. There are, though, two major modifications and changes in assumptions which need to be made.

The first is to move away from focusing solely on the connection between environmentally linked conflicts and violence to a broader framework which recognizes the possibility that such conflicts might lead to compromise, negotiation and peace. Homer-Dixon already concedes this to some degree when he notes that there is no evidence of wars being waged between states for environmental reasons. As the next chapter argues in relation to water, the expected water wars have not only failed to materialize but water-based conflicts have frequently resulted in an accommodation of interstate differences and a peaceful resolution. Ken Conca and Geoffrey Dabelko have pursued this peace-focused agenda by exploring the ways in which environmental issues can be deliberately targeted by international peacekeepers to contribute to the resolution of international disputes (Conca 1994; Conca and Dabelko 2002). Their argument is that parties involved in a complex political dispute are normally more willing to recognize their mutual responsibility for the management of shared eco-systems. As such, initiating environmentally related negotiations can contribute over the longer term to building the necessary trust and confidence for a broader political settlement. This logic, where peace is constructed through an enforced sharing of contested resources, is analogous to the European integration experience, where coal and steel were placed under supranational management as a symbolic gesture to break the pattern of European interstate conflict and war.

The second shift in assumptions is to place a much greater emphasis on the primacy of the role of politics in the generation of violent conflict, even where environmental factors might be highly visible. In practice, the evidence shows that subnational groups suffering from severe environmental stress either find adaptive solutions – such as migration, the use of developmental assistance or moves towards democratization – or else resign themselves passively to their fate. What rarely happens is that there is a bottom-up resistance which develops into a large-scale civil war. In part, this is because those who engage in burning forests or overgrazing croplands tend to see the result as a side-effect of their own actions or as an inevitable consequence of development and are not likely to blame the government. But, more importantly, the elites who are required to mobilize such violent action are most likely themselves to be the ones who benefit from such activities as deforestation or damming and large-scale irrigation projects. It is also easy for states and elites to legitimate such environmentally damaging activities as an integral part of a historic development process (J. McNeill 2000).

The role of politics, and particularly the interests and actions of elites, needs to be the centre of analysis, even when the physical and environmental sources of conflict are crucially important. The reality is that societies and differing social groups have regularly suffered from a multiplicity of grievances, many of which are environmentally induced. But most of these grievances do not result in wider collective action. What does translate some of them into violent disorder are primarily the actions and mobilizing abilities of elites who have direct interests to promote or safeguard through such collective action. There is normally also a deeper historical context, where long-standing practices of exploitation and exclusion are at the root of the environmental stresses and scarcities.

An example of this can be seen in the genocidal conflict which emerged in the Darfur region of Western Sudan in 2003 and has blighted the region since then. It is true that the roots of the conflict are environmental and the consequence of the progressive undermining of the delicate and interdependent balance between nomads and farmers because of the effects of desertification and the expansion of farms. In the 1980s, this resulted in a bitter struggle for diminishing resources and contributed to the famine in 1984 and 1985 (de Waal 1989). However, what is remarkable is how these competing groups succeeded after the famine, with the aid of international agencies, in finding adaptive solutions to their changing environmental conditions. What ultimately explains the descent into violence twenty years later is a combination of chronic neglect of the region by the state, the introduction of racist Arab supremacism from neighbouring countries, and the cynical manipulation of such extremist groups by the security clique within the Sudanese government to repress regional dissent through state-sponsored genocide (de Waal 2004; Flint and de Waal 2005). In Darfur, as in many other African civil conflicts, environmental factors are important elements in a broader picture of why intrastate conflicts are taking place. But it is the socio-political context and the deliberate actions of elites which are the more critical determinants of such conflicts.

Elites, resources and conflict

It is this attention to the interests and motivations of social elites that suggests one final reorientation of the Homer-Dixon approach. Homer-Dixon makes the case that the potential of the degradation and depletion of scarce renewable resources to cause violence is more evident than for more abundant non-renewable resources. But this focus on scarcity as the key variable is misconceived. What interests elites in certain resources is not primarily whether they are scarce (or abundant) but whether they are valuable. There are cases where a country can have an abundance of a particular resource, such as diamonds or timber, but where its economic value (due to global scarcity), and the power it provides to those who control it, make it an object of political contestation and violent conflict (de Soysa 2000: 125–7). In a statistical analysis of forty-seven armed civil conflicts from 1965 to 1999, the World Bank economist Paul Collier demonstrated a strong correlation between violent civil conflict and weak states heavily dependent on the export of valuable commodities. He further concluded that such wars were motivated primarily by economic incentives, most notably the greed of powerful elites for the possession and control of valuable and lootable resources. It is, he argues, such greed which is critical, rather than any abstract set of grievances, whether driven by environmental stress, economic inequality or political disenfranchisement (Collier 2000, 2003; Collier and Hoeffler 2001).

The significance of Collier's insight is that it highlights the dynamic way in which elite interests can interact, in certain social and economic settings, with a struggle over natural resources which contributes directly to violent conflict. This, in turn, has led to a number of attempts to understand the underlying political economy of post-Cold War civil conflicts (Berdal and Malone 2000; Renner 2002; Ballentine and Sherman 2003). This research has shown how many actors in these conflicts not only fund their armed revolts through such resource predation but also find themselves benefiting economically from the continuation rather than the resolution of the conflicts.

As such, these bloody and seemingly irrational and primitive conflicts can have a clear economic rationale and logic not always evident to outsiders (Keen 1998). The geographer Philippe Le Billon has provided a more precise taxonomy, as shown in table 6.1, of what types of resources are likely to lead, in conditions of strong political contestation, to what types of violent political conflict, along with their particular geographical locations. For example, he notes that oil and gas deposits which are concentrated in a fixed area but are located in the peripheral regions of a state will tend to promote secessionist conflicts, while resources such as alluvial diamonds or drugs which are diffused throughout a country and are easily lootable will tend towards violent fragmentation and warlordism (Le Billon 2001b: 572–5; see also Le Billon 2005). As such, Le Billon makes a distinction between point (i.e. fixed) and diffuse resources.

The more sophisticated analysis by Le Billon illustrates how the concept of environmental security can identify the ways in which the natural environment and its resources can contribute to the generation and prolongation of violent conflict. The proper overarching framework for this involves a recognition that, though resource depletion and environmental degradation are inevitably causes of conflict, normally such conflicts can be contained or resolved through human adaptive strategies and economic and political development. But, in certain circumstances, where there has already been significant political fragmentation and economic deterioration, environmen-

Table 6.1 Relation between resource characteristics and types of conflict

Resource characteristics	Point	Diffuse
Proximate	**State control/coup d'état**	**Peasant/mass rebellion**
	Algeria (gas)	El Salvador (coffee)
	Congo–Brazzaville (oil)	Guatemala (cropland)
	Colombia (oil)	Mexico–Chiapas (cropland)
	Iraq–Kuwait (oil)	Rwanda (coffee)
	Yemen (oil)	Senegal–Mauritania (cropland)
Distant	**Secession**	**Warlordism**
	Angola–Cabinda (oil)	Afghanistan (gems, timber)
	Chechnya (oil)	Angola (diamonds)
	Indonesia–Aceh–East Timor–West Papua	Burma (timber)
	(oil, copper, gold)	Cambodia (gems, timber)
	Morocco/Western Sahara (phosphate)	DR Congo (diamonds, gold)
	Nigeria–Biafra (oil)	Liberia (timber, diamonds)
	Papua New Guinea–Bougainville	Philippines (timber)
	(copper)	Sierra Leone (diamonds)
	Sudan (oil)	

Source: Le Billon (2005: 36).

tal and resource factors can play a significant role in the political power struggle sustaining violent civil wars. It is, though, the politics of these conflicts which remains pre-eminent, and the key question is to determine how environmental or resource factors might contribute to that political struggle. This issue is dealt with in greater detail in the following chapter, which compares and contrasts the insecurities and prospects for conflict in the geopolitical struggles for water and oil.

Conclusion: Environmental security and the new security agenda

The main conclusion to be drawn from this chapter is that the concept of environmental security needs to be used with care. Critics have rightly highlighted the danger of an exaggerated and alarmist projection of impending environmental crisis, which accepts neo-Malthusian assumptions in an uncritical and unquestioning manner. Environmental security also obviously requires thinking of security in a non-traditional and non-military context and recognizing that solutions will not depend primarily on military intervention. There is also a strong North–South dimension to the concept of environmental security, where complex equity issues and longer-term historical legacies need to be incorporated in forging policies which meet the interests of both North and South. The critical theory approach to environmental security rightly highlights the potential dangers of the concept being used as an instrument reflecting Northern rather than Southern concerns (see, for example, Dalby 2009; J. Barnett 2001).

Despite these dangers, the concept still has its clear advantages. At a basic level, the articulation of environmental security acts as a reminder of the most fundamental ecological roots of international security and human flourishing. There is, certainly, a natural and understandable tendency in security studies to focus on those threats which appear immediate and, because of their social nature, menacing and alarming. Thus it is understandable, for example, that the events of 9/11 and the associated fears of international terrorism have tended to marginalize concerns over environmental security, which has meant that research in this area has been less intensive in the 2000s than it was in the 1990s. But a continuing and longstanding commitment to environmental security acts as a reminder that humans do take daily risks with their natural environment which, over time, have a cumulative impact and can present potentially highly significant future security threats. This is, as argued above, particularly the case with global environmental challenges, such as climate change and biodiversity. In these fields, the security analyst is dependent on the professional judgements of others – scientists and economists in particular – but has a distinctive role to play as well.

The second area where the concept of environmental security adds value is in highlighting how the environment remains a critical security challenge to poor and developing states. Environmental security is an integral part of the human security approach, and the fact that many hundreds of millions of people around the world do not enjoy basic environmental security is a key indicator of human insecurity. There is clearly a strong developmental dimension to this problem; but it also has a vital security aspect where such adverse environmental conditions provide fertile ground, if not always a direct cause, for violent conflict.

Finally, bringing the environment back into security studies has the value of linking back to earlier traditions of thought which made connections between the environment and security. As noted earlier, naturalist theories, meaning theories positing nature as a cause of human events, became increasingly marginalized in the twentieth century as the conviction that human beings had mastered nature combined with ideologically driven confrontations between fascism, communism and liberalism (see Deudney 1999). In a similar fashion, the intellectual credentials of geopolitics, the environmentally sensitive study of military strategy, were discredited by its association with German and Soviet expansionism. The concept of environmental security has helped to revive these older traditions examining how environmental factors drive social and political events. Increasing attention has been given, for example, to how the particular ecologies of the Middle East, Africa and the Asia-Pacific have influenced the specific social, economic and political forms of life in these regions and contributed to their regional security complexes. Geopolitics itself has also come back into fashion, particularly among geographers, and this has in turn contributed to the growing study of how the uneven distribution of natural resources acts as a major source of global insecurity (Ó Tuathail, Dalby and Routledge 2006). The next chapter examines this in greater detail in relation to two of the most essential and contested natural resources – water and oil.

FURTHER READING

For an excellent general background to the multiple ways in which humankind has changed and transformed the environment, particularly during the twentieth century, see John McNeill, *Something New under the Sun* (2000). Ken Conca and Geoffrey Dabelko (eds), *Green Planet Blues* (2004), offers a complementary account of the emergence, evolution and key achievements of the international environmental movement. On climate change, a good introduction is Andrew Dessler, *Introduction to Modern Climate Change* (2012); the more detailed economic and political dimensions can be found in Dieter Helm and Cameron Hepburn (eds), *The Economics and Politics of Climate Change* (2009).

Some good readings relating to the Cornucopian and neo-Malthusian debates can be found in the edited collections *Debating the Earth: The Environmental Politics Reader* (Dryzek and Schlosberg 1998) and *International Politics:*

Enduring Concepts and Contemporary Issues (Art and Jervis 2000). A fuller flavour of this debate is given in the exchange between Norman Myers and Julian Simon in *Scarcity or Abundance? A Debate on the Environment* (1994). Other contributions to the debate include, on the more pessimistic side, Robert Heilbroner's *An Inquiry into the Human Prospect: Looked at Again for the 1990s* (1991) and Garret Hardin, *Living within Limits: Ecology, Economics and Population* (1993); the most influential recent Cornucopian account is Bjørn Lomborg, *The Skeptical Environmentalist* (2001).

The environmental scarcity–violent conflict hypothesis is set out in Thomas Homer-Dixon, *Environment, Scarcity and Violence* (1999), while *Ecoviolence: Links among Environment, Population and Security* (Homer-Dixon and Blitt 1998) provides case-studies of the application of the model. An excellent collection of the arguments for and against the Homer-Dixon thesis can be found in Paul Diehl and Nils Petter Gleditsch, *Environmental Conflict* (2001). The argument for thinking about environmental security in terms of conflict resolution is made in Conca and Dabelko, *Environmental Peacekeeping* (2002).

On the linkage between natural resource predation and violent conflict, see the collections of essays in Mats Berdal and David M. Malone (eds), *Greed and Grievance: Economic Agendas in Civil Wars* (2000), and Karen Ballentine and Jake Sherman (eds), *The Political Economy of Armed Conflict* (2003). Paul Collier presents his influential arguments on the primacy of greed against grievance in the co-authored book *Greed and Grievance in Civil Wars* (Collier and Hoeffler 2001). Philippe Le Billon's analysis from a political geography perspective can be found in *Fuelling War: Natural Resources and Armed Conflict* (2005). Michael Renner's *The Anatomy of Resource Wars* (2002) is a good overview of the whole issue.

As regards the concept of environmental security, the article by Jessica Mathews, 'Redefining security', in *Foreign Affairs* (1989), was probably the most influential in promoting the concept as the Cold War was dissolving. One of the most incisive critiques of the concept can be found in Marc Levy, 'Is the environment a national security issue?', in *International Security* (1995). The critical security and human security approaches to environmental security are given in Jon Barnett, *The Meaning of Environmental Security* (2001), and Simon Dalby, *Security and Environmental Change* (2009). For an excellent collection of articles debating environmental security, see Daniel Deudney and Richard Matthew (eds), *Contested Grounds: Security and Conflict in the New Environmental Politics* (1999).

Questions for Research and Discussion

1 How does the debate between so-called neo-Malthusians and Cornucopians affect our understanding of environmental security?
2 Is Homer-Dixon right to argue that there is a causal connection between environmental degradation and violent conflict?

3 To what extent and in what ways does the competition for natural resources lead to violent conflict?

4 To what extent is climate change a security issue?

WEBSITES

www.unep.org
The United Nations Environment Programme coordinates the environmental activities of the UN and is a central resource of relevant publications, research, multimedia sources and treaties.

www.wilsoncenter.org/program/environmental-change-and-security-program
The Environmental Change and Security Program at the Woodrow Wilson International Center for Scholars offers publications and multimedia on the relationship between the environment, security and conflict.

www.envirosecurity.org/
The Institute for Environmental Security is a dedicated institute which aims to increase political attention to environmental security as a means to help safeguard essential conditions for peace and sustainable development.

CHAPTER 7

The Struggle for Resources: Oil and Water

The previous chapter argued that environmental security can be seen, in part, as a revival of the tradition of geopolitics. Central to this tradition is the geopolitical struggle for natural resources. There are no more vital resources than water and oil. Fresh water is a basic necessity of life – for drinking, for producing food and for washing – and a key component of a modern and developed society. Oil is theoretically a less essential commodity in that there are alternatives or substitutes, but, in practice, modern industrial society is critically dependent on the relative cheapness and abundance of oil for providing a substantial part of the energy resources essential for modern living. During the twentieth century, human ingenuity and technological innovations manipulated water and oil resources in ways which have been central to modern advances in agriculture, industry, transport and general human welfare.

In reality, geopolitical concerns over these two key resources have always been present. In part, this is due to their uneven distribution. Water scarcity is particularly intense in regions and countries in the arid zone, such as the Middle East, Central Asia, South Asia and parts of sub-Saharan Africa. In contrast, petroleum reserves are concentrated most in the water-scarce countries of the Persian Gulf, though there are also significant supplies found in other parts of the world, such as the former Soviet Union, West Africa and the United States. It is this uneven distribution, in combination with the strategic importance accorded to water and oil, that feeds geopolitical anxieties. In the Persian Gulf region, Western concerns over energy security have been a background to multiple conflicts and interventions – the Gulf wars of 1990–1 and 2003 and the intervention into Libya in 2011 being only the most recent manifestations. The fear of water-based conflicts, again especially in the Middle East, has been similarly high (Gleick 1993; de Villers 1999; Zeitun 2011). In 1988, Boutros Boutros-Ghali, then Egypt's foreign minister, famously proclaimed that 'the next war in our region will be over the waters of the Nile, not politics' (quoted in Klare 2001: 12).

This chapter develops themes and arguments from the previous chapter, but with a more concentrated focus on the prospects of resource-based conflicts. The choice of the comparison between water and oil attempts to break down the sharp distinction made in much of the literature between renewable and non-renewable resources and their strategic implications. There are, in reality, many similarities and linkages between water and energy security.

These include issues relating to physical availability and potential scarcity. There are also similarities in the ways in which water and oil interdependencies potentially promote international cooperation as much as international conflict. In addition, both resources have security implications which involve multiple different parties and perspectives and are not limited just to the concerns of those dependent on the supply and import of these resources – there are also the legitimate concerns of those upstream and/or the exporters. There is besides a key human security dimension relating to those who do not have uninterrupted access to sufficient drinking water, sanitation or modern energy services. Furthermore, the critical impact on regional and global eco-systems from human use of water and oil provides a broader environmental dimension to the security picture.

The comparison between water and oil does, though, bring out certain key differences in how the struggle for these resources affects international security. The argument of the chapter is that the strategic implications of oil, and its threat to regional and international stability, are considerably greater than for water. But the core underlying reason for this is not physical scarcity or the distinction between renewable and non-renewable resources. It is about politics, particularly the international political economy, where oil is ultimately much more highly prized than water. This political dimension also involves the complex historical and sociological legacies of how certain natural resources, particularly oil, contribute to the generation of insecurities, both domestically and internationally.

Water security

This in no way diminishes the human tragedy of the global reality of water insecurity. It is estimated that currently more than 2 billion people are affected by water shortages in over forty countries; 1.1 billion do not have sufficient drinking water and 2.6 billion have no provision for sanitation (WHO/UNICEF 2000; Nickum 2010). It is also projected that by 2050 at least one in four people is likely to live in a country affected by chronic or recurring shortages of fresh water (Garner-Outlaw and Engelman 1997). As the global population grows, there will be a need for more water to ensure people's basic need for food, health and energy. Since in many of the most arid regions water is shared between different countries with often tense political relations, the increased competition for water is seen to be likely to contribute towards further exacerbating political and military tensions. Water insecurity appears destined to be an ever growing problem in the future.

Water is a highly emotive topic. It is rightly taken as an indictment of human achievement that we are still unable to ensure that everyone in the world has access to clean and freely available water. A United Nations report on the water crisis notes that, 'for many years over the past decades, 6,000 people, and mainly children under five, have died every day. Descriptions more severe than "a crisis" have been associated with events in which 3,000 people have lost their lives in a single day' (UNESCO 2003: 5). This is a salutary warning that the seriousness of the problem should not be underestimated and that there are highly significant human security and environmental security dimensions to the problem of water security. But getting to the root of this problem requires a clear-headed assessment of whether this is due primarily to physical scarcity or more to socio-economic and developmental factors.

How scarce is water?

In reality, the concept of water scarcity is less self-evident and easy to determine than is commonly imagined. One of the most commonly used benchmarks is that proposed by Malin Falkenmark, according to which countries exhibiting water availability of less than 2,740 litres per person per day should be considered water scarce (Falkenmark 1989). But among those countries falling into this category (see table 7.1) are a number that are relatively wealthy and which are clearly managing to survive apparently chronic water scarcity. For energy-rich countries such as Kuwait, the United Arab Emirates (UAE) and Saudi Arabia, part of the solution comes through desalination of the almost limitless salt water found on their shores (Lomborg 2001: 153). Singapore supplies most of its water needs through imports by tanker. Both options are clearly costly and would be unsustainable for most poorer developing countries. But these costs should not be exaggerated. The Jordanian water specialist Munther Haddadin estimates that the cost of desalination becomes a feasible option in countries with an average disposable income of $3,850 per year (Haddadin 2002: 215). This suggests, therefore, that water scarcity is not a problem if you have enough money; it is a problem for poor countries, but a problem which should become easier to resolve with the process of development.

Projections of future water scarcity also generally assume that per capita demand will remain constant or increase as populations grow. However, this ignores the countervailing logic that, as water scarcity increases and so the price of water rises, incentives for maximizing productivity and constraining demand should also grow. An analogy would be with the energy crises and oil price hikes of the 1970s, which resulted in significant increases in intensity of energy use in industrialized countries, along with measures to constrain the demand for oil.

In reality, the current practices and institutions of water management remain highly wasteful and inefficient, and there is much that can be done to increase productivity. The agricultural sector is the area where the greatest potential gains can be made, since it is here that nearly 70 per cent of global water is used. Israel, which is again a country formally in the category of

Table 7.1 Countries with chronic water scarcity (below 2,740 litres per capita per day): available water, litres per capita per day

	2000	2025	2050
Kuwait	30	20	15
United Arab Emirates	174	129	116
Libya	275	136	92
Saudi Arabia	325	166	118
Jordan	381	203	145
Singapore	471	401	405
Yemen	665	304	197
Israel	969	738	644
Oman	1,077	448	268
Tunisia	1,147	834	709
Algeria	1,239	827	664
Burundi	1,496	845	616
Egypt	2,343	1,667	1,382
Rwanda	2,642	1,562	1,197
Kenya	2,725	1,647	1,252
Morocco	2,932	2,129	1,798
South Africa	2,959	1,911	1,497
Somalia	3,206	1,562	1,015
Lebanon	3,996	2,971	2,533
Haiti	3,997	2,497	1,783
Burkina Faso	4,202	2,160	1,430
Zimbabwe	4,408	2,839	2,199
Peru	4,416	3,191	2,680
Malawi	4,656	2,508	1,715
Ethiopia	4,849	2,354	1,508
Iran	4,926	2,935	2,211
Nigeria	5,952	3,216	2,265
Eritrea	6,325	3,704	2,735
Lesotho	6,556	3,731	2,665
Togo	7,026	3,750	2,596
Uganda	8,046	4,017	2,725
Niger	8,235	3,975	2,573
Percentage of people suffering chronic scarcity	3.7%	8.6%	17.8%

Source: World Resources Institute (1998).

suffering water scarcity, has greatly increased its productivity by introducing drip irrigation and other efficiency measures. Sandra Postel has argued that the introduction of drip irrigation and the use of less water-intensive crops can achieve efficiency savings of up to 95 per cent and that, as of 1991, only 0.7 per cent of global irrigated land was being micro-irrigated (Postel 1999: 173; see also Charles and Varma 2010). Countries in arid zones can further alleviate their water problems by importing water-intensive crops such as grain, which requires over 1,000 cubic metres of water to produce 1 ton. This is what Tony Allan calls 'virtual water', and it is clearly part of the solution to water security problems in arid zones (Allan 2011). There is also clearly a logic for such water-stressed countries to make the transition from a predominantly agricultural to an industrial and urban society, where the water demands would be considerably reduced.

Water insecurity is additionally linked to the ingrained notion that water is a gift of nature and that it is somehow unjust to charge its full economic cost. The legacy of low prices has been one of wastefulness, a lack of incentives for conservation, and the embedding of powerful domestic constituencies resistant to any change in the subsidization and allocation of water. Moving to a commercial rate for water which is closer to the full cost is an essential but politically sensitive move, generally requiring not the dismantling of all subsidies but their targeting at those genuinely in need. Similar political sensitivities, and the necessity for a continuing regulatory role for the state, have to be taken into account in promoting other market-oriented measures such as the privatization of water systems or the development of water markets. Privatization, for example, can help in reducing water subsidies and public sector debt but it also needs to be managed in ways that do not exacerbate poverty and inequality. The failure to do this was well illustrated in Bolivia by the massive public protests in 2002 against the privatization of Cochabamba's water system, as a consequence of a mismanaged and corrupt process which resulted in water rates sky-rocketing and residents receiving bills representing a quarter or more of their income (Gleick et al. 2002). Overall, providing for water access rights and effective regulatory systems is critical to the successful management of problems of water insecurity.

The role and capacity of the state in this regard, therefore, is a critical variable. Traditional approaches and policies adopted by states are also increasingly questioned. For the past half century, the conventional approach has involved a geopolitical vision of water manipulation on a grand scale, with intensive pumping of groundwater, the construction of thousands of dams, and large-scale water diversions. These policies have in many ways been highly successful. Many water-borne diseases have been eradicated, and the extent of irrigated land increased from 50 million hectares in 1900 to 255 million hectares in 1995, making it possible to feed the additional 3.5 billion population. But these policies have had their limitations. Despite all these efforts, over 1 billion people remain without access to clean water. The environmental and human costs have also often been considerable, as seen in extensive soil degradation, groundwater depletion, forcible evacuations and damage to vital eco-systems. An influential report from the World Commission on Dams (2000) has highlighted the generally poor returns, the extensive environmental damage and the human rights abuses involved in the construction of large dams. The deliberate decision by the Soviet authorities to empty the Aral Sea in Central Asia to facilitate the irrigation of the region for the production of cotton is a classic example of such geopolitical engineering of water which fatally ignored the broader human security costs.

In many ways, the problem of water security has similarities to the global environmental security problems highlighted in the previous chapter, such as climate change and species preservation. The limits of traditional practices of water management have become increasingly apparent, and the simple model of state provision of security of supply has to be supplemented by more decentralized, market-oriented policies which increase water productivity and constrain demand (Wolff and Gleick 2002; Charles and Varma 2010). These problems also involve a human security concern both for the poorest and those without access to clean water and for the development of appropriate policies and technologies to meet these needs. In addition, the broader environmental consequences of water policies need to be more fully taken account of, often involving interstate cooperation. All these measures require sensitive and capable institutions and policy-making which can incorporate the multiple perspectives of water security and ensure the appropriate balance between state intervention and market-oriented policies. They are, though, clearly easier to implement for developed than for less developed countries, with their weaker social and political institutions.

Water: towards conflict or cooperation?

Conflict is an inevitable and endemic feature of the politics of water. As with any scarce and valuable resource, there are disputes about its appropriate allocation and use. Conflicts are apparent at both the domestic political and the interstate level. Within states, there are inevitably tensions between different users such as agriculturalists, industrialists, domestic users, hydro-power generators, leisure users and environmentalists. Policies such as privatization, as noted above, are also likely to generate political protest, particularly if they are mismanaged. Large-scale water projects, such as the building of dams, have increasingly become a focus of political mobilization. Water is inevitably a sensitive political issue between states as well, particularly between upstream and downstream states. Unlike other resources, water naturally flows across national borders. There are estimated to be 263 international water basins, approximately one-third of which are shared by more than two countries and nineteen between five or more countries. There are also as yet unknown numbers of transboundary aquifers (see Giordano and Wolf 2003).

There is, though, little empirical evidence that these water-related tensions have resulted in significant violent conflict at either the domestic or the international level. At the domestic intrastate level, multiple incidents can be found of water-related riots, revolts and the deliberate targeting of water resources as part of a domestic insurgency or terrorist campaign (see Gleick 1993). But the evidence that water scarcity itself has led to more protracted civil war is not so clear. The reasons for this are similar to the arguments set out in the previous chapter as to why resource scarcities are unlikely to lead to violent civil war. Water scarcity certainly affects the poor and dispossessed, and undoubtedly contributes to their misery and intermittent rebellion, but it is unlikely to motivate the interest of elites who are needed for the mobilization of large-scale organized violence. Water is not, in itself, a valuable enough resource for such violent inter-elite competition. Also, as argued above, the problem of water scarcity can potentially to lead to innovative solutions, whether in terms of measures to increase water productivity or of human migration towards cities, though these are admittedly more difficult for poorer developing states. As such, water scarcity can tend towards increasing societal adaptation and cooperation rather than conflict and confrontation (see Delli Priscolli 2000).

A similar movement towards cooperation rather than conflict is evident in relations between states over water. This was confirmed by a large-scale study of water conflict and cooperation completed in 2001 at Oregon State University, which tracked over 1,800 water-related interactions from 1948 to 1999 and found that incidents of cooperation greatly outnumbered those of conflict. The study also confirmed that there had been no modern wars fought over water (see Wolf, Yoffe and Giordano 2003). The Food and Agriculture Organization of the UN (FAO) has catalogued the impressive evidence of the many international agreements and treaties which have been established over the centuries to deal with water-related issues. In the period from 805 to 1984, the FAO identified over 3,600 water and navigational treaties, more than 200 of which were agreed in just the last fifty years (FAO 1978, 1984). The potential for water conflict has, therefore, frequently led to the establishment of institutions, whether defined legally through treaties or involving more informal and implicit agreements, which seek to spell out, however imperfectly, each country's rights and responsibilities towards a shared river.

International water disputes can, nevertheless, be severe and contribute to decades of political and military tensions (see Toset, Gleditsch and Hegre 2000; Griffiths and Houston 2008). This is particularly the case where one country within an international watershed, normally the regional hegemon, decides unilaterally to implement a major water project without involving neighbouring countries whose interests would also be greatly affected. Examples of this include Egypt's plans to build a high dam on the Nile in the 1950s and 1960s, which led to many years of tense relations with Sudan and Ethiopia. Turkey similarly introduced its highly ambitious GAP project on the Euphrates in the 1980s, which aimed to increase irrigation in south-east Turkey, without fully consulting and involving affected downstream countries such as Iraq and Syria. During the 1960s and early 1970s, India unilaterally constructed a barrage on the Ganges river at Farraka to channel more water to Calcutta, but at the expense of water available for irrigation in Bangladesh. All of these cases contributed significantly to political and regional tensions. Such water-related conflicts can also be less intentional, such as in Central Asia, where the newly independent states of the region lack the mutual political trust to re-establish the shared water management institutions which existed during the Soviet period.

Yet even in these cases the water-related conflicts have fallen short of leading to outright military conflict and have tended to delay, rather than rule out completely, the eventual establishment of a mutually acceptable institutional arrangement. The interesting question is why there is this tendency towards states seeking institutional treaty-based cooperative solutions rather than violent conflict or war. One important reason for this is the very nature of water being a shared resource. Theoretically, it is possible for an upstream state to consider that all the water in a river is its sole possession and that downstream users are merely granted a certain allocation. This notion of exclusive sovereignty is set out in the so-called Harmon doctrine, which some powerful upstream states, such as Turkey and China, have used to justify their unwillingness to agree to binding multilateral treaties. In practice, though, such a doctrine is difficult to defend even by the most ardent advocates, since it runs against international normative and legal developments such as the 1997 UN Convention on International Watercourses, which confirmed the need for equitable and cooperative management arrangements for international transboundary water resources. Upstream and downstream states also generally do have shared interests, so that building a dam may benefit both the upstream state through the provision of hydropower and the downstream states through increasing irrigation for land and better flood prevention. Such in-built interdependence has led many to advocate that states should forego considering water in terms of possessive rights, but rather see it in terms of the needs of all who use the water. Such an approach necessarily encourages a more cooperative and holistic approach (see Feitelson 2002).

A second factor is the more narrow military consideration that there is little practical military purpose in fighting a war over water. Much confusion over the prospects for water wars has arisen from exaggerated claims that the 1967 Arab–Israeli conflict and the 1982 Israeli invasion of Lebanon were driven by water considerations (Cooley 1984; Bulloch and Darwish 1993; Hillel 1994; Amery 2002). In reality, all serious in-depth studies of these wars identify deeper historical, political and geostrategic reasons for their outbreak (see Libiszewski 1995). The conflict over water was always more a function than a direct cause of these deeper roots of Arab–Israeli enmity (Lowi 1993; Zeitun 2011). Water is also ultimately not valuable enough a commodity to warrant the significant resources required to fight a war. If you assume that 70 per cent of water is used for low-value crops, then ultimately any war over water would primarily be over such low-value irrigation crops. An Israeli defence analyst expressed this clearly when he dismissed the claim that Israel had fought its wars over water: 'Why go to war over water? For the price of one week's fighting, you could build five desalination plants. No loss of life, no international pressure and a reliable supply you don't have to defend in hostile territory' (cited in Wolf 1998: 259).

A third factor can be attributed to the potential for external actors and institutions to play a positive role in promoting regional cooperative water arrangements. Water is an area where outside powers can present themselves as reasonably disinterested, since they generally have no direct strategic interest or need for the water which is in contention. It is also a functional area where the prospects for conflict prevention seem to be relatively favourable. Past evidence suggests that, before a conflict becomes too entrenched, external actors do have an opportunity to facilitate water agreements which can endure even the most intensive subsequent political and military disputes. A good example is the 1960 Indus Water Treaty, which was signed by India and Pakistan under World Bank stewardship and has survived the multiple subsequent Indo-Pakistani wars (Biswas 1992). There is also recognition that failure to implement a cooperative agreement early in a political dispute can lead to years of delay before a settlement can be reached, as can be seen over the Jordan or the Ganges. The 1999 Nile Basin Initiative is a good example of a more recent proactive and genuinely regional and multilateral attempt to ensure water security and to encourage regional integration (UNESCO 2003: 315).

From water to oil security

Oil and water are very different resources but there are similarities in the concerns and anxieties that are popularly expressed about them. As with worries over water scarcity, there are fears that oil is 'running out' and that future oil crises, like those of the 1970s, are bound to recur in the future. Oil, conflict and insecurity are also intimately associated in the popular consciousness, and, as with water, the major geographical focus of concern is the Middle East. Oil and water might not mix but, in political terms, they are seen to be highly combustible.

Are we running out of oil?

Ever since the oil price rises of the 1970s, there have been regular alarming projections that oil production has reached its peak and that a future of oil scarcity must be accepted (Gever 1986; P. Roberts 2004). This pessimistic outlook has been accorded scientific credibility by the geologist Colin Campbell and his associates, who have argued that the peak of global oil production has been, or is close to being, reached. When that peak is reached, oil supply will stall and the world will have to cope with a future of a fairly rapid decline in supply (Campbell 1997; Campbell and Laherrère 1998; Simmons 2005). Clearly, if this scenario is accepted, the political, economic and security implications of a world which suddenly has to cope with such oil scarcity, and with the rapid rises in prices associated with it, will be even more serious than the events of the 1970s. If this is true, governments can rightly be blamed for extraordinary complacency in the face of this major strategic challenge (Fleming 2000).

There is, though, an alternative way of understanding future oil supplies which is considerably less pessimistic. This is to adopt the more Cornucopian stance, in the tradition of Julian Simon, that it is fallacious to assume, as Campbell does, that energy resources are finite or that oil reserves are static. Rather, as Michael Lynch has argued, the starting point should be a recognition that the total resource base is likely to be large and that recoverable oil reserves are not a static or independently known quantity but rather a function of various complex factors, including technological knowledge, governmental polices and, most importantly, the price of oil (Lynch 1996). It is particularly when prices rise that oil reserves typically increase, since oil companies have a commercial incentive to explore for new oil and exploit additional oilfields that have become economically viable. Such a dynamic interaction between oil prices and oil reserves offers a much less deterministic understanding of global oil supplies and supports a greater optimism that they will meet future demand, at least until there is a transition to an appropriate and economically efficient alternative form of energy (Lynch 2002; Maugeri 2004).

This less pessimistic understanding of the dynamics of the oil industry is strengthened by the actual developments that have taken place since the oil crises of the 1970s. These were engineered principally by the cartel of predominantly Middle Eastern producer countries of the Organization of Petroleum Exporting Countries (OPEC). The response, however, was for the oil companies significantly to increase the exploration and production of oil among non-OPEC countries, whose reserves had earlier been too expensive to produce. As the OPEC countries continued to restrict production in order to maintain high prices, they found that their share of global oil production fell, from 56 per cent in 1973 to 29 per cent in 1985. When OPEC sought to regain market share, the price of oil plummeted. Oil companies have been active not only in finding new reserves but also in improving their use of technology so as to reduce costs and increase yields. While in the early 1980s it was thought impressive to extract 40 per cent of a field's reserves, this has increased to 70 per cent and even 90 per cent. The combined effects of the increase in non-OPEC production and advances in technology are that the amount of reserves has actually been expanding, as shown in figure 7.1, despite overall growth in consumption. The seeming paradox is that, over the last thirty years, ever increasing consumption of oil has actually made oil more plentiful rather than more scarce.

Increased costs have also created incentives for energy users to be more efficient in their use of oil and to seek to conserve supplies. In the same way

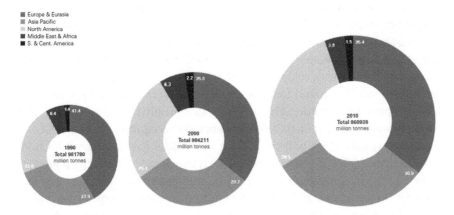

Figure 7.1 Distribution of proved oil reserves in 1990, 2000 and 2010 (percentages)
Source: BP Statistical Review of World Energy (June 2012).

that relatively simple measures such as drip irrigation can greatly reduce wastage of water, so various measures have been undertaken to improve energy productivity. Developed countries in particular have become much more efficient in their use of oil. In the US, greater efficiency in the use of its energy inputs has meant that, despite rises in oil imports, the overall energy costs for the booming US economy have declined, from 2.76 per cent of GDP in 1980 to about 1 per cent of GDP currently. During the same period, Germany and France have actually cut their consumption. Efficiencies in energy markets have also been encouraged by breaking up state-controlled monopolies, liberalizing markets and deregulating energy utilities (Buchan 2002; Goldthau and Witte 2009b). Measures to constrain domestic demand for oil and to promote energy conservation, for instance by introducing higher gasoline prices and government regulations to promote more efficient cars, have been part of this effort to increase energy productivity and to reduce the insecurities of oil dependence.

The success of this multi-pronged strategic response to the oil price rises and energy crises of the 1970s confirms that market-oriented policies, combined with appropriate governmental action and encouragement, are capable of meeting future energy needs. The dominant view, held by the International Energy Agency (IEA), is that there are ample and sufficient oil supplies to meet a projected doubling of demand, from about 85 million barrels a day in 2008 to 105 million barrels a day in 2030 (IEA 2012). However, one should add three qualifications to these projections. The first is that it is not the developed world that will be the major new source of demand but the developing world and the two-thirds of the world's population who either lack or have only intermittent access to modern energy services (Barton et al. 2004: 6). Currently, the greatest incremental demand for oil is coming from the developing countries in Asia, such as China and India, and this is only going to increase. The economies of these fast developing countries are also considerably more energy intensive than the industrialized countries in the Organization for Economic Cooperation and Development (OECD), and their economies are thus more vulnerable to the effects of oil price rises. The projected rise in demand from the developing world, which is most significantly impacted by the growth in demand for cars, means that there can still be a 'peak' in conventional oil considerably earlier than optimists would suggest. The second qualification is that it is also generally recognized that most of the increased supply of oil will come from the Middle East and not from non-OPEC countries. The challenge over the next two decades is to step up production capacity in the Middle East, from 20 million to 40 million barrels a day to meet increased demand. This will result in the global economy becoming more dependent on Middle Eastern oil, and this is nowhere more the case than in Asia, where the majority of Middle Eastern oil is already flowing. The regular political and military crises in the region naturally excite continuing energy security concerns.

The third qualification is an environmental one. It was noted in the previous chapter that climate change represents one of the most critical and difficult environmental security challenges. Oil consumption is one of the most significant causes of greenhouse gases, highlighting the potentially heavy environmental costs of our dependence on oil. Such perceived environmental costs have already encouraged governments to tax oil at higher rates than other energy resources and to promote greater diversification in the domestic mix of fuels. Natural gas, nuclear energy and renewable energy resources have all gained from their credentials as greener sources of energy. With China and India moving to a mass car society, there is justifiable concern whether the environment would survive the resulting increase in fossil fuel emissions. In this light, it is more plausible to envisage that it will ultimately be environmental factors that bring global dependence on oil to an end rather than a physical shortage of supply. As Sheikh Yamani, Saudi Arabia's former energy minister, reportedly quipped: 'the Stone Age came to an end not for a lack of stones, and the oil age will end, but not for a lack of oil' (quoted in Greider 2000: 5).

Oil: cooperation for energy security

There is a tendency, as with the impending threat of 'water wars', to think in terms of oil being inextricably linked to conflict and war. The rise of OPEC and the oil price hikes in the 1970s, coinciding with the 1973 Arab–Israeli conflict and the 1979 Iranian revolution, have firmly connected oil with Middle Eastern instability and endemic conflict with the West. The fear that oil is a weapon in the hands of the producing nations has remained embedded in Western popular consciousness. In the developing countries, the rise of OPEC has been viewed as one of the first effective Southern responses to

Northern domination and as a path to regaining control of their natural resources from avaricious multinational corporations. Oil politics and resource nationalism are perceived to be an integral feature of North–South conflict.

However, the fears of an endemic North–South confrontation, where the North is constantly held at the mercy of the oil-exporting states of the South, are exaggerated. Despite the rhetoric, the Arab oil weapon has been peculiarly ineffective, even in the 1973 war (see Al-Sowayegh 1984). In retrospect, it is clear that the oil price rises of the 1970s and the empowerment of the oil-producing states were due primarily to shifts in the fundamentals of supply and demand rather than to the assertion of Arab political muscle (Horsnell 2000: 7). In addition, the measures taken by the developed countries since the 1970s have greatly reduced the potential damage of politically related disruptions of supply. The promotion of integrated global markets, the diversification of supplies away from OPEC countries, the diversification in the domestic fuel mix, energy efficiencies and conservation, along with the establishment of strategic storage under the supervision of the IEA, have all contributed to a marked reduction of the energy security risks of physical disruptions of supply (Goldthau and Witte 2009a). The oil markets were barely disrupted by the Gulf wars in 1990–1 and 2003. If anything, the balance of political power shifted markedly in the North's favour, so that it was the major oil-exporting countries, such as Iran, Iraq and Libya, that suffered from politically inspired embargos on their oil exports during the 1990s (Morse 1999: 14). At the time of writing in 2012, the greatest threat to energy security comes from the prospect of an armed confrontation with Iran over its nuclear weapons programme.

Defining oil politics in terms of confrontation and zero-sum competition is also limiting and self-defeating. Just as with water, there is an alternative perspective which highlights the shared interests and the mutual interdependencies between upstream and downstream and between producing and importing countries. This, in fact, applies to what are properly considered to be the most pressing global energy security challenges: the volatility in the price of oil and the issue of whether investment will meet longer-term demand (Horsnell 2000: 8).

There is clearly a mutual interest between importing and exporting countries that oil prices do not fluctuate excessively. It is, though, a structural feature of oil markets that prices tend to be volatile, since it is particularly difficult to ensure that downstream crude oil supplies meet the upstream demand of refiners, whose demand in turn is extremely sensitive to macroeconomic conditions in the market as a whole. Oil markets also suffer from poor and opaque information about oil production. While all parties have a mutual interest in trying to ensure price stability, the difficult political issue is how the costs of adjustment are to be distributed. In practice, Northern governments have cushioned their customers from the impact of oil price rises, most notably through high taxation levels for gasoline products, which lessen the relative impact and magnitude of changes in prices. In contrast, the economies and populations of oil-producing countries, particularly those highly dependent on petroleum exports, suffer substantially from falls in prices (Mitchell 2002: 265). In addition, OPEC countries, and most notably Saudi Arabia, play a vital stabilizing role through maintaining spare production capacity which can be utilized to manage surges in demand. This role involves significant financial costs and finds the leading countries of OPEC acting in a much more cooperative and positive way in ensuring global energy security than is often popularly presented.

Ensuring that investment in oil production meets future demand also represents a mutual interest between the various interested parties. Oil-importing countries need to guarantee that there is sufficient investment so that what Paul Horsnell calls a 'fundamental discontinuity' does not emerge between supply and demand, the main reason for the high prices, oil crises and economic downturns of the 1970s (Horsnell 2000: 7; see also Andrews-Speed, Liao and Dannreuther 2002). Oil exporters are also interested in supply meeting demand, since experience has shown that a protracted period of 'fundamental discontinuity' would accelerate the transition away from oil to other sources of energy supply. However, the capital required to bring global oil production to the level of future demand is enormous, with costs estimated to be of the order of $5.5 billion per year for the Gulf States alone. One sign of a sense of greater mutual trust and shared interest is that the Gulf States are beginning to invite back their former foes, the oil multinationals, to provide the necessary capital, technology and expertise to maximize their downstream production. Probably the most critical energy security question is whether this convergence of interests and cooperation between the oil companies and the Middle Eastern OPEC states will be sufficiently timely and robust to ensure the required doubling of Middle Eastern production capacity by 2030.

The existence of shared interests and complex interdependence is nowhere more evident than in the relationship between Saudi Arabia, the largest oil exporter, and the United States, the largest oil importer. This relationship is also central to global energy security. Both the US and Saudi Arabia have a common interest in stable prices, set neither so high as to damage the global economy and undermine the Saudi interest in the long-term future of oil, nor so low as to undermine US domestic production and potentially destabilize pro-Western oil producers, not least Saudi Arabia itself. The US benefits from the role played by Saudi Arabia in promoting price stability through the provision of most of the global idle capacity and its willingness to discipline other oil producers whose interests drive them to seek to maximize revenues through high prices. Saudi Arabia, for its part, gains from the security guarantees that the US provides in the Persian Gulf region and further afield. It is this complex and delicate relationship between the US and Saudi Arabia which is the real lynchpin of global energy security.

Oil: geopolitics and global instability

Yet it is also the tensions and pressures evident in this critical US–Saudi energy relationship which reveal both the constraints on cooperation and the continuing role that geopolitics and fears of global instability play in international energy politics. At least part of the rationale for the US-led intervention into Iraq in 2003 was to secure a new pro-Western oil-rich state in the Gulf region which would limit US dependence on Saudi Arabia (Morse 2003; Klare 2004). For the Saudi state, it is just such US intervention-ism and its prominent military presence that invigorates popular domestic discontent and mobilizes its Islamist opposition, which is willing to use ter-rorist tactics to undermine the Saudi regime (Hegghammer 2010). This mix of geopolitical ambition among the major external powers and the internal instability of many oil-producing states makes oil a significant contribution to conflict and global insecurity. It is in these two aspects that the conflict-inducing dimensions of oil are different from those of water. Water simply does not have the economic value to excite the economic and strategic inter-ests of the major external powers and to contribute so clearly to domestic insecurities.

For some, the ideal world is one where energy security would be gained through the free operation of the market in a spirit of international coopera-tion. The European Union's green paper on energy security recognizes that markets ultimately provide the cheapest and most robust guarantee for energy security (European Commission 2001; Andrews-Speed 2004). However, it is not an ideal world, and oil has always been perceived by states as too vital for national security and too lucrative a business to be treated as just an ordinary economic commodity. Geopolitics, distrust between states and the influence of non-oil-related political conflicts have always been enmeshed in international oil politics. Thus, in the Middle East, the US ambition to act as the guarantor of energy security, most notably through providing the security of the Persian Gulf, has continually been frustrated by its failure to resolve the Arab–Israeli conflict and by its perceived partiality towards its Israeli ally. With the Middle East being globally regarded as unstable and unpredictable, international interest in other petroleum-rich regions has often resulted in competitive great power behaviour. The post-Soviet opening up of the Caspian Sea energy resources in the 1990s unleashed a major geopolitical struggle for power and influence. This has been called a new 'Great Game' which pits Russia against the US, and Turkey against Iran, and includes the intervention of China as a new global energy player.

The dilemmas facing China as it confronts its increasing energy security problems illustrate this broader geopolitical perspective. In 1993, China moved from being a net exporter to a net importer of oil, and, with the high growth rates it has achieved, its imports are projected to rise dramatically. By 2020, China is predicted to surpass the US as the largest importer of crude oil. The problem is that China's growing oil dependence will not only increase its vulnerability to variations in supply from the unstable Middle East but also its dependence on the US, which provides naval security for the navigation routes from the Middle East to the Chinese mainland (Lanteigne 2008; Andrews-Speed and Dannreuther 2011). China's dilemma is that its oil dependence makes it potentially open to US blackmail or strategic coercion. However, attempts by China to reduce this vulnerability and diversify its sources of supply also come up against geopolitical legacies of distrust and conflict. Efforts to gain access to Russia's energy reserves have met obstacles even with a post-Soviet warming of bilateral relations. China also competes with other oil-thirsty neighbours, such as Japan and India. Economic and political rationality would suggest that the most efficient way for China to resolve its energy security problems is through integration into global energy markets and encouraging extensive cooperation between its Asian neighbours, the United States and the oil-exporting countries (see Manning 2000; Salameh 2003; Andrews-Speed and Dannreuther 2011). However, it is far from inevitable that China will necessarily follow this course and that it will not be tempted to intervene more aggressively to ensure its energy needs.

The geopolitical tensions and competition between the major external powers also give a degree of political power and manoeuvrability to oil-exporting states. One of the most distinctive features of Middle Eastern politics is the way the local states have constantly manipulated the competing interests of the major external powers to protect their own independence and freedom of action. They have demanded and normally obtained generous terms, such as the provision of sophisticated military equipment, for granting access to their oil resources. They have also been highly resistant to any demands for extensive economic and political reforms at home, arguing that energy security depends on regime stability. The many years of European acquiescence to the military regime in Algeria, despite its suspension of democratic elections in 1991 and its appalling human rights record, are illustrative of such energy-driven pragmatism. Oil-exporting states can in addition insulate themselves from Western pressures for economic and political reform, since they are generally wealthy enough to avoid the imposition of World Bank or International Monetary Fund conditions. However, in the end, this preference for stability over reform only consolidates the perception and fear of longer-term instability. The 'Arab Spring' which was unleashed in 2011 has confirmed that pressures for economic and political change cannot be postponed indefinitely and that oil-rich states are as vulnerable as others to the pressure from popular protest.

The resource curse

The role of external powers is, though, only part of the picture explaining the instability found in many critical oil-producing regions. More important are the internal factors contributing to such instability. There is growing evidence that a country's dependence on the export of natural resources is itself a highly significant element in such instability. There is what has come to be called the 'resource curse', which is not limited to countries exporting oil but also affects countries exporting other internationally tradable primary commodities, such as diamonds, timber and drugs (for overview, see Ross 2012; as well as Karl 1997; Auty 2001). The main empirical support for the 'resource curse' is the statistical evidence that countries with a high ratio of natural resources to GDP have generally suffered from abnormally low growth rates (Sachs and Warner 2000). The effects are not just economic. Michael Ross (2001) has demonstrated that countries which have oil are less likely to be democratic. As the previous chapter has already explored, there is furthermore evidence that countries enjoying resource abundance are also more prone to civil wars (de Soysa 2000; Bannon and Collier 2003; Kaldor, Karl and Said 2007).

The reasons for this 'resource curse', with the possession of valuable resources appearing to have such damaging developmental and political consequences, are much debated (for a review, see Stevens 2003). For a start, there is no inevitability that resource wealth will lead to such negative consequences. Countries such as Norway, Australia and Botswana have all used their resource wealth to the general benefit of their economic and political development. But what the evidence does show is the difficulty of promoting such a positive outcome. Two main sets of reasons are provided for this. The first is primarily economic in nature and focuses on the capital-intensive and enclave nature of natural resource exploitation, which tends not to generate positive linkages to other parts of the economy such as agriculture or industry. Unlike countries suffering from water scarcity, for example, there is no powerful incentive to promote a shift towards manufacturing and other industrial activity. Scholars who have sought to explain why the resource-rich states of Latin America fell behind resource-poor East Asia in the 1970s and 1980s have tended to point to the way resource wealth in Latin America effectively impeded a shift towards the kind of export-oriented industrial development that invigorated the East Asian economies (see, for example, Mahon 1992; Wade 1992; Auty 1993).

The second and more political set of reasons for the 'resource curse' has developed from the concept of the 'rentier state', originally formulated with the oil-rich Middle Eastern states in mind (Mahdavy 1970; Behlawi and Luciani 1987; Chaudhry 1994). The concept of the rentier state refers to those countries which gain most of their income from the rents accruing directly to them through the export of primary commodities. Unlike states which have to rely on the taxation of their society, elites in rentier states enjoy a considerable degree of autonomy and disengagement from their populations. They have no immediate or necessary interest in the broader development of the economy of the state as a whole (for a comparison between Azerbaijan and Nigeria, see Bergeson, Haugland and Lundre 2000). The interest of the elites is focused on perpetuating their political dominance, and the economic advantages this provides, through the distribution of rents in exchange for political submission and subservience (Karl 1997). Such clientelistic networks, which tend to be backed up by extensive internal security forces, obstruct the development of civil society and the process of democratization (Ross 2001). To reverse the well-known quote: with 'no taxation, there is no representation'. Such clientelistic societies also tend towards weak judicial institutions, inadequate protection of property rights, and a culture of corruption. External actors, such as states or companies vying for preferential advantage, find it difficult not to contribute, through non-transparent economic and political deals, to the endemic corruption and subsequent weakening of state legitimacy.

Oil-rich rentier states are not necessarily unstable. Indeed, they can often have a perverse stability, being able to surmount internal and external opposition (see B. Smith 2004). The fact that Saddam Hussein survived defeat in the first Gulf War, the imposition of sanctions and the subsequent impoverishment of his people is testament to the power of oil-resourced clientelism and authoritarianism. Nevertheless, the threat of an internal coup or, as with Iraq, external intervention to replace the regime generates a sense of insecurity and perceptions of regional instability. To a certain degree, the amount of oil resources available to state elites makes a difference to regime stability. The prospect of severe internal instability is more evident for those states with limited oil reserves. In such states, the possibilities for patronage are more constrained, which means that, while central authority might be strong enough to resist challenges from the opposition, it may be too weak to extend control over all the peripheral parts of the country. The consequence can be long-term civil conflict and the extended civil wars seen in Angola, Sudan and Nigeria. In Angola, the central government has maintained control of the offshore oil resources, the capital city and much of the surrounding country, but it had to wage a long war against the UNITA opposition forces, who were themselves funded by the illicit sale of diamonds (Le Billon 2001b). In Nigeria and Sudan, the civil unrest is caused by central government's control of all of the resource revenue, while local communities get virtually nothing.

There are, therefore, powerful internal factors related to the 'resource curse' which contribute to the instability of many oil-exporting countries and regions. But the contributory role of external actors also needs to be included. Oil companies are by far the most important actors in terms of foreign investment in oil-rich regions such as the Middle East, the former Soviet Union and West Africa. However, they have to negotiate and reach agreements with the governments of these states. It is often difficult, particularly in a highly competitive market, to resist being implicated in the lack of transparency and corruption related to the oil revenues demanded by the state elites of oil-rich rentier states. Various initiatives, most notably the NGO-based 'Publish what you Pay' campaign and the British-promoted Extractive Industries Transparency Initiative (EITI), have sought to grapple with this problem. They seek to promote greater transparency from both companies and oil-producing governments over the revenues provided by resource rents, so as to support greater accountability, strengthen the power of citizens to challenge state policy, and weaken clientelistic practices. Certain studies suggest that such initiatives are potentially one of the most cost-effective ways to reduce the risk of conflict among resource-dependent countries (Collier and Hoeffler 2004). But the political obstacles to such enhanced transparency remain, in practice, very difficult to overcome (Shaxson 2009).

Conclusion

It is critical to keep in mind the vital roles that water and oil play in our modern civilization. Modern agriculture, industry, transportation and sanitation, and all the major advances in prosperity over the last century, have been intimately connected to the manipulation and utilization of the world's water and oil resources. It is quite natural, therefore, that access to these resources is seen not just as a technical or economic matter but also to do with security. The threat of disruption of supplies and the possibility of conflict are unavoidable strategic concerns.

Nevertheless, the security analyst has, as a scientist, to eschew unsubstantiated and excessively pessimistic projections of scarcities impending in the future and the deterministic fatalism that makes these lead inevitably to conflict. This excessive securitization of water and oil ignores the multiple technical and institutional ways in which resources such as water and oil can be maximized and used more efficiently, following a mix of effective regulation and market-based policies. Such pessimistic prognoses also ignore the evidence of the multiple ways in which interstate cooperation is possible in relation to water and energy. Nevertheless, the reality of conflicts and insecurities generated over the uneven distribution of these resources is inescapable. Here the security analyst as internationalist is required to incorporate the multiple perspectives of water and oil security: not just the concerns of the downstream/importers but also those of the upstream/exporters, along with the plight of the millions without access to easily available and cheap supplies of water and energy. In addition, there are security implications for the environment and fragile eco-systems. Resource security is a complex and multifaceted phenomenon.

But the core and central concern needs to be with the *politics* of water and oil. The strategic significance of resources lies in the role they play in the development of local and regional politics and, more broadly, in the international political economy. It is at this level that the heightened strategic significance of oil, as against water, and its particular potential for the generation of international insecurities are apparent. It is important, in this regard, to see how the possession of oil can contribute to repressive governments, poor development and weak civil societies. These domestic insecurities then generate the security fears of external actors, whose resulting interventions tend to exacerbate rather than resolve the underlying root sources of insecurity and conflict. The main contrast between oil and water is, in conclusion, that oil is such a valuable and internationally tradable resource that it has a particular capacity to excite internal conflict, weaken domestic stability, and involve the jealous security concerns of external powers.

FURTHER READING

For a good general review of the problems of water scarcity and irrigated agriculture, see Sandra Postel, *Pillar of Sand* (1999). For a comprehensive history of water and its impact on world politics, see Steven Solomon, *Water: The Epic Struggle for Wealth, Power and Civilization* (2010). For a good map of the world's water supplies and discussion of critical issues, refer to Maggie Black and Jannet King, *The Atlas of Water* (2009). Peter Gleick et al., *The World's Water* (2011), and the UN World Water Assessment Programme's *Managing Water under Uncertainty and Risk* (2012) provide a good set of articles on water topics and data.

On the issue of water security, a collection of classic papers on water disputes can be found in Aaron Wolf's *Conflict Prevention and Resolution in Water Systems* (2001). An analysis of water security which highlights the complex interconnections is the World Economic Forum's *Water Security: The Water–Food–Energy–Climate Nexus* (2011). Peter Gleick presents the case for water as a source of conflict in 'Water and conflict: fresh water resources and international security', in *International Security* (1993). Wolf challenges this and other accounts in 'Conflict and cooperation along international waterways', in *Water Policy* (1998). Wolf and his colleagues publish their findings in their water conflict and basins at risk project in 'International waters: identifying basins at risk', in *Water Policy* (Wolf, Yoffe and Giordano 2003). For a good general account of water politics and tensions in developing countries, see Arun Elhance, *Hydropolitics in the Third World* (1999), and Robert Griffiths and William Houston, *Water: The Final Resource* (2008). For a more specific assessment of the Middle East, see Mark Zeitun, *Power and Water in the Middle East* (2011).

The best history of the politics of oil is Daniel Yergin's *The Prize* (1991), and the same author covers the more recent period with *The Quest* (2011). For a good overarching overview of the politics of energy, see Brenda Shaffer, *Energy*

Politics (2009); a more sophisticated analysis is found in Timothy Mitchell, *Carbon Democracy* (2011). The concept of energy security is addressed in Roland Dannreuther, 'Energy security' (2010), and more empirical case studies are covered well in Jan H. Kalicki and David L. Goldwyn, *Energy and Security* (2005). Michael Klare's books *Resource Wars* (2001) and *Blood and Oil* (2004) highlight the potential conflicts over energy; Andreas Goldthau and Martin Witte, in *Global Energy Governance* (2009), bring out the potential for cooperation. For the role of the United States in global energy politics, see Doug Stokes and Sam Raphael, *Global Energy Security and American Hegemony* (2010). The impact of China on global energy politics is covered in Philip Andrews-Speed and Roland Dannreuther, *China, Oil and Global Politics* (2011).

For the arguments for and against the 'peak oil' thesis, compare Kyell Aleklett and Colin Campbell, 'The peak and decline of world oil and gas production', in *Minerals and Energy* (2003), and Michael Lynch, 'The new pessimism about petroleum resources', also in *Minerals and Energy* (2003). The 'peak oil' debate is extensively analysed in the UK Energy Research Council (UKERC), *The Global Oil Depletion Report* (2009). For an overview of the 'resource curse', see Michael L. Ross, *The Oil Curse* (2012), and Terry L. Karl, *The Paradox of Plenty* (1997). See the further reading recommendations in the previous chapter for items on the linkage between natural resource predation and violent conflict.

Questions for Research and Discussion

1 What is the likelihood that future wars will be fought over water?
2 To what extent is there international cooperation as well as conflict over ensuring that the global demand for oil is met?
3 Why do many resource-rich states suffer from the so-called resource curse?
4 Do you agree that wars are more likely over oil than over water?

WEBSITES

www.water.ox.ac.uk
The University of Oxford's Water Security Network, with links to various research projects on water security.

www.iea.org
The International Energy Agency – an intergovernmental organization within the OECD framework: it has a collection of data, country briefs, and multimedia on energy security and supply.

www.bp.com/sectionbodycopy.do?categoryId=7500&contentId=7068481
BP's influential annual *Statistical Review* for world energy. The website also provides a report on future projections, *Energy Outlook 2030*.

www.carnegieendowment.org/programs
The Carnegie Endowment for International Peace (CIEP) Energy and Climate Program brings together experts working in energy technology, environmental science, political economy, and security studies to develop practical solutions for policy makers around the world.

www.chathamhouse.org/research/eedp
The website of the Chatham House (Royal Institute for International Affairs) Energy, Environment and Development Programme has various reports and publications on energy security.

CHAPTER 8

People on the Move: Migration as a Security Issue

International migration is probably one of the most cited, yet also most contested, areas of the new security agenda. The perception that migration is properly considered a security threat is closely connected to global demographic trends, most notably the differential of fast population growth in the South as against ageing and declining populations in the North. The historian Paul Kennedy singled out this 'global population explosion' as one of the most challenging issues facing policy-makers in the twenty-first century, arguing that the growing inequalities in wealth between the 'haves' and the 'have-nots' would inevitably lead to 'great waves of migration' which would overwhelm traditional immigration controls (1993: 44). In a more alarmist and apocalyptic vein, he later argued that this might lead to a situation where the 'rich will have to fight and the poor will have to die if mass migration is not to overwhelm us all' (Connelly and Kennedy 1994).

Other studies have tended to avoid such extreme conclusions. But there have been a series of moves which have increasingly incorporated migration into security studies. In 1992, Myron Weiner influentially argued that migration had become 'high international politics' and that there was now the political imperative to deal with the 'global migration crisis' (Weiner 1992: 95; see also Weiner 1996). The post-Cold War rise in the numbers of refugees and the evidence of forced mass expulsion and ethnic cleansing have also elevated migration on to the security agenda (see Loescher 1992; Dowty and Loescher 1996). In terms of domestic politics, identity politics and the growing salience of ethnic, religious and national cleavages have led a number of more conservative commentators to warn that excessive immigration can threaten social and national integrity (Huntington 1997; Goldsborough 2000; Rowthorn 2003). Migration, particularly in Europe, has become an ever more important political issue, with the rise in popularity of far right parties and increasingly negative portrayals of migrants and asylum seekers (Sarrazin 2010; Laqueur 2012). As Ulrich Beck argues, migration raises all the fears and anxieties that modern societies experience in the face of the unpredictable and seemingly uncontrollable (Beck 1992: 147; see also Bauman 1998).

Yet it is precisely because of this potential for xenophobia and the rise of atavistic nationalism that many analysts have denied the legitimacy of making migration a security issue. For some, this follows from traditional realist assumptions according to which the study of security is limited to direct threats to survival and focuses on those actors seeking to use violence to achieve political objectives (Walt 1991; Freedman 1998). By this definition, migration simply does not meet the criteria for being a security threat. But such a rejection is not limited to realists. Social constructivists, particularly from the Copenhagen School (see chapter 2), support the widening of the security agenda and, in principle, the inclusion of the public discourse of immigration as a security threat. However, in practice, their main claim is that the 'securitization' of immigration should be understood as a retrogressive and illiberal move, which shifts migration from its proper realm of politics to the less accountable and exceptional realm of security.

The main argument of this chapter is that, suitably qualified, migration is a legitimate area for security studies, and it rejects the assumption that any linkage of migration with security is bound to lead to illiberal policies. But in arguing this the security analyst has a particularly challenging and difficult task in meeting the responsibilities, described in the introduction, built into the roles of scientist, internationalist and moralist.

In terms of the security analyst as scientist, the major task is to gain an overarching understanding of the dynamics of international migration and the pressures promoting and resisting such migratory moves, as well as a sense of whether, as many claim, there is a 'migration crisis'. This is a more complex and multidimensional phenomenon than popular perceptions would suggest. The challenge for the internationalist is, on the one hand, to recognize and understand the particular national policies and cultural perceptions of migration while, on the other, being able to transcend such national or regional perspectives. Migration in particular includes a complex and potentially fraught North–South dimension where Northern security-driven unilateralism tends to predominate over multilateral North–South cooperation. And, finally, for the security analyst as moralist, the challenge is to move beyond the simplistic debate which bifurcates migration into a security or non-security issue. The more interesting practical moral questions are about how security concerns over migration, which need to be seen as an inevitable structural consequence of the international state system, should be balanced with concerns over other values – such as freedom, prosperity and justice – which democratic societies hold to be important and which often facilitate as much as restrict the movement of peoples.

The chapter has three main parts. There is first an assessment of the major dynamics of international migration, looking especially at post-Cold War developments. The second part takes the case of European migration policies to see how difficult it is in practice for Northern countries to take an internationalist approach to the problems and issues of international migration. The final section revisits the issue of the legitimacy of the incorporation of migration as a security issue and challenges the 'securitization' approach to international migration.

How serious is the migration crisis?

The first point to note is that the popular perception that we are currently living in an unprecedented 'age of migration' – the title of one of the leading books on migration (Castles and Miller 2009) – is at the very least arguable. According to statistics provided by the United Nations Population Division, there were in 2010 214 million international migrants, representing 3.1 per cent of the world's population; of this number, roughly 2.2 per cent, or 10.5 million, are counted as refugees. This means that, in reality, 97 per cent of the world's population have not moved and continue to reside within their state's territory (Mills 1998). In historical perspective, contemporary migration is significantly smaller in scale than earlier migrations, such as the vast exodus from Europe to the New World in the late nineteenth century, or even than more recent migrations, such as from the Mediterranean countries to Europe in the 1960s and 1970s. Admittedly, there are significant migratory movements which are not included in the official statistics. International migration misses out mobility occurring within the borders of territorial states. It is estimated, for example, that over 150 million Chinese have migrated from the countryside to the cities, mainly to benefit from the dynamism of the coastal regions in the south (Goldstone 2002: 16). Figures on irregular immigration are also excluded; in the 1990s it was estimated to be about 5 million (although other estimates suggest up to 12 million) for the United States and a similar level for the European Union (Jordan and Duevell 2003: 67).

It is also a myth to think that the world's poorest and most desperate are swarming to enter the richer and more developed world. In reality, as Ronald Skeldon notes, international migration is economically and geographically a highly differentiated phenomenon. Those with the resources and capacity to penetrate the controls erected by industrialized countries normally come from what he calls the 'labour frontier', those regions on the 'periphery of the expanding core', such as Mexico for the United States and North Africa for Europe, or from pre-existing systems of circulation, such as Pakistan and India (Skeldon 1997: 144–70). Other poorer parts of the developing world, such as sub-Saharan Africa, the Middle East and Central Asia, are only weakly integrated into the global migration system, lacking the financial means to engage in international migration, and are home to most of the world's forced migrant populations (ibid.: 73). Refugees are disproportionately found in Asia and Africa (77 per cent at the end of 2010) as against Europe (15 per cent) and North America (4 per cent).

Nevertheless, there are legitimate reasons why developed countries feel distinctly challenged and even threatened by the trends in international migration. Of the 214 million international migrants, 127.7 million are in the developed world, where the proportion of migrants to overall population is 10.3 per cent, as against 1.5 per cent in the developing world (see table 8.1).

Table 8.1 Evolution of the number of international migrants in the world and major areas, 1970–2010

	Number of international migrants (millions)				International migrants as percentage of the population		
	1970	*1990*	*2000*	*2010*	*1970*	*1990*	*2010*
World	81.5	155.5	178.5	213.9	2.2	2.9	3.1
More developed	38.3	82.4	104.4	127.7	3.6	7.2	10.3
Less developed	43.2	73.2	74.0	86.2	1.6	1.8	1.5
Africa	9.9	16.0	17.1	19.3	2.8	2.5	1.9
Asia	28.1	50.9	51.9	61.3	1.3	1.6	1.5
Europe	18.7	49.4	57.6	69.8	4.1	6.9	9.5
Latin America and the Caribbean	5.8	7.1	6.5	7.5	2.0	1.6	1.3
North America	13.0	27.8	40.4	50.0	5.6	9.8	14.2
Oceania	3.0	4.4	5.0	6.0	15.6	16.2	16.8

Source: United Nations, Department of Economic and Social Affairs, Population Division (2011); *Trends in International Migrant Stock: Migrants by Age and Sex* (United Nations database, POP/DB/MIG/Stock/Rev.2011).

Almost all of the net growth of recent migration is also taking place in the developed countries, with North America growing by 22 million and Europe by 20 million in the decade 1990–2000. To put this recent expansion in historical context, Western Europe was home to 3.8 million foreign citizens in 1950, while now it has 69 million and rising.

Overall, this indicates that, though we are not currently living in an age of migration comparable to the late nineteenth century, underlying trends and dynamics point to the possibilities of returning to such an age. Three factors are particularly significant in this regard: the end of the structure of the Cold War; the dynamics of globalization; and the differentials in global demographic trends. These three dynamics are distinctive in the contradictory processes they unleash: on the one hand, they actively support and promote international migration and, on the other, they also instigate strong resistance and opposition to such migration. The nub of the problematic over contemporary international migration is that, while the opportunities and desire for migration are set to grow, the political conditions – such as the openness to migratory flows in the Americas and Oceania in the late nineteenth century – are unlikely to emerge to absorb this migration without significant political contestation or conflict.

Migration and the end of the Cold War

The end of the Cold War is a good example of these contradictory trends. In many ways, the Cold War was fought, at least in part, for the principle of the free movement of peoples. The ways in which communist countries placed severe restrictions on the right of exit, which was most evocatively symbolized by the brutality of the Berlin Wall, was viewed in the West as one of the most egregious denials of basic human rights by communist rule. During the Cold War, those who managed to escape to Western countries were generally viewed positively as having exercised their right to free movement rather than as potential security threats (Hollifield 2000: 81). The post-Second World War regime for refugees, built on the 1951 Geneva Convention and the establishment of the office of the United Nations High Commissioner for Refugees (UNHCR), benefited from the exigencies of the Cold War, being designed, in the late 1940s and early 1950s, to facilitate the flight of individuals from communist regimes (Loescher 2001). Similarly, the refugees who fled because of superpower-supported national liberation struggles or proxy civil war were often treated in a positive or even heroic light. The identification of the righteous 'refugee warrior', of whom the Afghan refugees/Mujahedin were the classic symbol, was a staple part of the Cold War struggle in the developing world (Loescher 1992: 12).

The end of the Cold War could have been expected to confirm and entrench these rights of free movement. There were certainly millions in the East and South who clearly expected that the end of the East–West divide would open up expansive new opportunities for movement abroad. In reality, though, the end of the Cold War has led to a distinctively less benign environment for international migration (Rudolph 2003: 606). In Western Europe, in particular, the prospect of mass East–West migrations was viewed as more of a source of insecurity than a positive assertion of human freedom. This exclusionary logic within Europe was also confirmed by the post-Cold War violent secessionist wars in the former Yugoslavia, which generated large numbers of refugees and contributed significantly to the growth of refugees, from about 8 million in the early 1980s to 18 million in 1992 (UNHCR 2000). Similarly, in a post-Cold War context of the disengagement of the superpowers from most conflicts in the developing world, the formerly heroic 'refugee warriors' were often transformed overnight into unprincipled and illegitimate actors, perpetuating senseless ethno-national conflicts and more than likely guilty of mass violations of human rights (Weiner 1996).

These contradictory dynamics are evident in the emergence of the post-Cold War practice of humanitarian intervention, which is covered more fully in chapter 4. The emergence of this norm reflects a generally positive move towards a recognition that states should no longer be able to claim sovereign immunity when they engage in mass abuse of their citizens, with their actions resulting in large-scale refugee movements. In Jeff Crisp's words, this also represents an implicit recognition that the presence or absence of refugees is a good 'barometer of human security and insecurity' (Crisp 2000: 1). In this regard, it was the plight of the Kurdish refugees fleeing Saddam Hussein in Iraq, and the Bosnians and Kosovar Albanians fleeing Serb 'ethnic cleansing', which contributed significantly to the development of the post-Cold War norm of humanitarian intervention and the understanding that sovereignty was no longer strictly juridical but must include a broader popular conception of the responsibility of states to their citizens (see Dowty and Loescher 1996; M. Barnett 1995).

However, there is also a darker side to this broadly beneficial post-Cold War development. In the Western interventions into the Balkans, the humanitarian impulse was combined with a more hard-nosed realist logic aimed at minimizing the movement and/or facilitating speedy repatriation of refugees, who were generally unpopular and unwelcome. Humanitarian intervention can, therefore, also be seen as part of a larger pattern of containment which seeks to limit or pre-empt refugee movements in regions of military conflict and instability. The ways in which the UNHCR, the main body responsible for refugees, has sought to redefine its own role to meet these contradictory trends highlight the moral ambiguities and difficulties. The UNHCR actively supported the move towards humanitarian intervention, assuming new responsibilities both for 'safe areas' within countries such as Iraq and Bosnia and for large numbers of 'internally displaced persons' (IDPs), who are not technically refugees as they have not crossed an international border. But this expansion of responsibilities has been seen by some critics as potentially undermining the commission's primary humanitarian responsibility, which is to protect refugees and to ensure that states do not evade their legal obligations to integrate or resettle bona fide refugees. For such critics, the UNHCR has *de facto* supported policies of containment and made itself complicit in the weakening of the international refugee regime (Barutciski 1998; M. Barnett 2001).

Migration and globalization

The dynamic of globalization has a similarly contradictory and push–pull impact on international migration. Much as the end of the Cold War promoted the perception of a more unified and seemingly free and mobile world, globalization has acted to 'compress time and space' and to blur national borders, thus concretely facilitating international migration. The twin revolutions in communications and transportation have made it both easier for potential migrants to learn about opportunities abroad and cheaper for them to leave their countries of origin. As compared to the eighteenth century, when British migrants would often promise to work three to six years to repay the one-way transportation costs, it typically costs less than $2,500 to travel anywhere legally and $1,000 to $20,000 illegally (Martin 2004: 405). Globalization has also consolidated the informal 'migration networks' between areas of emigration and immigration, providing potential migrants with information about opportunities for migration and helping them to cross national borders and remain abroad (Massey et al. 1998). These networks, in turn, are key to the well-known phenomenon of 'chain migration' or 'immigration begetting immigration'.

Globalization as a political ideology, like the liberal doctrines of human rights in the Western waging of the Cold War, has given further encouragement and support for migration. The economic assumptions of globalization encourage migration from lower- to higher-wage countries, as this increases allocative efficiencies, allowing the world to make the most efficient use of available resources and to maximize global production (Simon 1989). From a political science perspective, the dynamics of globalization entrench politically powerful economic interest groups in developed countries which depend on and encourage migrant labour (Freeman 1995). The movement towards international liberalization in trade in services, which can be seen as one of the most critical dynamics in contemporary globalization, has also raised the stakes in favour of labour mobility. This can be seen in the General Agreement on Trade and Services (GATS), where immigration laws restricting the movement of peoples were identified for the first time as a non-tariff barrier to trade in services (Keeley 2003). It is principally because of such globalization-driven economic pressures that European countries have moved away from the highly restrictive immigration policies introduced in the 1970s and towards seeking actively to recruit highly skilled migrants, or what the UK government has termed the 'brightest and the best', to fill the labour vacancies in the increasingly globalized services sector (European Commission 2000; Cornelius, Espenshade and Salehyan 2001; Home Office 2002). It is, thus, a myth that developed countries do not themselves encourage migratory movements.

However, such moves towards greater opportunities for legal high-skilled migration are invariably counterbalanced by draconian measures to limit lower-skilled migration and criminalize unauthorized irregular migration. This tends to take the form of increasingly tough policies towards asylum seekers and harsher action against irregular migration (Jordan and Duevell 2002). This reflects the inherently ambivalent popular attitude to globalization. While globalization can be seen to promote mutually advantageous labour mobility, it is also viewed as facilitating unwanted migration and human smuggling and criminal trafficking operations bypassing national border controls.

From the perspective of the hopeful migrant in the developing world, it is the mismatch between the ideology and the reality of globalization that is the most striking. It can appear particularly hypocritical that the developed countries preach the doctrine of economic liberalization and globalization while setting up strong and seemingly impenetrable borders to forestall the free movement of people. This sense of hypocrisy appears even greater to the extent that globalization increases the economic inequalities between the developed and the developing world. As has been noted before (see chapter 1), the global disparities in wealth have been growing rather than shrinking.

In 1975, high-income countries had per capita GDPs which were forty-one times those in low-income countries and eight times those in middle-income countries; in 2000, the ratio had grown to sixty-one times those in low-income countries and fourteen times those in middle-income countries (Martin 2004: 449). The conditions of poverty and enforced economic migration are further exacerbated by the depression of agricultural incomes in the South, which is largely a result of subsidies and protectionist agricultural policies in the developed countries.

Demographic trends and migration

Globalization, therefore, contributes significantly to the perceptions of global insecurity about the prospect of international migration. While it acts strongly to encourage such migratory movements, it also breeds Northern fears of uncontrolled movements of people, matched by Southern resentments at the barriers constructed to separate the 'world of plenty' from the 'world of want'. These tensions are further exacerbated by the third major factor intensifying international migration – demography.

The main impact of projected demographic trends is to make the developing world much more populous than the developed world. The principal reason for this is that the industrialized countries have all passed the so-called demographic transition, which is the technical term for a progressive and seemingly inexorable shift in society from a regimen of high birth and death rates to low birth and death rates (Chesnais 1992). The 'demographic transition' is not, though, a historical process unique to the industrialized countries but something all countries are either currently experiencing or will eventually face. The phenomenon of low fertility rates and an ageing and a declining population, which is currently the demographic reality in developed countries, is becoming or will become the demographic future of the rest of the world (Longman 2004; Eberstadt 2010). This is why the latest projections of the United Nations Population Division (UNPD) expect the seemingly inexorable global population growth, which has increased the world's population from 2 billion to 7 billion in 2011, to level off and stabilize at 9.15 billion in 2050 (see figure 8.1).

Nevertheless, the current reality of global differentials in fertility rates means that developing countries will account for almost all of the 3 billion extra people in the world's population. The population distribution between the developed and the developing world will, as a consequence, shift dramatically. By 2050, developing countries could represent 85 per cent of the global population, leaving the ageing populations of the North demographically marginalized (Goldstone 2010). A telling example of this is that, while currently the population of the European Union is roughly similar to that of the Middle East and North Africa (MENA), at 400 million, it is projected that, by 2050, the population of MENA will double, to around 800 million, while the

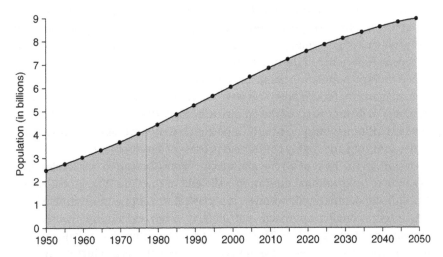

Figure 8.1 World population, 1950 to 2050 (projected)
Source: UN Population Division, *World Population Prospects: The 2006 Revision*, vol. 3: *Analytical Report* (New York: United Nations, 2010), p. 8.

European population will remain static or decline. Similarly, while in 2000 Europe and Africa had about an equal population, by 2050 Europe will have only 7 per cent as against Africa's 20 per cent share of the world's population (Martin 2004: 448). Much as Europe was the major source of migration in the nineteenth century, it can be expected that, if history repeats itself, Africa will be a major source of migration in the twenty-first century.

When these global demographic trends are taken into account, the multi-dimensional nature of the developmental and security challenges posed by global migration becomes more apparent. It explains one of the major sources of the insecurity felt in developed countries – the fear that the growing migratory influx will potentially undermine social cohesion. But such fears, while legitimate in their own right, need to be balanced by sensitivity to the developmental and security considerations of the developing countries. With fast-growing populations, a generally young age profile and large cohorts in the fifteen to twenty-nine age bracket, most governments in the developing world struggle to create the extra jobs required. One example of this challenge is in Iran, where there is a need to create 800,000 new jobs annually but where the government manages to produce only 400,000 (Vakil 2004: 47). In countries like Iran, often well-educated but unemployed young men naturally seek to emigrate to secure their economic future.

For developing countries, migration is not only an inevitable but a constitutive part of the developmental process (Skeldon 1997: 205). In developing countries, migration also has a security dimension, in that population growth combined with uneven development can contribute to a weakening of state capacity, to elite conflicts and to the potential mass mobilization of large cohorts of disaffected youth. These are the classic preconditions for insurrection and revolutionary change (Goldstone 1991, 2002). Migration and the ability to export surplus labour may not provide an immediate panacea for the problems of governance in developing and industrializing states. But the European experience in the nineteenth century, when the continent was itself experiencing a population boom and engaged in a fast process of industrialization, suggests that social pressures were alleviated by the ability to export huge numbers to distant parts of the empire (Chesnais 1992: 165; see also Bauman 1998). Migration is one potentially important 'safety valve' as countries engage in the daunting and highly conflictual process of development.

Overall, in the light of all the main factors contributing to the accelerating dynamic of international migration – the end of the Cold War, globalization and shifting demographic trends – it is critical to adopt a multidimensional and internationalist approach, particularly when examining the security dimensions of the problem. This involves a recognition that privileging the security concerns of receiving states is likely to be counterproductive and that it has to be balanced by an appreciation both of the security concerns of sending states and the way in which security and developmental goals are interlinked. This insight is developed more fully in the next section, which takes the example of how West European countries and the EU have approached the challenge of migration.

Europe and migration – the obstacles to internationalism

Western Europe and the European Union provide a good case-study for the challenges presented by these multiple trends promoting international migration to developed countries. Europe's cultural and national histories locate it somewhere between North America and Oceania, where immigration is a willed and recurrent phenomenon, and Japan, with its strong attachment to an ethnically pure national identity. Europe has also arguably faced the more dramatic challenge from immigration in recent years. As the International Organization for Migration (IOM) has remarked, 'during the 1990s, Europe became a continent of immigration', despite its projected self-image (IOM 2003). European societies are naturally and legitimately concerned about the implications of this profound shift, where a polyethnic reality is undermining the traditional conceptualization, however mythical in practice, of the homogeneous nation-state. More generally, Europe displays the classic symptoms of a declining and ageing population at its rich core, with a much poorer, younger and considerably more unstable and fast-growing periphery. Moreover, the enlarged European Union appears determined to strengthen control of its external borders, which now represent a 'welfare curtain' almost as strong and pervasive as the earlier Cold War 'iron curtain'. From both sides of this new curtain, the objective of keeping unwanted immigrants out appears to be the new security rationale of the post-Cold War European division (Huysmans 2000).

Despite the apparent dynamic towards closure of borders, there is nevertheless recognition that the pressures for and against migration are complex and that an effective policy requires a more nuanced and internationalist approach. This involves, first of all, an acknowledgement that immigration into Europe cannot be stopped completely. This is partly on account of human rights commitments, such as refugee protection and family reunification, but also because the European economy requires migrant labour. A UN report noted that, if Europe wants to keep its ratio of older people to active workers at 1995 levels, the EU will need 135 million immigrants by 2025 (UNPD 2000). Although they reject such an expansive policy, the European Commission and most European governments have nevertheless seen the need to establish legal channels for economic immigration, involving a decisive break from three decades of 'zero immigration' policy (see, for example, European Commission 2000). As mentioned above, European countries are now actively competing to secure the skilled migrant labour they see as critical for future economic growth.

But, in addition to providing legal channels for immigration, there needs also to be recognition that the negative controls and security measures against migration are blunt and ineffective instruments. At the very least, they need to be complemented by positive policies of prevention which seek to deal with the root causes for why migration is occurring. In practice, this involves pursuing an intensive dialogue with, and providing developmental support for, the principal countries sending migrants (Boswell 2003). Building 'fortress Europe' is, in this sense, counterproductive unless it is matched by intensive bridge-building. Furthermore, this more complex and nuanced policy demands greater cooperation and functional and cross-national coordination over immigration policy. This means ensuring that immigration policy involves not only law-enforcement officials but also those responsible for human rights and development and foreign policy, and, ideally, that this is coordinated at a regional EU level. Security is certainly one critical dimension of migration policy, but it can only work alongside and in coordination with the economic, humanitarian and international developmental objectives and responsibilities of European states.

In reality, though, this model of a balanced multidimensional and internationalist approach has consistently been undermined by political pressures for a more exclusionary approach. At the popular level, increases in asylum applications, the rise in irregular immigration and human trafficking, and the perceived linkages between migration and criminality and terrorism have fuelled the sense of immigration as an existential security threat. The political response has tended to prioritize unilaterally imposed policies driven by the desire for security and control. These include, for example, measures to restrict entry through strengthening borders, the introduction of carrier sanctions for airlines and the application of restrictive visa regimes. There are also measures to remove aliens and concepts such as 'safe third country' and 'safe country of origin' which permit aliens to be returned if they have arrived through another country or have their origin in a country deemed to be 'safe'. Policies towards neighbouring and other major sending countries have tended to focus narrowly on readmission agreements rather than on addressing immigration in a broader developmental framework. Not surprisingly, such agreements have often been difficult to conclude, as there is little incentive for sending countries to cooperate in the return of migrants. Controversial attempts to link development aid to return have foundered, not least because the value of immigrant remittances is often far greater than any promised provision of aid (Kapur and McHale 2003; Wucker 2004).

More generally, these unilaterally imposed and security-driven policy responses have had a number of other unintended or unexpected consequences. The exclusion of legal entry for immigrants has contributed to significant increases in asylum applications. This has not only overburdened asylum adjudication mechanisms but also incurred significant financial costs. The estimated $10 billion that European and other industrialized countries spend dealing with their 600,000 asylum applications dwarfs the $800 million they contribute to the operations of the UNHCR and the over 20 million people for which it has responsibility. As numbers of asylum seekers in Europe have increased as a result of the restrictions on legal avenues for immigration, so their treatment has become less generous, including, for example, detention in prison-like conditions and the adoption of ever more restrictive interpretations of the 1951 Refugee Convention. This has jeopardized the welfare of people who have a valid claim to refugee status and obstructed the flight of those with genuine fears for their well-being. The clamping down on asylum has also meant that clandestine irregular immigration has increased, with the development of a lucrative market in human smuggling and in coerced human trafficking, including the forced prostitution of women and children (Kyle and Koslowski 2001). This, in turn, has magnified the popular perception of links between immigration and criminality.

Such security concerns represent legitimate expressions of anxiety, and controls and exclusionary measures are an inevitable dimension of immigration policy. The challenge for Europe, though, is how to manage the potential security implications of immigration – such as trafficking, large-scale unwanted immigration, and criminal or terrorist links to migrant networks – without undermining those core 'European values', such as the commitment to freedom, human rights and justice, which are at the heart of the European liberal project. To do this requires viewing immigration from a broader perspective than a narrow strategic and economic calculus which exclusively privileges the interests of national or EU citizens. Furthermore, it requires the integration of migration policy into a broader developmental and security strategy seeking ultimately to export the European values of freedom and prosperity.

But this more internationalist approach to migration policy cannot be conceived as bringing short-term political gains. This is related particularly to the phenomenon of the 'migration hump', which is the empirical evidence that emigration actually increases as a country develops and only stabilizes and declines when the country is sufficiently industrialized and developed to entice inward migration. Past Italian out-migration and current in-migration illustrate this well. Similarly, the US experience with Mexico has shown that measures to promote Mexican development within arrangements of the North American Free Trade Area (NAFTA) increases rather than decreases short- to medium-term migration (see Martin 1993). The likelihood is that similar outcomes will emerge for Europe with the migrant-exporting countries of North Africa, particularly in the aftermath of the Arab Spring of 2011. As these countries move towards democratization and improve their economic prospects, it is likely that more rather than less outward migration will be encouraged. Preventive policies dealing with migration, seeking to resolve the 'roots of the problem', necessarily have to take a long-term and inevitably politically difficult perspective, which includes relatively generous provision for legal immigration.

Such a preventive approach does, though, create the political preconditions for establishing a more equitable system for dealing with asylum applications and a more generous European policy for giving protection to those fleeing persecution. Providing legal opportunities for immigration should reduce the numbers utilizing the asylum procedures for gaining entry and thus make it easier to concentrate on the needs of bona fide refugees. This should also help diffuse the practice of some European countries of accepting, through the UNHCR resettlement programmes, refugees from the main refugee-producing regions rather than limiting protection just to those who succeed in breaching the intensively controlled European borders, which now has its own dedicated EU border police called Frontex (Neal 2009). Ideally, this would lead to adoption of Gil Loescher and James Milner's proposal for an EU-wide resettlement programme which would 'aim to resettle 100,000 refugees a year, making a significant contribution to the resolution of protracted refugee situations' (Loescher and Milner 2003: 614). Although European leaders have not indicated that such generous provisions are yet politically possible, they do nevertheless agree that there is a convincing logic in favour of a common EU asylum policy.

Overall, the European example illustrates the potential gains and benefits of a multidimensional and internationalist approach to the general problem of international migration. It also highlights the fact that there is a significant absence, at both a regional and a global level, of an international regime dealing with migration. There have been suggestions for a global institution dealing with migration but, given the lack of consensus about the goals of such a regime and the extreme national sensitivities over the issue, there are doubts about its viability (for scepticism, see Hollifield 2000; for support, see Straubhaar 2000). But there is more justification for seeing such regimes develop on a regional level, and this is part of the dynamic of European integration, where migration and asylum issues have increasingly been incorporated into the institutions and policies of the EU (see Geddes 2008; Boswell and Geddes 2010). The challenge for the EU and its member states is to ensure that such multilateralism is promoted, not just to strengthen security controls and restrictionist measures but to consolidate an approach to international migration which ensures that legitimate security concerns are balanced with the other values integral to the principles of European integration, such as prosperity, freedom and justice.

Returning to the legitimacy of migration as a security issue

At the beginning of this chapter, it was noted how controversial and contested is the idea that migration should be treated as a security issue. There is, first, the realist critique that the promotion of immigration as a security threat simply represents a conceptual confusion and error which inappropriately uses the discourse and logic of security to deal with something which is essentially a social problem. Robert Jackson adopts this logic when he argues that immigration may certainly 'threaten the collective identity of the native-born population, in the sense that it may disrupt it and change it in the longer term; but immigration will not threaten the country's security and survival in the ordinary meaning of these terms' (2000: 195).

A negative stance is not, though, limited to the realist approach. It is also implicit in the constructivist approach adopted by the Copenhagen School and its theory of securitization (see chapter 2). There is certainly much more ambiguity here because this approach does recognize the growing popular consciousness of the perception of threat posed by immigration. And it is notable that securitization has been applied particularly extensively to the issue of immigration, and especially in the European context. Barry Buzan, Ole Waever and their collaborators elevated the concept of societal security – meaning essentially protection against threats to a social grouping's identity – to a status equal to that of traditional state security, focusing in particular on the perceived threats to 'European identities' through large-scale immigration (Waever et al. 1993; Buzan, Waever and de Wilde 1998). Didier Bigo has followed the same general approach through an examination of the securitization of immigration in Europe, arguing that the perceived threat of immigration has been cynically used by Europe's law-enforcement agencies – the police, customs and interior ministries – to promote their claims for a greater share of national resources in the context of a declining post-Cold

War external security threat (Bigo 1996, 2002). In a similar constructivist vein, Jef Huysmans explores the linkages between the European integration process and the securitization of migration, describing the latter as a parallel internal security project legitimating the exclusion of certain categories of people from the benefits of the European integration project by 'reifying them as dangers' (Huysmans 1995: 771; see also Huysmans 2000).

Much of the substance of these analyses of European migration practices and discourses only confirms the suggestions and recommendations in the arguments made above. In this sense, the securitization approach has been valuable in highlighting the multiple ways in which excessively security-driven policies are counterproductive and potentially dangerous to European traditions of civil liberties and humanitarianism. But where the securitization approach is problematic, and where it effectively mirrors the realist approach, is in its ultimate rejection of the legitimacy of treating migration as a security issue. Waever has continually asserted that the normative objective of the Copenhagen School is to encourage desecuritization, so as to treat topics such as immigration in a more appropriate political and democratic rather than national security framework (Waever 1995). Bigo's objection to security discourses over migration is in how they promote the empirically unfounded and morally objectionable 'security continuum' between immigration, unemployment, crime and terrorism (Bigo 1997). Similarly, Huysmans seeks to promote a deconstructivist sense of identity whereby the reification of stable identities, and the distinction between citizen and alien, is transformed by the ideal of the transitory nomad (Huysmans 1995). In all these cases, while the socially constructed intersubjective reality of the threat posed by immigration is recognized, it is at the same time challenged by the normative claim that such a threat construction is inappropriate, false or ethically wrong.

The approach adopted in this chapter, and in the book overall, is to challenge the separation of the political and the security realms. Instead, security considerations should be accepted as an integral part of the political process. This requires treating security not as an absolute but rather as a relative value: a value involving varying degrees of security and insecurity, and which is, moreover, only one – even though a highly important one – among others. In this sense, the value accorded to security should be determined not autonomously but only in relation to other core values which a society holds to be important, such as the commitment to freedom, to economic prosperity and to justice. This is particularly relevant for the issue of migration, where security concerns are inevitably mixed in with economic judgements and issues of civil liberties and human rights, with their associated humanitarian duties and obligations.

There is also a communitarian grounding – following the classical realist tradition argued for in chapter 2 – to the security dimension of international migration, which the securitization literature tends to avoid. From this perspective, whether desirable or not, controls on immigration represent a core and basic security responsibility for states. The legitimacy of these controls and the right of states to police their borders are deeply embedded in the political reality of an international system based on self-determining and sovereign political entities. A state-based international system, where humanity is divided and segmented into differing self-constituting national communities, entails that such communities have the right to determine who are to be members of that community and who are to be strangers. As the political theorist Michael Walzer argues, 'the primary good that we distribute to one another is membership in a human community', and, even though 'affluent and free countries are, like elite universities, besieged by applicants', they nevertheless have the right to 'decide on their own size and character' (1983: 32–3).

If this communitarian logic is accepted, then there is a legitimacy to the inclusion of security considerations in the determination of immigration policy and decisions on who is and who is not to be permitted to enter a particular national territory (for alternative cosmopolitan perspectives, see Carens 1987 and Cole 2000). States are legitimately highly sensitive to any perceived loss of control over human movements across their borders, not least because this is popularly seen to be a major failing in the state's primary security responsibilities. Similarly, one can legitimately argue that, while it is clearly unacceptable to conflate immigration with criminality and terrorism, there is nevertheless a justification for ensuring that immigration does not disrupt social integration and does not potentially introduce or entrench transnational criminal and/or terrorist networks if there is clear evidence that this might be the case. Security concerns are, therefore, an integral and inevitable part of the debate over immigration. As Christian Joppke bluntly puts it, when it comes to immigration, nation-states constitute 'rocks of facticity that defy universal justice and human rights' and are 'inclusionary and democratic on the inside but exclusionary and undemocratic on the outside' (Joppke 1999; see also Brubaker 1992).

This realist bluntness is refreshing in that it brings out clearly how security concerns are at the heart of immigration policies in even the most liberal and pluralist of countries. In this way, it is a useful corrective to those proclaiming a new age of post-national citizenship, where the capacity of states to limit or determine their citizenry has been undermined through the twin impact of globalization and the diffusion of universal human rights regimes (Bauboeck 1994; Soysal 1994; Jacobsen 1996). As the European case example has shown, states appear far from admitting defeat in their desire and capacity to institute broadly effective border controls.

But the communitarian and realist defences of security-driven controls, though justified as far as they go, have their limits. The post-nationalist critics do point to certain developments which qualify and undermine the exclusionary logic. They rightly emphasize that security does not represent the only frame of reference for dealing with immigration and human mobility. If it did, all states would look rather like the Soviet Union, which prohibited movements both out of and into the country and which kept its borders, in Stalin's words, 'under lock and key'. Liberal democracies, in particular, recognize that the pursuit of absolute security is self-defeating. In relation to immigration, this involves balancing security considerations with support for an economic and political freedom which requires a significant degree of transnational human mobility. There are, as noted above, the straightforward economic factors which encourage migration so as to enhance national prosperity. But even the less desired phenomenon of irregular migration is an inevitable by-product of a liberal regime of the cross-border movement of goods and people (Bhagwati 2003). As such, the insecurity of irregular or 'illegal' immigration is a necessary price for other economic and political freedoms.

In addition, the post-nationalist critics are right to emphasize the ways in which human rights regimes have constrained state powers of expulsion. The most significant external constraint of this nature is the 1951 Refugee Convention, which requires states to provide protection to those fleeing persecution. Human rights provisions at the domestic level, such as laws concerning non-discrimination, also regularize and give protection to alien residents in a country. The recognized right of family reunification for long-term residents is, in itself, a highly significant source of continued immigration into developed countries, though there have been recent shifts towards more restrictive policies in Europe and elsewhere (Joppke 2007).

Conclusion

The overall conclusion to be drawn is that, while it is right that immigration should not be treated exclusively as a security issue, this does not mean that security considerations are not legitimately part of the general debate about immigration. The important thing is to move beyond the rather simplistic framework which views immigration policy as a choice between a security-driven 'fortress' and an uncontrolled 'opening of the floodgates'. The more complex reality is that the more appropriate analogy for immigration controls is a net, where the key question is the size of mesh which best balances legitimate security concerns with the other values that society seeks to uphold, such as economic prosperity, freedom and international justice.

This chapter has sought to provide an overview of the nature of the security challenges presented by international migration. In this assessment, the more alarmist and exaggerated prognoses offered by some international relations accounts were rejected. International migration remains a broadly manageable phenomenon, but nevertheless the underlying trends, particularly the pressures of the end of the Cold War, globalization and demographic dynamics, point to a more challenging future, particularly since the global openness to migration is likely to remain limited. This chapter has further sought to adopt an internationalist approach which recognizes that migration presents security challenges not only for receiving states but also for sending states, and that migration is likely to be a major source of North–South tension. Managing the dynamics of migration is, therefore, important not only for the prospects for international development but also for international security. And, finally, the chapter reaffirms that there is a vital normative debate about migration, where the key issue is how the legitimate value accorded to the security concerns of states should be balanced with other core values, such as economic prosperity, freedom and justice.

FURTHER READING

For early post-Cold War assessments of the security implications of migration, see Myron Weiner, *The Global Migration Crisis: Challenge to States and to Human Rights* (1995), and Gil Loescher, *Refugee Movements and International Security* (1992). For analysis of the post-Cold War 'securitization' of migration, see Ole Waever and colleagues, *Identity, Migration and the New Security Agenda in Europe* (1993); Jef Huysmans, *The Politics of Insecurity: Fear, Migration and Asylum in the EU* (2005); and Elspeth Guild, *Security and Migration in the 21st Century* (2009).

For more general overviews of the phenomenon of global migration, see Stephen Castles and Mark Miller, *The Age of Migration* (2009); Bill Jordan and Frank Duevell, *Migration: The Boundaries of Equality and Justice* (2003); and Ronald Skeldon, *Migration and Development* (1997). For the classic analysis of the 'demographic transition', see Jean-Claude Chesnais, *The Demographic Transition: Stages, Patterns and Economic Implications* (1992). For an excellent comparative account between Germany, the UK and the US, see Christian Joppke, *Immigration and the Nation-State* (1999). For a more cosmopolitan assessment, see Yasmin Soysal, *Limits of Citizenship: Migrants and Postnational Membership in Europe* (1994).

For the more specifically European/EU responses to migration, see Andrew Geddes, *Immigration and European Integration: Towards Fortress Europe?* (2008); Christina Boswell and Andrew Geddes, *Migration and Mobility in the European Union* (2010); and Sandra Lavenex, *The Europeanisation of Refugee Policies: Between Human Rights and Internal Security* (2001).

For an analysis of forced migration, refugees and the role of the UN High Commission for Refugees, see Aristide Zolberg, Astri Suhrke and Sergio Aguyao, *Escape from Violence: Conflict and Refugee Crisis in the Developing World* (1989); and Gil Loescher, *The UNHCR and World Politics: A Perilous Path* (2001). For a penetrating critique of the post-Cold War challenges facing the UNHCR, see Michael Barnett, 'Humanitarianism with a sovereign face: UNHCR in the global undertow', in *International Migration Review* (2001).

Questions for Research and Discussion

1 Why has migration become increasingly perceived as a security issue in the post-Cold war period?
2 Is it legitimate to consider international migration as a security threat?
3 Have European migration policies since the end of the Cold war been too restrictive?

WEBSITES

www.iom.int
The official website of the International Organization for Migration, with policy papers and a migration law database.

www.unhcr.org
The offical website of the Office of the High Commissioner for Refugees, which is the principal international organization for the protection of refugees. It includes various publications, multimedia, data and current information.

www.un.org/esa/population/migration
A collection of publications and data from various UN bodies dealing with migration.

www.imi.ox.ac.uk/
The International Migration Institute at the University of Oxford – a major research centre which aims to advance understanding of the multi-level forces driving current and future migration processes.

PART IV

Asymmetric Power and Asymmetric Threats

CHAPTER 9

International Terrorism
and the Impact of 9/11

The terrorist attacks of 11 September 2001, which led to around 3,000 fatalities in New York and Washington, transformed the context of international security. The impact was felt most strongly in the developed world. Until 9/11, the countries of the industrialized West had enjoyed, as argued in chapter 1, the reassurance of the great power peace, with the end of the Cold War appearing to bring to an end the long historical era of the constant threat of, and preparation for large-scale interstate war. In this more benign security context, concerns could be focused on other challenges, with the resulting widening and enlarging of the security agenda to topics such as environmental degradation, the struggle for natural resources and immigration (see chapters 6–8). Where collective violence and war did still represent a major challenge, this was almost completely located in poorer or politically less mature regions, such as sub-Saharan Africa or the Balkans, where the impact on the North was primarily humanitarian rather than strategic (chapters 3–5). Violence and war was, nevertheless, something that happened to 'them' and not to 'us'. The principal impact of 9/11 was radically to subvert this confidence and self-assurance, demonstrating that violence and death could be inflicted on the richest and seemingly most secure parts of the North. The reassurance of the great power peace was shattered; violent aggression had found a new way to circumvent the defences of even the most privileged and best defended countries.

This sense of vulnerability was naturally felt most acutely in the country directly subject to the attacks – the United States. The shock to common wisdom was even stronger here. While the strategic dominance of the United States during the 1990s was seen to be broadly beneficial or at least unproblematic, this self-assurance was undermined by the vulnerabilities exposed by 9/11. Primacy and great power dominance now appeared as a double-edged sword, providing weakness and vulnerability as much as strength and resilience. Even in a strong country's homeland sanctuary, there were ways in which the weak, if sufficiently determined and creative, could circumvent the best-laid defences and accumulated military power. This, in turn, gave a new urgency to rethinking the security strategy of the US, with a particular focus on how to deal with threats which thrive on their asymmetric quality – on their ability to neutralize and circumvent the economic, political and military superiority of the United States and the North more broadly.

The unveiling of the National Security Strategy in 2002 represented the most significant attempt by the US government to define these new imperatives for international security and to set out a doctrine for fighting the 'war on terror', which it was presumed would have the same longevity as the Cold War doctrine of containment (White House 2002; see also Dannreuther and Peterson 2006). The real test came in 2003 with the intervention into and occupation of Iraq, which was considerably more controversial than the more limited humanitarian interventions of the 1990s. This was followed by the shift in fortunes in the US and NATO intervention in Afghanistan, where early victories over the Taliban led in the late 2000s to the return of a major insurgency and the resurrection of the Taliban as a military and political force. The projected withdrawal from Afghanistan in 2014 is set to provide an ambiguous and far from victorious culmination of the global 'war on terror'.

This period of heightened international security proved to be a boost for the fortunes of security analysts. As at the height of the Cold War, security studies came back into favour, and the security analyst has been courted by policy-makers and by markedly more generous research funding. But this more benign intellectual environment also has its dangers, the most critical of which is the potential loss of objectivity and the capacity to scrutinize and question the assumptions and policy outcomes of the new security discourse after 9/11.

In the introductory chapter, it was suggested that the security analyst has three main roles – as scientist, internationalist and moralist. Fulfilling these roles in the age of the 'war on terror' is particularly demanding. The challenge for the scientist is to make a judgement on the seriousness of the threat of international terrorism, at a time when this necessarily includes a strong subjective and psychological dimension. There is an irreducible 'constructed' dimension to the fear inculcated by terrorism, primarily by the terrorists themselves but also potentially by governments and other actors who might see an advantage in the 'securitization' of this threat. The challenge for the internationalist is to recognize and empathize with the hurt and vulnerabilities of the victims of international terrorism, but also to recognize that this is a multidimensional problem where there are 'root causes' which, while not justifying such terrorist acts, provide the broader context in which they potentially gain a sympathetic audience. The internationalist perspective also requires a recognition that the 'war on terror' is perceived and understood differently in different places; for example, for many countries in the South, it has often been seen as a distraction from the more urgent 'human security' challenges of poverty, intrastate conflict, HIV/AIDS, water scarcity and environmental degradation (Berdal 2005: 13–14; see also Ayoob and Zierler 2005). Finally, the 'war on terror' makes particularly complex normative demands on the security analyst as moralist. There is a strong need to make judgements about whether the value accorded to security, greatly enhanced in the aftermath of 9/11, has protected or threatened to undermine other core values, most notably those of freedom and civil liberties, prosperity and international justice.

This chapter has two parts. The first provides a more general overview of understanding the phenomenon, nature and development of international terrorism, which culminated in the events of 9/11. The peculiarly subjective and psychological dimension of terrorism as a threat to international security is identified, as well as the danger that counter-terror campaigns can potentially mimic the terrorist tactics of their opponents and lead to a dangerous escalation of violence. To avoid this, a key counter-terror goal is the building of trust with those communities providing passive or active support to the target terrorist organizations.

The second part of the chapter examines the conduct of the US-directed 'war on terror' since 2001 and argues that its successes have been significantly qualified by a failure to address the concerns of these broader communities. Two roots for this failure are identified: the first is the assumption that the terrorist attacks were due primarily to a visceral and unconditional hatred of the United States and its values; the second is the belief that the principal reason for US vulnerability was its unwillingness to assert the freedom consonant with its power and interests, as well as its subjection to a variety of constraints, including the demands of allies, multilateral regimes and institutions, and international law. President Barack Obama has attempted to address these key failures and, while redirecting US foreign policy in a more multilateral and less ambitious fashion, has nevertheless struggled to overcome the more deep-seated legacies of the 'war on terror', most notably in Afghanistan.

International terrorism: Its nature and pathologies

The security analyst enters into a definitional minefield in dealing with terrorism. The hoary old maxim that 'one man's terrorist is another man's freedom fighter' highlights the divide between those who see terrorism as ineradicably evil and those who see it as potentially redeemable through the justice of the cause it promotes. The strong – in particular, powerful states – generally have a more negative view of terrorism than the weak, the disenfranchised and the unjustly excluded. The problems of defining it are also matched by the difficulties of making accurate assessments of the seriousness of the threat of international terrorism. This is particularly the case when the empirical grounds for such potential threats are inevitably subjective and speculative, such as the 'low probability but high risk' threat of terrorist attacks using weapons of mass destruction, as discussed in the next chapter. The security analyst also has the challenge of transcending the historical and cultural particularities of the experience and perceptions of terrorism of different countries. Overall, terrorism is a complex and multidimensional problem which does not submit easily to clear definitions and analytical categories.

Towards a definition of terrorism

Nevertheless, a good starting point is to recognize that terrorism, unlike liberalism, communism or conservatism, is not an ideology but a method. As a method of political violence, it is ideologically neutral. Historically, terrorism has been a tactic utilized by a wide array of ideological movements: states, ethno-nationalists, religious and millenarian movements, extreme left-wing and right-wing groups, and single-issue fanatics, such as anti-abortionists and animal rights movements, have all variously engaged in terrorism at certain times (see Wilkinson 2003). As with war, the nature and contexts of terrorism are constantly shifting and evolving. What remains distinctive is, as Raymond Aron observed, that 'an act of violence is labelled "terrorist" when its psychological effects are out of proportion to its purely physical results' (Aron 1966: 170). For the terrorist, the direct physical target is either insignificant or irrelevant: the intended target is the larger political community, in whom the act is deliberately aimed to engender a sense of terror and psychological fear which will, it is hoped, change the target's behaviour, attitudes and policies. Terrorism is, thus, a particularly effective strategy for the weak, a method to attempt to apply strategic coercion to a more powerful actor when the conditions for alternative forms of coercion, such as a sustained guerrilla campaign, are insufficient or absent (see Münkler 2005: 100).

It is for this reason that most definitions of terrorism highlight the role of non-state actors, such as the US State Department's definition of terrorism as 'politically motivated violence perpetrated against non-combatant targets by subnational groups or clandestine agents' (US State Department 2004: ix). But this restriction of terrorism to non-state actors by definitional fiat is problematic. It is important to remember, as the human security perspective would require, that most of the victims of terror in the last hundred years have been victims of state-imposed regimes, whether in Nazi Germany, Stalin's Soviet Union, the military dictatorships in Latin America, or Middle Eastern tyrannies such as under Saddam Hussein (for a sobering account of Saddam's reign of terror, see Makiya 1998). States also continue to sponsor terrorist groups in a clandestine way. Excluding states from being potential agents of terrorism also crucially misses out the complex but critical dynamic whereby states fighting terrorist groups often come to adopt similar methods to their opponents, leading to a vicious spiral of unconstrained violence and an embedding of a culture of terrorism. Contemporary examples of this include Algeria during the 1990s, where radical Islamists and the military regime were equally guilty in their acts of terror, and where the resulting violence spiralled uncontrollably, and in Russia, where the Russian army's responses to the Chechen acts of terror have themselves been terroristic (on Algeria, see

Martinez 2000 and Souaidia 2001; on Chechnya, see Politkovskaia 2003 and Tishkov 2004).

Both states and non-state actors can use terrorism tactically or strategically. Tactical terrorism is where the acts of terror are part of a broader strategy, whether military or political, such as the 'gun and olive branch' approach adopted by ethno-nationalist groups such as the PLO and the IRA. Here the acts of terror are not expected to change the behaviour of the target state by themselves, but are intended to contribute to that desired outcome within the context of a broader politico-military campaign. As in the insurgency in Iraq, it is often a difficult and much debated question as to where the line between guerrilla action and terrorism is to be drawn. There is no such difficulty with strategic terrorism, because the expectation in these cases is that the acts of terror will themselves be sufficient to achieve the desired political ends. The aim is, in Lawrence Freedman's words, 'to use acts of violence to influence a whole political system' (2005: 163). Strategic terrorism is a political short-cut to achieving objectives which generally require a more sustained political and military strategy. In the Second World War, the allied strategic bombing of Germany attempted such a short-cut, seeking to win the war through undermining the will of the German people (see Hastings 1999; Grayling 2006). Strategically if not morally, al-Qaeda is attempting to achieve a similar objective, believing that it can accelerate the retreat of the West from the Middle East through undermining the West's moral will.

One way to circumvent some of the divisiveness in defining terrorism is to focus on the act of terrorism rather than on the perpetrators and the justice of their associated cause (Jenkins 1998: v). Internationally, this has been the approach which has managed to gain greater cooperation and support. Thus the United Nations has agreed to various conventions on terrorism, outlawing, for example, acts such as the hijacking of aircraft (1973), the taking of hostages (1979) and the financing of terrorism (2001) (IISS 2001). This approach also has the advantage of identifying a more realistic and effective strategy in countering the threat of terrorism. Focusing on the criminality and illegality of acts of terrorism does not require condemning all organizations which engage in terrorist acts as irredeemably evil or their cause as *a priori* illegitimate. Rather, the simple assertion is that acts of terrorism, whatever their causes, are themselves inherently wrong, morally and legally. The Geneva Conventions are well known for prohibiting the indiscriminate targeting of civilians by conventional armies, but it is less well known that the same conventions prohibit non-state actors, such as guerrilla groups, from doing so as well (1977 Geneva Protocol II). The aim of counter-terrorism strategy should be, therefore, to embed and enforce these laws and norms. This is, in a sense, a civilizational ambition: to seek to outlaw a certain class of acts as being illegitimate and fundamentally unjust as a method of political conflict, making terrorism as illegitimate an international norm as slavery, apartheid and imperialism.

The seriousness of the threat

Despite this moral imperative, there is little sign that terrorism is going out of fashion. Since the end of the Cold War, the evidence points rather to the opposite, with the attractions and visibility of acts of international terrorism increasing, even before 9/11. What has been most striking in this dynamic is the greater lethality of major terrorist incidents. Brian Jenkins argued from the experience of international terrorism in the 1970s that 'terrorists want a lot of people watching and a lot of people listening and not a lot of people dead' (1975: 15). Indiscriminate mass slaughter would, he argued, be counterproductive to terrorist groups by alienating the broader communities from whom they gained their support. The principal impact of 9/11 was radically to undercut this reassuring received wisdom. It confirmed the clear trend in international terrorism away from ethno-nationalist to religiously sanctioned terrorism, whose more maximalist and apocalyptic goals seemingly justify terror on a much larger scale (see Hoffmann 2006; Laqueur 1996; Juergens-meyer 2000). This, in turn, has added credibility to the claim that, were these new terrorist groups to have access to weapons of mass destruction, they would have little inhibition about using them (Stern 1999; Perry 2001). The inexorable rise in the phenomenon of suicide bombings, which multiplied dramatically in the mid-2000s in Iraq and Afghanistan in particular (see figure 9.1), has been the most potent symbol of a new, more deadly, and seemingly irrational fanaticism, though it also appeared to be in decline in 2011 (see Gambetta 2005; Pape 2005a; Atran 2006; Pape and Feldman 2010).

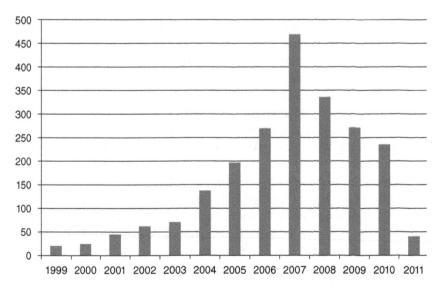

Figure 9.1 Suicide attacks worldwide, yearly average from 1999 to 2011
Source: Chicago Project on Security and Terrorism, 'The Suicide Attack Database', updated 14 November 2011, at http://cpost.uchicago.edu/.

There is, though, a need to make a couple of qualifications to this picture of a devastating and omnipresent threat of international terrorism. The first is that the 'war on terror', as promulgated by the US administration, is explicitly defined as dealing with the threat of 'terrorists with a global reach', thus excluding terrorism limited to within national borders. In practice, this excludes the vast majority of terrorist acts, which remain primarily domestic challenges within countries such as Russia (Chechnya), Sri Lanka, Colombia, Algeria, Turkey, Iraq and elsewhere. Overall, apart from outlier years like 2001, the numbers of deaths caused by international terrorism in any one year are not particularly numerous, counted in the hundreds rather than the thousands. To take an extreme example, in the year 1994–5, sixteen US citizens died from international terrorism as compared to fifty-nine victims of lightning. Such a comparison might be facile, but the general point remains that the threat of international terrorism, defined in terms of probable loss of human life, is significantly less serious than the millions of victims of the 'new wars' in Africa or the daily loss of infant life from lack of access to clean water.

But the threat of international terrorism is not simply reducible to such quantifiable indicators. As highlighted above, the seriousness of the threat of terrorism has a 'constructed', intersubjective and psychological dimension to it. The effect of 9/11 was in promoting a generalized fear among Americans and others in the developed world of their essential vulnerability. After 9/11, international terrorism, as exemplified by al-Qaeda, had clearly developed a sophisticated capacity to target some of the critical weak links in the complex and globalized structures of modern society (Homer-Dixon 2002). As an organization, al-Qaeda does not conform to the traditional hierarchical structures of ethno-nationalist terrorist organizations: it is a much flatter and amorphous grouping, more of a network or 'network of networks', and symbolically akin to a virus in its capacity to bypass traditional defences and to penetrate and to propagate deep into its target societies (Arquilla and Ronfeldt 1997; Sageman 2008). It is this shady, elusive and religio-mystical quality of al-Qaeda, its mix of fanaticism and organizational cunning, which has made the threat seem so ever present. In all of this, the role of the media has been crucial, in providing the terrorist acts with the necessary exposure to a wider audience and in constructing their visual and symbolic quality of societal vulnerability and fearfulness (B. Hoffmann 2006: 131–55; Nacos 2000; Baudrillard 2003).

It is not just individuals who feel vulnerable, though. States are also acutely sensitive to the implications of terrorist campaigns. However, this fear is more symbolic and subjective than direct and immediate. Governmental fear is rarely that terrorism represents a direct strategic threat to the state, akin to an army amassing on one's borders. In practice, terrorist campaigns, particularly strategic terror campaigns, have been notably unsuccessful and have tended to strengthen rather than weaken societal morale and state resilience.

The threat has more of a normative or moral quality, directed at some of the key underlying norms and practices of the international state system. Thus international terrorism breaks the cardinal rule that it is the state that holds the monopoly of the use of violence; it also deliberately breaks the basic tenets of international humanitarian law, most notably the prescription against the deliberate targeting of innocent civilians. But states are probably most sensitive to the fact that international terrorism, as perpetrated by groups like al-Qaeda, seeks to undermine confidence in the state's primary duty – its ability to provide security for its citizens. It is not surprising that, in the face of such terrorist attacks, states tend to assume a strongly realist and communitarian logic, focusing all efforts on eliminating or radically reducing this radical challenge to their authority.

There is, finally, one further dimension to assessing the seriousness of the contemporary threat of international terrorism. This is an area which shades into the metaphysical and theological. One of the consequences of the rise of al-Qaeda is that religious conceptions, most notably the sense of some wider struggle between good and evil, have gained in public prominence and discourse (see, for example, Berman 2003; Elshtain 2003; Ignatieff 2004; Rengger and Jeffery 2005). The ways in which, with the activities of al-Qaeda, the sacred and the divine have been conflated with unerring self-belief, intolerance and terror have provided a stark reminder of the dark possibilities of human evil. The shock of 9/11 was, in this sense, a direct riposte to some of the Panglossian expectations of the post-Cold War period, which was expected to usher in the 'end of history' (Fukuyama 1992). It was also a reminder that the greatest threats to security remain human-directed social violence, and that human progress has far from eradicated this. However, the counter-reaction to 9/11 has also highlighted the potential danger that the objects of the attacks, through self-righteousness and a belief in an elemental struggle between good and evil, come to mimic the tactics of their opponents, leading to a bloody escalation of violence and conflict (Eagleton 2005: 12; Gray 2008). The anthropologist Renée Girard (1977) called this the scapegoat mechanism, whereby the role of religion is to transfer the violent impulses and alienation of society on to an alien 'other', and through its ritual sacrifice satisfy the demands for revenge. The danger here is that both sides, the terrorist and the counter-terrorist forces, see themselves as innocent victims and thus justified in escalating the level and ferocity of the violence so as to gain the required revenge.

Countering terrorism

For all these reasons, acts of terrorism, particularly on the scale of 9/11, present significant challenges to states. The almost inevitable tendency, as noted above, is to revert to a realist logic, because the government's credibility in ensuring the safety of its citizens has been directly challenged. Governments are required to respond to the strong public pressure to engage in immediate action, to assuage the desire for revenge, and to bring the perpetrators of the attack to justice. In addition, they are under considerable pressure to minimize, or ideally to eliminate, the prospect of further such attacks. The real test of the success of a terrorist organization is the ability to wage a sustained campaign, demonstrating that the organization has the capacity to strike at will and thus revealing to the general population the impotence of the state's authority. In such a struggle, the state's very legitimacy is at stake.

War can, as a consequence, appear the natural designation for such a struggle (Lesser 1998a: 94–6). Particularly after an event such as 9/11, nothing less than its recognition as an act of war appears to meet the urgency of the moment. In addition, international terrorism frequently gains protection, or receives support, from foreign states, such as the Taliban government's support for al-Qaeda in Afghanistan, where military intervention appears to be the only realistic option, given the limits of international legal procedures. A further benefit of applying the war paradigm is that potentially it resolves one of the key strategic advantages of terrorist groups – their ability to gain the protection of the laws and norms of the democratic society they simultaneously seek to destroy. The military-dominated approach means that one can be rather less fastidious about the evidence than would be required in a court of law; suspects can, given their status as enemy forces, be eliminated rather than apprehended; and the rules over such practices as detention and interrogation can be more malleable than in less exceptional or 'securitized' conditions.

There are, though, significant disadvantages to adopting such an approach. In an early critique of the concept of a 'war on terror', Michael Howard noted that it would potentially have the counterproductive effect of legitimizing the actions of terrorist groups by according them 'a status and dignity that they seek and which they do not deserve' (2002: 8–9). Declaring a 'war on terror' potentially makes the terrorists warriors, or prisoners of war, rather than criminals. The language of war also puts an excessive burden on the military to gain swift results, while the reality is that most successful counter-terror campaigns are normally the result of the slow and painstaking work of police and intelligence operatives in a concerted international effort (Andreani 2004: 36–8). War further presumes the objective of an ultimate victory, which is not only unrealistic but ultimately meaningless when directed against a method such as terrorism. Defining some more realistic and pragmatic conception of what success means is a critical objective if the public is not to be subjected to the anxiety and disillusionment of an endless and unwinnable war (A. Roberts 2005: 121–4).

Although there are clearly significant problems with adopting a war paradigm, approaching counter-terrorism purely within a criminological paradigm is not without its problems. As Michael Ignatieff has pointed out, governments are confronted with particularly acute moral dilemmas when dealing with terrorism and are sometimes called to commit 'lesser evils' to protect their citizens from the 'greater evils' intended by the terrorists. Thus he notes that:

> the suppression of civil liberties, surveillance of individuals, targeted assassination, torture, and pre-emptive war put liberal commitments to dignity under such obvious strain, and the harms they entail are so serious, that, even if mandated by peremptory majority interest, they should only be spoken of in the language of evil. (Ignatieff 2004: 18)

The argument that the democratic state's struggle against terrorism will require some actions which do not follow the conventions and laws of liberal democracy is a common refrain throughout all counter-terror campaigns (see Wilkinson 2001). When armed groups seek to kill and destroy indiscriminately, the state's duty to the security of its citizens has to take priority over the civil liberties and protections enjoyed by society in less threatened times. But both how this balance is to be sustained and how to ensure that 'exceptional measures' do not become normalized and routinized are properly the focus of popular and intellectual debate (for example, on the issue of torture, see Lukes 2005; Bellamy 2006). Overall, the critical objective is to ensure that, whatever campaign is conducted, the general perception is sustained that the response is proportionate as well as effective (English 2010; Jackson and Sinclair 2011).

In this regard, it is important to realize that there are two audiences needing to be convinced and reassured: the domestic audience and the audience of those potentially sympathetic to the goals and objectives of the terrorists. For the domestic audience, a two-pronged offensive and defensive strategy is demanded. The offensive strategy is focused primarily on targeting those individuals and groups which seek to attack you and doing what is required to forestall such attacks. Pre-emption, or more properly prevention, is a legitimate aspect of such an offensive strategy (Freedman 2004: 84–108). But it should not overshadow the continuing importance of deterrence and containment, which remain vital tools of counter-terrorism. Many aspects of terrorist organization and practice, and the broader support terrorist groups receive, can be effectively deterred (see Stevenson 2004; Trager and Zagorcheva 2005–6). In addition, the defensive strategy is a critical complement to the more offensive strategies. It is clearly vital that the ability of terrorist groups to succeed in hitting their desired targets should be as limited as possible. Civil defences, homeland security and critical infrastructure protection are all key elements of this defensive strategy (see Howitt and Pangi 2003).

But this mix of defensive and offensive strategies, essential to respond to the concerns and fears of the domestic audience, has to be carefully calibrated so as not to alienate the community which might not explicitly support, but might be sympathetic towards, the terrorists' cause. A key objective of counter-terrorism must be to undermine this support by delegitimizing the tactics of the terrorist organization and showing that there are legitimate, non-criminal ways to resolve the root causes behind popular alienation and disaffection. As Cronin (2011) notes, terrorist campaigns do come to an end, and this is generally when local support declines or evaporates. The danger is particularly that, in pursuing the other dimensions of the counter-terror strategy, this critical third strategic prong is not accorded sufficient attention. In Northern Ireland, the British military learnt through hard experience that, if 'one kills one IRA terrorist, one recruits five more'. It is particularly important, therefore, that the counter-terror campaign is conducted in ways which reassure rather than alienate the broader community from whom terrorist organizations draw their ultimate sustenance.

The 'war on terror' in practice

It is precisely in this vital third dimension of counter-terrorism strategy, the strategy which seeks to alienate and disconnect the terrorist organizations from the communities in which they gain support, that the US-led 'war on terror' has been the most deficient. One should, though, recognize that on the other two dimensions of a counter-terror strategy – the offensive and the defensive – there have been significant gains and successes. On the offensive side, the Taliban was initially overthrown in Afghanistan, core leaders of al-Qaeda, including Osama bin Laden, have been destroyed or captured, and, probably most critically, camps that had trained thousands of jihadists during the 1990s have been closed down. On the defensive side, the increased domestic security measures in the US, such as in airline security, and the centralization of policy-making in one body – the Department of Homeland Security – have contributed to the success of avoiding a further attack on the US mainland. As noted earlier, the critical objective for a successful terrorist campaign is to mount a sustained campaign, so that the state appears powerless to protect its citizens. Al-Qaeda and transnational jihadism have singularly failed to do this, most especially in relation to the United States.

But these successes must be counterbalanced by the relative failure in convincing the outside world, most notably the Muslim community but also traditional allies such as those in Europe, that the 'war on terror' has successfully addressed the main sources of alienation and resentment from which extremist Islamism, and the propagation of transnational jihadism, gain their support. The reasons for this key failing are certainly intimately connected to the US-led wars and occupations of Iraq and Afghanistan, though it was the former war which has been most divisive. The story of the mix of hubris and misjudgement that led to the pursuit and conduct of the war in Iraq has been extensively described elsewhere (see Clarke 2004; J. Mann 2004; L. Diamond 2005; Phillips 2005). But the Iraq war was itself a symptom of two more fundamental, and fundamentally flawed, assumptions which flowed from the initial US response to the events of 9/11. These are what might be called 'the two fallacies' of post-9/11 US strategic thinking which have been seriously critiqued internally in the US only with the Obama administration. The first is that the reason why the US was attacked in this terrible way was primarily on account of a deep hatred of the US and all its values. The second is that the US found itself so vulnerable because it had been unnaturally 'constrained', so there was a need to reassert US primacy and superiority.

The 'they hate us' approach

For an American audience seeking to understand the calamity of 9/11, the argument that these events were driven by a visceral hatred of the United States has an immediate appeal. Such an explanation gives a metaphysical meaning to what would otherwise appear to be a random and incomprehensible act of mass violence. As President Bush noted in his address to Congress on 21 September 2001: 'They hate our freedoms: our freedom of religion, our freedom of speech, our freedom to vote and assemble . . . These terrorists kill not merely to end lives, but to disrupt and end a way of life' (quoted in Byman 2003: 143). By identifying the events of 9/11 as part of the American struggle for freedom, the 'war on terror' can be contextualized within the grand narrative of the epic struggles fought by the US against fascism and communism in the twentieth century. As Paul Berman argues in this vein, Islamism and Ba'athism (the ideology of the Iraqi and Syrian regimes) should be seen as just the latest manifestations and Middle Eastern variants of totalitarian counter-reactions to a liberalism 'which tries to encourage individual freedom, and tries to keep religion and government in separate corners, and to encourage open debate, and in these several ways to inculcate a public habit of rational decision-making' (2003: xii–xiii).

The sense that liberalism and the values which the US holds most dear are under threat from the enemies behind 9/11 provides a powerful rallying call for decisive and radical action. It also has the advantage of appearing to call a spade a spade and of resisting the clamour for appeasement. If the problem is, as Jean Bethke Elshtain argues, that 'they loathe us because of who we are and what our society represents' (2003: 3), then the US is not going to be able to protect itself by changing its policies. The roots of Islamist terror are not, therefore, found in the US military presence in Saudi Arabia or the close strategic relationship between the US and Israel. Rather, the sources are found in an internal civil war within the Middle East, where a fascistic Islamist ideology has emerged which celebrates extremism, intolerance and repression and seeks to impose its will through violence (see Pipes 2002; Berman 2003). The roots of this are, in Bernard Lewis's influential interpretation, found in the longer historical narrative where the Muslim world has consistently failed to adapt to decline relative to Europe and the West (Lewis

2002, 2003). Radical Islam, in this broader perspective, is just the latest manifestation of the unwillingness of the Muslim world to recognize that the
weaknesses are found primarily in the internal culture and politics of the
region and the tendency, instead, to blame the West and Western values and
imperialism for Muslim failures. If 9/11 is seen in this light as the dangerous
consequence of a totalitarian Middle Eastern movement which hates the West
and Western values, then the US has a clear strategic justification for intervening forcefully to attempt to support those local forces in favour of pluralism, liberal values and human rights (Gordon 2003; more generally, see
Daalder and Lindsay 2003).

But do 'they' really hate us?

There are, though, problems in this 'they hate us' approach to the challenge
of Islamist radicalism. The first is that it tends to exaggerate the degree to
which Islamists, or political actors in the Middle East more generally, are
actually interested in 'us'. The West is certainly an obsession, but it is not the
Western culture of political debate or protection of human rights, or even
the moral attitude to women or homosexuals, which is central to this obsession. Rather, it is the ways in which the West is perceived to act in the Middle
East and the Muslim world which form the principal target. It is the policies
of the West, not its moral and political systems, that are the main source of
resentment and about which, as discussed below, there are legitimate reasons
for disquiet.

But, beyond this, it is also a mistake to see the rise of political Islam as
primarily a reaction to the West or a displacement of internal problems on
to a malevolent West. The real roots of the rage and sense of alienation are
firmly grounded in the perceived economic, social and political failures of
the states found in the Middle East. The rise of political Islam is driven by the
very modern challenges that these failures present, rather than by a counter-
reaction to the West. As a result, the Islamist desire to reconstruct a pristine
Islamic community, which would wrench itself from dependence on the
West, should not be taken strictly at face value. It is an ideological response
to, and rooted in, the failure of the secular state in the Middle East to deliver
security, justice and prosperity. It is this failure, and its multiple complex
causes, which need to be the focus in understanding the roots of radical
political Islam, rather than concentrating solely on the anti-Western and
anti-liberal sentiments of its ideologies (see, for example, Zubaida 1993: ch.
6; Halliday 1996: ch. 4; Tripp 2000b).

This sociological rather than theological approach also provides a more
nuanced and differentiated understanding of radical Islam. An associated
problem with the 'they hate us' approach is that it tends to make a simple
division between those Muslims who like us (i.e. moderates) and those who
dislike us (i.e. extremists), where a battle between 'good and evil' is fought

between Western-supporting democrats and totalitarian Islamists. This does little justice to the reality of multiple Islamisms, which range from moderates accepting the democratic rules of the game (for example, the Justice and Development Party in Turkey) to radical anti-systemic transnational terrorist organizations (see Eickelman and Piscatori 1996; Mandaville 2007). A more differentiated account would also make a critical distinction between those politically radical fundamentalist groups inspired in the 1990s by the Iranian revolution and the subsequent emergence of the more socially conservative neo-fundamentalism associated with the Taliban and al-Qaeda. As Olivier Roy has argued, the earlier Iranian-inspired Islamist wave has gradually lost its radical transnational commitment to revolution and international terrorism, increasingly limiting its political ambitions to specific national territories (Roy 1999). This has happened in Iran itself, as the demands of state consolidation have gained ascendance over the claims of the global *umma* (Muslim community) (Zubaida 1997; Ansari 2003). A similar domestication and territorialization of political struggle can also be seen in Lebanon, Palestine and Turkey, with radical Islamist groups such as Hizbullah, Hamas and Refah gradually incorporated into the national political scene. It is not unduly optimistic to hope that, in these cases, Islamism might actually contribute to the development of a more pluralistic and democratic polity, given the right regional and international conditions (see Kramer 1997; Ehteshami 1999). This is being tested directly in countries such as Egypt and Tunisia after their democratic revolutions in 2011 brought to power Islamist parties.

But this nationalization and potential secularization of political Islam has inevitably meant a loss of revolutionary ardour. Neo-fundamentalism has emerged to fill this vacuum and preserve the dream of a Muslim world without territorial divisions. This new variant of Islamism has been strongly influenced by the practice of re-Islamization, of introducing stricter Islamic practices of moral conduct, in practically all of the (even most secular) Arab states from the 1980s onwards (O. Roy 2004: 92–7). Its inspiration comes from the Sunni sources of conservative Islam, such as Wahhabism from Saudi Arabia or Deobandism from South Asia, and which has, as compared to political Islam in Iran, a strongly exclusionary attitude to women and an aggressive intolerance towards Shi'a Muslims, Christians and Jews (O. Roy 1994; Kepel 2004). The resultant neo-fundamentalist ideology is, as Roy argues, less explicitly political or interested in the concept of an Islamic state and much more obsessed with the minutiae of the strict implementation of sharia law (O. Roy 2004: 97–9). In this way, it has similarities with fundamentalist movements in other religions, where the main concern is with individual salvation, whereby one is 'born again' into a pristine new condition radically discontinuous from the social condition of one's previous life.

The majority of these neo-fundamentalists are quietist and apolitical and seek to promote a transnational caliphate to escape the banalities and alienation of everyday life. However, a minority have become politically radicalized and have been susceptible to the ideology of al-Qaeda, where jihad is promoted as a personal duty to promote the Islamic political ideal. But what is important sociologically is that the typical al-Qaeda recruit is not one whose political identity is necessarily closely connected to a national territory or even to the Middle East region. For most Muslims living in the Middle East, the claim that the struggle for freedom comes through attacking the 'far enemy', the United States, holds little credibility. Where it does have a stronger resonance is in migrant and diaspora communities, where it is now estimated that 80 per cent of known jihadis live, marginalized from the host society and physically disconnected from one another (Atran 2006: 135; see also Sageman 2004, 2008). What is attractive to these adherents is not specific nationalist struggles but the broader sense of global injustice and political repression, which reflects their own sense of alienation and disaffection, and the possibilities for humanity's violent redemption. The appeal is not dissimilar to the radical populist movements of the 1960s and 1970s, with an audience now present as much in the Muslim suburbs of Europe as in the Middle East.

Should 'they' not hate us (at least a bit)?

A further problem with the 'they hate us' approach is that it does tend to locate all the problems on the 'internal civil war' within the Muslim world. The problem here is that, in making the necessary adjustment to ensure that the Middle East takes greater responsibility for its own problems, the influence and negative impact of external powers are minimized or ignored. But this is potentially as one-sided and blind to political reality as the Islamist claim that the West is responsible for all the travails of the region. As mentioned above, the main roots of anti-Westernism are not principally about culture but about politics and a strong disenchantment with Western policies and political legacies. It is critical to recognize that European and American actions and legacies have, in various ways, contributed to the Middle Eastern crisis. The reflexive distrust of the West in the Middle East is not without foundation and cannot simply be reduced to a deep sense of resentment and jealousy.

The important fact is that the West has been so deeply involved with the strategic dynamics, the politics and the economics of the Middle East that it is almost impossible to disentangle the internal and the external factors behind its political crises. European imperial powers were behind the creation of most of the states of the region, with their artificial borders and complex ethnic and confessional differences. The strategic demands for British imperial control meant that initial experiments in democracy were manipulated by the strategic need to ensure a subservient pro-British oligarchical elite, thereby undermining Middle Eastern faith in democracy. The strategic dictates of the Cold War ensured the protection of pro-Western authoritarian regimes, with the accompanying extravagant flow of arms and aid to ensure regime stability (see Halliday 2005: ch. 4). The overriding demand for energy security has similarly played a vigorous role in dampening Western demands for economic and political reform, which might potentially rein in the predatory and neo-patrimonial 'rentier state' practices of most Middle Eastern countries, as discussed in chapter 7. It is not surprising, in this context, that Western proclamations of the values of democracy and human rights appear to be contradictory, as became apparent in the Western response to the Arab Spring.

The complex and highly interpenetrated way in which the internal and external have contributed to the crisis in the Middle East is nowhere seen more clearly than in the rise of the phenomenon of al-Qaeda itself. The roots of al-Qaeda are found in the Cold War superpower contest in Afghanistan, where the United States supported the Afghan guerrilla movement and encouraged radical Islamist groups to support the Afghans in their anti-Soviet struggle (Kepel 2002; Burke 2003). With the then dominant perceived threat of Iranian radicalism, the United States supported the more conservative neo-fundamentalist agenda promoted by the key US allies of Saudi Arabia and Pakistan. The rise of the Taliban in the late 1990s, and its military victories which led to control of over 80 per cent of the country, were a strategic success for Pakistan and Saudi Arabia which the US, at least initially, supported. It was only very late in the day, and really only after 9/11, that the US finally understood how the conservative religious trend it had seemingly benignly encouraged had been transformed into the West's most dangerous enemy.

The strategic implications of the 'they hate us' approach

The first major consequence of adopting the 'they hate us' approach is significantly to overestimate the political strength and the credibility of the extremist strand of Islamism represented by al-Qaeda. Certainly, the period of neglect of developments in Afghanistan, and the subsequent recruitment of thousands of jihadists in the training camps of that country, had created a very significant threat to international security. But, as Fawaz Gerges has persuasively demonstrated, the ideological claim that the Islamist struggle should move from targeting the 'near enemy' – meaning the local rulers in Muslim states – to the 'far enemy' of the United States was driven primarily by political failure, most notably the successful repression of radical jihadist groups in Middle Eastern states such as Egypt, Syria and Jordan (Gerges 2005: ch. 4; 2011). For most people in the Middle East, the claim that a political solution could be found by bypassing the political struggle within these repressive states and targeting the US appeared quixotic and politically unrealistic. The initial success of the US campaign in Afghanistan, and the closure of the training camps and operational capacities of al-Qaeda, should only have confirmed this. If this action had been followed by positive moves to resolve some of the core conflicts in the region, such as reinvigorating the Arab–Israeli peace process, support for the transnational jihadist ideology among the broader Muslim and Middle Eastern community could have been expected to diminish much quicker than has actually been the case.

This leads to the second major consequence of the 'they hate us' approach. Instead of promoting a politico-military strategy, which would have combined effective military intervention with a restrained and positive diplomatic and political strategy aimed at undercutting the appeal of transnational jihadism in the Middle Eastern and Muslim world, a far more ambitious strategy was adopted which ultimately acted only to confirm suspicions of US imperialistic ambitions. Once the problem was defined as an all-out ideological battle between liberalism and totalitarianism and between 'good and evil', rather than the isolation of an extremist and unrepresentative version of Islamist fundamentalism, the solution came to be seen as requiring a fundamental and radical recasting of the political order of the Middle East. It was this solution which was articulated in the neo-conservative vision for the Middle East which had been marginalized before 9/11 but thereafter gained the support of the Bush administration, in large part because it appeared to provide a persuasive answer to the problem that 'they hate us' (for an extreme but representative example, see Frum and Perle 2003).

The core of this vision was that, against all previous received wisdom, the liberation of Iraq from the forces of illiberalism and totalitarianism would cut the Gordian knot and lead to the resolution of the more general Middle East crisis. Once Saddam Hussein's regime was overturned and the moderate Iraqi opposition was permitted to rebuild the country and to institute the first Arab democracy in the region, anti-Westernism and anti-Zionism would decline and the underlying roots of Islamist extremism and international terrorism would be extirpated. This, however, wilfully ignored the far deeper structural problems within Iraq, which could not be neatly solved by a battle between the forces of liberalism and autocracy, but rather reflected a complex inter-ethnic and interconfessional struggle within the political economy of a neo-patrimonial 'shadow state', where the very foundations of national unity and civilized state–society relations needed to be reconstructed from the bottom up (Tripp 2000a: ch. 6; 2002–3). As the United States became inevitably sucked into this complex internal Iraqi struggle, the perception that it was a major contributor, rather than a solution, to the problems in the Middle East only emboldened anti-Western sentiment and the groundswell of support for radical Islam and terrorist actions. It was only with Barack Obama's presidency in 2008 and a much heralded redefining and redrawing of US policy in the Middle East that the reputation of the US has partially recovered.

The 'unshackling' of the United States

The second major fallacy of US post-9/11 strategy is closely connected to the 'they hate us' approach in that its effect was also to promote a more activist and radical strategic response. As with the belief that the causes of 9/11 were due to the hate and jealousy of others, the idea that the US was unnaturally constrained and shackled offered an explanation for US vulnerability. The image of a 'shackled' US presented a picture of a country which was passive and disengaged rather than focused and proactive, too concerned about the interests of others rather than those of ordinary Americans, and too subservient to the multiple international obligations attendant on US global leadership to give sufficient attention to American national interests. These multiple constraints, it was argued, had acted to prevent the US from responding sufficiently promptly to those forces seeking its destruction, who were willing to experiment with any means, however criminal, to circumvent US conventional superiority.

The image was thus of a Gulliver bound down by the Lilliputians. The post-9/11 strategic imperative was to break these bonds and reassert US power and leadership. The US was no longer to be the 'reluctant sheriff' (Haas 1997), as it had been called during the 1990s, but a proactive and interventionist sheriff, who was 'bound to lead' (Nye 1991). The doctrinal confirmation for this new role was established in the 2002 US National Security Strategy (NSS). In earlier post-Cold War US security strategies, the temptation to assert US primacy had been resisted because of the fear that it would be perceived as arrogant. There was no such compunction in the 2002 NSS, where the fact that the US enjoyed 'a position of unparalleled military strength' was celebrated as a means of forging a 'balance of power that favors freedom' (White House 2002: iv). The new post-9/11 strategic context, where the threat is presented less by 'conquering states than by failing states' (ibid.: 1), also required a radically different posture, relaxing the constraints which had earlier reduced the freedom of US action during the Cold War. In particular, the structure of deterrence, which had sacrificed the defence of US citizens for the sake of strategic stability, was no longer relevant. Now US primacy meant that threats to its national interests should be actively pre-empted rather than passively deterred. At its logical extreme, a US empire was no longer a temptation but a strategic necessity (Boot 2004; Ferguson 2004; for a review of the 'empire' debate, see M. Cox 2004).

The assumed strategic requirement for the US to 'unshackle' its power provided an impetus not only radically to restructure the Middle East but also to redefine US attitudes to issues of global governance. International regimes and institutions, which the US had traditionally valued as integral components of a multilateral liberal international order, were now judged strictly by their utility. Where these institutions supported and concretely helped to secure US interests, then they were valued; where they were perceived to dilute or make more difficult the attainment of these interests, then the US preference was to act alone or with a 'coalition of the willing'. And where there was a suspicion that international norms and institutions were being used directly to constrain and limit US freedom of action, such as parts of the UN or the International Criminal Court, US hostility was now itself unconstrained. There was also the underlying suspicion that the US was vulnerable to unscrupulous states gaining a strategic advantage by cheating on the norms of behaviour of the international regimes and institutions of which they were formally members. If this was the case, the US also needed to be freed from such institutional constraints. A similar logic was applied to the application of international law. The practice of 'extraordinary rendition' meant that presumed terror suspects could be imprisoned, interrogated and potentially tortured in prisons throughout the world. At Guantánamo Bay and in the Abu Ghraib prison in Iraq, the Bush administration interpreted the laws and conventions on detention and torture in ways which, many fear, denude them of their protective functions (see Danner 2004; Levinson 2004; Amnesty International 2005).

The strategic implications of the 'unshackling' of the US

The main impact of the process of the 'unshackling' of the United States has been a significant loss of international authority and prestige which the Obama administration has sought to restore. The efficacy of the 'unshackling' approach rests on the assumption that key interests are most efficiently and effectively defended through the visible manifestation of supremacy of power and will. The problem is that, from the perspective of the less powerful, such explicit invoking and legitimation of the inequalities of international power can appear arrogant, with the ensuing taint of illegitimacy and imperialism. The end result might be effective demonstrations of compulsory power ('hard power'), but with a subsequent loss of relational power ('soft power') (Nye 2004; for a more general review of the nature of power, see M. Barnett and Duvall 2005). In contrast, where power is channelled and constrained through persuasion and where there is a genuine attempt to gain the support of others, compromise might be required, but at the gain of legitimacy and longer-term durability (see Deudney and Ikenberry 1999; Ikenberry 2001, 2011a).

The contrast between the 1991 and 2003 wars in Iraq is illustrative of this. In 1991, the US used the forum of the United Nations to construct an international coalition, which included not only transatlantic allies but also the Soviet Union, China and key Arab and Muslim states. The necessary compromise for such a global consensus was agreement on a limited war, aimed at the liberation of Kuwait rather than the direct overthrow of Saddam Hussein and the Iraqi regime (see Dannreuther 1992; Freedman and Karsh 1994). Even though Saddam Hussein remained in power, the international prestige of the

US was greatly enhanced and provided the opportunity for American leadership in the most sustained period of Middle East peacemaking in the history of the region. In 2003, in contrast, the US willingly circumvented the UN, intervening in Iraq without an express UN mandate and with only a few of its most loyal allies. Most European and Middle Eastern allies were simply excluded or ignored. The result was the decisive overthrow of Saddam Hussein, but the intervention suffered from a lack of perceived legitimacy and sustainability. Most critically, the 'unshackling' approach, with its imperial temptation, has ignored the fact that traditional empire-building is now viewed as illegitimate and that, as a consequence, the strategic odds tend to favour those forces resisting foreign occupation (for why democracies lose small wars, see Merom 2003).

Overall, the image of an 'unshackled' United States has had a detrimental impact on the moral struggle for 'hearts and minds' which has to be a key component of the 'war on terror'. As mentioned earlier, the key objective of counter-terrorism is to persuade the broader communities which might be sympathetic to the goals of the terrorist organizations that the methods used by the terrorists are illegitimate and criminal. In this 'hearts and minds' struggle, the behaviour and methods used by those fighting terrorism will inevitably come under close scrutiny. The image of the 'unshackling' of the US, however reassuring for a domestic audience, is distinctly less effective for these broader external communities. The sense that the US has significantly devalued its support for multilateral governance and international regimes and institutions has alienated even traditional allies, such as in Europe. The impression that the US seeks to intervene directly to overturn the existing order in the Middle East, without the advice and support of key allies in the region, has similarly revived fears of US imperialism. And the visible disregard for some of the main principles of the rule of law in Guantánamo Bay and Abu Ghraib, together with the practice of extraordinary rendition, has had a particularly damaging impact on US prestige and moral stature. It has been difficult for the US convincingly to argue that, in the 'war on terror', it has not itself made decisions and taken actions which mimic terrorist methods and which have stooped to the same moral level as its terrorist opponents. The use of drones to continue to target terrorist suspects, as discussed more fully in chapter 11, indicates that the challenges and dilemmas over the US conduct of its 'war on terror' have continued into the Obama administration.

Conclusion

Overall, the events of 9/11 and the subsequent waging of the 'war on terror' represented significant challenges for the security analyst. International security was radically transformed by these terrorist attacks, and the new security environment requires new priorities and frameworks of analysis. In this new context, there is a strong temptation to return to the comforting realist paradigm of the Cold War, where state security is paramount and where international terrorism replaces the threat of Soviet aggression. But this would be unfortunate. Alternative anti-realist theoretical traditions provide many useful insights and differing perspectives on the post-9/11 security environment. The constructivist approach, for example, highlights the multiple and complex ways in which the threat of international terrorism is intersubjectively constructed and securitized. The 'critical security' approach offers a valuable anti-statist and radical perspective where Northern claims to be fighting a struggle between 'good and evil' can rightly be questioned and challenged. And the human security approach acts as an important reminder of the continuing insecurities experienced by the poor and suffering far distant from the 'war on terror' (Jackson et al. 2011; Jackson and Sinclair 2012).

Nevertheless, the threat to international security of transnational jihadism is real, not least in its pervasive psychological impact, and states have a vital and key role in protecting their citizens from large-scale terrorist attack. How to assess this threat, and its implications, is a key obligation for the security analyst, requiring the differing roles identified earlier of scientist, internationalist and moralist. The main challenge for the scientist is to assess the seriousness of the threat of international terrorism. The argument of this chapter is that the threat of transnational jihadism, as exemplified by al-Qaeda, was significantly reduced by the initial campaign in Afghanistan. Since then, al-Qaeda and its affiliates have been able to stage occasional attacks but have not demonstrated the capacity for a sustained campaign which would represent a truly strategic threat to Western interests. For its part, the war in Iraq followed by the upsurge in the insurgency in Afghanistan has done more to revive than to lessen the support for extremist transnational jihadism, but with the added feature that the basis of support is now being found as much in the suburbs of Europe and other parts of the Muslim diaspora as in the Middle East. However, with the projected withdrawal from Afghanistan in 2014 and the evidence of the Arab Spring of 2011, it does appear that Islamist extremism, if not more conservative political Islam, is increasingly a less significant political force in the Muslim world.

The main duty of the security analyst as internationalist is to resist the conception of the 'war on terror' as a simple morality tale of 'good versus evil'. This does not mean a stance of moral relativism but it does require a refusal to accept essentialist cultural generalizations, which posit an incommensurable clash of cultures between Islam and the West. This chapter argues that, in reality, the sociological roots of transnational jihadism are narrower than the popular image of the 'war on terror' suggests, and that the drivers of the crisis that it reflects are not primarily religious but secular

– the problem of state failure in the South, as set out in chapter 3. It is these broader and deeper sources of insecurity, the subjects of the wider security agenda, which need to be kept in perspective, even when international terrorism dominates the security discourse.

Finally, there is the role of security analyst as moralist, which is perhaps the most challenging task in the post-9/11 environment. The argument of this book is that security is a vital and positive value and that states have a primary obligation to ensure the security of their citizens. With events of the scale and destructiveness of 9/11, it is natural that renewed priority will be given to security and that states will revert to a more realist and communitarian moral posture, with a generally adverse effect on other core societal values, such as freedom, prosperity and justice. But the 'war on terror' has generally gone too far in this direction, to an extent that the search for a condition of absolute security has materially damaged traditions of civil liberties, economic freedom and international justice. Guantánamo Bay and Abu Ghraib prison have been the most potent symbols of this. The 'war on terror' has highlighted the complex interrelationship between security and freedom. Security does not come ultimately from the assertion of an absolute freedom but from a freedom constrained by law and justice. It is this defence of a shackled and law-driven freedom, negating the absolute freedom of terror, which is the proper arena for a 'war against terror'.

FURTHER READING

For the best general books on international terrorism, see Bruce Hoffmann, *Inside Terrorism* (2006); Martha Crenshaw, *Explaining Terrorism* (2010); and Walter Laqueur, *A History of Terrorism* (2001). For problems of how to respond to terrorism, see Richard English, *Terrorism: How to Respond* (2010), and Paul Wilkinson, *Terrorism versus Democracy: The Liberal State Response* (2001). For analyses of the 'new terrorism', see Peter Newman, *Old and New Terrorism* (2009); Ian Lesser, *Countering the New Terrorism* (1998); and David Benjamin and Steve Simon, *The Age of Sacred Terror* (2002). For more on the religious sources of contemporary terrorism, see Marc Juergensmeyer, *Terror in the Mind of God* (2000); for a pessimistic projection of the prospects for WMD terrorism, see Jessica Stern, *The Ultimate Terrorists* (1999); and for the phenomenon of suicide bombing, see Diego Gambetta (ed.), *Making Sense of Suicide Missions* (2005), and Robert Pape, *Dying to Win* (2005) and Robert Pape and James K. Feldman, *Cutting the Fuse* (2010).

On the ethical debates about the significance of 9/11 and the 'war on terror', see the combative arguments of Jean Bethke Elshtain, *Just War against Terror* (2003), and Paul Berman, *Terror and Liberalism* (2003); the liberal dilemmas exposed in Michael Ignatieff, *The Lesser Evil: Political Ethics in the Age of Terror* (2004); and the more radical critique by Terry Eagleton, *Holy Terror* (2005) and John Gray, *Black Mass* (2008).

For the roots of the Middle East crisis, which lies behind the rise of al-Qaeda and transnational jihadism, the best overview is provided in Fred Halliday, *The Middle East in International Relations* (2005). See also Raymond Hinnebusch, *The International Politics of the Middle East* (2003), and Barry Rubin, *The Tragedy of the Middle East* (2002). More specifically on the role and rise of radical Islam, the richest and most provocative account is provided by Olivier Roy in *Globalised Islam* (2004), as well as in his earlier book *The Failure of Political Islam* (1994). Key other accounts are by Gilles Kepel, *Jihad: The Trail of Political Islam* (2002); Fawaz Gerges, *The Far Enemy* (2005) and *The Rise and Fall of al-Qaeda* (2011); and Marc Sageman, *Understanding Terror Networks* (2004) and *Leaderless Jihad* (2008).

Finally, for accounts of the US foreign policy revolution which led to the 'war on terror' and the interventions into Iraq and Afghanistan, see Jason Burke, *The 9/11 Wars* (2011); Jim Mann, *Rise of the Vulcans* (2004); and the neo-conservative polemic of David Frum and Richard Perle, *An End to Evil: How to Win the War on Terror* (2003). For a good if critical account of the problems of the Afghan campaign, see Sherard Cowper-Coles, *Cables from Kabul* (2011). To place this in a broader historical context, see John Lewis Gaddis, *Surprise, Security and the American Experience* (2004), and John Ikenberry, *Liberal Leviathan* (2011a). Of the multiple critiques of US foreign policy under the Bush administration, a good but partial selection includes David Calleo, *Follies of Power* (2009); Richard Clarke, *Against All Enemies* (2004); Larry Diamond, *Squandering Victory* (2005); Mark Danner, *Torture and Truth* (2004); and Michael Mann, *Incoherent Empire* (2003).

Questions for Research and Discussion

1 Why is the definition and meaning of terrorism so contested? Can a satisfactory definition of terrorism nevertheless be established?
2 In what ways has international terrorism evolved since the end of the Cold War?
3 How has the United States responded to the terrorist attacks of 9/11? How effective have been these responses?

WEBSITES

www.rand.org/topics/terrorism-and-homeland-security.html
RAND is a world leader in research on terrorism, counter-terrorism, counter-insurgency and homeland security. All of the reports and publications are available online.

http://cpost.uchicago.edu
The Chicago Project on Security and Terrorism (CPOST) maintains a complete worldwide knowledge base of suicide attacks and attackers, martyr videos, and terrorist groups profiles.

CHAPTER 10

Proliferation of Weapons of Mass Destruction

There is an intimate relationship between weapons of mass destruction (WMD) and terror. During the Cold War, Wohlstetter's phrase the 'delicate balance of terror' aptly identified this relationship (Wohlstetter 1959). The Orwellian reality was that peace had become equated with the threat of mass terror. The paradox was that this appeared to be the basis for a stability that was more resilient than in earlier periods. As argued in chapter 1, one consequence of the nuclear age has been the dampening of the threat of great power war, since nuclear weapons dramatically change the calculus of the instrumentality of war for achieving political objectives. It was, at least in part, this unravelling of the strategic logic of the nuclear revolution which brought about the peaceful ending of the nuclear-driven confrontation between East and West. The reductions in nuclear arsenals and the remarkable process of disarmament from the mid-1980s onwards formed a crucial symbol and catalyst for the termination of this all-consuming ideological confrontation.

Since the end of the Cold War, two narratives about the continuing role and purpose of nuclear weapons and other WMD have emerged. The first suggests that the end of superpower rivalry and the new degree of trust and amity in international relations herald a strategic devaluation of nuclear weapons. In the post-Cold War period, the strategic imperative is to sustain the momentum of disarmament and arms control so as progressively to reduce and ultimately to eliminate their perceived strategic utility. Even if the abolition of such weapons might be difficult, even if desirable, at least marginalizing them from playing a substantive role in the management of interstate relations is considered an achievable goal. The highlight of this relatively optimistic post-Cold War narrative was the 1995 Extension Conference of the Nuclear Non-Proliferation Treaty (NPT), when it appeared both that the nuclear weapons states were committed to progressive disarmament and that the non-nuclear weapons states were equally committed to foregoing the nuclear option.

There has been an alternative post-Cold War narrative, though, which has been considerably less sanguine. One significant catalyst for this was the discovery, after the first Gulf War in 1990–1, that Iraq had a more advanced nuclear programme than had previously been thought, along with extensive chemical and biological weapons programmes. These discoveries not only contributed to much greater attention being given to chemical and biological weapons than had been the case during the Cold War. They also provided an alarming indication that certain states, characteristically called 'rogue states', were willing to cheat and dissimulate their legal commitments to the WMD order, most significantly in relation to the NPT, so as to gain protection and increase their international stature. This more pessimistic 'rogue state' counter-narrative turned even darker with the terrorist attacks of 9/11, which made it more intuitively plausible that non-state groups would willingly contemplate WMD terrorism. For the United States in particular, this conflation of terrorism with WMD proliferation, as noted in the previous chapter, appeared to demand a strategic revolution which overturned Cold War assumptions and practices. From this more urgent perspective, the alternative 'marginalist' narrative depicts a benign post-Cold War world which no longer exists and promotes Cold War mentalities and practices which are no longer relevant.

With such competing narratives, the role of the security analyst is challenging, particularly in seeking to balance the tripartite functions of scientist, internationalist and moralist. For the security analyst as scientist, there is the problem of how to provide an assessment of the threat of WMD proliferation, where the probability of the use of such weapons might be very low but the consequences, should they ever be used, would be potentially catastrophic. There are also more basic and fundamental questions about how to understand the dynamics of proliferation – the relative weight to give to such factors as rationality, culture, identity and norms, which in turn reflect substantive IR theoretical debates. As an internationalist, the security analyst is necessarily challenged by a nuclear order which is structurally inequitable and where that inequity has a strong North–South dimension. If, as T. V. Paul (1999) argues, nuclear weapons are 'great equalizers', how does one justify such inequality and avoid the perception of 'strategic orientalism', where the South is denied these weapons on account of its perceived irrationality and immaturity? Constructing an equitable bargain between North and South in this regard is critical. And, as moralist, the security analyst needs constantly to be aware of the inherent immorality of nuclear strategy, given that the threat of indiscriminate slaughter is central to its operation. The question here is whether there are prudential 'realist' considerations which justify such intrinsically immoral practices, so as to safeguard key international public goods, such as order and stability, which would not otherwise be adequately provided.

This chapter seeks to offer a critical overview of these key concerns and issues. The first section addresses the theoretical and conceptual issues surrounding the question of proliferation. There are, it is argued, a number of underlying assumptions and perspectives which critically influence the ways in which the problem is perceived and constructed. In particular, there is a fundamental debate about the value to accord to deterrence in ensuring strategic stability and the role that defence and prevention should play, particularly in the post-Cold War period. The second section provides a more detailed account of the evolution of post-Cold War strategy, with attention given to the shift from the 'marginalist' to the 'rogue state' narrative. The third section provides an assessment of the contemporary threats posed by WMD proliferation, where it is argued that, though there is no reason for complacency, a number of these threats are exaggerated.

Indeed, the key argument of this chapter is that an undue focus on certain low probability threats, such as WMD terrorism, can ultimately be counterproductive. This is particularly the case if the resulting policies undermine the complex set of bargains and mutually agreed arrangements that have hitherto reduced the incentives for the possession and use of WMD. As argued in chapter 1, one of the key consequences of the Cold War reliance on nuclear weapons was the advantage that this gave to defence, to the extent of making great power war increasingly unthinkable (see Jervis 1989). The danger of the post-Cold War revision of nuclear and WMD strategy is that this shifts the balance towards the perceived advantage of offensive action so as to pre-empt dangers from 'rogue states' and terrorists before they emerge. The danger here is that this generates an 'ideology of the offensive', with all its broader potential for undermining international security (Snyder 1984). The increased risk that the United States or Israel might unilaterally attack Iran so as to prevent its nuclear weapons programme is the key contemporary example of this potential threat to international security.

Proliferation in theory

Nuclear weapons were central to the Cold War. They were, in many ways, a Cold War obsession and a principal reason why the confrontation assumed such a military and uniquely existential character. The shadow of the mushroom cloud, the threat that civilization itself was potentially at risk from the conflict, provided a constant background to the political reality of the Cold War (Schell 1982; Sagan 1983–4). The centrality of nuclear weapons was also seen in the way they transformed the nature of military strategy. As Bernard Brodie noted as early as 1946, 'thus far the chief purpose of our military establishment has been to win wars. From now on its chief purpose must be to avert them' (1946: 69).

This radical and revolutionary implication of the proliferation of nuclear weapons was not incorporated overnight into strategic thinking. The belief that nuclear weapons could secure a military advantage, and that they continued to have war-fighting utility, was never completely lost. Some strategists consistently refused to accept, and thought it dangerously naive to believe, that nuclear weapons had changed the essential Clausewitzian characteristics of war (see, for example, Kissinger 1957; Gray 1976). However, once the United States lost its early monopoly and itself became vulnerable to Soviet nuclear attack, the conviction that a nuclear war would be too destructive to contemplate grew stronger. War prevention, at least in cases where nuclear weapons would be used, became a central strategic objective.

Civilian strategists, drawn from academia or from think tanks such as the RAND Corporation and the International Institute for Strategic Studies (IISS), led the way in thinking through the radical implications of such a war-avoidance strategy (Brodie 1959; Schelling 1960; Bull 1961; Schelling and Halperin 1961). Their work rested on two core assumptions. First, that the employment of nuclear weapons would be self-defeating because of the danger that any use might escalate to a devastating nuclear exchange; and, second, that the proliferation of nuclear weapons was inherently dangerous and would increase the threat of war unless carefully managed. Where these strategists differed from earlier scholars was that they did not see the solution to be secured through disarmament or the abolition of nuclear weapons. This was judged to be unrealistic when these weapons were already in the arsenals of two ideologically opposed and competing superpowers. They argued, instead, that avoidance of nuclear war depended on the more realizable goal of inducing a sense of equality and parity between the two superpowers, where both sides could be assured that they could always respond in kind to any attack or provocation from the other. A stable system of mutual deterrence was the key objective, requiring mutually agreed regimes of control for nuclear weapons (so-called arms control) rather than simple disarmament. And the core foundation, and most paradoxical aspect, of this regime of arms control was the institutionalization of a mutual agreement to ensure both sides were equally vulnerable to massive nuclear attack – the so-called doctrine of MAD, or 'mutual assured destruction'.

MAD, as the acronym suggests, was the most radical and counter-intuitive innovation of the nuclear age (see Freedman 2003: 232–42). The key agreement buttressing MAD was the Anti-Ballistic Missile (ABM) Treaty of 1972, which essentially prohibited the construction of defences against long-range intercontinental nuclear attacks coming from either the United States or the Soviet Union. The reassurance this agreement provided was that both sides could feel confident that they would not be vulnerable to a successful preemptive strike – that, in the official terminology, they would preserve a 'second strike' capability against any initial strike. MAD was also a mechanism which sought to place limits on the 'vertical' proliferation of weapons in the Soviet and US arsenals. Until the mid-1980s, the success here was limited, despite the various strategic arms control agreements, as both sides greatly increased the numbers of nuclear weapons in their possession. But the logic of MAD, which suggested that strategic stability could also be attained through far fewer weapons so long as the principle of mutual vulnerability was preserved, provided the intellectual reassurance for the far more radical nuclear disarmament initiated by presidents Gorbachev and Reagan in the USSR and the US in the late 1980s. MAD, as a core structure of the East–West nuclear relationship, ultimately played a critical role in its dismantlement.

There was, though, a vital second pillar to the Cold War nuclear order. This pillar dealt with the other potential dynamic of nuclear proliferation – the 'horizontal' proliferation to other states in the international system. The 1968 Nuclear Non-Proliferation Treaty provided formal expression of this, limiting the countries with the right to a nuclear capability to those already in possession of such weapons: the US, the USSR, the UK, France and China (Shaker 1980). The treaty, therefore, institutionalized a division between nuclear weapons states (NWS) and non-nuclear weapons states (NNWS). The inherent inequality of the agreement led certain countries, among them India, Pakistan, Israel, and France, to refuse to sign the treaty (though France did join in 1992). But, for the majority of NNWS, the treaty provided an avenue to avoid the expensive, and destabilizing, path of nuclear weapons acquisition. Moreover, the NWS made certain commitments and reassurances to the NNWS which were attractive in their own terms – these were, first, that the NWS would be committed to nuclear disarmament; second, that NNWS could rely on 'negative security' commitments that no NWS would ever use nuclear weapons against a NNWS; and, third, that the NNWS would have the right to access technology for the civilian use of nuclear power, most notably for developing nuclear energy.

Proliferation: may more be better?

During the Cold War, the nuclear order based on these two pillars – deterrence through MAD and restraint through the NPT – enjoyed, as William Walker argues, a significant degree of international legitimacy (Walker 2004: 28). But the two pillars could appear potentially contradictory in their internal logic. If, on the one hand, deterrence, as set out in MAD, worked in avoiding war between East and West and ultimately in bringing peace, then what was the justification for the NPT's denial of these benefits to other countries and conflict situations? Why if deterrence worked in one context should it not be expected to work in others?

Kenneth Waltz is probably the most famous scholar to focus on this internal contradiction (but see also Bueno de Mesquita and Riker 1990; Lavoy 1995). Indeed, he has consistently argued that the proliferation of nuclear weapons to other states would be beneficial and promote stability. In a seminal paper written in 1981, he argued that 'more may be better' in terms of the spread of nuclear weapons (Waltz 1981; see also Waltz 1990). For Waltz, the positive benefits of nuclear proliferation flow from the logic of neo-realism. In an anarchic 'self-help' system, the best way for a state to dissuade an aggressor from attacking is through an effective deterrent, and nuclear weapons provide just such a deterrent. Moreover, they provide a highly durable deterrent, since their mere possession fosters extreme caution and a desire to avoid war from other states. For Waltz and other thinkers such as Martin Van Creveld (1993), it is precisely this nuclear-induced caution that is key to understanding the causes of the great power peace.

Where Waltz goes further is in arguing that the benefits of nuclear restraint should be extended to other countries and regions. He has argued that, just as deterrence worked in avoiding a war between two mortal enemies, the Soviet Union and the United States, then it would also work its conflict-subduing effects in other hostile situations, such as that between India and Pakistan (Sagan and Waltz 2003: 109–24). Following the same logic, Mearsheimer argued in 1991–2 that Ukraine should hold on to the nuclear weapons left on its territory after the collapse of the Soviet Union (Mearsheimer 1993). For realists like Waltz and Mearsheimer, it is only ethnocentric prejudice which limits nuclear weapons to the North and does not permit their benefits to be distributed to other states and conflict situations in the South.

However, few analysts or leaders have found such 'proliferation optimism' ultimately convincing. Scepticism is focused particularly on the underlying neo-realist assumption of states as uncomplicated rational actors who always act so as to maximize their self-interest. Scott Sagan has argued, often in debate with Waltz, that aspirant nuclear states cannot be expected to conform to such rationalist expectations (Sagan and Waltz 2003: ch. 2). In contrast to Waltz's assumption of states as rational utility-maximizing actors, Sagan sees them as complex bureaucratic organizations which often act in incoherent ways and have their own imperfect 'bounded' conceptions of rationality, and where there is constant competition between different interest groups whose parochial interests can assert a disproportionate influence on policy-making. The influence of the military in nuclear policy is particularly significant in this regard.

Given these limitations of 'rationality', it is legitimate to doubt whether all states, particularly those with very different political cultures, will consistently be able to manage the delicate balancing act required for a resilient and effective nuclear deterrent structure. Indeed, the actual history of the Cold War does not itself inspire confidence, with the evidence now available that nuclear war was only just averted during the Cuban missile crisis (May and Zelikow 1997). Sagan and other authors have also documented the multiple near misses and accidents concerning nuclear weapons during the Cold War (Blair 1993; Sagan 1993; Busch 2004). The historical record suggests, therefore, that luck and good fortune, as much as deliberate design, contributed significantly to the success of deterrence in bringing the Cold War to an end. For nuclear pessimists like Sagan, it would be an unwarranted leap of faith to believe that Cold War deterrence systems will always work in other conflicts with differing conditions, structures and cultures. Reasons of prudence, such sceptics argue, promote a restrictive policy towards proliferation.

The normative and civilizational dimension

The assumptions of the rational actor model which underpin the optimistic nuclear proliferation stance are also challenged by constructivist scholars. They offer a further alternative perspective on the dynamics of proliferation. As noted in chapter 2, constructivism questions the explanatory power of the rationalist agency-driven emphasis on strategic interaction, of which 'rational deterrence theory' is a prime example. From a constructivist perspective, the problem with such a rationalist theory is that it ignores the complex socio-historical process through which WMD have come to be identified as illegitimate and not part of civilized warfare. As Richard Price and Nina Tannenwald have demonstrated with their case-studies on chemical and nuclear weapons, this was not something that emerged naturally or uncontroversially (Price 1995; Tannenwald 1999; see also Paul 2009). In contrast to neo-realist theory, which takes the status of WMD as an 'objective given', these accounts showed how such a designation emerged only after a determined effort to accord these weapons a 'taboo' status which was far from evident to others. For example, the dropping of nuclear bombs in Japan was not, at the time, seen as different in kind from the equally destructive conventional bombing of Tokyo or Dresden and other cities in Germany. For many strategists in the early twentieth century, chemical weapons were even seen as more humanitarian, as well as more effective, than traditional conventional weaponry (Price and Tannenwald 1996: 127–8).

For constructivists, therefore, the role of nuclear and other WMD in international relations is not to be understood solely in terms of how they deter actors from doing what they would otherwise wish to do. It is also about how they represent socially powerful norms which define the very interests and identities of states. The designation of certain weapons as weapons of 'mass destruction' acts independently to constrain their use, as states have committed themselves to mutual agreements that these are 'taboo weapons' which no civilized nation should use. In this way, the conduct of modern war can no longer be seen as constrained solely by rational self-interest, but also by certain norms of behaviour which, in certain instances, preclude what might be the most effective and 'rational' course of action. This applies to the norms against the use of chemical, biological and nuclear weapons, where their potential military utility is proscribed by the internalized norm of non-use. Such norms are, in this sense, counterweights to a realist Hobbesian state of nature, since they 'constrain the practice of self-help in the international state system' (Price and Tannenwald 1996: 145).

Constructivists tend in their policy prescriptions to promote a liberal internationalist agenda of strengthening and consolidating these norms of international behaviour. Arms control agreements, moves towards nuclear disarmament, and strengthening treaties such as the NPT are generally viewed favourably. There is similarly a positive evaluation of the role of 'moral entrepreneurs', enlightened public opinion and non-government actors in consolidating a progressive move towards a more norm-based and legal international order, where war and its barbaric practices are reduced if not entirely eliminated (see Keck and Sikkink 1998). The landmines campaign, which resulted in the Ottawa Convention in 1997, represented, in this sense, a constructivist-supported continuity with earlier campaigns to outlaw chemical and biological weapons and to promote nuclear disarmament (Price 1998). As with WMD, the aim was to make landmines, which for many military strategists have an invaluable military function, into 'taboo' weapons which no civilized country would contemplate using.

But are these norms universal?

Such constructivist and liberal internationalist activism does, though, depend on an implicit distinction between the 'civilized', who respect and act on these progressive norms, and the 'uncivilized', who reject or fail to abide by them. If there were no uncivilized to convert, there would be no need to promote norms in the first place. There are, though, two potential criticisms of this implicit good/bad or civilized/uncivilized bifurcation: the first is a conservative scepticism at the presumed power of liberals to convert the wicked from their 'bad' ways; the second is a critical response to balk at the neo-imperialist connotations of such civilizational language, particularly given that it emanates mainly from liberal opinion in the North.

The first conservative sceptical critique emphasizes that norms are not the same as laws and, particularly in the international sphere, that there are only weak mechanisms for enforcing them. The inherent limitation is that such international norms are generally respected by those who are 'good' or are willing to be converted, but that there will always be those who persist in flouting them. More insidiously, there is also the prospect that such violators will pretend formally to be abiding by the norm, such as not seeking to develop WMD, but will secretly cheat, using the protection that their formal adherence to the norm provides to gain strategic advantage.

In essence, this is the classic conservative critique of arms control (see Gray 1992). From this perspective, 'good' states, such as democracies, which abide by arms control agreements and voluntarily limit their military capacities, potentially place themselves at a disadvantage in relation to 'bad' states, which pretend to abide by the same agreements but actually violate them. This, in particular, is one lesson of the 1930s, when arms control and disarmament arguably weakened and left the democracies unprepared against the threat from Nazi Germany. The danger here, conservative sceptics argue, is the unwarranted belief that, once a norm such as the stigmatization of WMD is universally confirmed, this is itself sufficient for that norm to be respected. In reality, there remain many reasons why states, not least at moments of military necessity, might seek to possess, threaten to use, or actually use such 'outlawed' weapons. The structural problem of arms control, from this perspective, is that it can paradoxically advantage the 'bad' states against the norm-abiding 'good states'. For arms control hawks during the Cold War, it was this implicit assumption of moral equality between the US and the USSR embedded within the structure of MAD that was perceived to be so dangerous, since it provided the opportunity for the Soviet Union to cheat and to gain strategic advantage (Goure, Kohler and Harvey 1974; Gray 1976; Whetten 1976).

It is essentially the same sceptical logic which has promoted the alternative 'rogue state' narrative, where the key danger in terms of WMD proliferation is perceived to be those 'bad' states which seek to gain advantage by cheating on their international obligations. In this context, the sole reliance on deterrence, which was the policy of MAD, is deemed inappropriate, since it limits the options of the 'good states', providing a status and implicit moral equality with 'rogue states' which is not justified. For those states which have a clearly revisionist policy and which refuse consistently to abide by the rules of international behaviour, deterrence needs to be supplemented by a preventive capability that permits law-abiding states to act promptly to curtail their WMD ambitions. Arms control agreements which limit or constrain the strategic capacity for 'good states' to be able to respond to such threats need to be revised or ignored. For those promoting this more interventionist line, MAD's prohibition against the right to build missile defences which would protect Western countries from attacks by countries such as Iran and North Korea represents a classic example of how arms control can paradoxically increase the power of 'rogue states' and weaken the capacity of law-abiding states to respond (Gaffney 2001: 31–2).

But who decides who is 'good' and 'bad'?

But a key question is who decides what or who is to be considered good or bad or civilized and uncivilized? For many in the South, this charged moral discourse can appear to have a neo-imperialist resonance, which ascribes rationality and strategic responsibility to the North and irrationality, cultural backwardness and strategic irresponsibility to the South (see Krause and Latham 1999). Terms such as 'rogue state' and 'axis of evil' similarly replicate the language and images of imperialism, with its civilizing mission to convert the barbaric practices of the unenlightened (Gong 1984; Ayoob and Zierler 2005). For those countries with practical experience of colonialism, the resonance of the language of civilization, now expressed in terms of norms and international law, can easily be interpreted as a cynical exercise to perpetuate the structural inequalities of the system, not least of which is the inequality in the nuclear order (Mutimer 2000: 151). India is the key Southern country which has consistently challenged such inbuilt inequality by refusing to sign the NPT and by then developing its own nuclear weapons (Walker 1998: 512). Iran has also regularly raised the perceived double standards of Western toleration of Israel's nuclear capability while coming down harshly on its own alleged nuclear ambitions (Khan 2010).

This leads to a further problem of this good/bad, civilized/uncivilized distinction. It is that many countries do not neatly fit into this black and white division. In terms of the NPT, these include countries such as Brazil, Argentina, Egypt, Turkey and South Korea, which are fully abiding by the terms of the NPT but which have certainly been tempted in the past to develop their indigenous capability, and might do so again if circumstances were to change (K. Campbell, Einhorn and Reiss 2004). For these countries, the benefits of NPT are not just in constraining nuclear proliferation in their neighbourhood but also in limiting the power and strategic advantages of the nuclear-possessing great powers, including the United States. The danger here is that the new powers and capabilities justified by the US and other nuclear weapons states to counter the perceived threat of 'rogue states' could also damage the bargain with the broader set of non-nuclear weapons states, increasing their sense of threat and their temptation to develop their own nuclear capacity. Even between the existing nuclear weapons states, such fears are not absent, because China and Russia (themselves fitting uneasily into the good/bad distinction) are concerned that the strategic shifts of the US to deal with 'rogue states' might also be aimed at reasserting US strategic dominance over them, thus fatally undermining the principles of mutual restraint articulated by MAD (for independent confirmation that these fears are not ungrounded, see Lieber and Press 2006).

Proliferation in practice

All of these various debates and perspectives are evident in the ways in which WMD proliferation has been addressed since the end of the Cold War. As noted above, the most significant shift has been from the dominance of the 'marginalist' narrative to a 'rogue state' counter-narrative.

For those promoting the 'marginalist' narrative, the period from 1986 to 1995 can perhaps be seen as a 'golden decade' for arms control enthusiasts. The key turning point was the agreement between presidents Gorbachev and Reagan to sign the Intermediate-Range Nuclear Forces Treaty (INF). This treaty was distinctive and radical for two main reasons. First, it eliminated a whole class of weapons and included substantial quantitative reductions, something not contemplated in earlier US–Soviet agreements. And, second, it included and institutionalized verification procedures and mechanisms which were far more extensive and intrusive than had ever been considered before. These two major innovations – genuine reductions for disarmament and emphasis on transparency and verification – were to establish the principles of the arms control dynamic over the next decade.

The results of this 'golden decade' are impressive. This can be seen most dramatically in Europe. From a situation where Europe represented an armed camp, with massive conventional and nuclear forces ready to attack from either side of the East–West border, the continent became practically nuclear-free, with large-scale reductions in conventional forces and the introduction of highly sophisticated measures to ensure mutual transparency and confidence. The relationship between the US and the Soviet Union/Russia was similarly transformed. Various strategic arms control agreements (START I and II, the 2003 SORT, and the new START which came into force in 2011) promised to reduce weapons deployed on either side from their peak of almost 30,000 to about 1,500 by 2018. Concern for 'mutual assured safety' became a more significant core of their relationship than 'mutual assured destruction', with intensive joint cooperation taking place to eliminate or properly safeguard the weapons accumulated by the Soviet Union (Krepon 2001, 2003). The Nunn–Lugar Cooperative Threat Reduction programme provided significant US financial support for Russia in these endeavours.

Verification and disarmament measures were also strengthened in other areas (for an overview, see Andemicael and Mathiason 2005). The nuclear watchdog, the International Atomic Energy Agency (IAEA), had its verification powers strengthened in 1997 with the Model Additional Protocol. In 1993, the Chemical Weapons Convention was signed, which included provision for a permanent verification and inspections body. The symbolic culmination of this highly productive period for arms control was the 1995 NPT Renewal Treaty, where the treaty was extended indefinitely, and a number of countries, such as China and France, finally signed up to it. In addition, the promise of further disarmament appeared to be confirmed by agreements to end nuclear tests by moving towards a Comprehensive Test Ban Treaty (CTBT) and to stop the further production of weapons-grade fissile material by negotiating a Fissile Material Cut-Off Treaty (FMCT).

This impressive record of arms control and disarmament provided the background for the immediate post-Cold War dominance of the 'marginalist' narrative. With the end of the Cold War, nuclear weapons were seen by most analysts to have lost their strategic centrality. In the absence of major threats to international security, there was perceived to be a corresponding reduction in the deterrent function to be played by nuclear weapons. Adapting to this changed strategic environment, marginalists argued that nuclear forces should not only be smaller but also be kept off alert status and made more difficult to use. Thus Michael Mazarr proposed that there should be only 'virtual' nuclear arsenals, whose lack of readiness would mean that much effort and work would be needed to consider their use (Mazarr 1995; see also Feiverson 2000). There also emerged in 2008 a movement for a comprehensive and complete disarmament, which was named the Global Zero movement (see figure 10.1 for its proposals for full global disarmament by 2030) and which included unlikely signatories such as Henry Kissinger, George Shultz, Sam Nunn and Bill Perry (Perkovich and Acton 2008; Cortright and Vayrynen 2010). Although most nuclear weapons states saw this as too radical a

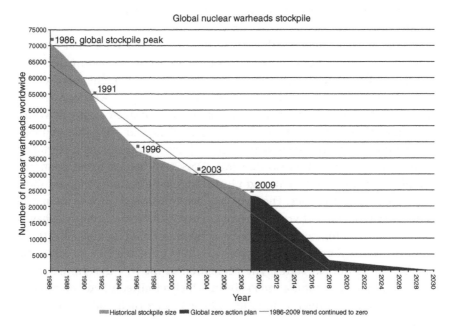

Figure 10.1 Global nuclear warheads stockpile and Global Zero action plan
Source: Global Zero, *Global Zero Action Plan*, February 2010.

proposal, there was still much greater recognition that the utility of nuclear weapons had now declined and that they should be understood principally as 'weapons of last resort' (Quinlan 1993).

The 'marginalist' narrative promoted three key non-proliferation policy priorities. The first was the need to develop and enhance verification and inspection regimes so as to increase transparency, make cheating less easy, and generally provide reassurance that arms control regimes were being effectively policed. The second was the need for non-proliferation norms to be institutionalized and consolidated through multilateral treaties and international regimes. The 'marginalist' logic was that the more states were tightly bound by multilateral commitments and agreements, the better it would be for non-proliferation and international security. And the third feature was that not all the practices and institutions of the Cold War should be jettisoned. In particular, the basic principles of MAD – the need for symmetrical reductions to preserve parity and mutual vulnerability – were to be maintained between nuclear weapons states, most notably between the US and Russia, so as to preserve mutual trust and confidence.

The 'rogue state' counter-narrative

It is, though, this continuing genuflection to the Cold War East–West paradigm which the alternative narrative to nuclear 'marginalism' challenged most strongly. From this alternative perspective, strategic attention to WMD proliferation needs to shift from an East–West context, and its associated Cold War practices, to a North–South axis, and a recognition that one has entered, as a number of commentators have argued, a 'second nuclear age' radically different from the first (Payne 1996; Gray 1999). The discovery of Iraq's nuclear programme and its chemical and biological weapons demonstrated to these critics that many states still saw a strategic utility in WMD. The strategic response, it was argued, required new and tougher counter-proliferation measures, such as the strict regime of inspections undertaken by the UN Special Commission on Iraq (UNSCOM) to verify that country's complete WMD disarmament, and ultimately the right to use military force to ensure such compliance. The Iraqi case was followed by proliferation concerns over Iran, where it was discovered in 2002 that it was secretly engaged in a nuclear enrichment programme in contravention of its NPT obligations; and over North Korea, which simply withdrew from the NPT in 2003 and proclaimed its nuclear status. The perception of the NPT in terminal crisis was accentuated when India and Pakistan, which admittedly had never joined the NPT, conducted nuclear tests in 1998, asserting their coming of age as nuclear powers.

It was in the United States that the policy implications of this 'rogue state' counter-narrative was most vigorously pursued (Roberts 1993; Litwak 2000). The shift in US thinking also reflected the growing influence of groups within the US hostile towards arms control during the George W. Bush administration. These individuals promoted a much more forceful US counter-proliferation policy, along with significant changes in the nature and content of the role of the US nuclear deterrent, which the Obama administration has had difficulty in reversing. The 2001 Nuclear Posture Review set out clearly that the US saw a continuing strategic need for nuclear weapons: first, as providing a capacity for retaliation against the use of chemical and biological attacks, where US treaty commitments precluded responses in kind; and, second, as providing a capability to destroy WMD-filled deep bunkers which would not be able to be destroyed through conventional weapons. The review also confirmed that the US would need to keep open the possibility of testing nuclear weapons in the future, thus precluding it from signing the CTBT (Gabel 2004–5; Payne 2005).

This counter-narrative also radically challenged the 'marginalist' narrative in its distrust of multilateral agreements and independent international regimes for verification and inspections. The Bush administration was particularly notable for its scepticism and hostility towards traditional arms control. The working assumption of the administration appeared to follow the 'arms control paradox', where arms control is either unnecessary because you trust your partners or impossible because you distrust them. Thus the administration argued that traditional East–West arms control was unnecessary between the US and post-Soviet Russia since mutual trust now prevailed.

The 2003 SORT agreement differed fundamentally from earlier strategic arms agreements by requiring neither the verification nor the elimination of weapons. Similarly, the US justified its unilateral withdrawal from the ABM Treaty as, in part, reflecting this changed and more trusting US–Russian relationship. It saw no reason for Russia to feel threatened by defences which were being built to counter the threats from the new proliferators such as Iran and North Korea.

In pursuing these counter-proliferation policies towards these 'rogue states', the Bush administration was determined to keep its strategic options open and flexible, even if this upset traditional arms control practices. Thus the counter-narrative suggested that not only was there a need for the US deterrent structure to be adapted, but defensive measures, such as national missile defences, also had to be developed, and the option of pre-emptive or preventive war to nip potential proliferators in the bud needed to be preserved. From this perspective, MAD was a Cold War relic which was no longer relevant and should not be allowed to act as an obstacle to establishing much-needed defensive measures. Similarly, traditional arms control provisions for verification and transparency were received sceptically by these more hawkish elements, leading to the Bush administration's refusal to contemplate such verification regimes for biological weapons or fissile material production. The fear was that such measures were likely to strengthen the hand of those who cheat rather than those who abide by the rules. The preference of the Bush administration was for measures, such as the Proliferation Security Initiative, which strengthened the capacity of states – rather than unaccountable international institutions – to ensure that counter-proliferation obligations were observed (Valencia 2005; see also Joseph 2005).

In the previous chapter, it was noted that the 'war on terror' had led to a perceived need within the US to 'unshackle' itself from the constraints and international obligations which, it was feared, had left it uniquely vulnerable. This ambition of 'unshackling the US' is clearly evident in American non-proliferation policy. For many critics, particularly those who continue to hold to the 'marginalist' paradigm, it is this 'unshackling' logic, where the US cuts away at its Lilliputian ropes, which is the greatest threat to non-proliferation. For some, it is the US which should really be seen as the 'rogue state', since it has consistently undermined the non-proliferation regimes which build trust and mutual cooperation and has furthermore developed its own expansive nuclear strategies, which have only bred fear and suspicion among many states.

But US nuclear strategy is not static, and the Obama administration reaffirmed a more traditional multilateralist approach which involved a 'resetting' of relations with Russia and the successful conclusion of the new START treaty, which came into force in 2011. The US is also not the only nuclear weapons state to be revising its nuclear strategy. France, for example, has adapted its strategy to preserve the option of using its nuclear weapons against chemical and biological attacks by states or terrorist groups (see Yost 2005). In addition, it is a mistake to see the US as the sole, or even the most significant, cause of other states developing their WMD capabilities. To do this is to fall into the 'they hate us' fallacy noted in the previous chapter, where all the most serious threats to international security in this case come from an obsession with the US. In reality, most of the reasons why states might consider proliferating WMD have little directly to do with the US; similarly, many of the reasons why they decide not to develop WMD are disconnected from US policy. It is to the core root causes of proliferation that we now turn.

Assessing the nature of the threat

The first point to make is that successive bleak projections of nuclear proliferation have failed to materialize. There is a popular nuclear variant of neo-Malthusianism (see chapter 6) which, as with the environmental version, the historical record fails to support. As figure 10.2 demonstrates, there has actually been a steady decline in the number of countries with nuclear weapons or programmes since the 1960s. The fears expressed, for example, by John F. Kennedy in the early 1960s of rapid horizontal proliferation have simply failed to materialize.

In the 1960s, twenty-three countries had weapons, were conducting weapons-related research, or were discussing the pursuit of weapons: Argentina, Australia, Brazil, Canada, China, Egypt, France, India, Israel, Italy, Japan, Norway, Romania, South Africa, Spain, Sweden, Switzerland, Taiwan, the United Kingdom, the United States, the USSR, West Germany, and Yugoslavia. In the 1980s, nineteen countries had weapons or were conducting weapons-related research: Argentina, Brazil, Canada, China, France, India, Iran, Iraq, Israel, Libya, North Korea, Pakistan, South Africa, South Korea, Taiwan, the United Kingdom, the United States, the USSR, and Yugoslavia. In 2012, in addition to the eight states with nuclear weapons, Iran and North Korea are suspected of having active nuclear weapons programmes.

It is, thus, the record of proliferation restraint that most needs to be explained. A number of factors are significant here. First, it is a myth to believe that it is easy to develop nuclear weapons. It is actually a complex and difficult engineering and technological challenge which requires considerable expense, technical scientific expertise and a sophisticated industrial infrastructure. It is generally recognized that only states can meet these basic requirements, making nuclear weapons development something too difficult for non-state actors such as terrorist groups. In addition, although the discovery of the Pakistani scientist A. Q. Khan's nuclear black market has heightened fears of increased access to illicit nuclear material, such illegal markets have generally been limited to enabling technology and knowledge

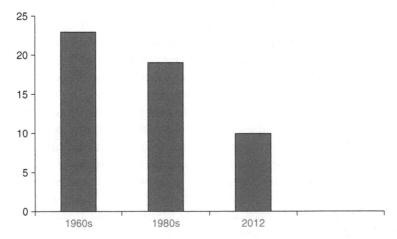

Figure 10.2 Countries with nuclear weapons or programmes (number of programmes)
Source: Cirincione, Wolfstal and Rajkumar (2005: 20; updated to 2012).

rather than providing direct access to ready-made nuclear weapons or weapons-grade enriched uranium (Cirincione, Wolfstal and Rajkumar 2005: 247–9). Even for relatively industrially sophisticated countries like Iran and North Korea, which are also willing to devote huge resources to their efforts, the path towards developing a nuclear capacity is far from straightforward or easy (Montgomery 2005: 157–63).

A further disincentive to prospective proliferators is the salience and strength of the norm against the possession and use of nuclear weapons. It is here that the constructivist approach is particularly relevant. The NPT is notable for its near universality – only India, Pakistan and Israel have yet to sign the treaty, making it the most widely adhered to arms control treaty in history. The principal international effect of the NPT has been to delegitimize the quest to develop nuclear weapons or, at the very least, to raise significantly the costs of doing so. This can be seen in the contrast between France's first nuclear weapons test in 1960, which was the cause of open national celebrations, and India's tests in 1974 and 1998, which had to be done secretly and which invited international opprobrium. As Iran and North Korea have found to their cost, it is very difficult to develop nuclear weapons in a clandestine way and not be found out eventually. The international consequences of being caught 'cheating' are serious – most states either would not be willing to contemplate them or feel that the putative benefits would outweigh the costs. Lawrence Freedman put it well when he said of this internal paradox of nuclear weapons that they 'reinforce the autonomy of states while, at the same time, they provide the most profound reflection of their ultimate interdependence' (Freedman 2003: 464). Most states do not wish to court the negative interdependence that comes from failing to respect their NPT obligations.

The role of the United States as a key constituent element constraining nuclear proliferation also needs to be recognized. The NPT agreement was itself an outcome of a US and Soviet resolve to counter proliferation, which was jointly viewed to be potentially damaging to their mutual interests (Jones 2006: 12). One of the main mechanisms to dissuade key allies, such as Germany and Japan, from developing their own nuclear weapons was by providing the 'positive security' commitment of extended deterrence, where the US nuclear umbrella was extended to these states. In the post-Cold War unipolar system, the US role of providing strategic reassurance to its key allies continues to be critical in dissuading them from developing their own nuclear capability. If countries like Japan, South Korea, Saudi Arabia and Turkey were to feel less secure about the strategic commitment of the US, this would be a significant factor leading them to reassess their position towards nuclear weapons (K. Campbell, Einhorn and Reiss 2004: 321–3).

Why then the temptation towards proliferation?

This does raise the question of why, then, some states continue to seek to develop a nuclear capability despite the multiple constraints and obstacles. The simple answer is that it is generally only when states feel deeply insecure that they are willing to contemplate the costs of such a pursuit. In regions of the world where the level of insecurity (at least between states) is not so high, such as in Latin America, Africa and the South Pacific, it has been possible to formalize nuclear weapons-free zones. As noted above, a pacified Europe after the Cold War has now become practically free of nuclear weapons. However, the major regional gaps in the global non-proliferation map are in the Middle East, South Asia and East Asia, where regional insecurities are such as to provide a permissive environment for nuclear proliferation (Solignen 2007).

For Israel, India and Pakistan, it is their involvement in intensive regional conflicts which makes nuclear weapons appear vital to their perceived national interest. For Iran and North Korea, the deep sense of regional insecurity is the strongest underlying driver for their nuclear weapons programmes. For Iran, the searing experience of the Iran–Iraq war, which included chemical attacks by Iraq during the late 1980s, is a dominant factor (Takeyh 2004–5: 53; Khan 2010). Clearly, though, for both Iran and North Korea, the threatening posture of the US further accentuates their insecurity and resulting drive for nuclear weapons. Indeed, it is these nuclear programmes, and their potential cessation, which provide these states with a bargaining card they would not otherwise possess for negotiating directly with the US.

Status and prestige are also undoubtedly further ingredients in the drive for states to acquire nuclear weapons. It is not lost on most weaker states in the international system that nuclear weapons are the 'great equalizers', and that their possession grants a degree of protection from attack by stronger actors which no other weapon provides (Paul 1999). In the post-Cold War unipolar system, where US conventional military superiority is overwhelming, the role of nuclear weapons in neutralizing this coercive monopoly is strategically tempting. As one Indian general reportedly concluded, the one lesson from the first Gulf War was that 'you do not challenge the United States unless you possess nuclear weapons'. India has also been the most vocal country in arguing that the NPT order is essentially illegitimate in freezing the international status quo and thereby denying India, and other emerging countries, their rightful international recognition as key regional powers. To be a nuclear weapons state does inevitably convey a certain international status, which continues to be valuable to declining powers like France and the UK. But, by the same token, for many rising powers it is an order which appears to have been arbitrarily frozen at the particular distribution of power in 1968, and one which seeks furthermore to perpetuate Northern domination over the South.

What does effective non-proliferation require?

The NPT represents, therefore, a problematic and contested international order. For the security analyst as internationalist, this structural inequality and its North–South implications are significant. However, even India has not sought to abolish the NPT, and most states would agree that the NPT bargain, though imperfect, contributes to international stability.

The key challenge is, though, to set out the 'red lines' to establish which changes to this order can be accommodated without undermining it, and which simply cannot be permitted because otherwise the whole order would collapse. The problem here is exacerbated by the fact that the existing nuclear weapons states are hardly consistent. Israel's secret development of nuclear weapons and its chemical and biological weapons programmes have never been seriously challenged by the United States. Similarly, with the US–India nuclear agreement of 2005, the United States has implicitly recognized India as a nuclear weapons state and overturned the sanctions it had hitherto applied to express its opposition to Indian proliferation (Potter 2005; Thyagaraj and Thomas 2006). For their part, Russia and China have been at least complicit in the nuclear weapons programmes in Pakistan, North Korea and India.

In terms of practical politics, one can say that there are effectively two tiers of aspirant nuclear states. There is, first, the tier of India, Pakistan and Israel, where proliferation has already taken place and where it is highly unlikely that international action would persuade these countries to give up their nuclear capability. For this tier of countries, a delicate balance is required between expressing continuing international opposition to the way they wilfully ignore the NPT and ensuring that, as *de facto* NWS, they comply fully with the non-proliferation measures adopted by the recognized NWS. The second tier of states is that of North Korea and Iran, where there is, in contrast, a greater, if far from guaranteed, prospect of forging an international consensus to act more decisively. It is in relation to this tier that the non-proliferation 'red lines' probably need to be drawn, since the NPT would be gravely endangered if North Korea and Iran were to succeed in becoming nuclear weapons states, or, at the very least, were to do so without significant international resistance and serious long-term costs.

Given that the stakes are so high, military options cannot be excluded. But, as the counter-proliferation war against Iraq in 2003 has demonstrated, the unintended consequences of such military enforcement are considerable. Similar military operations against Iran and North Korea are generally seen to be extremely problematic. And, as noted above, the only sustainable long-term way to dissuade these countries (and others in the future) is to undercut the main cause of proliferation – the deep insecurity experienced by these states. It is such an insecurity-reducing strategy which ultimately helped to end Libya's WMD aspirations in 2003. The US, particularly with the Obama administration, has seen similar multilateral diplomatic paths – forged by the EU-3 (Germany, France, the UK) in Iran and by the six-party talks over North Korea – as the main, if not the sole, avenue for the desired resolution of these crises. However, the continuing Western frustration over Iran's intransigence and lack of compromise has led to increasing calls, particularly from Israel, for military options to be considered more seriously.

Beyond these more immediate challenges, there are other more precautionary measures which contribute to non-proliferation objectives. One of the key factors reducing the danger of nuclear proliferation is the difficulty of obtaining fissile materials. There have been various suggestions and proposals to improve international cooperation in this regard, seeking to make, as far as is practically possible, all nuclear weapons grade material as secure as the gold in 'Fort Knox' (Allison 2004a: 64; United Nations 2004; Perkovich et al. 2005). The Cooperative Threat Reductions (CTR) programme in Russia is seen as a key element in this, and there have been proposals to extend such programmes and practices to other parts of the world (Krepon 2003; Gottemoeller 2005).

A key area of global concern is also focused increasingly on the principal structural weakness of the NPT, the way in which it permits non-nuclear weapons states to enrich uranium for civilian nuclear use which can then easily be diverted to a weapons programme. The world would be much safer, particularly given that nuclear energy is becoming more and more attractive, if the enrichment of uranium was limited to existing NWS but where supply of such fuel was guaranteed to NNWS. However, for this to be accepted internationally requires NNWS to agree to it, which in turn requires the NWS to be meeting their side of the NPT bargain. The justified suspicion that the NWS simply do not take seriously their treaty obligations to move towards full and comprehensive disarmament is a serious obstacle to the achievement of non-proliferation goals. It is this recognition which led to the surprising resurgence in 2008 of the Global Zero movement, who have called for a world without nuclear weapons (see figure 10.1). Even some traditional arms control sceptics have subscribed to the radical demands of this movement (for example, see O'Hanlon 2010).

The threat of WMD terrorism

The analysis so far has concentrated on what might be called the traditional concerns of arms control, where the central focus is on states and on the proliferation of nuclear weapons. For some, though, this is an anachronistic and even dangerously complacent understanding of the dynamic nature of the WMD threat. Even before the terrorist attacks of 9/11, there was a burgeoning concern about the prospects of terrorist groups using weapons of mass destruction to further their objectives (see, for example, Betts 1998; Falkenrath et al. 1998; Stern 1999; Lavoy, Sagan and Wirtz 2000). The events of 9/11, though the weapons used were low-tech and did not involve WMD, have accentuated the fear that WMD terrorism is now an even more likely future development. Advances in biotechnology have also raised fears that biological weapons, for which the necessary materials are generally easily available, have gained in strategic utility and destructiveness (Dando 2001; Koblentz 2003). This perception of a radically changing strategic threat is captured by George W. Bush's fears that, now 'armed with a single vial of biological agent or a single nuclear weapon, small groups of fanatics or failed states can gain the power to threaten great nations, threaten world peace' (quoted in Joseph 2005: 377).

The question of how to assess the seriousness of this threat and, as a consequence, what resources should be allocated to it, is one of the most difficult challenges facing any security analyst. At one level, the threat is clearly very serious. The events of 9/11 demonstrated that, as argued in the previous chapter, certain terrorist groups wish to inflict mass casualty attacks. A number of these groups, most notably Aum Shinrikyo and al-Qaeda, have also expressed interest in developing a WMD capability. The prospect of WMD terrorism, moreover, adds a new vulnerability to states, as the normal instruments of deterrence against WMD attacks are unlikely to be effective and preventive action cannot always be guaranteed to work. It is hard to avoid the conclusion that civilian populations need to be able to defend themselves against such prospective attacks (Betts 1998: 36–41). For government leaders and their security services, the prospect of a 9/11 repeat but with a biological or nuclear weapon naturally and rightly causes deep concern and anxiety (Garrett 2001).

However, to gain a better sense of the nature and extent of the threat, a distinction needs to be made between, on the one hand, the expressions of interest by terrorist groups in WMD and, on the other, their actual capability to develop and use them (Tucker 2000a; Parachini 2003). Expression of interest does not, in itself, convert into capability or will. Moreover, expression of interest in WMD by terrorist groups is generally limited to those with a strongly religious or apocalyptic conviction. Such groups are the least concerned about the negative impact of deliberately and indiscriminately causing mass civilian casualties and deaths. Aum Shinrikyo is the paradigmatic example of an apocalyptic cult terrorist group for which, under the psychotic leadership of Ashoko Asahara, the use of WMD became a central obsession and strategic goal. Al-Qaeda is also another significant potential WMD user, evident in the consideration given to the spraying of biological agents by agricultural fertilizer planes as a possible option for the 9/11 attacks. But al-Qaeda also has, along with its religiously inspired maximalist goals, more narrow and identifiable political goals which might make the use of WMD less attractive compared to conventional means of attack, particularly if these can result in the same objective of mass casualties and widespread terror. For more traditional ethno-nationalist terrorist groups, WMD probably hold little attraction, as any potential use would so undermine the legitimacy of their political goals, both domestically and internationally, that it would be difficult to justify the expense of their development and use.

It is, though, the second stage of converting the expression of interest in WMD to developing the actual capability their use which is the most difficult. It is here too that the post-Cold War conflation of nuclear, chemical, biological and radiological weapons into the single category of 'weapons of mass destruction' needs to be carefully deconstructed (see Cirincione, Wolfstal and Rajkumar 2005: 3–4). It is only nuclear and biological weapons which have a truly mass destructive capacity, in the sense of the ability to cause thousands of casualties with near-simultaneous effect. Fortunately, it is regarding these weapons that the difficulties of developing such capabilities are most severe. As noted above, it is generally recognized that the development of nuclear weapons is beyond the capacity of any non-state actor and that, moreover, access to the necessary fissile material is severely restricted (Frost 2005: 9). For biological weapons, it is easier to obtain the basic pathogens, but it is very difficult to develop virulent strains and to be able to handle them, because they are generally very unstable. It is even more difficult to disseminate these pathogens in a form which would cause mass casualties. In particular, the technology required for aerosolized dispersal is extremely complicated to master (Leitenberg 2005: viii). It is notable that Aum Shinrikyo, despite substantial funds, a highly permissive environment and ample scientific expertise, including twenty university-trained microbiologists working in well-equipped laboratories, was unable to 'obtain virulent strains of pathogens, nor was it apparently capable of working successfully with the strains that it did have' (Leitenberg 2004: 28).

The result is that Aum Shinrikyo terrorists switched to chemical nerve agents, which are easier to deliver, for their attacks on the Japanese city of

Matsumoto in 1994 and on the Tokyo subway in 1995. Chemical weapons are primarily tactical rather than strategic weapons and are not adaptable for mass casualty attacks. Moreover, the Aum Shinrikyo attacks were similar to all other terrorist incidents using chemical or biological agents to date, in that decidedly low-tech delivery systems were used – plastic bags in the Tokyo subway case. Such crude delivery methods are potentially capable of inflicting tens or hundreds of casualties but not the mass casualty numbers predicted by most alarmist scenarios. The same more limited casualty rates are also likely to result from radiological or 'dirty' bombs – which involve using conventional weapons to disperse radioactive material – since such bombs would be unlikely to kill anyone immediately, except as a result of the conventional explosives themselves, and in the longer term would probably increase only marginally the rate of deaths from cancer among those affected (Frost 2005: 77).

What conclusions should be drawn from the evidence of generally exaggerated fears of WMD terrorism? The first is that the threat cannot simply be ignored, as there are extreme terrorist groups that wish to obtain a WMD capability. Also, any terrorist attack using WMD, however relatively light the resulting casualties, would potentially have a disproportionate psychological effect – the main objective of terrorist groups in any case. But the threat of WMD terrorism needs to be kept in proportion (Kamp 1996; Tucker 2000a; Parachini 2003). There is a danger that the focus on WMD proliferation to non-state actors distorts the reality that the principal threat of such proliferation comes from states, which are the actors with the resources to develop these weapons and which are more likely to be convinced of the strategic utility of their possession. There is also a real danger of conflating the threat of terrorism with state-directed WMD proliferation, something which has been central to the intellectual justification of the US-led 'war on terror', the intervention into Iraq in 2003 and potentially for a military attack on Iran. In reality, these are two discrete and separate areas of concern, since it is highly unlikely that states seeking to develop their indigenous WMD capability would be willing to hand over their hard-earned 'crown jewels' to terrorist groups they cannot be sure of controlling.

In addition, the fact that deterrence is unlikely to be as effective against terrorist groups should not lead to costly alternative measures which potentially weaken other aspects of non-proliferation and broader security policy. Deterrence might be less central to WMD terrorism, but it is a mistake to believe that terrorist groups do not have some valuable assets they would be loath to lose (Trager and Zagorcheva 2005–6). Preventive strategies to deal with many terrorist groups, such as al-Qaeda, are also not dissimilar to those to be used against state proliferators – in particular, the broader civilizational goal to persuade both state and non-state actors of the essential illegitimacy of the possession and use of WMD. And in terms of defending one's population from a WMD terrorist attack, this should be done in conjunction with other measures dealing with a range of other possible security threats. For example, the effect of a bioterrorist attack would not be dissimilar to a flu pandemic – for instance, of avian flu – and the likelihood of that occurring is considerably greater than that of a comparable deadly bioterrorist attack. The fact that in US fiscal year 2006 the US planned to spend $1.76 billion on biodefence research as against only $120 million for work on influenza indicates the danger of post-9/11 distortions in threat assessments (Leitenberg 2005: 7).

Conclusion

Overall, the challenges for the security analyst in addressing the perceived and actual threat posed by WMD proliferation are considerable. But the starting point is the one indicated by Bernard Brodie at the beginning of the nuclear age: that 'everything about the atomic bomb is overshadowed by the twin facts that it exists and its destructive power is fantastically great' (Brodie 1946: 52). It is this capacity for near simultaneous destruction, and the fact that its avoidance is dependent on the frailties of human beings, who have not shown much restraint in the past in using all the destructive powers available to them, which make the issue so urgent. The threat of nuclear weapons is that one false step could usher in a new tragic reality whose contours are difficult to determine. The threat posed by chemical and biological weapons, whose strategic utility is substantially reduced by their unreliability, is ultimately that they lie in the shadow of nuclear weapons. Any large-scale use of such weapons would inevitably invite a nuclear response with all its assured destructive power.

The quest to ensure that these weapons are never used again must, therefore, be a central concern for all security analysts. The fact that one mistake would be potentially catastrophic underlines the seriousness of the endeavour. However, this does not mean that the security analyst should lose the capacity to exercise his or her roles as scientist, internationalist and moralist. In terms of the security analyst as scientist, there is the need to resist the temptation to exaggerate the threat of proliferation from both states and non-state actors. As argued above, the actual record shows that horizontal proliferation among states has been considerably less widespread than many expected; and there is not yet much evidence of terrorist groups gaining an effective WMD capability. But there is also a need to recognize that the 'golden decade' of disarmament and arms control ground to a halt in the late 1990s and that there is now a distinctly more pessimistic mood. This is, in part, due to more brazen attempts to bridge the proliferation barrier, such as those by India, Pakistan, North Korea and Iran; and, in part, it is due to the acknowledged nuclear weapons states appearing to reaffirm both the strategic utility of nuclear weapons and their distrust of arms control measures which might constrain that potential use.

For the security analyst as internationalist, it is the interstate bargains which have traditionally helped to limit proliferation which need to be identified and affirmed. These bargains are essentially twofold. First, there is the bargain between the recognized nuclear weapons states who agreed, in the context of the Cold War superpower nuclear stand-off, that international security depends on no state gaining a position of dominance or primacy. This remains the continuing value of MAD. The danger now is that the implicit stability-producing bargain of MAD is potentially at risk through a deliberate US drive to gain a position of nuclear primacy over its main peer competitors, Russia and China (Lieber and Press 2006). The second bargain is between the nuclear weapons states and the non-nuclear weapons states, where the essential bargain is agreement by NNWS not to seek to obtain such weapons so long as the NWS demonstrate genuine commitment to disarmament and to guaranteeing access to the non-military benefits of nuclear power. The hawkish scepticism towards multilateral arms control agreements adopted by the Bush administration represented a significant challenge and threat to this other major bargain underpinning the international nuclear order, though the Obama administration has provided at least some temporary reassurance of support for traditional arms control. However, ultimately, it is the regional insecurities in the Middle East and South Asia which are the principal causes of proliferation. But the interlocking and mutually supportive networks of non-proliferation norms and international regimes also represent invaluable instruments to facilitate the goal of reducing the temptation to obtain WMD. In their absence, the international climate for encouraging non-proliferation is significantly damaged.

Finally, as moralist, the security analyst needs to be constantly reminded of the immorality of the threat of use, as well as the actual use, of WMD. A prudential realist commitment to the value of nuclear deterrence is not incompatible with the liberal internationalist and constructivist goal of delegitimating the use of these weapons. It is here that there is convergence in the principles of non-proliferation and counter-terrorism, providing a reverse image to the link between WMD and terrorism noted at the beginning of this chapter. Much like terrorism, WMD cannot be disinvented. However, the ultimate overarching objective for both policy approaches remains a morally charged one – to consolidate the civilizational norm that the threat or use of WMD is wrong and immoral in the same way as the threat or use of terrorist acts is morally abhorrent.

FURTHER READING

For a comprehensive overview of the state of proliferation, see Joseph Cirincione, Jon B. Wolfsthal and Miriam Rajkumar, *Deadly Arsenals: Nuclear, Biological and Chemical Threats* (2005). For post-Cold War developments, see William Walker, *Weapons of Mass Destruction and International Order* (2004). For a practitioner's perspective, see Richard Butler, *Fatal Choice: Nuclear Weapons and the Illusion of Missile Defence* (2001). For collections of key essays and articles on nuclear proliferation, see Michael E. Brown et al., *Going Nuclear* (2010), and Harsh V. Pant, *Handbook of Nuclear Proliferation* (2012).

For a historical background, see the excellent Lawrence Freedman, *The Evolution of Nuclear Strategy* (2003); and Edward Spiers, *A History of Chemical and Biological Weapons* (2010). For a general overview of the strategic implications of nuclear weapons, see Robert Jervis, *The Meaning of the Nuclear Revolution* (1989).

The debate between proliferation 'optimists' and 'pessimists' is best covered in Scott D. Sagan and Kenneth N. Waltz, *The Spread of Nuclear Weapons* (2003). For the constructivist perspective, see Richard Price and Nina Tannenwald, 'Norms and deterrence: the nuclear and chemical weapons taboos' (1996). For a strong hawkish critique of arms control, see Colin S. Gray, *House of Cards: Why Arms Control Must Fail* (1992). For the rise of the 'rogue state' counter-narrative, see Robert Litwak, *Rogue States and US Foreign Policy* (2000), and Keith B. Payne, *Deterrence in the Second Nuclear Age* (1996); for a radical critique of this narrative, see David Mutimer, *The Weapons State: Proliferation and the Framing of Security* (2000). For the ideas of moving towards 'Global Zero' or a world without nuclear weapons, see George Perkovich and James Acton, *Abolishing Nuclear Weapons* (2008).

Investigations of why states decide on or abstain from nuclear proliferation are pursued in Kurt M. Campbell, Robert J. Einhorn and Mitchell B. Reiss (eds), *The Nuclear Tipping Point* (2004); and T. V. Paul, *Power versus Prudence* (2000) and *The Tradition of Non-Use of Nuclear Weapons* (2009). There are good overviews of contemporary arms control policy prescriptions in William E. Potter and Gaukhar Mukhatzhanova (eds), *Forecasting Nuclear Proliferation in the 21st Century* (2010); James M. Acton, *Deterrence during Disarmament* (2011); Michael A. Levi and Michael E. O'Hanlon, *The Future of Arms Control* (2005); Michael Krepon, *Cooperative Threat Reduction, Missile Defence and the Nuclear Future* (2003); and Graham Allison, *Nuclear Terrorism: The Ultimate Preventable Catastrophe* (2004).

On the rising fear and concern about WMD terrorism, see the influential article by Richard K. Betts, 'The new threat of mass destruction', in *Foreign Affairs* (1998), followed by Jessica Stern, *The Ultimate Terrorists* (1999). For more evidence-based and less alarmist accounts see Michael Levi, *On Nuclear Terrorism* (2007); Jonathan Tucker (ed.), *Toxic Terror: Assessing the Terrorist Use of Chemical and Biological Weapons* (2000); and John Parachini (ed.), *Motives, Means and Mayhem: Assessing Terrorist Use of Chemical and Biological Weapons* (2005).

Questions for Research and Discussion

1 How convincing is Waltz's argument that 'more' nuclear weapons is 'better'?

2 Is the fact that nuclear weapons have not been used since 1945 the result of the development of an international norm of non-use of nuclear weapons?
3 What threat to international security is posed by horizontal proliferation and how might this best be addressed?
4 How worried should we be about the threat of WMD terrorism?

WEBSITES

www.wilsoncenter.org/program/npihp
The Nuclear Proliferation International History Project is a major study of international nuclear history through archival documents, oral history interviews and other empirical sources.

www.carnegieendowment.org/programs
The Carnegie Nuclear Policy Program is a leading source of expertise and policy thinking on nuclear industry, non-proliferation, security and disarmament.

www.iaea.org
The official website of the International Atomic Energy Agency, with access to books, factsheets, bulletins and links to more specialized resources.

www.globalzero.org
Global Zero is an NGO that promotes a world without nuclear weapons and provides policy briefs and multimedia resources.

CHAPTER 11

Cyber-Warfare and New Spaces of Security

One of the themes taken up throughout this book is the close interconnection between war and security and changes in the social world more broadly. The use of historical sociology in chapter 2 demonstrated how processes of state-building had left Northern and Southern states with different trajectories of war and insecurity. The previous chapter discussed how the development of nuclear weapons changed the nature of the battlefield, strategy and tactics, at least for the major powers in possession of such weapons. The intertwining of technology, social change, warfare and security has thus formed a core concern of security studies. Needless to say, none of these factors has remained static over time. An emerging research field in international security (as well as political science and the social sciences more generally) concerns whether we are currently observing an epochal shift such as that brought about by technologies such as the telegraph, tanks and aircraft in the twentieth century, or gunpowder, printing and deep sea navigation in the fifteenth and sixteenth centuries. These technological changes were connected to deep and wide-ranging transformations in warfare and social organization as a whole.

Does the beginning of the twenty-first century represent the threshold of such a transformation? Authors such as Peter Singer (2009) argue that an ensemble of technologies emerging in the latter part of the twentieth century have begun fundamentally to change society, warfare and security. These technologies centre around the internet, and associated social media networks such as Facebook and Twitter, and the so-called revolution in military affairs involving the integration not just of information technology but of robotics leading to a change in who fights wars, where and when. The manifestations of these changes are to be found in the development of 'cyber-war', the conduct of the US-led invasions and occupations of Iraq and Afghanistan and in revolutionary events in the Middle East – the 'Arab Spring' that began in early 2011. This chapter examines these claims and asks what the degree of change really is.

Changing conflicts, changing technologies

The idea that both technical progress and social change alter the strategic environment – and thereby the means by which wars are fought – is neither particularly obscure nor new. The English historian A. J. P. Taylor famously argued that the First World War was a 'war by timetable', the German strategy of striking quickly against France being determined by the relatively slow pace of railway development in Russia, necessitating a pre-emptive attack through Belgium at the more quickly mobilized French. Changes in technology become consequential in the minds of strategists, however, when they appear to give one state an advantage over others. At the end of the Cold War, and most especially after the 1991 Gulf War, some US strategists came to believe that new technologies in guided weapon systems, robotics and, above all, the internet had given the US a supreme advantage that it was imperative to pursue and maintain. They described this as a 'revolution in military affairs' (RMA) that held the possibility of 'solving many of the strategic dilemmas the United States faces in the post-Cold War world' (Metz and Kievit 1995: 2; Der Derian 2009: 28; Singer 2009: 180–1). The origins of this idea lay not in US military doctrine, however, but in that of their defunct Soviet adversary.

'Military technical revolutions" and the Soviet origins of the RMA

Soviet strategists, notionally basing their analyses on Marxist premises, were schooled in grounding military adaptations in technological and social change. In the 1970s and 1980s, Soviet military theorists began to speak about a 'military technical revolution' that could give the US an advantage in future conflict (Krepinevich 2002: 16). Influenced perhaps by the rather crude technological determinism of Soviet dialectical materialism, these theorists argued that 'advanced technologies, especially those related to informatics and precision-guided weaponry employed at extended ranges', were tending to 'the point where quality is becoming far more important than quantity, revolutionizing the nature of warfare'. This 'military technical revolution', the Soviets believed, would entirely change the strategic environment: instead of so-called sequential operations and distinct front-lines, entire states would become the battlefield, with targets precisely selected and swiftly destroyed. A 'reconnaissance strike complex' based on these technologies might even come to replace nuclear weapons capability (ibid.: 6).

According to the Soviet military theorists and the US analysts who took up their ideas, this military technical revolution – or revolution in military affairs – represented a paradigmatic change in warfare such as that seen in previous epochs. Indeed, when the Soviets initially spoke of 'military technical revolution', they were referring to the ensemble of technologies that emerged in the First World War and were brought to devastating effect in the Second: tanks, aircraft and aerial bombing, submarines, and radio (Der Derian 2009: 28–9). Andrew Krepinevich, a proponent of the idea of RMA, defined such revolutions as occurring 'when the application of new technologies into military systems combines with innovative operational concepts and organizational adaptation to alter fundamentally the character and conduct of military operations' (2002: 3). The revolution in military affairs of the late twentieth and early twenty-first century would therefore form part of a pattern visible in previous military history – of transformative technologies, allied to comprehensive social change, which certain powers were able to harness to gain a lasting advantage over others.

Such an epochal shift, argued the RMA theorists, was central to the very rise of the modern European state from the fifteenth to the seventeenth centuries – discussed in chapter 3 in connection with Charles Tilly's claim that 'war makes states'. Technologies such as gunpowder and deep-water navigation both encouraged and permitted the founding and expansion of unitary states. These were not automatic developments, however: most of the technologies central to this process had been known in the Chinese empire for centuries (Wallerstein 1974b: 63). Therefore, according to the proponents of the idea of the RMA, transformation requires adaptation to the new technologies (Krepinevich 2002: 3). The use of gunpowder and artillery undermined the special position of armoured cavalry in the early modern armies, thereby feeding into a process of the breakdown of power of feudal aristocracies: deep-sea navigation permitted the use of these gunpowder technologies against non-European societies and eventually the rise of England as predominant maritime power (Singer 2009: 183).

The gaps between these revolutions in military affairs are decreasing, as is the time it takes for their effects fully to be felt (Singer 2009: 183). RMA theorists usually identify two, or possibly three, moments of military technical revolution that have been foundational to the international system over the past two centuries. The first of these (in some ways a finalization of the initial development of the modern state) took place in the first half of the nineteenth century and was associated with the changes between the French Revolution and the US civil war. The key aspects of this RMA were railways, the telegraph system, ironclad ships and repeater rifles – in short, the beginnings of industrialized warfare (Krepinevich 2002: 4). Thus, the RMA consisted of the tactical innovations in weaponry, the increased speed of battlefield communication and a strategic change (the movement of armies via railways) that reflected wider social changes. Failure to adapt to these changes led to defeat. The Napoleonic wars had been fought with breech-loading muskets and armies manoeuvring in open field. Those who retained these tactics in the changed environment were swiftly annihilated. The military technical revolution of the mid-nineteenth century transformed the innovations of earlier epochs rather than simply overturning them, however: for example, the *levée en masse* of the French Revolution, the mass army infused with a sense of national mission, was transformed into the huge conscript forces that in many cases forged an identity of disparate local provinces.

The revolution to which RMA theorists were most attracted, however, was that which (they argue) took place between the First and Second World War

(Der Derian 2009: 28–9). The First World War represented in some ways a fulcrum point: the later battles of the American civil war resembled those of the First World War, with trenches, movements determined by railway and telegraph, and attrition under heavy artillery and machine gun fire (Krepinevich 2002: 4). However, the First World War also saw the introduction of technologies that would come to full fruition only in the 1920s and 1930s – technologies such as tanks, aircraft, radio and telephone communication. The struggle between those who perceived the transformative capabilities of such technologies and those who remained wedded, if not to the old, to using the new in the manner of the old endows the interwar period with a great sense of retrospective pathos. As British and French generals ignored or down-played the new technologies, their German counterparts were planning the blitzkrieg that would sweep through Europe (Der Derian 2009: 27). The devo-tees of the new age of war in the 1930s were seized by both terror and fasci-nation – especially for air power and the idea that 'the bomber will always get through' (Betz and Stevens 2011: 83). It is perhaps for this reason that the proponents of the idea of a new RMA in the late twentieth and early twenty-first century were so taken with the example of the interwar period (Der Derian 2009: 27).

The Second World War demonstrated the devastating effect of an ensemble of new technologies, allied to appropriate command structures, deployed against those who had failed to adapt to them. The German blitzkrieg was made possible by the preceding decades of technological innovation and soon swept away the French forces who had planned for a war of position rather than manoeuvre (Krepinevich 2002: 3). However, the example of blitzkrieg should give some pause to simplistic notions of the RMA: after all, Germany lost the war simply by being bled dry by opponents with greater manpower (the USSR) or industrial resources (the US). Futhermore, the war ended in what might be considered a new and perhaps even more significant revolution in military affairs: the development of nuclear weapons. As previous chapters of this book have indicated, the enormous destructive power of these weapons appeared to change the nature of war. Tactical systems and weapons designed for conventional war between symmetric enemies seemed almost useless: if the theory of mutual assured destruction were true, then the only weapons that mattered in such competition were nuclear ones and the only important decisions were those to be taken *before* any first strike. This was less important for the asym-metrical warfare carried out (and often lost) against recalcitrant parts of the superpowers' own spheres of influence in Afghanistan or Vietnam, but it seemed to accelerate the trend by which 'the decisiveness of major war has been diminishing' (Betz and Stevens 2011: 76). The attraction of the idea of a new RMA, to its adherents in the US at least, was that it might restore such decisiveness to war and in particular reinforce the hegemony of the US (Singer 2009: 185).

The post-Cold War RMA and its proponents

The first inklings of the idea of a new revolution in military affairs were raised in the US in the late 1980s, when Pentagon strategists began to assimilate the ideas of their Soviet adversaries (Metz and Kievit 1995: 5). However, the concept began to win wider acceptance after the Gulf War of 1991 – a conflict in which the proponents of RMA believed 'various systems and networks began to realize the enormous potential of integrated operations' (Krepinevich 2002: 8). The Gulf War, according to the RMA theorists, showed the way to the future. In that conflict, the US had won swiftly and apparently decisively on the basis, RMA theorists argued, of the new information technology and precision-guided weaponry such as so-called smart bombs. A note of caution should be sounded about how much of the US victory depended on such technology and how much on facing an adversary depleted after nearly a decade of war with Iran and the loss of its superpower patron, the Soviet Union: 93 per cent of the US bombs dropped in the Gulf War were 'dumb' (Singer 2009: 58). However, the conflict was the first US war in which the logistics of the military were computerized, and this may have had an effect: the US commander Norman Schwarzkopf believed as much, saying, 'I couldn't have done it without the computers' (quoted ibid.).

The idea that widespread computer use, and most of all the internet, has wrought epochal social change reflected in battlefield strategy and tactics is central to the theory of the RMA. Here the military theorists of the Pentagon find themselves with strange bedfellows, including post-Marxist radical social theorists such as Manuel Castells (2009) or Michael Hardt and Antonio Negri (2001). The basic idea of such theorists is that the epoch of industrial modernity, with its hierarchical organizations, sovereign nation-states, and politics based on the clash between identifiable interests of labour and capital, has passed. Instead we now live in a 'network society'. Hardt and Negri, beneath a blizzard of language about rhizomes, transversality and nomadism, identify much the same thing. This network society was a flattened one in which 'nodes' of information were able to communicate directly with one another, obviating the need for large and territorially based hierarchies. The implications for war and security seemed, to those who accepted this thesis, profound: those powers that adapted correctly to the change would be able to exercise predominance over those who did not, and the United States was perfectly positioned to take advantage of its lead in information technology to grasp such hegemony (Singer 2009: 185). James Der Derian notes an address by the US chief of staff that speaks of how 'our present Army is well-configured to fight and win in the late Industrial Age . . . we have begun to move into Third Wave Warfare, to evolve a new force for a new century' (quoted in Der Derian 2009: 16). The notion of 'network-centric warfare' is not solely an American one, however: one of the key texts in the genre is

Unrestricted Warfare by two strategists for the Chinese People's Liberation Army, Qiao Liang and Wang Xiangsui (Betz and Stevens 2011: 76).

In the atmosphere of US triumphalism that pervaded discussions of international security after the Gulf War and the collapse of the Soviet Union, it was in the Pentagon where the idea of RMA was taken most seriously. A group of analysts associated with the Naval War College and the 'Office for Strategic and Budget Assessments' began to propose the idea as the foundation for a new US strategy. These analysts included men such as Vice Admiral Arthur Cebrowksi, Andrew Krepinevich, Jeffrey Cooper and – often described as a guru of sorts for the RMA enthusiasts – Andrew Marshall (Der Derian 2009: 27). Marshall seems early in the 1970s to have latched on to the idea that increases in micro-processing power would change warfare significantly, although apparently disavowing the 'revolution' label as a tactical exaggeration.

What were the components of the claimed revolution in military affairs? First of all came the advantages conferred by precision bombing at a distance: smart bombs and cruise missiles. Non-nuclear combat still depends, to put it rather crudely, on killing one's enemies by inserting lethal objects of some sort into them. Since the invention of projectiles – which allow one to threaten the enemy while being less at risk by virtue of distance – a balance has been struck between accuracy and distance (Metz and Kievit 1995: 4). One can be fairly certain of striking a deadly blow with a sword in hand-to-hand combat, less so with a bow and arrow, more so again with a firearm. The massive destruction wrought by aerial bombing relied until the 1980s more or less on flying directly above the target for any real degree of accuracy – conventional missiles from the Nazi V-2 to the Iraqi scud being notoriously inaccurate. Computer precision-guided weapons such as cruise missiles have become much more accurate, enabling the holders of such weapons (the US, in the main) to threaten massive destruction with apparent impunity, suggesting to some analysts the replacement of close-range encounters entirely with such weaponry (ibid.).

Again, a note of caution should be sounded here. The US made extensive use of smart weaponry in the 'shock and awe' campaign at the beginning of the 2003 invasion of Iraq. Yet, as outlined below, it would be difficult to describe the result of the following war as a victory for the United States. In part at least, this is ascribable to the difference between combat and occupation: one can pound an enemy into submission via computer-controlled weaponry but cannot rule a country day-to-day on that basis (although, as mentioned below, unmanned UAV drones may represent attempts to do precisely this). Moreover, these technologies can be seen as simply an extension of the 'Western way of war': utilizing superior technologies to remain at a distance from the battlefield and thereby to preserve the lives of Western combatants perceived to rank more highly in a racialized structure of life.

There is thus an important political dynamic behind the development of precision-guided munitions. Since the upheaval occasioned by American losses in Vietnam, US strategists have sought consistently to avoid high casualties (Singer 2009: 60). Precision-guided weaponry serves this political purpose.

These so-called precise, stand-off conventional strikes form the more tangible and pedestrian end of the RMA (Metz and Kievit 1995: 4). Strategists such as Andrew Marshall and Arthur Cebrowski were interested in how to harness information technology in 'network-centric warfare' to give the US a decisive advantage over its competitors (Singer 2009: 180). Cebrowski explained the meaning of this phrase, more often invoked than defined, as comprising three 'themes': a change from 'platform' to 'network', a change from 'actors as independent' to being part of a 'continuously adapting ecosystem', and the 'importance of making strategic choices to adapt or even survive in such changing ecosystems' (Cebrowski and Garstka 1998: 1). As with much of the RMA literature, Cebrowski borrows the language of the business press to obscure rather than explain, but the essence of the concept seems to be a shift from business making products (or soldiers using weapons) to networks of 'content' or information about the battlefield (ibid.: 2). 'Lock-in' had allowed certain technology companies a generation-long advantage: US strategy should seek to do likewise with network-centric warfare (ibid.: 3).

The RMA in theory and practice: Afghanistan and Iraq

The dream behind network-centric warfare was that what Clausewitz called 'the fog of war' would be lifted by the new information networks (Singer 2009: 185). Knowing what is going on, and ensuring that everyone has the same such information, is an almost insurmountable obstacle in combat. The proponents of network-centric warfare imagined that, with every combatant becoming a 'node' transmitting and exchanging information through online systems, war would become 'an essentially frictionless engineering exercise' (ibid.). This would confer on the US the advantage of 'speed of command', enabling 'forces to organize from the bottom up – or to self-synchronize – to meet the commander's intent' and thereby 'to offset a disadvantage in numbers, technology, or position' (Cebrowski and Garstka 1998: 5).

In retrospect, it is tempting to view the idea of network-centric warfare as an example of late twentieth-century 'dot com' hype, based firmly on the idea that an epochal change had taken place in the US economy and society in the 1990s and warfare had to follow suit (Cebrowski and Garstka 1998: 2). Some of the claims Cebrowski gives, such as Windows reducing Apple to a 'niche' producer or that the US economy was on a 'steady growth path', seem rather dated and good examples of why one should avoid drawing conclusions too strongly from possibly temporary phenomena. Nonetheless, the RMA theorists did win a consequential hearing in the Pentagon in the run-up to the US invasion of Iraq. Identifying innovation in information technology as one aspect of a US hegemony to be extended and preserved, the neo-conservative team of advisors around President George W. Bush fully accepted the premises of the RMA and network-centric warfare, increasing funding for such technologies by $20 billion on entering office (Singer 2009: 187).

The idea that 'speed and agility can take the place of mass' (Donald Rumsfeld, quoted in Singer 2009: 187) in network-centric warfare heavily influenced US post-invasion planning for the attack on Iraq. Rumsfeld created the 'Office of Force Transformation' and appointed Cebrowski to run it. Buoyed by the initial success of the invasion and occupation of Afghanistan, the proponents of the RMA argued that Iraq could be defeated with far fewer troops than the 680,000 of the 1991 Gulf campaign, initially suggesting 20,000, then revising the figure upwards to 135,000 at the insistence of experienced generals. This campaign of 'shock and awe', it was claimed, would be a version of blitzkrieg for the information age, utilizing the advantages of an RMA to overwhelm the enemy swiftly (ibid.:188).

What was the actual impact of the putative RMA on the invasion and occupation of Iraq and Afghanistan? Both campaigns defeated the initial resistance of the state very quickly – a little over three weeks in the case of Iraq and not much more in Afghanistan. Given the immense gap between the capabilities of the protagonists, it is difficult to say to what degree the new doctrines of network-centric warfare made a difference. It is difficult to imagine the US, a military power stronger than all its nearest competitors put together, losing in open field to the ramshackle forces of Southern states battered by years of war or sanctions. There may have been a 'force-multiplier' effect: the invasion of Iraq was accomplished with about one-fifth of the forces used in the 1991 Gulf War, while Afghanistan was initially conquered with only a few US special forces troops in alliance with Afghan opponents of the Taliban government.

Winning the invasion was merely a prelude to the far more difficult task for the US of mounting an occupation that would achieve strategic goals. When US forces were withdrawn from Iraq and scheduled for withdrawal from Afghanistan, President Barack Obama pointedly avoided using the word 'victory' (McGreal 2011). In Afghanistan, the ousted Taliban were being invited to join in negotiations about a post-occupation government, while in Iraq the widespread belief was that Iran was the true victor of the conflict. Several thousand US lives, and many more Afghans and Iraqis, had been lost in the interim.

Can it be said, then, that the so-called revolution in military affairs was a failure, or failed to live up to the hype? US and allied forces in Iraq and Afghanistan were very well equipped with information technology, each unit having a 'blue force tracker' that allowed them to know the location of every other unit. Reports were transmitted in enormous volumes of emails: it is these that formed the basis of the 'Wikileaks' disclosures made by Private

Bradley Manning. The prevalence of 'blue on blue incidents' (i.e. friendly fire) in that material indicates that the military network did not greatly dispel the fog of war even on the US side. 'Friction' persisted, with the computer equipment breaking down or running out of batteries (Singer 2009: 180). Yet perhaps the fundamental mistake made by the proponents of the RMA was to believe that networks would allow them to turn war into an engineering exercise rather than understanding its fundamentally political nature – and the fact that it has at least two sides. The opponents of the occupation, unsurprisingly, did not oblige US military networks with their information. In the end, the US began to stabilize (partially) the situation in Iraq only by making political decisions to cut its losses and work with its opponents: the Sunni 'Sons of Iraq' militia, who were turned against their former al-Qaeda allies, and the bloc of pro-Iranian Shi'a politicians and militiamen who would eventually form the government. In doing so, they turned away from notions of the 'revolution in military affairs' and towards (perhaps equally flawed) doctrines of colonial counter-insurgency.

Post-human warfare? US strategy and the rise of drones and robots

If the occupations of Iraq and Afghanistan did not see the epochal change in warfare foretold by the RMA theorists, a shift in the personnel of war was certainly visible. US forces began significantly to make use of various kinds of unmanned aerial vehicles (UAVs, or 'drones') and their land-borne counterparts in both combat and support roles. By 2008, there were twenty-two different kinds of robotic system operating in the US occupation forces in Iraq. When the US first invaded the country, there were no robotic systems in operation: by 2004 there were 150, and by 2008 the figure was projected to reach 12,000 (Singer 2009: 32).

These robots perform a variety of roles: on the ground they are used to transport materiel, for bomb disposal and even for combat. In the air they are used for intelligence gathering, bombing and assassination. On land the PackBot, a box-shaped robot with caterpillar tracks, is usually equipped with a camera and bomb disposal equipment (Singer 2009: 23). A similar machine, the 'Talons' system, is used by the US occupation forces in Iraq. The makers of the Talon also produce the so-called SWORDS robot, a version of the Talon with added weaponry that can be operated by remote control. Three of these were sent to Iraq and used in combat, but their guns were not fired: the US military has yet to give permission for such an action. In addition, US soldiers use a robot resembling a remote-controlled car, called MARCBOT, and to which they sometimes attach mines with which to attack anti-occupation forces. A plethora of such robots, often inspired by animals such as dogs or snakes, are being developed primarily for use by the US military: they have yet to use weapons in combat, however, perhaps reflecting concerns that they might point the guns the wrong way. Indeed, in 2007 a semi-autonomous cannon malfunctioned at a military display in South Africa, killing nine soldiers (Lin 2011).

While commanders have reservations about using unmanned or remote-controlled weapons systems on the ground, there is no such reticence about their use in the air. Undoubtedly the most significant use of unmanned military technology has occurred in the development of UAVs. The most notorious of these is the 'Predator' drone. The Predator, a relatively large piece of equipment about the size of a biplane, is flown by remote control by 'pilots' located in the US or any one of a reported sixty bases around the world – often with a local technician – in Afghanistan, for example – involved as well (Turse 2011). Drone use has grown enormously since the 2003 invasion of Iraq: in 2002 the US spent around $550 million on UAVs, a figure that had risen to $5 billion in 2011 (Lorenz, von Mittelstaedt and Schmitz 2011). In total, US forces by 2008 (including the notionally civilian CIA, which oversees most drone attacks in Pakistan) held 5,331 such drones in its inventory (Singer 2009: 57).

Aerial drones were originally used for surveillance and target designation but were soon adapted for attack purposes in Afghanistan (Singer 2009: 34). An eco-system of drones occupies the skies of Baghdad, from small 'Ravens' manually launched by soldiers themselves to enormous 'Hawk' spy drones mapping the entire country (ibid.: 37). President Obama proved far more willing to use aerial drone attacks – for example, in assassinating US citizen Anwar Al-Awlaki in Yemen – than his predecessor, George W. Bush. Whereas President Bush sanctioned, on average, one drone attack every forty-seven days, the average for President Obama was one every four days (Lorenz, von Mittelstaedt and Schmitz 2011). Of the 308 drone strikes since 2004, 256 took place under Barack Obama (Rushing 2011). So far, US UAVs are reported to have killed 2,300 people, according to some reports 20 per cent of them being civilians (Lorenz, von Mittelstaedt and Schmitz 2011). Many of these strikes have been in Yemen or Pakistan, the advantage of the drone being that it can be used to carry out killings in countries in which the US is not officially involved in conflict and without introducing ground troops. The Pentagon has begun to reconfigure the location of its overseas bases, mostly around the Arabian peninsula and East Africa, to permit most effective drone use (Turse 2011).

The most significant advantage of drone warfare, perhaps, is that it is comparatively cheap. Drones cost much less to build and operate than manned aircraft: a 24-hour manned reconnaissance mission requires eight F-15 planes, fifteen pilots and ninety-six mechanics, whereas a similar UAV mission requires only three drones, four operators and thirty-five mechanics (Santamaria 2011). One 'Reaper' drone costs ten times less than an F-22 'Raptor' fighter (Lorenz, von Mittelstaedt and Schmitz 2011). Indeed, so impressive has the cost-effectiveness of drones been that, in 2006, the US Senate Armed Forces Committee mandated that spending must be specially justified when it is *not* on unmanned technology (Singer 2009: 65). The US plans to spend $30 billion on drones up to the year 2020 (Rushing 2011).

What are the implications of the increasing use of unmanned weapons systems? The phenomenon has encouraged the belief that the use of drones and ground robots and the 'augmentation' or 'enhancement' of human soldiers will 'change the rules of the game' of war (Singer 2009: 376). This claim conjures up a vision akin to that of the *Terminator* film franchise, as networks of robotic weapons systems engage in combat against one another or potentially against hapless humans. Of course, the future is impossible to predict, but certainly one of the central arguments over unmanned weapons systems is whether they should be given the autonomy (which actually some already possess) to decide by algorithm when to take human life (Lin 2011). There have been remote-controlled weapons for actually rather a long time (both the USSR and Nazi Germany used them in the Second World War) but autonomous killing machines would mark a new era.

The question is indeed a troubling one, but again begins from technical rather than political premises and is therefore likely to misread the impact of these technologies. The salient characteristic, particularly of US UAVs, is that their use has been limited to what Laleh Khalili calls 'liberal counter-insurgency' (Khalili 2012: 5). The political imperative of the preservation of the lives of occupying soldiers – thereby attempting to avoid the domestic discontent that hampered the Vietnam War – has led to the development of these technologies that 'take our sons and daughters out of harm's way' (Rushing 2011). Yet, although killing may be becoming automated, dying most certainly is not: one report on drones in the technophile *Wired* magazine described how 'CIA drones kill large groups without knowing who they are' (Ackerman 2011). It is no accident that Israel has been the leading developer and user of drone technologies (Lorenz, von Mittelstaedt and Schmitz 2011) and that Turkey was the first state after the US and Israel to begin developing its own UAVs for use against Kurdish guerrillas. UAVs and unmanned ground systems are an extension in some sense of the air and technical superiority usually enjoyed by the counter-insurgent side in asymmetrical warfare.

Might robotic conflict between 'peer competitors' emerge, thereby changing the nature of war and strategy? There are already around forty states pursuing such technologies, in addition to non-state actors such as Hizbullah and the Libyan rebels who overran Muammar Gaddafi's regime in October 2011 (Rushing 2011). The US has strongly resisted the export of its UAV technology except to close allies, but this has not prevented other states from buying or developing their own – especially China, whose manufacturers have developed twenty-five new varieties of drones. Iran has also developed its own UAV, although the effectiveness of the device is in some doubt (Lorenz, von Mittelstaedt and Schmitz 2011). Again, it is difficult to tell the impact of these changes, although the trend is clearly in favour of the greater use of unmanned vehicles. It may be that this trend exacerbates, rather than over-turns, the decline in the perceived utility of massed ground combat between 'peer competitors' that has been observable since the beginning of the nuclear weapons age (Betz and Stevens 2011: 76). Next this chapter discusses the idea that a change is coming to international security that may mark such an epochal change: so-called cyber-war.

Cyber-war and cyber-battlespace

The notion of 'cyber-war' is closely related to that of 'network-centric warfare' or the revolution in military affairs. Indeed, with some versions of the ideas it can be difficult to distinguish between the two, but we can make a rough distinction by defining the idea of cyber-war as the transformation of the 'metaphorical place in which machine-mediated communications occur' into a space of combat (Betz and Stevens 2011: 13). This means, in the main, the internet, the World Wide Web that is accessed through it, and the physical infrastructure from which this interaction emerges. The idea of cyber-space as an additional realm of conflict (in the manner of air, land, sea or, in some readings, space) has become commonplace in the US military, to the extent that a cyber-command was established in 2010 (Lynn 2010: 101). The networks and infrastructure under the command of this body are indeed vast, compris-ing 15,000 networks, 7 million devices and 90,000 human operatives (ibid.: 100).

The idea of cyber-space as a new domain of war, and hacking of various kinds as a new tactic, has given rise to a great deal of speculation about the impact of cyber-attacks by terrorists, criminals or so-called rogue nations. For example, it is commonly repeated that the US has experienced cyber-attacks, especially from China (Klimburg 2011: 44), although one often struggles to find verifiable information about the number, nature or origin of these. At one end, these claims shade into rather breathless fantasies about the havoc likely to be wreaked by unknown entities on the infrastructure of modern life controlled by online networks (examples of which are to be found in Betz and Stevens 2011: 91–3). Such scenarios typically emphasize the dependence of most societies on cyber-space and therefore their vulnerability; the cheap-ness and universality of the technology required for an attack and therefore the widespread capacity for non-state actors to mount one; and the anonym-ity (and therefore impossibility of deterrence) with which a cyber-attack could be carried out. The fear of such an attack is such that US defence officials have threatened retaliation with conventional weaponry if subject to one: in the words of one Department of Defense spokesman: 'if you shut down our power grid, maybe we'll put a missile down one of your smokestacks' (quoted in Lin 2011).

What, however, is a cyber-attack, and how much impact is cyber-space likely to have on war and strategy? We have already dealt with the idea of network-centric warfare. Here we focus on the methods of cyber-attacks, such as they are. Perhaps the most widely known of these is the 'distributed denial of service' attack. An attack of this kind consists of causing a particular institution's servers to become clogged – a larger version of the phenomenon of downloads slowing down when there are many users on the same wireless network. The particular methods may vary – sending huge volumes of email requests through the servers or using up the bandwidth of the connection – but these attacks are difficult to attribute to a particular agency because they appear to be the outcome of many individual actions (Klimburg 2011: 41). Easier to ascribe to a particular origin (or at least to identify as having a point of origin) are viruses spread through the download-ing of data, which may then be able to control the infected system or acquire intelligence such as through logging key strokes. A group of computers con-trolled via such a virus is known as a 'botnet', and is a favourite tactic of online mafias.

What are the examples of such attacks used against the state, rather than simply for fraud? Political hacker groups such as 'Anonymous' have used denial of service attacks against state and corporate targets or have hacked into agencies such as the FBI when these have acted against perceived infringe-ments of the freedom of the internet (Williams 2012). One US defence analyst claims that more than one hundred intelligence agencies 'are engaged in trying to pierce the digital computer networks of the US military' (Lynn 2010: 107). No evidence is provided for this claim, but it would be surprising if such activity were not going on, and if the US were not reciprocating.

The best-known examples of 'cyber-war' come from Russia and China. There are two well-known instances, at least with the tacit support of the state, in Russia's relations with its neighbouring former Soviet republics. In 2007, Estonia experienced a massive denial of service attack that affected the banking system and the Parliament. Immediately before the war with Georgia in August 2008, denial of service attacks were launched against Georgian government websites and the country's routers were attacked: information on how to do this was provided on a number of Russian websites (Betz and Stevens 2011: 30). Did these cause significant damage, enough to speak, as the Estonian prime minister did, of a battle 'simply' between 'good and evil' (Klimburg 2011: 55)? Indeed, Estonia attempted to invoke the NATO charter to call its allies in defence (Farwell and Rohozinski 2011: 32). The cyber-attacks on Estonia and Georgia were undoubtedly malicious and harmful, but it would be something of an exaggeration to describe them as 'crippling' (ibid.) or to envisage them as fearful harbingers of an era of cyber-war. Esto-nian banks were shut down for an hour and a half on 9 May 2007, and for a further two hours on 10 May, and Estonian MPs were unable to send emails for several days. Georgia seems to have lost little from the cyber-attack, perhaps even gaining in the battle of online public opinon (Betz and Stevens 2011: 32).

The threat of Chinese cyber-attack is a recurrent theme in US and other Western literature on the topic (see Brimley 2010; Inkster 2010; Klimburg 2011). According to one US defence analyst, 'the PLA has integrated cyber-warfare units into its standard field-army organisation from 2003 onwards' and the Chinese government has encouraged a para-governmental network of perhaps 100,000 hackers (Klimburg 2011: 46). According to the same analyst, two-thirds of cyber-attacks on the US and EU originate from the Chinese mainland (ibid.: 44). Little concrete evidence is provided in defence of this figure, but there do appear to have been cyber-attacks from sites in the People's Republic. In 2003 the Pentagon claimed to have identified a series of attacks on its systems emanating from China, which they dubbed 'Titan Rain' (Inkster 2010: 55). In the run-up to the 2008 Beijing Olympics, Tibetan activists reported attacks against thousands of their computers: similar claims have been made by Taiwan and Western targets. China itself appears to fear for its own cyber-security given both the large (but decreasing) volume of Asian internet traffic that passes through the US and historic Western dominance over the medium (ibid.: 62–4).

What is definitely known is that the internet in China, as elsewhere, is an area of political contestation and one over which the Chinese Communist Party is keen to exercise control through the so-called Great Firewall of China and other measures. Google engaged in a high-profile confrontation with the Chinese government over these measures (Brannigan 2010). This has in some ways helped the Chinese regime, in that Chinese internet users now tend to use different applications from Europeans and North Americans – Baidu rather than Google and Ren Ren rather than Facebook. There are also large numbers of 'patriot hackers', variously encouraged, permitted or supported by the government, who take it upon themselves to launch cyber-attacks against those they consider enemies of the country (Klimburg 2011: 48). The People's Liberation Army is alleged to set up online identities through which they intervene on debates in blogs to steer them in pro-regime directions (Inkster 2010: 57).

None of these techniques are unknown to Western powers. After revealing thousands of diplomatic and military cables, the website Wikileaks was subject to a severe denial of service attack, 'apparently from hackers friendly to the point of view of the US government', which led to the withdrawal of hosting rights for the site from commercial providers (Arthur and Halliday 2010). The US air force, among other organizations, has also been accused of setting up online 'sock puppets' – automated identities to be used to comment on blogs and chatrooms to steer conversations (Monbiot 2011). In fact, two of the apparently most successful uses of cyber-warfare are alleged to have been carried out by the US. The first of these is a very early example: an explosion on the Trans-Siberian gas pipeline in 1982. Claims about this incident are hotly disputed, but a former US National Security official claimed that the CIA engineered flaws in the Canadian software used to control the pumps on the pipeline, resulting in malfunctions and a huge explosion (Safire 2004). Former KGB sources deny that there was any such interference (Medetsky 2004). Of more recent vintage, but also within the realm of murky denials of responsibility, is the so-called Stuxnet incident of 2010. Stuxnet was a computer virus, a 'worm' that infected systems at the Iranian nuclear facility at Natanz (Farwell and Rohozinski 2011: 23). It infected 60,000 computers in total, only about half of them in Iran. No responsibility was claimed for the attack, but the United States and Israel were widely assumed to be responsible.

Did Stuxnet show the future of cyber-war? If so, the future is not as terrifying as is sometimes made out. Estimates of the effectiveness of the worm vary, but at the highest it seems to have resulted in a 23 per cent slowdown of work at Natanz rather than a complete shut-down (Farwell and Rohozinski 2011: 29). The virus was 'quickly and effectively disarmed' when Iran turned to the internet to 'crowd-source' solutions to the problem (ibid.: 27). Furthermore, Stuxnet was 'air-gapped' – that is, it had to be introduced into the system, probably by a flash memory drive, rather than operating directly over the internet (ibid.: 24). It is difficult to know exactly how the worm was introduced, but if it had to be physically inserted then this suggests an operative on the inside – closer to traditional, difficult sabotage operations based on long-term intelligence than to a crippling and sudden attack from nowhere.

It is likely, of course, that more effective viruses than Stuxnet will be developed and used to further aims in the conflict between states. However, the very 'deliberate ambiguity' (Farwell and Rohozinski 2011: 27) with which Stuxnet was employed suggests limitations on cyber-war. Analysts of this field often display a concern with whether a cyber-attack would constitute an act of war, even though no 'kinetic exchange' takes place. The US argues that it would (Lin 2011). Does this change the nature of security strategy? If we agree with Clausewitz that war is an extension of politics, then it probably does not (Betz and Stevens 2011: 93). Any serious cyber-attack on civilian infrastructure would certainly cause large numbers of deaths (planes hitting runways, cars crashing into one another at traffic lights, and so forth) and would therefore not only invite retaliation but *be carried out with some aim in mind*. In that case, it would be entirely counterproductive not to claim responsibility: how would one bend the enemy to one's will if he is ignorant of who you are or what you want (ibid.: 95)? Contrary to popular belief, even al-Qaeda operates with such strategic logic. It is possible that a deranged nihilist might mount a completely unattributable cyber-attack, but this remains within the same realm of possibility, for example, as someone poisoning the water supply for no reason. If cyber-attacks are seen as a tactical addition to the armoury of war, then it becomes perhaps more reasonable to speak of 'cyber-skirmish' rather than 'cyber-war' (ibid.: 97).

Social networks, cyber-revolutions and security

Cyber-attacks and network-centric warfare represent one side of the (perceived) impact of new technology on global politics – that of conflict between states; on the other lies what we might call the 'revolution in political affairs'. Since at least the early years of the twenty-first century, analysts have claimed that online networks, mobile telephony and, especially, social media have led to a rash of popular uprisings, insurgencies and revolutions, from the so-called colour revolutions in former Eastern bloc states through to the 'Arab Spring' and the global anti-capitalist 'Occupy' movement. In some versions of this argument, these technologies and networks are inherently amenable to a liberal version of democracy and therefore to the spread of US influence (Bremmer 2010; Shirky 2011). In others, these events reflect the arrival of 'a new sociological type': the graduate 'with no future' but with access to social media that allow them to channel their frustrations into non-hierarchical movements (Mason 2012a).

The effect of social media, particularly on the overthrow of authoritarian regimes, is hotly disputed. Clayton Shirky argues that the 'use of social media tools –text messaging, e-mail, photo sharing, social networking and the like – does not have a single preordained outcome', but 'these tools probably do not hurt in the short run and might help in the long run' and 'have the most dramatic effects in states where a public sphere already constrains the actions of the government' (Shirky 2011: 29). Shirky claims, in an argument apparently tailored for debates within the US State Department before the Arab Spring, that social media cannot simply be used instrumentally to promote US goals (assumed to be democratic ones) but rather it is the slow growth of a free media environment that will best serve that end (ibid.: 40). However, and here we find the common thread with notions of network-centric warfare, mobile text messaging and internet services allow 'larger, looser groups' to 'take on some kinds of coordinated action, such as protest movements and public media campaigns, that were previously reserved for formal organizations' using 'what the military calls "shared awareness"' (ibid.: 35). Such an idea is reflected in what has become a common understanding in some of the movements under discussion – for example the 'Occupy' protests, which made much of their formally non-hierarchical consensus decision-making structure.

A particularly strong version of this argument is put forward by Paul Mason, who does not accept the rather uncritical faith in the US of other writers on the topic (Shirky 2011: 29; Bremmer 2010: 87). Mason claims that the economic crisis that began in 2008 created a flammable social situation comparable to that of the late nineteenth century: 'a large and radicalised intelligentsia, a slum-dwelling class finding its voice through popular culture, and a weakened proletariat, still wedded to the organisations and traditions of 20 years before' (Mason 2012). The impact of social media on the uprisings of 2011 represented a delayed version of the similar impact of information technology on business, culture and industry in the preceding decade. The key aspect of these media, again, is that they form a network whose utility increases to each user the more users there are. It is the development of mobile telephones, even more than laptops, that permits the formation of such networks and the utilization of a 'suite' of applications: 'Facebook is used to form groups, covert and overt – in order to establish those strong but flexible connections. Twitter is used for real-time organisation and news dissemination, bypassing . . . the mainstream media. YouTube and the Twitter-linked photographic sites . . . provide instant evidence of the claims being made' (ibid.). These technologies, Mason claims, have encouraged a wave of global popular protest as 'memes' of street protest and the occupation of public space spread through the new networks (ibid.).

These points are made from a standpoint broadly sympathetic to the aims of the protestors. Yet, even where government and commentators are hostile to waves of collective action, they still point to the alleged impact of new network technologies. For example, a common theme during the riots in English cities in the summer of 2011 was the claim that youth gangs were using instant messaging services on Blackberry smartphones (a more secure network than ordinary text messages) to coordinate the riots (Halliday 2008). The parallel is indeed ironic when one considers the call by UK media and government figures to restrict or shut down these services just after previous Western condemnation of Middle Eastern states seeking to do exactly the same thing (Bremmer 2010: 91). However, a London School of Economics study found that, although Blackberry phones were certainly the communication method of choice during the riots, the causes behind them seem largely to have been familiar ones – poverty, alienation and dislike of the police (Lewis et al. 2011).

Scholars such as Evgeny Morozov make the point that the internet and associate technology may even serve the purpose of authoritarian control. The medium tends to promote the titillating, the trivial and the pornographic over serious public discourse and therefore may distract rather than empower the citizenry (Morozov 2011). It may produce 'slacktivism', in which people consider their political commitments absolved by joining a Facebook group or signing an online petition. Also sites like Facebook and Twitter can actually provide an immense source of information for secret police and security services of various kinds to track and suppress dissent. They are places of surveillance as much as liberation. Among bloggers and activists of, for example, the Egyptian revolution themselves there seems little enthusiasm for the notion of a 'Facebook revolution'. Hossam el-Hamalawy, a revolutionary journalist and writer of the prominent blog '3arabawy', relates that, under the Mubarak regime, independent media such as blogs did become an important source of uncensored information (el-Hamalawy 2011). The internet had a role, argues el-Hamalawy, but this was most prominent in conveying the events of the revolution to its supporters abroad. More important was the wave of strikes that began in Egypt (a country where only 25 per cent of the population has internet access) among workers who for the most part did not have Twitter or Facebook. When the Mubarak regime cut off internet access on the weekend of the 28 January 2011, the resulting protests – organized by leafleting and simply walking through areas calling on people to join – were even larger. Satellite TV also played a role: the activists were able to put a statement on Al-Jazeera publicizing where demonstrations would begin (ibid.).

What then is the role of the new networks? For the most part both the boosters and detractors of the idea agree that 'saying that people want a revolution because of "social media" is akin to saying that people want a revolution because of the telephone' (Morozov 2011). However, the telephone was not an inconsequential technology – for example, in the Russian Revolution, even where very few members of the population had access to one – and the new social networks may be the same. They may operate, like 'cyber-warfare', mainly at a tactical level. Twitter is often used for information about where demonstrations are going on, how to outwit police, and so on, endowing confrontations with a greater fluidity and mobility. Mobile phones are even more widespread for this purpose. However, the people giving out such information must trust and respect one another in ways that are more likely to be the result of patient political work or ideological identification than online-only encounters. It is possible that these networks are changing the way contentious street politics happens – even the ease with which it can happen – but not the underlying reasons.

Conclusion

Vladimir Lenin described the early years of the twentieth century as an 'epoch of wars and revolutions'. Does the beginning of the twenty-first century mark an era of cyber-wars and information revolutions? The evidence surveyed in this chapter suggests that, at the very least, we must differentiate between the effects of different technologies, and the levels at which their impact may be felt, in order to answer this question correctly.

Much has been made of the 'revolution in military affairs' and its effect on US strategy after the Cold War. What is certain is that the idea of an ensemble of remote-controlled and autonomous weaponry, and the integration of battlefield information through various information networks, strongly influenced the planning for war in Iraq and Afghanistan. The failure of the US to achieve its strategic aims in these campaigns may be taken as a judgement on some of the more extravagant claims made for 'network-centric warfare'. A lasting change may have emerged in the US wars on Iraq, Afghanistan and elsewhere in the use of robotic systems. The numbers of these have increased significantly, and they do now influence strategic decisions – for example, about the placement of bases and the response to the perceived threat of Islamist groups based in remote areas of countries such as Pakistan or Yemen. However, it is yet to be seen whether this technology can be extended from the realm of 'liberal counter-insurgency', to which it is particularly well suited, and into geopolitical competition among peers.

What of the potential of cyber-space as an arena and technique of combat? As we have seen, the dependence of most societies on this infrastructure means that vulnerability to cyber-attacks is real. Yet, at least in the examples seen so far in the Baltic region, the Russo-Georgian war of 2008 and the Stuxnet worm, the results have been less than devastating. It seems that cyber-war is more of a tactical than a strategic innovation. The same can be said for the idea of political revolutions inspired and effected through online networks. These social media have certainly been important for activists, but the entry to them (through personal trust and ideological affinity) and the power they mobilize (street fighting, protests, strikes) remain those of the pre-internet age. All things may change, of course, but at present it seems that the new technologies of the late twentieth and early twenty-first century may have changed aspects of how wars and revolutions happen, but not yet why.

FURTHER READING

The subject of technological change, international security and society naturally tends to attract more speculative writing than others, especially with regards to 'cyber-war' and social networking. Peter Singer's *Wired for War* (2009) addresses most of the topics discussed in this chapter, albeit in rather breathless and uncritical fashion, and puts forward a strong assertion that robot technology in particular is irrevocably changing the nature of warfare. James Der Derian's *Virtuous War: Mapping the Military–Industrial–Media–Entertainment Complex* (2009) covers similar ground, with particularly good material on the 'revolution in military affairs' and its affinities to the obsession with airpower and blitzkrieg between the First and Second World War: it is constructed more as a travelogue than a conventional work of social science, however, and some readers may be unfamiliar with Der Derian's references to thinkers such as Walter Benjamin and Paul Virilio.

The main policy documents outlining the case for 'network-centric warfare' and the RMA are publicly available and can be read online: these are Arthur Cebrowski and John Garstka, 'Network-centric warfare: its origin and future', in *Proceedings of the US Naval Institute* (1998); Steven Metz and James Kievit's pamphlet on *Strategy and the Revolution in Military Affairs* (1995); and Andrew Krepinevich's *The Military-Technical Revolution* (2002). Richard A. Clarke and Robert Knake argue for cyber-war as an imminent threat in *Cyber-War* (2010), while David Betz and Tim Stevens's paper for the International Institute for Strategic Studies *Cyberspace and the State* (2011) takes a more sanguine view of the threat. There are a number of books on unmanned weapons systems, mostly concerning their technical specifications: however, the US congressional report *Rise of the Drones: Unmanned Systems and the Future of War* (2010) outlines the place of drones in current US strategy, while Medea Benjamin's *Drone Warfare* (2012) takes a more critical look at the technology from the point of view of its victims. Much of the debate around drones concerns the ethics and legality of their use – Patrick Lin's 'Drone-ethics briefing', in *The Atlantic* (2011), provides a good introduction.

The debate over the impact of social media on politics is also quite polarized. Clay Shirky's *Here Comes Everybody: The Power of Organizing without Organizations* (2008) puts the case that social media are overturning existing models of society, while Evegeny Morozov's book *The Net Delusion: The Dark Side of Internet Freedom* (2012) makes the more pessimistic opposite argument. Paul Mason's *Why It's Kicking Off Everywhere: The New Global Revolutions* (2012) presents a 'network'-based account of the wave of global popular unrest in 2011, including the Arab revolutions, conclusions that are questioned by Miriyam Aouragh and Anne Alexander's 'Sense and nonsense of Facebook revolutions' in the *International Journal of Communication* special issue on 'Arab Revolutions and New Media' (2011).

Questions for Research and Discussion

1 Has the so-called revolution in military affairs really revolutionized the way wars are conducted since the end of the Cold War?
2 To what extent is cyber-warfare a serious new threat to international security?
3 Have the internet and social media advanced freedom in the world?

WEBSITES

www.rand.org/topics/cyber-warfare.html
RAND research which provides recommendations to military and civilian decision-makers on methods of defending against the damaging effects of cyber-warfare.

www.wired.com/dangerroom/
Wired magazine's 'Danger Room' blog covers contemporary developments concerning national security and cyber-warfare.

http://droneswatch.org/
Droneswatch is a campaigning organization to monitor and regulate the use
of drones.

www.arabawy.org/
3arabawy blog by Hossam el-Hamalawy, an example of a very popular and
influential Egyptian activist blogger.

Conclusion: The Challenges for the Future

This book provides one distinctive approach to the unravelling of the complex realities of post-Cold War international security. It embraces the intellectual liberation of the broader security agenda, incorporating non-traditional but increasingly salient issues such as migration, resource scarcity and environmental security. It also reflects the increasing recognition of the inherent complexities of the phenomena of international security – how, in dealing with security issues, one confronts the unknown as much as the known; the subjective as much as the objective reality; issues where the policy options are often unclear and indeterminate; and stakes which are often very high, involving the protection of values deemed critical to the interests of the actors concerned. The task of the security analyst is inevitably challenging and demanding.

A key theme running through the book is the need for such an analyst to balance three different but inevitably interconnected roles: those of scientist, internationalist and moralist. The scientific role is arguably the most critical, demanding a rigorous evaluation of the most significant dangers and threats to international security through analysis based on the best evidence available. In many parts of this book, this involves puncturing some of the more gloomy and pessimistic scenarios and threat assessments. The book demonstrates that many fears – such as of imminent environmental catastrophe, or impending resource scarcity, or migration-induced conflict, or terrorist use of weapons of mass destruction – often involve exaggerated claims which come to be significantly qualified and moderated by more dispassionate and evidence-based analysis. While focusing on contemporary dangers, the book also recognizes the benefits to international security of the end of the Cold War: the consolidation of the great power peace, the ending of the East–West ideological division, the reduction in nuclear arsenals, the reinvigoration of the United Nations, and the increasing role played by humanitarian concerns in seeking to resolve civil wars and to subdue internal repression. Although security studies inevitably tends to be a 'gloomy science', this is no reason to ignore advances made or to overestimate the dangers that are present.

The second role of the security analyst, as internationalist, involves the intellectual challenge of transcending the limitations of a narrow cultural or national perspective on international security issues. There is a natural, and perhaps inevitable, tendency within security studies to assume the primacy of a specifically national or Western conceptualization of the key security challenges. There is nothing illegitimate in itself in such a focus. As argued in various sections in the book, states assume a strongly realist and communitarian response to developments perceived to be directly threatening to their own citizens, as with fears of uncontrolled migration, the growth of international terrorism, or WMD proliferation. But the book consistently argues that a comprehensive conceptualization of international security demands broader perspectives, rooted in an understanding of global historical processes, of the multiple ways in which relations between states have developed and the legacies they have left, and of the complex mix of local, regional and international sources of conflict and insecurity. A key theme has been how the East–West Cold War framework has shifted to a North–South context, where the core issues are inequalities of wealth and political status and the resentments these have generated. It is from the South, particularly from the so-called arc of crisis from North-East Asia through the Middle East to sub-Saharan Africa, that many of the most critical security threats have their origin. Durable solutions to such threats and conflicts require a multidimensional approach, where the security analyst contributes by bringing out more clearly the complex set of interrelations and differing perspectives.

The security analyst as moralist provides the broader overarching normative context. Again, a key theme of the book is its refusal to accord security an exceptional status, somehow beyond politics and divorced from moral considerations. Security is not part of an amoral realm, separate from humanitarian or other normative concerns. Rather, it is an irreducible and integral part of politics, where politics is itself understood as a process of contestation of values, and where security is one value, however critical, alongside others such as freedom, prosperity and justice. As a result, the security analyst cannot remain detached from the value-charged debate over the politics of international security. For example, the suffering of the destitute caught up in conflicts in desperately poor parts of the world raises questions of international justice which cannot be ignored. The implementation of security measures has economic costs, threatening the prosperity which ultimately provides the core foundation of security. And the balance between freedom and security, values which are literally inseparable, must be foremost in the security analyst's mind. There is a constant need to wrestle with the paradox that the quest for security by states can potentially provide the conditions both for freedom and for subjugation.

In balancing these three roles of the security analyst, the book pursues a constructive dialogue between the major theoretical traditions in international relations. There has been no attempt to impose a rigid theoretical straitjacket. Theories have been treated as competing, and often complementary, analytical lenses which help the analyst to identify patterns of order in the complex flux of international developments. Theories prove their utility by the extent to which they illuminate the issues under examination. It is this pragmatic approach, eschewing predetermined theoretical preferences, which this book has followed.

Nevertheless, the book generally welcomes the post-Cold War shift from rationalist-dominated accounts, most notably that of neo-realism, to constructivist theories, where the intersubjective and normative dimensions of contemporary international security can more adequately be incorporated. While neo-realism has certainly retained powers of explanation, constructivist theories have provided new and richer insights. Thus securitization theory provides renewed understanding of how security issues are intersubjectively constructed; human security provides a salutary reminder of the insecurities of the poor and dispossessed and the suffering they endure, not least from the states which formally should provide their protection; and the various strands of critical security highlight the Northern-dominated and masculinist logic of much of the dominant security discourse. As this book argues, these various contributions have reinvigorated the liberal internationalist tradition, where the struggle for a more cosmopolitan law-based international order is seen as the precondition for international security.

However, while welcoming these developments away from a rigidly neo-realist perspective, the book qualifies them in two important ways. First, the tradition of historical sociology provides a supplement to constructivist accounts. The contribution that historical sociology offers is in its more hard-nosed materialist account of how norms and values can be instrumentally manipulated and offers a corrective to some of the idealist tendencies in constructivist scholarship. This tradition also provides a historical depth to the understanding of how social power has emerged over the longer-term historical trajectory, and how this has led to the contemporary distribution of power, with its multiple inequalities and divisions. In addition, historical sociology provides a more sophisticated conceptualization of the state which neither reifies it, as in neo-realism, nor seeks to dissolve it, as in certain variants of liberal internationalism. Rather, as argued throughout this book, the state is best understood as a Janus-faced actor, certainly a source of much of the violence and aggression of modern times, but also as a vital source of communal identity and the civilizing and disciplining of other social forces and actors. Historical sociology points to the strategic imperative of the need to strengthen and empower states, rather than to seek to dissolve or undermine them, and in so doing to create both the infrastructural power to promote synergistic state–society relations and the framework for peaceful political and economic interchange.

The second qualification is in the proposed revival of the normative tradition of classical realist thought. The argument here is that this tradition, which has a close affinity to liberal communitarian thought, highlights the imperfect and messy nature of international behaviour, where universal moral aspirations constantly conflict with the empirical realities of state political interest, of differing cultures and communities of value, and of the complex vein of historical legacies and memories of resentment. The value of the realist tradition is that it inculcates a certain scepticism of expectations of a radical normative transformation, advocating a moral prudentialism which recognizes the limits of international sympathy and the primacy that states, as the most powerful actors in the system, accord to the interests of their own citizens over and above those of foreigners. It is also a precaution-ary warning that grand schemes for international change need to be very carefully managed if they are not to have multiple unintended consequences which undermine rather than strengthen international security.

Anxieties for the future

The influence of these more historically sensitive and critical accounts ensures that this book avoids a too optimistic or Panglossian expectation for interna-tional security. As argued above, the end of the Cold War has brought many advances to international security, and many of the more alarmist fears emerging since the end of the Cold War have been shown to be exaggerations and distortions of the reality. But, in avoiding the dangers of excessive secu-ritization, it is important not to fall into the trap of complacency and an underestimation of present dangers and threats. One observation and conclu-sion of this book is that post-Cold War developments have also contributed to a deterioration of much of the international security environment. The early post-Cold War optimism, which led most notably to the revitalization of the United Nations, has increasingly foundered on a number of seemingly intractable problems. These include the prevalence of ethnic conflict, such as in the former Yugoslavia, sub-Saharan Africa and Afghanistan; the rise of transnational terrorism dedicated to indiscriminate slaughter; and the fraying of the restraints on WMD proliferation. International trust, which is the essential glue of international security, has become increasingly tested and strained.

Security analysts are not, though, good at gazing at crystal balls and pre-dicting the future. This is not surprising, as the international system is complex, with a seemingly insignificant event or development in one part of the world capable of triggering an unprecedented crisis in the system as a whole. The way in which the strategically forgotten Afghanistan of the 1990s became the incubator for the most serious terrorist challenge ever encoun-tered is symptomatic of this, as is the apparent initial success of the interven-tion into Afghanistan in 2002 and seeming defeat of the Taliban turning into a prolonged and revived insurgency by the very same Taliban forces. But this recognition of the indeterminacy of the future does not mean that the secu-rity analyst is absolved from articulating concerns over contemporary trends and developments which appear to presage dangers in the future. For this author, two concerns have the power to keep me, at times, awake at night – these are, first, doubts about the capacity of the international system, and most critically the more powerful developed countries, to manage the devolution of power from North to South over the coming decades; and, second, the security implications of the evident strategic shift, particularly after 9/11, from the Cold War tradition of defensive balance to offensive primacy.

International security and the devolution of power

The twentieth century was marked by a significant devolution of power from the North to the South. The termination of the European empires and the process of decolonization devolved political sovereignty and territorial integrity to multiple new states. As of 2012, there are 193 states at the UN, as compared to the fifty-one original signatories of the UN Charter in 1945. This remarkable process of political liberation, which has consolidated a strong anti-imperialist norm, is a highly significant development. But this formal political equality coexists with considerable economic and political inequalities, where the North continues to dominate economic and political power. The major failure of the century which has passed was the inability to make much inroad into bridging this divide. In fact, global inequality has tended to increase rather than diminish, despite relative success stories such as in East Asia. During the last century, only one country managed to make the transition into the developed Northern world – Japan. Even with the fast growth in China and India in the twenty-first century, these two dynamic economies still have large-scale poverty and will remain developing countries for at least the next few decades.

It is as much a security as a developmental challenge to ensure that the international system in the twenty-first century does a better job in promoting global prosperity and a more equitable distribution of that wealth. One parameter identifying the magnitude of this challenge is demographic. As noted in chapter 8, the world's population is projected to grow from the present-day 7 billion to over 9 billion in the year 2050 before it is expected to level off. Almost all of this demographic growth is going to take place in the South. For the Southern countries concerned, this will add considerably to the difficulties of managing the complex process of economic development. For the North, the temptation will be to sustain its current political and economic dominance, accentuating the already existing inequalities, despite at the same time becoming demographically more marginal. Such consolidation of the North–South divide can only be expected to increase international tensions. The next forty to fifty years are, therefore, a highly critical period.

The challenge is particularly acute in ensuring that the processes of development in fast-growing countries, which inevitably bring with them severe dislocation, a popular sense of alienation and social unrest, are managed in ways which do not threaten broader international security. Most of the core security threats identified in this book will only be resolved by such successful management, along with intensive North–South cooperation. Global environmental challenges, such as climate change, will only intensify in the process of the devolution of economic power to the South, as is already seen in the shift to mass car societies in China and India. Global migration pressures, particularly into the land of plenty in the North, will inevitably increase. The pressure on vital energy resources, such as oil and water, will also intensify, with the high prices for oil an indication of this. More generally, the danger of the emergence of extreme ideologies, breeding on the resentments of perceived global injustices and the dislocations and alienation of local development, can be expected to remain a potent source of conflict. The devolution of power through the spread of more sophisticated weaponry, most notably in terms of WMD, adds to the magnitude of the challenges ahead.

The developed Northern countries, with their economic, political and military capacities, naturally and rightly have a special responsibility for managing this complex process of transition. The difficulty is that the developmental demands of the South are far from homogeneous. Table 3.1 (p. 72) gives a typology which distinguishes between globalizing, praetorian and failed states in the South. This schema provides an inevitably rough but useful way of identifying and differentiating the key challenges. For those globalizing states where substantial progress has already been made, such as China or India or Brazil, the critical task is to encourage and welcome their emergence as rising powers, to see their economic development as an opportunity rather than a threat, and to accommodate their rightful claims to be more fully incorporated into the institutions and regimes of global governance. This is not going to be easy to manage. Tensions are apparent with China's failure to adopt the democratic norm which underpins the Western security community and with India's demand to be a nuclear weapons state, despite the requirements of the Nuclear Non-Proliferation Treaty. Both countries, as with most others in the South, have painful memories of past colonial injustices. In the North, domestic political forces also raise strong internal fears of how these rising economic giants might threaten their economic and political gains.

In terms of the so-called praetorian states, where the regimes in power form one of the main obstacles to developmental progress, the challenge is in identifying the most effective ways of encouraging economic and political reform. One dimension of this was discussed in chapter 7, where the resource wealth of a number of these countries often leads import-dependent states to compromise demands for political and economic reform on the altar of energy security. The empirical record of external actors, such as the main international financial institutions and developmental agencies, is also one of a general failure to encourage effective reforms in the absence of conditions which are already propitious for such reforms. There is, unfortunately, no easy blueprint for development. Paradoxically, one of the main obstacles is a consequence of the historical process of the devolution of power, which has created sovereign states whose ruling elites are simply uninterested in economic and political development. However, the 'Arab Spring' in the Middle East indicates that popular pressure, reacting to the sense of humiliation at the continued predations of the ruling authoritarian regimes, has the power to subvert and challenge these unjust structures of power. The challenge for the rest of the international community is to support these nascent forces for political democratization.

These dilemmas are, though, more acute with the third category of failing or failed states. The picture here is not necessarily all gloomy. As argued in chapter 4, progress has been made in rejuvenating the UN and other bodies for the task of taking over control of failed states and reconstructing them into more effective and sustainable states. But, as was also noted, the post-Cold War record is mixed, with as many failures as successes. The challenge here is to ensure effective interventions which do not create a dependency culture and do not resurrect fears of imperialist imposition. Even more critical is ensuring that domestic support for such action from the richer and more capable states is sustained and that the human security demand for a 'preferential option to the poor' is preserved. The danger of the Western withdrawal from Afghanistan, scheduled for 2014, is that the country will again descend into the lawless anarchy of the 1990s and be forgotten by the outside world.

In essence, the challenge for the North is not to turn away from these complex challenges which will be critical to future international security. The main danger is that the desired devolution of power is perceived as a threat to existing values and power relations, encouraging an inward-looking and protectionist attitude. The economic recession which has afflicted most of the developed world since 2008 has only accentuated the dangers of such a shift to a beggar-my-neighbour approach. If this does materialize, it would be a recipe for a return to the conditions of the 1930s, with all their tragic consequences.

From the primacy of defence to offence

The Cold War system can be seen in retrospect to have been a relatively static and conservative order, despite the rhetoric on both sides about their revolutionary credentials and their deep mutual animosity. The military stalemate, which was consolidated and entrenched by the nuclear stand-off, created a system, as described in chapter 10, based on the principles of mutual balance and the preservation of the existing status quo, with a strategic primacy accorded to defence over offence.

There were, certainly, other processes and dynamics which challenged this dominant East–West security management system. Decolonization, and the devolution of power to the South, created new actors which sought to disrupt the hegemonic status quo. Paradoxically, however, the end result was ultimately a strengthening of the system, as the newly formed states defended the principles of territorial integrity and the inviolability of borders even more fervently than those powers which had originally granted them their political independence. Globalization was arguably a more potent disruptive force, empowering actors which transcended or ignored state borders, threatening the legitimacy of the states to which they were formally subordinated. Many of these transnational processes provided substantive benefits, most notably in terms of economic integration, but there were others, such as transnational terrorism and global crime, whose power and influence represent severe threats to international order.

Overall, though, the Cold War period was characterized by an increasingly effective and seemingly durable East–West management system. Indeed, its success was ultimately instrumental in dissolving the root causes of the conflict, leading to the dramatic reduction in the level of militarized East–West confrontation and ultimately the demise of the Soviet empire. In practice, though, the dismantling of the Cold War system did not result, at least immediately, in the dissolution of the practices and norms underlying its management. Rather, these principles and norms were strengthened so as to enhance international cooperation in resolving the legacies of the residual Cold War insecurities and in confronting new emerging challenges. The network of Cold War institutions, such as the UN and NATO, were given new powers and enhanced legitimacy to pursue their security management roles. Cold War security regimes, such as the NPT and other arms control regimes, including the various inspection agencies monitoring the compliance of state parties, were strengthened. And for even more complex and intractable issues, such as climate change or the hitherto sacrosanct principle of sovereign immunity, concerted attempts were made to construct regimes which would facilitate cooperation based on mutual respect and common interests

However, during the course of the 1990s and 2000s, this familiar Cold War conservative order, based on principles of balance and the primacy of defence, became increasingly frayed. There were multiple factors behind this, making it difficult to determine the precise causal linkages. In part, its weakening was due to the unique power capacities possessed by the United States in the absence of its Soviet competitor, with no alternative power centres apparently capable of matching or attempting to balance the combined accumulation of American military, economic and political power. In the aftermath of 9/11, the US sought to 'unshackle' itself from those international commitments and norms which it felt constrained its autonomy of action. During this period, a weakened Russia became increasingly resentful that its voice in international affairs was being ignored and that developments appeared to threaten rather than enhance its position. Russia found itself increasingly an opponent rather than a partner in international security operations, such as in Bosnia and Kosovo in the 1990s and in Libya and Syria in 2011–12. China experienced a similar sense of wilful neglect when its new-found wealth and confidence was not translated into the international influence it believed was its due. Even loyal European allies from the Cold War period found that their advocacy and influence were increasingly ineffective, as was harshly revealed in the US decision to invade Iraq in 2003 in the absence of a European consensus on the war.

The high point of this shift to a strategy of strategic offence based on military predominance was reached in the aftermath of 9/11 and was formally codified in the 2002 US National Security Strategy, where it was argued that 'America is now threatened less by conquering states than by failing ones. We are menaced less by fleets and armies than by catastrophic technologies in the hands of the embittered few' (White House 2002: 1). The US took on itself the strategic imperative to act pre-emptively against terrorist groups and 'rogue states' which openly defy and challenge the principles of the legitimacy of the broader international order. The disastrous consequences of the post-2003 occupation of Iraq effectively undermined this hubristic overextension of the United States. The election of Barack Obama to the presidency in 2008 heralded a significant shift in US foreign policy outlook which helped to restore, at least initially, relations with both Russia and China and with European allies. Suspicion and distrust of the US in the Middle East was also partly dissolved by the US support for the Arab Spring and the unleashing of indigenous political change in the region.

The situation has, therefore, improved significantly from the time of writing of the first edition of this book in 2006, when the Iraqi civil war was at its height, Israel and Lebanon were engaged in a bloody war, the threat of al-Qaeda was still strong, and the authoritarian structures of power in the Middle East appeared to be unassailable. Nevertheless, in late 2012 there still remain significant international tensions and causes for concern. The economic recession has weakened the West but not necessarily diluted its interventionist tendencies. The NATO engagement in Libya in 2011 appeared to restore the Western appetite for humanitarian intervention. And the continued intransigence of Iran in relation to its nuclear programme has again raised the spectre of a Western-led pre-emptive military strike against the Iranian regime. In the meantime, Russia and China have not only become economically and militarily stronger but also remained politically authoritarian and strongly resistant to the doctrine of offensive intervention on humanitarian grounds promoted by Western countries. Russia and China joined together to support the Syrian regime in its counter-offensive against its internal armed insurrection in 2011–12 and ensured that no decision by the United Nations would permit any form of external armed intervention. Both countries also remain firmly opposed to any military action against Iran.

These differences in strategic approach among the major powers reflect some fundamental divergences in ideology and understanding of international relations. For Russia and China, as for many of the emerging powers, the principles of sovereignty and non-intervention are paramount and should be respected even if the domestic political regimes do not meet the 'Western' norms of democracy and respect for human rights. For the United States, and for the West more generally, there remains the conviction that the international order should, as Raymond Aron terms it (1966: 99–104), be 'homogeneous' rather than 'heterogeneous' and where democracy and capitalism have an ideological supremacy. In cases where these values are egregiously assaulted, the Western presumption remains that external intervention is not only justified but asserts a certain moral obligation. However, in conditions where the West no longer has the capability merely to assert its strategic preferences, the danger is that these fundamental ideological differences will result in international paralysis and increasing international tension. The impotence of the great powers to be able to cooperate effectively to deal with the challenges presented by Iran, North Korea, Israel/Palestine and multiple other conflicts has, as a consequence, worrying echoes of 1914. The hope, and the challenge for the security analyst, is to find and articulate a renewed international consensus which can support the construction of an order that brings genuine stability, security and prosperity.

Questions for Research and Discussion

1 What are the major challenges for international security into the future?
2 How does the decline of the West affect international security over the next coming decades?

WEBSITES

www.dni.gov/nic/NIC_2025_project.html
The official website of the National Intelligence Council, which published an influential report entitled *Global Trends: 2050*.

www.acus.org/program/strategic-foresight-initiative
The Atlantic Council's Strategic Foresight Initiative, which seeks to enhance understanding of the potential impact and the policy implications of long-term global trends, disruptive change, and strategic shocks. There are also a number of useful publications.

References

Acharya, A. (2001) *Constructing a Security Community in Southeast Asia: ASEAN and the Problem of Regional Order*. London: Routledge.

Acharya, A. (2003–4) 'Will Asia's past be its future?', *International Security*, 28(3): 165–80.

Acharya, A. (2004) 'How ideas spread: whose norms matter? Norm localization and institutional change in Asian regionalism', *International Organization*, 58(2): 239–76.

Acharya, A. (2009) *Whose Ideas Matter? Agency and Power in Asian Regionalism*. Ithaca, NY: Cornell University Press.

Ackerman, S. (2011) 'CIA drones kill large groups without knowing who they are', *Wired.com*, 4 November, at www.wired.com/dangerroom/2011/11/cia-drones-marked-for-death/#more-62270 (accessed 10 April 2012).

Acton, J. M. (2011) *Deterrence during Disarmament*. London: Routledge.

Adebajo, A. (2002) *Building Peace in West Africa: Liberia, Sierra Leone, and Guinea-Bissau*. Boulder, CO: Lynne Rienner.

Adler, E., and Barnett, M. N. (eds) (1998) *Security Communities*. Cambridge: Cambridge University Press.

Adler, E., and Greve, P. (2009) 'When security community meets balance of power: overlapping regional mechanisms of security governance', *Review of International Studies*, 35: 59–84.

Agamben, G. (1998) *Homo Sacer: Sovereign Power and Bare Life*. Stanford, CA: Stanford University Press.

Agamben, G. (2005) *States of Exception*. Chicago: University of Chicago Press.

Ajami, F. (1991) *The Arab Predicament: Arab Political Thought and Practice since 1967*. Cambridge: Cambridge University Press.

Ajami, F. (1998) *Dream Palaces of the Arabs: A Generation's Odyssey*. New York: Pantheon.

Aleklett, K., and Campbell, C. J. (2003) 'The peak and decline of world oil and gas production', *Minerals and Energy: Raw Materials Report*, 18(1): 5–20.

Allan, T. (2011) *Virtual Water: Tackling the Threat to our Planet's most Valuable Resource*. London: I. B. Tauris.

Allen, C. (1995) 'Understanding African politics', *Review of African Political Economy*, 22(65): 301–20.

Allen, C. (1999) 'Warfare, endemic violence and state collapse', *Review of African Political Economy*, 26(81): 367–84.

Allison, G. (2004a) 'How to stop nuclear terror', *Foreign Affairs*, 83(1): 64–74.

Allison, G. (2004b) *Nuclear Terrorism: The Ultimate Preventable Catastrophe*. New York: Times Books.

Amery, H. (2002) 'Water wars in the Middle East: a looming threat', *Geographical Journal*, 168(4): 313–23.

Amnesty International (2005) *Guantánamo and Beyond: The Continuing Pursuit of Unchecked Executive Power*. London: Amnesty International (also at www.amnesty. org).

Anand, M. (2010) 'Empowering paradise? The ESDP at ten', *International Affairs*, 85(2): 227–46.

Anand, M. (2011) 'European defence policy from Lisbon to Libya', *Survival*, 53(3): 75–90.

Andemicael, B., and Mathiason, J. (2005) *Eliminating Weapons of Mass Destruction: Prospects for Effective International Verification*. Basingstoke: Palgrave.

Anderson, B. (1991) *Imagined Communities: Reflections on the Origins and Spread of Nationalism*. London: Verso.

Anderson, L. (2004) 'Antiquated before they can ossify: states that fail before they form', *Journal of International Affairs*, 58(1): 1–16.

Anderson, M. (1996) *Frontiers: Territory and State Formation in the Modern World*. Cambridge: Polity.

Anderson, M. B. (1999) *Do No Harm: How Aid Can Support Peace – Or War*. Boulder, CO: Lynne Rienner.

Anderson, T. L., and Leal, D. R. (1991) *Free Market Environmentalism*. Boulder, CO: Westview Press.

Andreani, G. (2004) 'The "war on terror": good cause, wrong concept', *Survival*, 46(4): 31–50.

Andrews-Speed, P. (2004) 'A European approach to energy security', in F. Godemont, F. Nicolas and T. Yakushiji (eds), *Asia and Europe: Cooperating for Energy Security*. Paris: Institut Français des Relations Internationales.

Andrews-Speed, P., and Dannreuther, R. (2011) *China, Oil and Global Politics*. London: Routledge.

Andrews-Speed, P., Liao, X. J., and Dannreuther, R. (2002) *The Strategic Implications of China's Energy Needs*, Adelphi Paper 346. Oxford: Oxford University Press.

Angell, N. (1912) *The Great Illusion*. London: Heinemann.

Annan, K. (1999) *Facing the Humanitarian Challenge: Towards a Culture of Prevention*. New York: United Nations.

Annan, K. (2000) *'We the Peoples': The Role of the United Nations in the 21st Century*, at www.un.org/millennium/sg/report (accessed October 2006).

Ansari, A. L. (2003) *Iran, Islam and Democracy: The Politics of Managing Change*. London: Royal Institute of International Affairs.

Aouragh, M., and Alexander, A. (2011) 'Sense and nonsense of Facebook revolutions', *International Journal of Communication*, 5 [special issue].

Aradau, C. (2004) 'Security and the democratic scene', *Journal of International Relations and Development*, 7(4): 388–413.

Aris, S. (2009a) 'A new model of Asian regionalism: does the Shanghai Cooperation Organisation have more potential than ASEAN?', *Cambridge Review of International Affairs*, 22(3): 451–67.

Aris, S. (2009b) 'Tackling the "three evils": Shanghai Cooperation Organisation (SCO) – a regional response to non-traditional transnational security challenges in Central Asia', *Europe–Asia Studies*, 61(5): 457–82.

Aron, R. (1966) *Peace and War: A Theory of International Relations*. London: Weidenfeld & Nicolson.

Arquilla, J., and Ronfeldt, D. (eds) (1997) *In Athena's Camp: Preparing for Conflict in the Information Age.* Santa Monica, CA: RAND.

Art, R. J., and Jervis, R. (eds) (2000) *International Politics: Enduring Concepts and Contemporary Issues.* Harlow: Longman.

Arthur, C., and Halliday, J. (2010) 'WikiLeaks fights to stay online after US company withdraws domain name', *The Guardian,* 3 December, at www.guardian.co.uk/media/blog/2010/dec/03/wikileaks-knocked-off-net-dns-everydns (accessed 10 April 2012).

Ashley, R. K. (1998) 'Untying the sovereign state: a double reading of the anarchy problematique', *Millennium,* 17(2): 227–62.

Asmus, R. D. (2010) *A Little War that Shook the World: Georgia, Russia and the Future of the West.* Basingstoke, Palgrave Macmillan.

Atran, S. (2006) 'The moral logic and growth of suicide terrorism', *Washington Quarterly,* 29(2): 127–47.

Austin, J. L. (1962) *Sense and Sensibilia.* Oxford: Clarendon Press.

Ausubel, J. H. (1996) 'The liberation of the environment', *Daedalus,* 125(3): 1–18.

Auty, R. M. (1993) *Sustaining Development in the Mineral Economies: The Resource Curse Thesis.* London: Routledge.

Auty, R. M. (2001) *Resource Abundance and Economic Development.* Oxford: Oxford University Press.

Axworthy, L. (2001) 'Human security and global governance: putting people first', *Global Governance,* 7(1): 19–23.

Ayoob, M. (1995) *The Third World Security Predicament: State Making, Regional Conflict and the International System.* Boulder, CO: Praeger.

Ayoob, M. (2002) 'Humanitarian intervention and state sovereignty', *International Journal of Human Rights,* 6(1): 81–102.

Ayoob, M. (2004) 'Third world perspectives on humanitarian intervention and international administration', *Global Governance,* 10(1): 99–118.

Ayoob, M., and Zierler, M. (2005) 'The unipolar concert: the North–South divide trumps transatlantic differences', *World Policy Journal,* 22(1): 31–42.

Baaz, M. E., and Stern, M. (2009) 'Why do soldiers rape? Masculinity, violence, and sexuality in the armed forces in the Congo (DRC)', *International Studies Quarterly,* 53(2): 495–518.

Baechler, G. (1999) *Violence through Environmental Discrimination: Causes, Rwanda Arena and Conflict Model.* Dordrecht: Kluwer Academic Press.

Baldwin, D. (1989) *Paradoxes of Power.* Oxford: Blackwell.

Baldwin, D. (ed.) (1993) *Neorealism and Neoliberalism: The Contemporary Debate.* New York: Columbia University Press.

Baldwin, D. (1997) 'The concept of security', *Review of International Studies,* 23(1): 5–26.

Ballentine, K., and Sherman, J. (eds) (2003) *The Political Economy of Armed Conflict: Beyond Greed and Grievance.* Boulder, CO: Lynne Rienner.

Bannon, I., and Collier, P. (eds) (2003) *Natural Resources and Violent Conflict: Options and Actions.* Washington, DC: World Bank.

Barkawi, T., and Laffey, M. (1999) 'The imperial peace: democracy, force and globalization', *European Journal of International Relations,* 5(4): 403–34.

Barkin, S. (1998) 'The evolution of the constitution of sovereignty and the emergence of human rights norms', *Millennium*, 27(2): 229–52.

Barnett, H., and Morse, C. (1963) *Scarcity and Growth: The Economics of Natural Resource Availability*. Baltimore: Johns Hopkins University Press for Resources for the Future.

Barnett, J. (2001) *The Meaning of Environmental Security*. London, Zed Books.

Barnett, J., and Adger, W. N. (2007) 'Climate change, human security and violent conflict', *Political Geography*, 26(8): 639–55.

Barnett, M. (1995) 'The new UN politics of peace: from juridical sovereignty to empirical sovereignty', *Global Governance*, 1(1): 79–97.

Barnett, M. (1997) 'Bringing in the New World Order: liberalism, legitimacy and the United Nations', *World Politics*, 49(4): 526–51.

Barnett, M. (2001) 'Humanitarianism with a sovereign face: UNHCR in the global undertow', *International Migration Review*, 35(1): 244–77.

Barnett, M. (2002) *Eyewitness to a Genocide: The United Nations and Rwanda*. Ithaca, NY: Cornell University Press.

Barnett, M. (2003) 'What is the future of humanitarianism', *Global Governance*, 9(3): 401–16.

Barnett, M., and Duvall, R. (2005) 'Power in international politics', *International Organization*, 59(1): 39–75.

Barnett, M., and Weiss, T. J. (eds) (2008) *Humanitarianism in Question: Politics, Power and Ethics*. Ithaca, NY: Cornell University Press.

Barton, B., Redgewell, C., Ronnie, A., and Zilman, D. N. (eds) (2004) *Energy Security: Managing Risk in a Dynamic Legal and Regulatory Environment*. Oxford: Oxford University Press.

Barutciski, M. (1998) 'Involuntary repatriation when refugee protection is no longer necessary', *International Journal of Refugee Law*, 10(1–2): 236–55.

Bauboeck, R. (1994) *Transnational Citizenship: Membership and Rights in International Migration*. Aldershot: Edward Elgar.

Baudrillard, J. (2003) *Spirit of Terrorism and Other Essays*. London: Verso.

Bauman, Z. (1998) *Globalization: The Human Consequences*. Cambridge: Polity.

Beck, U. (1992) *Risk Society: Towards a New Modernity*. London: Sage.

Beck, U. (1999) *The World Risk Society*. Cambridge: Polity.

Beckerman, W. (1995) *Small is Stupid: Blowing the Whistle on the Greens*. London: Duckworth.

Behlawi, H., and Luciani, G. (eds) (1987) *The Rentier State*. London: Croom Helm.

Beitz, C. R. (1979) *Political Theory and International Relations*. Princeton, NJ: Princeton University Press.

Belin, J. (1956) *La Suisse et les Nations Unies*. New York: Carnegie Endowment.

Bellamy, A. J. (2006) 'No pain, no gain? Torture and ethics in the war on terror', *International Affairs*, 82(1): 121–48.

Bellamy, A. J. (2008) *Responsibility to Protect*. Cambridge: Polity.

Bellamy, A. J., Williams, P., and Griffin, S. (2010) *Understanding Peacekeeping*. Cambridge: Polity.

Benjamin, D., and Simon, S. (2002) *The Age of Sacred Terror*. New York: Random House.

Benjamin, M. (2012) *Drone Warfare*. New York: OR Books.

Berdal, M. (1993) *Whither UN peacekeeping?*, Adelphi Paper 281. London: Brassey's for the International Institute for Strategic Studies.

Berdal, M. (1994) 'Fateful encounter: the United States and UN peacekeeping', *Survival*, 36(1): 30–50.

Berdal, M. (2003) 'How "new" are the "new wars"? Global economic change and the study of civil war', *Global Governance*, 9(4): 477–502.

Berdal, M. (2005) 'The UN's unnecessary crisis', *Survival*, 47(3): 7–32.

Berdal, M., and Leifer, M. (1996) 'Cambodia', in J. Mayall (ed.), *The New Interventionism 1991–1994: United Nations Experience in Cambodia, Former Yugoslavia, and Somalia*. Cambridge: Cambridge University Press, pp. 25–58.

Berdal, M., and Malone, D. (eds) (2000) *Greed and Grievance: Economic Agendas in Civil Wars*. Boulder, CO: Lynne Rienner.

Berger, T. U. (1998) *Cultures of Anti-Militarism: National Security in Germany and Japan*. Baltimore: Johns Hopkins University Press.

Bergeson, H., Haugland, T., and Lundre, L. (2000) *Petro-States: Predatory or Developmental?* Oslo: ECON and Fridtjof Nansen Institute.

Berman, P. (2003) *Terror and Liberalism*. New York: W. W. Norton.

Betts, R. K. (1998) 'The new threat of mass destruction', *Foreign Affairs*, 77(1): 26–41.

Betz, D. J., and Stevens, T. (2011) *Cyberspace and the State: Toward a Strategy for Cyber-Power*, Adelphi Paper 424. London: Routledge for the International Institute for Strategic Studies.

Bhagwati, J. (2003) 'Borders beyond control', *Foreign Affairs*, 82(1): 98–104.

Bierstecker, T. J., and Weber, C. (eds) (1996) *State Sovereignty as Social Construct*. Cambridge: Cambridge University Press.

Bigo, D. (1996) *Polices en réseaux: l'experience européenne*. Paris: Presses de Sciences Po.

Bigo, D. (1997) 'Sécurité et immigration: vers une gouvernementalité par l'inquiétude', *Conflits et Cultures*, 31(2): 13–38.

Bigo, D. (2002) 'Security and immigration: toward a critique of the governmentality of unease', *Alternatives*, 27(1): 63–92.

Bildt, C. (1998) *Peace Journey: The Struggle for Peace in Bosnia*. London: Weidenfeld & Nicolson.

Biswas, A. K. (1992) 'Indus water treaty: the negotiating process', *Water International*, 17(4): 201–9.

Black, M., and King, J. (2009) *The Atlas of Water: Mapping the World's Most Critical Resource*. London: Routledge.

Blair, B. (1993) *The Logic of Accidental Nuclear War*. Washington, DC: Brookings Institution.

Bobbitt, P. (2002) *The Shield of Achilles: War, Peace and the Course of History*. London: Penguin.

Boot, M. (2004) *The Savage Wars of Peace: Small Wars and the Rise of America's Power*. New York: Basic Books.

Booth, K. (1991) 'Security and emancipation', *Review of International Studies*, 17(4): 313–26.

Booth, K. (2007) *Theory of World Security*. Cambridge: Cambridge University Press.

Boswell, C. (2003) 'The "external dimension" of EU immigration and asylum policy', *International Affairs*, 79(3): 619–38.

Boswell, C., and Geddes, A. (2010) *Migration and Mobility in the European Union*. Basingstoke: Palgrave Macmillan.

Boulden, J. (2004) *Dealing with Conflict in Africa: The United Nations and Regional Organizations*. Basingstoke: Macmillan.

Boutros-Ghali, B. (1992) *An Agenda for Peace: Preventive Diplomacy, Peacemaking and Peace-Keeping*. New York: United Nations.

Brannigan, T. (2010) 'Google to end censorship in China over cyber attacks', *The Guardian*, 13 January, at www.guardian.co.uk/technology/2010/jan/12/google-china-ends-censorship (accessed 10 April 2012).

Brauch, H. G. (2005) *Environment and Human Security: Towards Freedom from Hazard Impacts*. Bonn: United Nations Institute for Environment and Human Security Intersections.

Bremmer, I. (2010) 'Democracy in cyberspace', *Foreign Affairs*, 89(6): 86–92.

Bretherton, C., and Vogler, J. (1999) *The European Union as a Global Actor*. London: Routledge.

Brimley, S. (2010) 'Promoting security in common domains', *Washington Quarterly*, 33(3): 119–32.

Brodie, B. (1946) *The Absolute Weapon*. New York: Newcourt Brace.

Brodie, B. (1959) *Strategy in the Missile Age*. Princeton, NJ: Princeton University Press.

Brooks, S. G. (1997) 'Dueling realisms', *International Organization*, 51(3): 445–77.

Brooks, S. G., and Wohlforth, W. C. (2008) *World out of Balance: International Relations and the Challenge of American Primacy*. Princeton, NJ: Princeton University Press.

Brown, L. (1965) 'Population growth, food needs and production problems', in *World Population and Food Supplies 1980*. Madison, WI: American Society of Agronomy, pp. 17–20.

Brown, L. (1977) *Redefining National Security*. Washington, DC: Worldwatch.

Brown, L. (1995) *Who Will Feed China?: Wake-Up Call for a Small Planet*. London: Earthscan.

Brown, L., and Kane, H. (1994) *Full House: Reassessing the Earth's Population Carrying Capacity*. New York: W. W. Norton.

Brown, M. E. (1995) 'The flawed logic of NATO expansion', *Survival*, 37(1): 34–52.

Brown, M. E., Coté, O. R., Lynn-Jones, S. M., and Miller, S. E. (eds) (2000) *The Rise of China: An International Security Reader*. Cambridge, MA: MIT Press.

Brown M. E., Coté, O. R., Lynn-Jones, S. M., and Miller, S. E. (eds) (2009) *Primacy and its Discontents: American Power and International Stability*. Cambridge, MA: MIT Press.

Brown, M. E., Coté, O. R., Lynn-Jones, S. M., and Miller, S. E. (eds) (2010) *Going Nuclear: Nuclear Proliferation and International Security in the 21st Century (An International Security Reader)*. Cambridge, MA: MIT Press.

Brown, M. E., Lynn-Jones, S. M., and Miller S. E. (eds) (1996) *Debating the Democratic Peace*. Cambridge, MA: MIT Press.

Brown, O., Hammill, A., and McLeman, R. (2007) 'Climate change as the "new" security threat: implications for Africa', *International Affairs*, 83(6): 1141–54.

Brown, N. (1989) 'Climate, ecology and international security', *Survival*, 31(6): 519–32.

Brubaker, R. (1992) *Citizenship and Nationhood in France and Germany*. Cambridge, MA: Harvard University Press.

Brubaker, R., and Laitin, D. D. (1998) 'Ethnic and nationalist violence', *Annual Review of Sociology*, 24(1): 423–52.

Buchan, D. (2002) 'The threat within: deregulation and energy security', *Survival*, 44(3): 105–16.

Buckley, M. (2001) 'Russian perceptions', in M. Buckley and S. N. Cummings (eds), *Kosovo: Perceptions of War and its Aftermath*. London: Continuum, pp. 156–75.

Bueno de Mesquita, B., and Riker, W. H. (1990) 'An assessment of the merits of selective nuclear proliferation', *Journal of Conflict Studies*, 26(2): 283–306.

Bull, H. (1961) *The Control of the Arms Race*. London: Weidenfeld & Nicolson.

Bull, H. (1977) *The Anarchical Society*. London: Macmillan.

Bull, H. (1984a) *Intervention in World Politics*. Oxford: Oxford University Press.

Bull, H. (1984b) 'The emergence of a universal international society', in H. Bull and A. Watson (eds), *The Expansion of International Society*. Oxford: Oxford University Press, pp. 117–26.

Bulloch, J., and Darwish, A. (1993) *Water Wars: Coming Conflicts in the Middle East*. London: Victor Gollancz.

Burgess, J. P., and Owen, T. (eds) (2004) 'Symposium on human security', *Security Dialogue*, 35(3): 345–88.

Burke, J. (2003) *Al-Qaeda*. London: I. B. Tauris.

Burke, J. (2011) *The 9/11 Wars*. London: Allen Lane.

Busch, N. E. (2004) *No End in Sight: The Continuing Menace of Nuclear Proliferation*. Lexington: University Press of Kentucky.

Bush, G. (1991) 'A new world order?', speech to the House of Representatives, 6 March.

Butler, J. (2004) *Precarious Life: the Powers of Mourning and Violence*. London: Verso.

Butler, R. (2001) *Fatal Choice: Nuclear Weapons and the Illusion of Missile Defence*. Boulder, CO: Lynne Rienner.

Butts, K. (1999) 'The case for DoD involvement in environmental security', in D. Deudney and R. A. Matthew (eds), *Contested Grounds: Security and Conflict in the New Environmental Politics*. Albany: State University of New York Press.

Buzan, B. (1991) *People, States and Fear: An Agenda for International Security Studies in the Post-Cold War Era*. Hemel Hempstead: Wheatsheaf.

Buzan, B. (1997) 'Rethinking security after the Cold War', *Cooperation and Conflict*, 32(1): 5–28.

Buzan, B., and Waever, O. (2003) *Regions and Powers: The Structure of International Security*. Cambridge: Cambridge University Press.

Buzan, B., Waever, O., and de Wilde, J. (1998) *Security: A Framework for Analysis*. Boulder, CO: Lynne Rienner.

Byman, D. L. (2003) 'Al-Qaeda as an adversary: do we understand our enemy?', *World Politics*, 56(1): 139–63.

Calleo, D. (2009) *Follies of Power: America's Unipolar Fantasy*. Cambridge: Cambridge University Press.

Callinicos, A. (2007) 'Does capitalism need the state system?', *Cambridge Review of International Affairs*, 20(4): 533–49.

Campbell, C. (1997) *The Coming Oil Crisis*. Brentwood: Multi-Science.

Campbell, C., and Laherrère, J. (1998) 'The end of cheap oil?', *Scientific American*, 278(3): 78–84.

Campbell, D. (1992) *Writing Security: United States Foreign Policy and the Politics of Identity*. Minneapolis: University of Minnesota Press.

Campbell, D. (1998) *National Deconstruction: Violence, Identity and Justice in Bosnia*. Minneapolis: University of Minnesota Press.

Campbell, K. M., Einhorn, R. G., and Reiss, M. B. (eds) (2004) *The Nuclear Tipping Point: Why States Reconsider their Nuclear Choices*. Washington, DC: Brookings Institution.

Caplan, R. (2005) *International Governance of War-Torn Territories: Rule and Reconstruction*. Oxford: Oxford University Press.

Carens J. (1987) 'Aliens and citizens: the case for open borders', *Review of Politics*, 49(2): 251–73.

Carr, E. H. (1964) *The Twenty Years' Crisis, 1919–1939*. New York: Harper & Row.

Castells, M. (2009) *The Information Age: Economy, Society and Culture*, Vols 1–3. Oxford: Wiley-Blackwell.

Castles, S., and Miller, M. J. (2009) *The Age of Migration*. Basingstoke: Palgrave.

Cebrowski, A. K., and Garstka, J. J. (1998) 'Network-centric warfare: its origin and future', *Proceedings of the US Naval Institute*, January, at www.kinection.com/ncoic/ncw_origin_future.pdf (accessed 10 April 2012).

Centeno, M. A. (2003) *Blood and Debt: War and the Nation-State in Latin America*. Philadelphia: Pennsylvania State University Press.

Chabal, P., and Daloz, J. P. (1999) *Africa Works: Disorder as a Political Instrument*. Oxford: Currey.

Chalecki, E. L. (2012) *Environmental Security: A Guide to the Issues*. Santa Barbara, CA: Praeger.

Charles, C., and Varma, S. (2010) *Out of Water: From Abundance to Scarcity and How to Solve the World's Water Problems*. London: Financial Times and Prentice- Hall.

Chaudhry, K. A. (1994) 'Economic liberalization and the lineages of the rentier state', *Comparative Politics*, 27(1): 1–25.

Chesnais, J.-C. (1992) *The Demographic Transition: Stages, Patterns and Economic Implications*. Oxford: Oxford University Press.

Chesterman, S. (2001) *Just War or Just Peace? Humanitarian Intervention and International Law*. Oxford: Oxford University Press.

Chesterman, S. (2004) *You, the People: The United Nations, Transitional Administration, and State Building*. Oxford: Oxford University Press.

Child, J. (1992) *The Central American Peace Process, 1983–1991: Sheathing Swords, Building Confidence*. Boulder, CO: Lynne Rienner.

Chomsky, N. (2000) *Rogue States*. London: Pluto Press.

Christensen, T., and Snyder, J. (1990) 'Chain gangs and passed bucks: predicting alliance patterns in multipolarity', *International Organization*, 44(2): 137–68.

Cirincione, J., Wolfstal, J. B., and Rajkumar, M. (2005) *Deadly Arsenals: Nuclear, Biological and Chemical Threats*. Washington, DC: Carnegie Endowment for International Peace.

Clapham, C. (1985) *Third World Politics: An Introduction*. London: Croom Helm.

Clarke, R. (2004) *Against All Enemies: Inside America's War on Terror*. New York: Free Press.

Clarke, R. A., and Knake, R. (2010) *Cyber War*. New York: Ecco.

Claude, I. L. (1956) *Swords into Ploughshares*. New York: Random House.

Claude, I. L. (1962) *Power and International Relations*. New York: Random House.

Clausewitz, C. von (1984 [1832]) *On War*. Princeton, NJ: Princeton University Press.

Cohn, C. (1987) 'Sex, death and the rational world of defense intellectuals', *Signs*, 12(4): 687–718.

Coker, C. (2001) *Humane War: The New Ethics of Postmodern War*. London: Routledge.

Cole, P. (2000) *Philosophies of Exclusion: Liberal Political Theory and Immigration*. Edinburgh: Edinburgh University Press.

Colley, L. (1992) *Britons: Forging the Nation, 1707–1837*. New Haven, CT: Yale University Press.

Collier, P. (2000) 'Doing well out of war: an economic perspective', in M. Berdal and D. Malone (eds), *Greed and Grievance: Economic Agendas in Civil Wars*. Boulder, CO: Lynne Rienner.

Collier, P. (2003) *Breaking the Conflict Trap: Civil War and Development Policy*. Washington, DC: World Bank.

Collier, P., and Hoeffler, A. (2001) *Greed and Grievance in Civil Wars*. Washington, DC: World Bank.

Collier, P., and Hoeffler, A. (2004) 'The challenge of reducing the global incidence of civil war', Copenhagen Consensus Paper, at www.copenhagenconsensus.com/Files/Filer/CC/Papers/Conflicts_230404.pdf (accessed October 2006).

Commission on Human Security (2003) *Human Security Now: Protecting and Empowering People*. New York: Commission on Human Security.

Conca, K. (1994) 'In the name of sustainability: peace studies and environmental discourse', *Peace and Change*, 19(2): 91–113.

Conca, K., and Dabelko, G. D. (eds) (2002) *Environmental Peacekeeping*. Washington and Baltimore: Woodrow Wilson Center Press and Johns Hopkins University Press.

Conca, K., and Dabelko, G. D. (eds) (2004) *Green Planet Blues: Environmental Politics from Stockholm to Johannesburg*. Boulder, CO: Westview Press.

Connelly, M., and Kennedy, P. (1994) 'Must it be the Rest against the West?', *Atlantic Monthly*, December: 61–9.

Cooley, J. (1984) 'The war over water', *Foreign Policy*, 54: 3–26.

Cooper, R. (1999) 'The long peace', *Prospect*, 40: 22–5.

Cooper, R. (2003) *The Breaking of Nations: Order and Chaos in the Twenty-First Century*, London: Atlantic Books.

Cornelius, W. A., Espenshade, T., and Salehyan, I. (2001) *The International Migration of the Highly Skilled*. La Jolla, CA: Center for Comparative Integration Studies.

Cortright, D., and Vayrynen R. (2010) *Towards Nuclear Zero*, Adelphi Paper 410. London: Routledge for the International Institute for Strategic Studies.

Cowper-Coles, S. (2011) *Cables from Kabul: The Inside Story of the West's Afghanistan Campaign*. London: HarperPress.

Cox, M. (2004) 'Empire, imperialism and the Bush Doctrine', *Review of International Studies*, 30(4): 585–608.

Cox, M. (2005) 'Beyond the West: terrors in Transatlantia', *European Journal of International Relations*, 11(2): 203–33.

Cox, R. (1986) 'Social forces, states and world orders: beyond international relations theory', in R. O. Keohane (ed.), *Neo-realism and its Critics*. New York: Columbia University Press.

Cramer, C. (2002) 'Homo economicus goes to war: methodological individualism, rational choice and the political economy of war', *World Development*, 30(11): 1845–64.

Crenshaw, M. (2010) *Explaining Terrorism: Causes, Processes and Consequences*. London: Routledge.

Crisp, J. (2000) *People on the Move: Security Challenges at the Turn of the Millennium*. Geneva: Geneva Centre for Security Policy.

Cronin, A. K. (2011) *How Terrorism Ends: Understanding the Decline and Demise of Terrorist Campaigns*. Princeton, NJ: Princeton University Press.

Daalder, I. H., and Lindsay, J. M. (2003) *America Unbound: The Bush Revolution in Foreign Policy*. Washington, DC: Brookings Institution.

Dabelko, G. D., Lonergan, S., and Matthew, R. A. (1999) 'State of the art review on environment, security and development cooperation', at www.eldis.org/static/Doc1676.htm (accessed October 2006).

Dalby, S. (1999) 'Threats from the south: geopolitics, equity and environmental security', in D. Deudney and R. A. Matthew (eds), *Contested Grounds: Security and Conflict in the New Environmental Politics*. Albany: State University of New York Press.

Dalby, S. (2002) *Environmental Security*. Minneapolis: University of Minnesota Press.

Dalby, S. (2009) *Security and Environmental Change*. Cambridge: Polity.

Dando, M. (2001) *The New Biological Weapons*. London: Lynne Rienner.

Danner, M. (ed.) (2004) *Torture and Truth: America, Abu Ghraib and the War on Terror*. New York: New York Review of Books.

Dannreuther, R. (1992) *The Gulf War: A Political and Strategic Analysis*, Adelphi Paper 264. London: Brassey's for the International Institute for Strategic Studies.

Dannreuther, R. (1999) 'The political dimension: authoritarianism and democratization', in L. Fawcett and Y. Sayegh (eds), *The Third World beyond the Cold War*. Oxford: Oxford University Press, pp. 34–55.

Dannreuther, R. (1999–2000) 'Escaping the enlargement trap in NATO–Russian relations', *Survival*, 41(4): 145–64.

Dannreuther, R. (2001) 'War in Kosovo: history, development and aftermath', in M. Buckley and S. N. Cummings (eds), *Kosovo: Perceptions of War and its Aftermath*. London: Continuum, pp. 12–29.

Dannreuther, R. (ed.) (2004) *European Union Foreign and Security Policy: Towards a Neighbourhood Strategy*. London: Routledge.

Dannreuther, R. (2010) 'Energy security', in J. P. Burgess (ed.), *The Routledge Handbook of New Security Studies*. London: Routledge.

Dannreuther, R., and Kennedy, J. (2007) 'Historical sociology in sociology: British decline and US hegemony with lessons for international relations', *International Politics*, 44(4): 369–89.

Dannreuther, R., and Peterson, J. (eds) (2006) *Security Strategy and Transatlantic Relations*. London: Routledge.

de Soysa, I. (2000) 'The resource curse: are civil wars driven by rapacity or paucity?', in M. Berdal and D. Malone (eds), *Greed and Grievance: Economic Agendas in Civil Wars*. Boulder, CO: Lynne Rienner.

de Villers, M. (1999) *Water Wars: Is the World's Water Running Out?*, London: Weidenfeld & Nicolson.

de Waal, A. (1989) *Famine that Kills: Darfur, Sudan, 1984–5*. Oxford: Clarendon Press.

de Waal, A. (2004) 'Darfur: counter-insurgency on the cheap', *London Review of Books*, 26(15): 25–8.

Delli Priscolli, J. (2000) 'Water and civilization: using history to reframe water policy debates and to build ecological realism', *Water Policy*, 1(6): 623–36.

Deng, Y. (2008) *China's Struggle for Status: The Realignment of International Relations*. Cambridge: Cambridge University Press.

Der Derian, J. (1990) 'The (s)pace of international relations: simulation, surveillance and speed', *International Studies Quarterly*, 34(4): 295–310.

Der Derian, J. (2009) *Virtuous War: Mapping the Military–Industrial–Media–Entertainment Complex*. London: Routledge.

Desch, M. C. (2003) 'It is kind to be cruel: the humanity of American realism', *Review of International Studies*, 29(3): 415–26.

Dessler, A. (2012) *Introduction to Modern Climate Change*. Cambridge: Cambridge University Press.

Dessler A., and Parson, E. A. (eds) (2010) *The Science and Politics of Global Climate Change: A Guide to the Debate*. Cambridge: Cambridge University Press.

Deudney, D. H. (1990) 'The case against linking environmental degradation with national security', *Millennium*, 19(3): 461–76.

Deudney, D. H. (1999) 'Bringing nature back in: geopolitical theory from the Greeks to the global era', in D. Deudney and R. A. Matthew (eds), *Contested Grounds: Security and Conflict in the New Environmental Politics*. Albany: State University of New York Press, pp. 25–60.

Deudney, D. H., and Ikenberry, G. J. (1999) 'The nature and sources of liberal international order', *Review of International Studies*, 25(2): 179–96.

Deudney, D. H., and Matthew, R. A. (eds) (1999) *Contested Grounds: Security and Conflict in the New Environmental Politics*. Albany: State University of New York Press.

Deutsch K. W., et al. (1957) *Political Community in the North Atlantic Area: International Organization in Light of Historical Experience*. Princeton, NJ: Princeton University Press.

Diamond, J. (2006) *Collapse: How Societies Choose to Fail or Survive*. London: Penguin.

Diamond, L. (2005) *Squandering Victory: The American Occupation and the Bungled Effort to Bring Democracy to Iraq*. New York: Holt.

Diamond, L., and Plattner, M. F. (eds) (1996) *The Global Resurgence of Democracy*. Baltimore: Johns Hopkins University Press.

Diehl, P., and Gleditsch, N. P. (eds) (2001) *Environmental Conflict*. Boulder, CO: Westview Press.

Dillon, M., and Lobo-Guerrero, L. (2008) 'Biopolitics of security in the 21st century: an introduction', *Review of International Studies*, 34(2): 265–92.

Dillon, M., and Neal, A. (eds) (2008) *Foucault on Politics, Security and War*. London: Palgrave Macmillan.

Downs, G. W. (ed.) (1994) *Collective Security beyond the Cold War*. Ann Arbor: University of Michigan Press.

Dowty, A., and Loescher, G. (1996) 'Refugee flows as grounds for international action', *International Security*, 21(1): 43–71.

Doyle, M. (1983a) 'Kant, liberal legacies and foreign affairs, part 1', *Philosophy and Public Affairs*, 12(3): 204–35.

Doyle, M. (1983b) 'Kant, liberal legacies and foreign affairs, part 2', *Philosophy and Public Affairs*, 12(4): 325–53.

Doyle, M. (1986) 'Liberalism and world politics', *American Political Science Review*, 80(4): 1151–61.

Doyle, M. (1997) *Ways of War and Peace*. New York: W. W. Norton.

Dryzek, J. S., and Schlosberg, D. (eds) (1998) *Debating the Earth: The Environmental Politics Reader*. Oxford: Oxford University Press.

Duffield, J. S. (1994–5) 'NATO's functions after the Cold War', *Political Science Quarterly*, 109(5): 763–87.

Duffield, J. S. (1998) *World Power Forsaken: Political Culture, International Institutions, and German Security Policy after Unification*. Stanford, CA: Stanford University Press.

Duffield, M. (2001) *Global Governance and the New Wars: The Merging of Development and Security*. London: Zed Books.

Duffield, M. (2007) *Development, Security and Unending War*. Cambridge: Polity.

Dunne, T., and Wheeler, N. J. (2004) ' "We the peoples": contending discourses of security in human rights theory and practice', *International Relations*, 18(1): 9–23.

Durch, W. J. (ed.) (1993) *The Evolution of UN Peacekeeping: Case Studies and Comparative Analyses*. New York: St Martin's Press.

Eagleton, T. (2005) *Holy Terror*. Oxford: Oxford University Press.

Eberstadt, N. (1998) 'Demography and international relations', *Washington Quarterly*, 21(2): 33–52.

Eberstadt, N. (2010) 'The demographic future', *Foreign Affairs*, 89(6): 54–64.

Economy, E. (2010) *The River Runs Black: The Environmental Challenge to China's Future*. Ithaca, NY: Cornell University Press.

Ehrlich, P. (1968) *The Population Bomb*. New York: Ballantine.

Ehrlich, P., and Ehrlich, A. H. (1991) *The Population Explosion*. New York: Touchstone.

Ehteshami, A. (1999) 'Is the Middle East democratizing?', *British Journal of Middle East Studies*, 26(2): 199–218.

Eickelman, D. F., and Piscatori, J. P. (1996) *Muslim Politics*. Princeton, NJ: Princeton University Press.

Eizenstat, S. E., Porter, J. E., and Weinstein, J. M. (2005) 'Rebuilding weak states', *Foreign Affairs*, 84(1): 134–46.

Elhance, A. (1999) *Hydropolitics in the Third World: Conflict and Cooperation in International River Basins*. Washington, DC: US Institute of Peace Press.

Elshtain, J. B. (1987) *Women and War*. New York: Basic Books.

Elshtain, J. B. (2003) *Just War against Terror: The Burden of American Power in a Violent World*. New York: Basic Books.

English, R. (2010) *Terrorism: How to Respond*. Oxford: Oxford University Press.

Enloe, C. (1990) *Bananas, Beaches and Bases: Making Feminist Sense of International Politics*. Berkeley: University of California Press.

Enloe, C. (2004) *The Curious Feminist: Searching for Women in the New Age of Empire*. Berkeley: University of California Press.

Enzensberger, H. M. (1994) *Civil Wars: From L.A. to Bosnia*. New York: Vintage.

Ericksonn, J. E. (ed.) (1999) 'Symposium: Observers or advocates: on the political role of the security analyst', *Cooperation and Conflict*, 34(3): 311–52.

Esty, D. C., Goldstone, J. A., Gurr, T. D., et al. (1995) *State Failure Task Force Report*. McLean, VA: Science Applications International Corporation.

Esty, D. C., Goldstone, J. A., Gurr, T. D., et al. (1998) *State Failure Task Force Report: Phase II Findings*. McLean, VA: Science Applications International Corporation.

Etzioni, A. (2004) 'A self-restrained approach to nation-building by foreign powers', *International Affairs*, 80(1): 1–17.

EU (2003) *A Secure World in a Better World: European Security Strategy*. Brussels: European Union.

European Commission (2000) *Communication from the Commission to the Council and the European Parliament on a Concerted Strategy for Immigration and Asylum*, COM (2000) 757 Final. Brussels: European Commission.

European Commission (2001) *Towards a European Strategy for the Security of Energy Supply*. Brussels: European Communities.

Evans, G. (2009) *Responsibility to Protect*. Washington DC: Brookings Institution.

Evans, P. (1995) *Embedded Autonomy: States and Industrial Transformation*. Princeton, NJ: Princeton University Press.

Evans, P. (ed.) (1997) *State–Society Synergy: Government and Social Capital in Development*. Berkeley: International and Area Studies, University of California.

Falk, R. (1971) *The Endangered Planet: Prospects and Proposals for Human Security*. New York: Random House.

Falkenmark, M. (1989) 'The massive water shortage in Africa: why isn't it being addressed?', *Ambio*, 18(2): 112–18.

Falkenrath, R. A., Newman, R. D., et al. (1998) *America's Achilles Heel: Nuclear, Biological and Chemical Terrorism and Covert Attack*. Cambridge, MA: MIT Press.

FAO (1978) *Systematic Index of International Water Resources Treaties, Declarations, Acts and Cases, by Basin*, Volume 1. Rome: Food and Agriculture Organization.

FAO (1984) *Systematic Index of International Water Resources Treaties, Declarations, Acts and Cases, by Basin*, Volume II. Rome: Food and Agriculture Organization.

Farber, H., and Gowa, J. (1995) 'Politics and peace', *International Security*, 20(2): 123–46.

Farer, T., Archibugi, D., Brown C., et al. (2005) 'Roundtable: Humanitarian intervention after 9/11', *International Relations*, 19(2): 211–50.

Farwell, J. P., and Rohozinski, R. (2011) 'Stuxnet and the future of cyberwar', *Survival*, 53(1): 23–40.

Feil, S. R. (1998) *Preventing Genocide: How the Early Use of Force might have Succeeded in Rwanda*. New York: Carnegie Corporation.

Feitelson, E. (2002) 'Implications for shifts in the Israeli water discourse for Israeli–Palestinian water negotiations', *Political Geography*, 21(3): 293–318.

Feiverson, H. A. (ed.) (2000) *The Nuclear Turning Point: A Blueprint for Deep Cuts and De-alerting of Nuclear Weapons*. Washington, DC: Brookings Institution.

Ferguson, N. (2004) *Colossus: The Price of America's Empire*. New York: Penguin.

Fierke, K. M. (2007) *Critical Approaches to International Security*. Cambridge: Polity.

Finer, S. (1975) 'State- and nation-building in Europe: the role of the military', in C. Tilly (ed.), *The Formation of National States in Western Europe*. Princeton, NJ: Princeton University Press, pp. 84–163.

Finkel, S., and Rule, J. B. (1986) 'Relative deprivation and related theories of civil violence: a critical review', in K. Lang and G. Lang (eds), *Research in Social Movements*. Greenwich, CT: JAI Press.

Finkelstein, M. S., and Finkelstein L. S. (1966) *Collective Security*. San Francisco: Chandler.

Finnemore, M. (2003) *The Purpose of Intervention: Changing Beliefs about the Use of Force*. Ithaca, NY: Cornell University Press.

Fleming, D. (2000) 'After oil', *Prospect*, 57: 24–8.

Flint, J., and de Waal, A. (2005) *Darfur: A Short History of a Long War*. London: Zed Books.

Forsythe, D. (1989) *Human Rights in World Politics*. Lincoln: Nebraska University Press.

Frank, A. G. (1967) *Capitalism and Underdevelopment in Latin America*. New York: Monthly Review Press.

Freedman, L. (1989) *The Evolution of Nuclear Strategy*. London: International Institute for Strategic Studies.

Freedman, L. (1998) 'International security: changing targets', *Foreign Policy*, 110: 48–63.

Freedman, L. (2003) *The Evolution of Nuclear Strategy*. 3rd edn, Basingstoke: Palgrave.

Freedman, L. (2004) *Deterrence*. Cambridge: Polity.

Freedman, L. (2005) 'Strategic terror and amateur psychology', *Political Quarterly*, 76(2): 161–70.

Freedman, L., and Karsh, E. (1994) *The Gulf Conflict, 1990–1991: Diplomacy and War in the New World Order*. London: Faber.

Freeman, G. P. (1995) 'Modes of immigration politics in liberal democratic states', *International Migration Review*, 26(4): 881–913.

Friedberg, A. L. (1993–4) 'Ripe for rivalry: prospects for peace in multipolar Asia', *International Security*, 18(3): 5–33.

Friedberg, A. L. (2005) 'The future of US–China relations: is conflict inevitable?', *International Security*, 30(2): 7–45.

Frost, R. M. (2005) *Nuclear Terrorism after 9/11*, Adelphi Paper 378. London: Routledge for the International Institute for Strategic Studies.

Frum, D., and Perle R. (2003) *An End to Evil: How to Win the War on Terror*. New York: Random House.

Fukuyama, F. (1992) *The End of History and the Last Man*. London: Hamish Hamilton.

Fukuyama, F. (2004) *State-Building: Governance and World Order in the 21st Century*. Ithaca, NY: Cornell University Press.

Gabel, J. (2004–5) 'The role of US nuclear weapons after September 11', *Washington Quarterly*, 28(1): 181–95.

Gaddis, J. L. (1992–3) 'International relations theory and the end of the Cold War', *International Security*, 17(3): 5–58.

Gaddis, J. L. (2004) *Surprise, Security and the American Experience*. Cambridge, MA: Harvard University Press.

Gaffney, F. J. (2001) 'Bush, missile defence, and the critics', *Commentary*, May: 29–36.

Gambetta, D. (ed.) (2005) *Making Sense of Suicide Missions*. Oxford: Oxford University Press.

Garner-Outlaw, T., and Engelman, R. (1997) *Sustaining Water, Easing Scarcity: A Second Update*. Washington, DC: Population Action International.

Garrett, L. (2001) 'The nightmare of bioterrorism', *Foreign Affairs*, 80(1): 76–89.

Garthoff, R. (1985) *Detente and Confrontation: American–Soviet Relations from Nixon to Reagan*. Washington, DC: Brookings Institution.

Geddes, A. (2008) *Immigration and European Integration: Towards Fortress Europe*. Manchester: Manchester University Press.

Gellner, E. (1983) *Nations and Nationalism*. Oxford: Blackwell.

Gellner, E. (1994) *Conditions of Liberty: Civil Society and its Rivals*. London: Hamish Hamilton.

Gerges, F. (2005) *The Far Enemy: Why Jihad Went Global*. Cambridge: Cambridge University Press.

Gerges, F. (2011) *The Rise and fall of al-Qaeda*. Oxford: Oxford University Press.

Gever, J. (1986) *Beyond Oil: The Threat to Food and Fuel in the Coming Decades*. Cambridge, MA: Ballinger.

Giddens, A. (1997) *The Nation-State and Violence*. Berkeley: University of California Press.

Giddens, A. (1999) *Runaway World: How Globalization is Reshaping our Lives*. London: Profile.

Gilbert, M. (1983) *Winston S. Churchill*, Volume VI: *Finest Hour, 1938–1941*. London: Heinemann.

Gilpin, R. G. (1984) 'The richness of the tradition of political realism', *International Organization*, 53(4): 631–68.

Ginifer, J. (1996) 'Development within UN peace missions', *International Peacekeeping*, 3(2): 41–63.

Giordano, M. A., and Wolf, A. T. (2003) 'Sharing waters: post-Rio international water management', *Natural Resources Forum*, 27: 163–71.

Girard, R. (1977) *Violence and the Sacred*. Baltimore: Johns Hopkins University Press.

Glaser, C. (1997) 'The security dilemma revisited', *World Politics*, 50(1): 171–201.

Gleditsch, N. P. (2001) 'Armed conflict and the environment', *Journal of Peace Research*, 35(3): 381–400.

Gleick, P. (1993) 'Water and conflict: fresh water resources and international security', *International Security*, 18(1): 79–112.

Gleick, P., Wolff, G. H., Chalecki, E. L., and Reyes, R. (2002) 'The privatisation of water and water systems', in P. Gleick et al., *The World's Water*, Volume 3. Washington, DC: Island Press.

Gleick, P., et al. (2011) *The World's Water*, Volume 7. Washington DC: Island Press.

Goh, E. (2007–8) 'Great powers and hierarchical order in Southeast Asia', *International Security*, 32(3): 113–57.

Goldgeier, J. M., and McFaul, M. (1992) 'A tale of two worlds: core and periphery in the post-Cold War era', *International Organization*, 46(2): 467–91.

Goldsborough, J. (2000) 'Out-of-control immigration', *Foreign Affairs*, 79(5): 89–101.

Goldstone, J. A. (1991) *Revolution and Rebellion in the Early Modern World*. Berkeley: University of California Press.

Goldstone, J. A. (2002) 'Population and security: how demographic change can lead to violent conflict', *Journal of International Affairs*, 56(1): 3–21.

Goldstone, J. A. (2010) 'The new population bomb', *Foreign Affairs*, 89(1): 31–43.

Goldthau, A., and Witte, J. M. (eds) (2009a) *Global Energy Governance: The New Rules of the Game*. Washington DC: Brookings Institution.

Goldthau, A., and Witte, J. M. (2009b) 'Back to the future or forward to the past: strengthening markets and rules for effective global energy governance', *International Affairs*, 82(2): 373–90.

Gong, G. (1984) *The Standard of 'Civilization' in International Society*. Oxford: Clarendon Press.

Gordon, P. H. (2003) 'Bush's Middle East vision', *Survival*, 45(1): 155–66.

Gore, A. (1992) *Earth in the Balance: Ecology and the Human Spirit*. Boston: Houghton Mifflin.

Gottemoeller, R. (2005) 'Cooperative threat reduction beyond Russia', *Washington Quarterly*, 28(2): 145–58.

Gouré, L., Kohler, F. D., and Harvey, M. L. (1974) *The Role of Nuclear Forces in Current Soviet Strategy*. Miami: Center for Advanced International Studies, University of Miami.

Gow, J. (1997) *Triumph of the Lack of Will: International Diplomacy and the Yugoslav War*. London: Hurst.

Gray, C. S. (1979) 'Nuclear strategy: the case for a theory of victory', *International Security*, 4(1): 54–87.

Gray, C. S. (1976) *The Soviet–American Arms Race*. Farnborough, Saxon House.

Gray, C. S. (1992) *House of Cards: Why Arms Control Must Fail*. Ithaca, NY: Cornell University Press.

Gray, C. S. (1997) *Post-Modern War: The New Politics of Conflict*. London: Routledge.

Gray, C. S. (1999) *The Second Nuclear Age*. Boulder, CO: Lynne Rienner.

Gray, J. (2008) *Black Mass: Apocalyptic Religion and the Death of Utopia*. London: Penguin.

Grayling, A. C. (2006) *Among the Dead Cities*. London: Bloomsbury.

Greenwood, C. (1993) 'Is there a right of humanitarian intervention?', *The World Today*, 49(2): 34–40.

Greider, W. (2000) 'Oil on political waters', *Nation*, 271(12): 5–6.

Gries, P. H. (2004) *China's New Nationalism: Pride, Politics and Diplomacy*. Berkeley: University of California Press.

Griffiths R., and Houston, W. (2008) *Water: The Final Resource: How the Politics of Water Will Affect the World*. Petersfield: Harriman House.

Guild, E. (2009) *Security and Migration in the 21st Century*. Cambridge: Polity.

Gurr, T. R. (1970) *Why Men Rebel*. Princeton, NJ: Princeton University Press.

Haas, E. B. (1953) 'The balance of power: prescription, concept or propaganda', *World Politics*, 5(4): 442–77.

Haas, E. B. (1958) *The Uniting of Europe: Political, Economic and Social Forces*. London: Stevens.

Haas, P. M. (1990) *Saving the Mediterranean: The Politics of International Environmental Cooperation*. New York: Columbia University Press.

Haas, R. (1997) *The Reluctant Sheriff: The United States after the Cold War*. New York: Council on Foreign Relations.

Habermas, J. (2000) 'Bestialität und Humanität', in R. Merkel (ed.), *Der Kosovo-Krieg und das Völkerrecht*. Frankfurt am Main: Suhrkamp, pp. 51–65.

Haddadin, M. J. (2002) 'Water issues in the Middle East: challenges and opportunities', *Water Policy*, 4(3): 205–22.

Haftendorn, H. (1991) 'The security puzzle: theory-building and discipline-building in international security', *International Studies Quarterly*, 8(1): 129–53.

Hall, J. A. (1985) *Powers and Liberties: The Causes and Consequences of the Rise of the West*. Oxford: Blackwell.

Hall, J. A., and Zhao, D. X. (1994) 'State power and patterns of late development', in J. A. Hall (ed.), *Coercion and Consent: Studies in the Modern State*. Cambridge: Polity.

Halliday, F. (1994) *Rethinking International Relations*. Basingstoke: Macmillan.

Halliday, F. (1996) *Islam and the Myth of Confrontation: Religion and Politics in the Middle East*. London: I. B. Tauris.

Halliday, F. (2005) *The Middle East in International Relations: Power, Politics and Ideology*. Cambridge: Cambridge University Press.

Halliday, J. (2008) 'London riots: how blackberry messenger played a key role', *The Guardian*, 8 August, at www.guardian.co.uk/media/2011/aug/08/london-riots-facebook-twitter-blackberry (accessed 10 April 2012).

el-Hamalawy, H. (2011) 'Social media, workers and the Egyptian revolution', *3arabawy*, 2 October, at www.arabawy.org/2011/10/02/video-social-media-workers-and-the-egyptian-revolution (accessed 10 April 2012).

Hansen, L. (2000) 'The little mermaid's silent security dilemma and the absence of gender in the Copenhagen School', *Millennium*, 29(2): 285–306.

Hansen, L. (2006) *Security as Practice: Discourse Analysis and the Bosnian War*. London: Routledge.

Hardin, G. (1993) *Living within Limits: Ecology, Economics and Population*. Oxford: Oxford University Press.

Hardin, G. (1998 [1968]) 'The tragedy of the commons', *Science*, 162(1): 243–8; repr. in J. S. Dryzek and D. Schlosberg (eds), *Debating the Earth: The Environmental Politics Reader*. Oxford: Oxford University Press.

Hardt, M., and Negri, A. (2001) *Empire*. Cambridge, MA: Harvard University Press.

Hartmann, F. H. (1982) *The Conservation of Enemies: A Study in Enmity*. Westport, CT: Greenwood Press.

Hastings, B. (1999) *Bomber Command*. London: Pan.

Hauge, W., and Ellingsen, T. (2001) 'Causal pathways to conflict', in P. Diehl and N. P. Gleditsch (eds), *Environmental Conflict*. Boulder, CO: Westview Press, pp. 36–57.

Hegghammer, T. (2010) *Jihad in Saudi Arabia: Violence and Pan-Arabism*. Cambridge: Cambridge University Press.

Heilbroner, R. (1991) *An Inquiry into the Human Prospect: Looked at Again for the 1990s*. New York: W. W. Norton.

Helm, D., and Hepburn, C. (eds) (2009) *The Economics and Politics of Climate Change*. Oxford: Oxford University Press.

Herbst, J. (1989) 'The creation and maintenance of national boundaries in Africa', *International Organization*, 43(4): 673–92.

Herbst, J. (1990) 'War and the state in Africa', *International Security*, 14(4): 117–39.

Herbst, J. (2000) *States and Power in Africa: Comparative Lessons in Authority and Control.* Princeton, NJ: Princeton University Press.

Heydemann, S. (ed.) (2000) *War, Institutions and Social Change in the Middle East.* Berkeley: University of California Press.

Hill, C. (1993) 'The capabilities–expectations gap, or conceptualizing Europe's international role', *Journal of Common Market Studies*, 31(3): 305–28.

Hillel, D. (1994) *Rivers of Eden: The Struggle for Water and the Quest for Peace in the Middle East.* Oxford: Oxford University Press.

Hinnebusch, R. (2003) *The International Politics of the Middle East.* Manchester: Manchester University Press.

Hironaka, A. (2005) *Neverending Wars: The International Community, Weak States and the Perpetuation of Civil War.* Cambridge, MA: Harvard University Press.

Hirst, P. (1997) 'The global economy: myths and realities', *International Affairs*, 73(3): 409–35.

Hobden, S., and Hobson, J. M. (eds) (2002) *Historical Sociology of International Relations.* Cambridge: Cambridge University Press.

Hobson, J. M. (2004) *The Eastern Origins of Western Civilization.* Cambridge: Cambridge University Press.

Hoffmann, B. (2006) *Inside Terrorism.* Rev. edn, New York: Columbia University Press.

Hoffmann, S. (1996) *The Ethics and Politics of Humanitarian Intervention.* Notre Dame, IN: University of Notre Dame Press.

Holbrooke, R. (1999) *To End a War.* New York: Modern Library.

Hollifield, J. F. (2000) 'Migration and the "new" international order: the missing regime', in B. Ghosh (ed.), *Managing Migration: Time for a New International Regime?.* Oxford: Oxford University Press.

Holzgrefe, J. L., and Keohane, R. O. (eds) (2003) *Humanitarian Intervention: Ethical, Legal and Political Dilemmas.* Cambridge: Cambridge University Press.

Home Office (2002) *Secure Borders, Safe Haven: Integration with Diversity in Modern Britain.* London: Stationery Office.

Homer-Dixon, T. (1991) 'On the threshold: environmental changes as causes of acute conflict', *International Security*, 16(2): 76–116.

Homer-Dixon, T. (1994) 'Environmental scarcities and violent conflict: evidence from cases', *International Security*, 19(1): 5–40.

Homer-Dixon, T. (1999) *Environment, Scarcity and Violence.* Princeton, NJ: Princeton University Press.

Homer-Dixon, T. (2001) *The Ingenuity Gap.* London: Vintage.

Homer-Dixon, T. (2002) 'The rise of complex terrorism', *Foreign Policy*, 128: 52–62.

Homer-Dixon, T. (ed.) (2009) *How the Twin Crises of Oil Depletion and Climate Change Will Define the Future.* Toronto: Random House.

Homer-Dixon, T., and Blitt, J. (eds) (1998) *Ecoviolence: Links among Environment, Population and Security.* Lanham, MD: Rowman & Littlefield.

Hooper, C. (2000) *Manly States: Masculinities, International Relations, and Gender Politics.* New York: Columbia University Press.

Horsnell, P. (2000) *The Probability of Oil Market Disruption: With an Emphasis on the Middle East.* Houston: James A Baker III Institute for Public Policy, Rice University.

Howard, M. (2002) 'What's in a name?', *Foreign Affairs*, 81(1): 8–13.

Howard, P., and Homer-Dixon, T. (1998) 'Environmental scarcity and violent conflict: the case of Chiapas', in T. Homer-Dixon and J. Blitt (eds), *Ecoviolence: Links among Environment, Population and Security*. Lanham, MD: Rowman & Littlefield.

Howitt, A. M., and Pangi, R. L. (eds) (2003) *Countering Terrorism: Dimensions of Preparedness*. Cambridge, MA: MIT Press.

Howorth, J. (2007) *Security and Defence Policy in the European Union*. Basingstoke: Palgrave.

Hunt, D. (1989) *Economic Theories of Development: An Analysis of Competing Paradigms*. New York: Harvester Wheatsheaf.

Huntington, S. P. (1968) *Political Order in Changing Societies*. New Haven, CT: Yale University Press.

Huntington, S. P. (1991) *The Third Wave: Democratization in the Late Twentieth Century*. Norman: University of Oklahoma Press.

Huntington, S. P. (1993) 'The clash of civilizations?', *Foreign Affairs*, 72(3): 22–49.

Huntington, S. P. (1996) 'The West unique, not universal', *Foreign Affairs*, 75(6): 28–46.

Huntington, S. P. (1997) 'The erosion of American national interests', *Foreign Affairs*, 76(5): 28–49.

Hurewitz, J. C. (1969) *Middle East Politics: The Military Dimension*. New York: Praeger.

Hurrell, A. (1992) 'Collective security and international order revisited', *International Relations*, 11(1): 37–55.

Hurrell, A. (1998) 'An emerging security community in South America', in E. Adler and M. Barnett (eds), *Security Communities*. Cambridge: Cambridge University Press, pp. 228–64.

Huth, P. K. (1996) *Standing your Ground: Territorial Disputes and International Conflict*. Ann Arbor: University of Michigan Press.

Huysmans, J. (1995) 'Migrants as a security problem: dangers of "securitizing" societal issues', in R. Miles and D. Thränhardt (eds), *Migration and European Integration: The Dynamics of Inclusion and Exclusion*. London: Pinter.

Huysmans, J. (2000) 'The European Union and the securitization of migration', *Journal of Common Market Studies*, 38(5): 751–77.

Huysmans, J. (2005) *The Politics of Insecurity: Fear, Migration and Asylum in the EU*. London: Routledge.

ICISS (2001a) *The Responsibility to Protect*. Ottawa: International Development Research Centre for the International Commission on Intervention and State Sovereignty.

ICISS (2001b) *The Responsibility to Protect: Research, Bibliography and Background*. Ottawa: International Development Research Centre for the International Commission on Intervention and State Sovereignty.

IEA (2012) *World Energy Outlook 2012*. Paris: International Energy Agency.

Ignatieff, M. (1998) *The Warrior's Honour: Ethnic War and the Modern Conscience*. New York: Henry Holt.

Ignatieff, M. (2000) *Virtual War: Kosovo and Beyond*. London: Chatto & Windus.

Ignatieff, M. (2004) *The Lesser Evil: Political Ethics in the Age of Terror*. Princeton, NJ: Princeton University Press.

IISS (International Institute for Strategic Studies) (2001) 'Defining terrorism', *Strategic Comments*, 7(9): 1–2.

Ikenberry, G. J. (2001) *After Victory: Institutions, Strategic Restraint, and the Rebuilding of Order after Major Wars*. Princeton, NJ: Princeton University Press.

Ikenberry, G. J. (2011a) *Liberal Leviathan: The Origins, Crisis and Transformation of the American World Order: The Rise, Decline and Renewal*. Princeton, NJ: Princeton University Press.

Ikenberry G. J. (2011b) 'The future of liberal world order', *Foreign Affairs*, 90(3): 56–68.

Ikenberry, G. J., and Tsuchiyama, J. (2002) 'Between balance of power and community: the future of multilateral security cooperation in the Asia-Pacific', *International Relations of the Asia-Pacific*, 2(1): 69–94.

Inkster, N. (2010) 'China in cyberspace', *Survival*, 52(4): 55–66.

Institute of International Studies (2005) *Small Arms Survey 2005: Weapons at War*. Oxford: Oxford University Press.

International Commission on Intervention in Kosovo (2000) *The Kosovo Report*. Oxford: Oxford University Press.

International Rescue Committee (2008) *Mortality in the Democratic Republic of Congo: An Ongoing Crisis*, at www.rescue.org/sites/default/files/migrated/resources/2007/2006-7_congomortalitysurvey.pdf (accessed 5 January 2011).

IOM (2003) *World Migration 2003: Managing Migration – Challenges and Responses for People on the Move*. Geneva: International Organization for Migration.

IPCC (International Panel on Climate Change) (2007) *Climate Change: Synthesis Report*. Geneva: IPCC.

Jackson, R. (1990) *Quasi-States: Sovereignty, International Relations, and the Third World*. Cambridge: Cambridge University Press.

Jackson, R. (1993) 'The weight of ideas in decolonization: normative change in international relations', in J. Goldstein and R. O. Keohane (eds), *Ideas and Foreign Policy*. Ithaca, NY: Cornell University Press.

Jackson, R. (2000) *The Global Covenant: Human Conduct in a World of States*. Oxford: Oxford University Press.

Jackson, R., and Sinclair, S. J. (eds) (2012) *Contemporary Debates on Terrorism*. London: Routledge.

Jackson, R., Smith M. B., Gunning, P. J., and Jarin, L. (2011) *Terrorism: A Critical Introduction*. Basingstoke: Palgrave Macmillan.

Jackson, R. H., and Rosberg, C. G. (1982) 'Why Africa's weak states persist: the empirical and the juridical in statehood', *World Politics*, 35(1): 1–24.

Jacobsen, D. (1996) *Rights across Borders: Immigration and the Decline of Citizenship*. Baltimore: Johns Hopkins University Press.

James, A. (1990) *Peacekeeping in International Politics*. Basingstoke: Macmillan for the International Institute for Strategic Studies.

Jenkins, B. (1975) 'International terrorism: a new mode of conflict', in D. Carlton and C. Schearf (eds), *International Terrorism and World Security*. London: Croom Helm.

Jenkins, B. (1998) 'Foreword', in I. O. Lesser (ed.), *Countering the New Terrorism*. Santa Monica, CA: RAND, pp. iii–xiv.

Jervis, R. (1978) 'Cooperation under the security dilemma', *World Politics*, 30(2): 167–94.

Jervis, R. (1984) *The Illogic of American Nuclear Strategy*. Ithaca, NY: Cornell University Press.

Jervis, R. (1989) *The Meaning of the Nuclear Revolution: Statecraft and the Prospect of Armageddon*. Ithaca, NY: Cornell University Press.

Jervis, R. (1991–2) 'The future of world politics: will it resemble the past?', *International Security*, 16: 39–73.

Jervis, R. (2002) 'Theories of war in an era of leading-power peace', *American Political Science Review*, 96(1): 1–14.

Joffé, G. (1984) 'Europe's American pacifier', *Foreign Policy*, 58: 64–82.

Johnson, C. (2002) *Blowback: The Costs and Consequences of the American Empire*. London: Time Warner.

Johnson, C. (2004) *The Sorrows of Empire: Militarism, Secrecy, and the End of the Republic*. New York: Metropolitan Books.

Johnston, A. I. (1995) *Cultural Realism: Strategic Culture and Grand Strategy in Ming China*. Ithaca, NY: Cornell University Press.

Johnston, A. I. (2003a) 'Is China a status quo power?', *International Security*, 27(4): 5–56.

Johnston, A. I. (2003b) 'Socialization in international institutions: the ASEAN way and international relations theory', in G. J. Ikenberry and M. Mastanduno (eds), *International Relations Theory and the Asia-Pacific*. New York: Columbia University Press.

Johnston, A. I., and Evans, P. (1999) 'China's engagement with multilateral security institutions', in A. I. Johnston and R. S. Ross (eds), *Engaging China: The Management of an Emerging Power*. London: Routledge.

Jones, B. D. (2011) 'Libya and the responsibility to protect', *Survival*, 53(3): 51–60.

Jones, C. (2006) 'The axis of non-proliferation', *Problems of Post-Communism*, 53(2): 3–16.

Jones, D. M., and Smith, M. L. R. (2007) 'Making process, not progress: ASEAN and the problem of regional order', *International Security* 32(1): 148–84.

Jones, R. B. J. (1995) *Globalization and Interdependence in the International Political Economy*. London: Pinter.

Joppke, C. (1999) *Immigration and the Nation-State*. Oxford: Oxford University Press.

Joppke, C. (2007) 'Beyond national models: civic integration policies for immigrants in Western Europe', *West European Politics*, 30(1): 1–22.

Jordan, B., and Duevell, F. (2002) *Irregular Migration: The Dilemmas of Transnational Mobility*. Cheltenham: Edward Elgar.

Jordan, B., and Duevell, F. (2003) *Migration: The Boundaries of Equality and Justice*. Cambridge: Polity.

Joseph, J. (2005) 'The exercise of national sovereignty: the Bush administration's approach to combating weapons of mass destruction proliferation', *Nonproliferation Review*, 12(2): 373–87.

Juergensmeyer, M. (2000) *Terror in the Mind of God: The Global Rise of Religious Violence*. Berkeley: University of California Press.

Kagan, R. (2003) *Of Paradise and Power: America and Europe in the New World Order*. New York: Alfred A. Knopf.

Kagan, R. (2008) *The Return of History and the End of Dreams*. London: Atlantic Books.

Kahl, C. H. (1998–9) 'Constructing a separate peace: constructivism, collective liberal identity, and democratic peace', *Security Studies*, 8(2/3): 94–144.

Kaldor, M. (2012) *New and Old Wars: Organised Violence in a Global Era*. 3rd edn, Cambridge: Polity.

Kaldor, M., Karl, T. L., and Said, Y. (eds) (2007) *Oil Wars*. London: Pluto Press.

Kalicki, J. H., and Goldwyn, D. L. (eds) (2005) *Energy and Security: Toward a New Foreign Policy Strategy*. Washington, DC: Woodrow Wilson Center Press.

Kalyvas, S. N. (2001) ' "New" and "old" civil wars: a valid distinction?', *World Politics*, 54(1): 99–118.

Kamp, K.-H. (1996) 'An overrated nightmare', *Bulletin of the Atomic Scientists*, 52(4): 30–5.

Kang D. C. (2007) *China Rising: Peace, Power and Order in East Asia*. New York: Columbia University Press.

Kaplan, R. D. (1994a) *Balkan Ghosts: A Journey through History*. New York: Vintage.

Kaplan, R. D. (1994b) 'The coming anarchy', *Atlantic Monthly*, 273(2): 44–76.

Kaplan, R. D. (1996) *The Ends of the Earth: A Journey at the Dawn of the 21st Century*. New York: Random House.

Kaplan, R. D. (2010) 'The geography of Chinese power', *Foreign Affairs*, 89(3): 22–41.

Kapur, D., and McHale, J. (2003) 'Migration's new payoff', *Foreign Policy*, 130: 49–57.

Karl, T. L. (1997) *The Paradox of Plenty: Oil Booms and Petro-States*. Berkeley: University of California Press.

Katsumata, H. (2006) 'Establishment of the ASEAN regional forum: constructing a "talking shop" or a "Norm Brewery" ', *Pacific Review*, 19(2): 181–98.

Katzenstein, P. J. (ed.) (1996) *The Culture of National Security: Norms and Identity in World Politics*. New York: Columbia University Press.

Kaufman, S., Little, R., and Wohlforth W. C. (eds) (2007) *The Balance of Power in World History*. Basingstoke: Macmillan.

Kaufmann, C. (1996) 'Possible and impossible solutions to ethnic civil wars', *International Security*, 20(4): 136–75.

Keck, M., and Sikkink, K. (1998) *Activists beyond Borders: Advocacy Networks in International Politics*. Ithaca, NY: Cornell University Press.

Keeley, C. B. (2003) 'Globalization transforms trade–migration equation', *International Migration*, 41(1): 87–92.

Keen, D. (1998) *The Economic Functions of Violence in Civil Wars*, Adelphi Paper 320. Oxford: Oxford University Press.

Kelly, K., and Homer-Dixon, T. (1998) 'Environmental scarcity and violent conflict: the case of Gaza', in T. Homer-Dixon and J. Blitt (eds), *Ecoviolence: Links among Environment, Population and Security*. Lanham, MD: Rowman & Littlefield.

Kennedy, P. (1993) *Preparing for the Twenty-First Century*. New York: Vintage.

Keohane, R. O. (1984) *After Hegemony: Cooperation and Discord in the World Political Economy*. Princeton, NJ: Princeton University Press.

Keohane, R. O. (2002) 'Ironies of sovereignty: the European Union and the United States', *Journal of Common Market Studies*, 40(4): 743–65.

Keohane, R. O., and Nye, J. S. (2000) 'Globalization: What's new? What's not? (And so what?)', *Foreign Policy*, 118: 104–19.

Kepel, G. (2002) *Jihad: The Trail of Political Islam*. Cambridge, MA: Harvard University Press.

Kepel, G. (2004) *The War for Muslim Minds: Islam and the West*. Cambridge, MA: Belknap Press.

Kerr, M. (1965) *The Arab Cold War: A Study of Ideology in Politics*. Oxford: Oxford University Press.

Khalili, L. (2011) 'Gendered practices of counter-insurgency', *Review of International Studies*, 37(4): 1471–91.

Khalili, L. (2012) *Time in the Shadows: Confinement in Counterinsurgencies*. Stanford, CA: Stanford University Press.

Khan, S. (2010) *Iran and Nuclear Weapons: Protracted Conflict and Proliferation*. London: Routledge.

Khong, Y. F. (2001) 'Human security: a shotgun approach to alleviating human misery?', *Global Governance*, 7(3): 231–7.

Kim, Y. (2003) *The Resource Curse in a Post-Communist Regime: Russia in Comparative Perspective*. Aldershot: Ashgate.

Kirchheimer, O. (1966) 'The transformation of the Western European party systems', in J. La Palombara and M. Weiner (eds), *Political Parties and Political Development*. Princeton, NJ: Princeton University Press.

Kissinger, H. (1957) *Nuclear Weapons and Foreign Policy*. New York: Harper.

Kissinger, H. (1965) *The Troubled Partnership: A Re-Appraisal of the Atlantic Alliance*. New York: McGraw Hill.

Kissinger, H. (1994) *Diplomacy*. New York: Simon & Schuster.

Klare, M. (2001) *Resource Wars: The New Landscape of Global Conflict*. New York: Henry Holt.

Klare, M. (2004) *Blood and Oil: The Dangers and Consequences of America's Growing Dependency on Imported Petroleum*. New York: Metropolitan Books.

Klimburg, A. (2011) 'Mobilising cyber power', *Survival* 53(1): 41–60.

Klotz, A. (1995) *Norms in International Relations: The Struggle against Apartheid*. Ithaca, NY: Cornell University Press.

Koblentz, G. D. (2003) 'Biological terrorism: understanding the threat and America's response', in A. M. Howitt and R. L. Pangi (eds), *Countering Terrorism: Dimensions of Preparedness*. Cambridge, MA: MIT Press.

Koslowski, R. (1999) 'A constructivist approach to understanding the European Union as a federal polity', *Journal of European Public Policy*, 6(4): 561–78.

Koslowski, R., and Kratochwil, F. (1995) 'Understanding change in international politics: the Soviet empire's demise and the international system', in R. N. Lebow and T. Risse-Kappen (eds), *International Relations Theory and the End of the Cold War*. New York: Columbia University Press, pp. 127–66.

Kramer, G. (1997) 'Islamist notions of democracy', in J. Beinin and J. Stork (eds), *Political Islam*. London: I. B. Tauris.

Kramer, M. (2009) 'The myth of no-NATO-enlargement pledge to Russia', *Washington Quarterly*, 32(2): 39–61.

Krasner, S. D. (1995) *Sovereignty: Organized Hypocrisy*. Princeton, NJ: Princeton University Press.

Krause, K. (1996) 'Insecurity and state formation in the global military order: the Middle Eastern case', *European Journal of International Relations*, 2(3): 319–54.

Krause, K. (1998) 'Critical theory and security studies: the research programme of "Critical Security Studies"', *Cooperation and Conflict*, 33(3): 298–333.

Krause, K. (2004) 'The key to a powerful agenda, if properly defined', *Security Dialogue*, 35(3): 367–8.

Krause, K., and Latham, A. (1999) 'Constructing non-proliferation and arms control: the norms of Western practice', in K. Krause (ed.), *Culture and Security: Multilateralism, Arms Control and Security Building*. London: Frank Cass, pp. 23–54.

Krause, K., and Williams, M. C. (1996a) 'Broadening the agenda of security studies: politics and methods', *Mershon International Studies Review*, 40(2): 229–54.

Krause, K., and Williams, M. C. (1996b) *Critical Security Studies: Concepts and Cases*. Boulder, CO: Lynne Rienner.

Krepinevich, A. F. (2002) *The Military-Technical Revolution: A Preliminary Assessment*. Washington, DC: Center for Strategic and Budgetary Assessments.

Krepon, M. (2001) 'Moving away from MAD', *Survival*, 43(2): 81–95.

Krepon, M. (2003) *Cooperative Threat Reduction, Missile Defence and the Nuclear Future*. Basingstoke: Palgrave.

Kupchan, C. (2002) *The End of the American Era: US Foreign Policy and the Geopolitics of the 21st Century*. New York: Alfred A. Knopf.

Kupchan, Charles A., and Kupchan, Clifford A. (1991) 'Concerts, collective security and the future of Europe', *International Security*, 16(1): 114–61.

Kupchan, Charles A., and Kupchan, Clifford A. (1995) 'The promise of collective security', *International Security*, 20(1): 52–61.

Kyle, D., and Koslowski, R. (2001) *Global Human Smuggling: Comparative Perspectives*. Baltimore: Johns Hopkins University Press.

Kynge, J. (2004) 'China is the workshop of the world, but it is becoming the rubbish tip too', *Financial Times*, 27 July, p. 15.

Labs, E. (1997) 'Offensive realism and why states expand their war aims', *Security Studies*, 6(4): 1–49.

Lake, D. (1992) 'Powerful pacifists: democratic states and war', *American Political Science Review*, 86(1): 24–37.

Lancaster, C. (2005) 'Development in Africa: the good, the bad, the ugly', *Current History*, 104(682): 222–7.

Lanteigne, M. (2008) 'China's maritime security and the "Malacca dilemma"', *Asian Security*, 4(2): 143–61.

Laqueur, W. (1996) 'Post-modern terrorism', *Foreign Affairs*, 75(5): 24–36.

Laqueur, W. (2001) *A History of Terrorism*. New Brunswick, NJ: Transaction Books.

Laqueur, W. (2012) *After the Fall: The End of the European Dream and the Decline of a Continent*. New York: Thomas Dunne Books.

Lavenex, S. (2001) *The Europeanisation of Refugee Policies: Between Human Rights and Internal Security*. Aldershot: Ashgate.

Lavoy, P. R. (1995) 'The strategic consequences of nuclear proliferation', *Security Studies*, 4(4): 699–711.

Lavoy, P. R., Sagan, S. D., and Wirtz, J. J. (eds) (2000) *Planning the Unthinkable: How New Powers Will Use Nuclear, Chemical and Biological Weapons*. Ithaca, NY: Cornell University Press.

Lawson, L., and Rothchild, D. (2005) 'Sovereignty reconsidered', *Current History*, 104: 228–35.

Layne, C. (1994) 'Kant or cant: the myth of the democratic peace', *International Security*, 19(2): 5–49.

Le Billon, P. (2001a) 'Angola's political economy of war: the role of oil and diamonds, 1975–2000', *African Affairs*, 100(398): 55–80.

Le Billon, P. (2001b) 'The political ecology of war: natural resources and armed conflicts', *Political Geography*, 20(5): 561–84.

Le Billon, P. (2005) *Fuelling War: Natural Resources and Armed Conflict*, Adelphi Paper 373. London: Routledge for the International Institute for Strategic Studies.

Leitenberg, M. (2004) *The Problem of Biological Weapons*. Stockholm: Swedish National Defence College.

Leitenberg, M. (2005) *Assessing the Biological Weapons and Bioterrorism Threat*. Carlisle, PA: Strategic Studies Institute.

Lepgold, J. (1998) 'NATO's post-Cold War collective action problem', *International Security*, 23(1): 5–55.

Lesser, I. O. (1998a) 'Countering the new terrorism: implications for strategy', in I. O. Lesser (ed.), *Countering the New Terrorism*. Santa Monica, CA: RAND, pp. 85–144.

Lesser, I. O. (ed.) (1998b) *Countering the New Terrorism*. Santa Monica, CA: RAND.

Levi, M. (2007) *On Nuclear Terrorism*. Cambridge, MA: Harvard University Press.

Levi, M. A., and O'Hanlon, M. E. (2005) *The Future of Arms Control*. Washington, DC: Brookings Institution.

Levinson, S. (2004) 'Torture in Iraq and the rule of law in America', *Daedalus*, 133(3): 5–9.

Levy, M. A. (1995) 'Is the environment a national security issue?', *International Security*, 20(2): 35–62.

Lewis, B. (2002) *What Went Wrong? The Clash between Liberalism and Modernity in the Middle East*. London: Weidenfeld & Nicolson.

Lewis, B. (2003) *Crisis of Islam: Holy War and Unholy Terror*. London: Weidenfeld & Nicolson.

Lewis, P., Newburn, T., Taylor, M., and Ball. J. (2011) 'Rioters say anger with police fuelled summer unrest', *The Guardian*, 5 December, at www.guardian.co.uk/uk/2011/dec/05/anger-police-fuelled-riots-study (accessed 10 April 2012).

Libiszewski, S. (1995) *Water Disputes in the Jordan Basin Region and their Role in the Resolution of the Arab–Israeli Conflict*. Zurich: Center for Security Studies and Conflict Research.

Lieber, K. A., and Press, D. G. (2006) 'The end of MAD: the nuclear dimension of US primacy', *International Security*, 30(4): 7–44.

Liefer, M. (1989) *ASEAN and the Security of South-East Asia*. London: Routledge.

Lin, P. (2011) 'Drone-ethics briefing: what a leading robotics expert told the CIA', *The Atlantic*, 15 December, at www.theatlantic.com/technology/archive/2011/12/drone-ethics-briefing-what-a-leading-robot-expert-told-the-cia/250060/ (accessed 10 April 2012).

Little, R. (1981) 'Ideology and change', in B. Buzan and R. J. Barry Jones (eds), *Change and the Study of International Relations: The Evaded Dimension*. New York: Continuum, pp. 30–45.

Little, R. (2007) *The Balance of Power in International Relations: Metaphors, Myths and Models*. Cambridge: Cambridge University Press.

Litwak, R. (2000) *Rogue States and US Foreign Policy*. Washington, DC: Woodrow Wilson Center Press.

Loescher, G. (1992) *Refugee Movements and International Security*. London: Brassey's.

Loescher, G. (2001) *The UNHCR and World Politics: A Perilous Path*. Oxford: Oxford University Press.

Loescher, G., and Milner, J. (2003) 'The missing link: the need for comprehensive engagement in regions of refugee origin', *International Affairs*, 79(3): 595–617.

Lomborg, B. (2001) *The Skeptical Environmentalist: Measuring the Real State of the World*. Cambridge: Cambridge University Press.

Longman, P. (2004) 'The global baby bust', *Foreign Affairs*, 83(3): 64–79.

Lonsdale, J. (1981) 'States and social processes in Africa: a historiographical survey', *African Studies Review*, 24(2/3): 139–225.

Lorenz, A., von Mittelstaedt, J., and Schmitz, G. P. (2011) 'Messengers of death: are drones creating a new global arms race?', *Der Spiegel Online*, 21 October, at www.spiegel.de/international/world/0,1518,792590,00.html (accessed 10 April 2012).

Lowi, M. (1993) 'Bridging the divide: transboundary resource disputes and the case of West Bank water', *International Security*, 18(1): 113–38.

Lukes, S. (1974) *Power: A Radical View*. London: Macmillan.

Lukes, S. (2005) 'Liberal democratic torture', *British Journal of Political Science*, 36(1): 1–16.

Lundestad, G. (1998) *'Empire' by Integration: The United States and European Integration, 1945–1997*. Oxford: Oxford University Press.

Lustick, I. S. (1997) 'The absence of Middle Eastern great powers: political "backwardness" in historical perspective', *International Organization*, 51(4): 653–83.

Luttwak, E. N. (1999) 'Give war a chance', *Foreign Affairs*, 78(4): 36–44.

Lynch, M. C. (1996) 'The analysis and forecasting of petroleum supply: sources of error or bias', in D. H. El Mallakh (ed.), *Energy Watchers*, Volume VII. Boulder, CO: International Research Center for Energy and Economic Development.

Lynch, M. C. (2002) 'The new energy crisis: separating threats from hysteria', *Energy Policy*, 30(1): 1–2.

Lynch, M. C. (2003) 'The new pessimism about petroleum resources: debunking the Hubbert model', *Minerals and Energy: Raw Materials Report*, 18(1): 21–32.

Lynn, W. J. (2010) 'Defending a new domain', *Foreign Affairs*, 89(5): 97–108.

Lynn-Jones, S. (1995) 'Offense–defense theory and its critics', *Security Studies*, 4(1): 660–91.

McCalla, R. (1996) 'NATO's persistence after the Cold War', *International Organization*, 50(3): 445–75.

MacFarlane, N. S. (1985) *Intervention and Regional Security*, Adelphi Paper 196. London: Brassey's for the International Institute for Strategic Studies.

MacFarlane, N. S. (2002) *Intervention in Contemporary World Politics*. Oxford: Oxford University Press.

McGreal, C. (2011) 'Barack Obama declares Iraq war a success', *The Guardian*, 14 December, at www.guardian.co.uk/world/2011/dec/14/barack-obama-iraq-war-success (accessed 10 April 2012).

McInnes, C. (2002) *Spectator Sport War: The West and Contemporary Conflict*. Boulder, CO: Lynne Rienner.

Mackinlay, J., and Chopra, J. (1992) 'Second generation multinational operations', *Washington Quarterly*, 15(3): 113–21.

McMahon, P. C. (2004–5) 'Rebuilding Bosnia: a model to emulate or to avoid', *Political Science Quarterly*, 119(4): 569–93.

McNeill, J. R. (2000) *Something New under the Sun: An Environmental History of the Twentieth Century*. New York: W. W. Norton.

McNeill, W. H. (1983) *The Pursuit of Power: Technology, Armed Force and Society since AD 1000*. Oxford: Blackwell.

Mahbubani, K. (1992) 'The West and the Rest', *National Interest*, 28: 3–13.

Mahbubani, K. (2008) *The New Asian Hemisphere: The Irresistible Shift of Global Power to the East*. New York: PublicAffairs.

Mahdavy, H. (1970) 'The pattern and problems of economic development in rentier states: the case of Iran', in M. A. Cook (ed.), *Studies in Economic History of the Middle East*. Oxford: Oxford University Press.

Mahon, J. E. J. (1992) 'Was Latin America too rich to prosper?', *Journal of Development Studies*, 28(2): 241–64.

Makiya, K. (1998) *Republic of Fear: The Politics of Modern Iraq*. Berkeley: University of California Press.

Mandaville, P. (2007) *Global Political Islam*. London: Routledge.

Mandelbaum, M. (1998–9) 'Is major war obsolete?', *Survival*, 40(4): 20–38.

Mandelbaum, M. (1999) 'A perfect failure', *Foreign Affairs*, 78(5): 2–8.

Mandelbaum, M. (2010) *The Fragile Superpower: America's Global Leadership in a Cash-Strapped Era*. New York: PublicAffairs.

Mann, J. (2004) *Rise of the Vulcans: The History of Bush's War Cabinet*. New York: Viking.

Mann, M. (1986) *The Sources of Social Power*, Volume I: *A History of Power from the Beginning to AD 1760*. Cambridge: Cambridge University Press.

Mann, M. (1993) *The Sources of Social Power*, Volume II: *The Rise of Classes and Nation States, 1760–1914*. Cambridge: Cambridge University Press.

Mann, M. (1994) 'In praise of macro-sociology: a reply to Goldthorpe', *British Journal of Sociology*, 45(1): 37–54.

Mann, M. (2003) *Incoherent Empire*. New York: Verso.

Manning, R. A. (2000) 'The Asian energy predicament', *Survival*, 42(3): 73–88.

Marten, K. Z. (2004) *Enforcing the Peace: Learning from the Imperial Past*. New York: Columbia University Press.

Martin, P. (1993) *Trade and Migration: NAFTA and Agriculture*. Washington, DC: Institute for International Economics.

Martin, P. (2004) 'Migration', in B. Lomborg (ed.), *Global Crises, Global Solutions*. Cambridge: Cambridge University Press.

Martinez, L. (2000) *The Algerian Civil War: 1990–1998*. London: Hurst.

Mason, P. (2012a) 'Global unrest: how the revolution went viral', *The Guardian*, 3 January, at www.guardian.co.uk/world/2012/jan/03/how-the-revolution-went-viral (accessed 10 April 2012).

Mason, P. (2012b) *Why it's Kicking off Everywhere: The New Global Revolutions*. London: Verso.

Massey, D. S., Arango, J., Hugo, G., et al. (1998) *Worlds in Motion: Understanding International Migration at the End of the Millennium*. Oxford: Oxford University Press.

Mathews, J. T. (1989) 'Redefining security', *Foreign Affairs*, 62(2): 162–77.

Matthew, R. A. (2002) 'In defense of environment and security research', *Environmental Change and Security Project Report*, 8: 109–24.

Maugeri, L. (2004) 'Oil: never cry wolf: why the petroleum age is far from over', *Science*, 304: 1114–15.

Maurseth, P. (1964) 'Balance-of-power thinking from the Renaissance to the French Revolution', *Journal of Peace Research*, 1(2): 120–36.

May, E. R., and Zelikow, P. D. (eds) (1997) *The Kennedy Tapes: Inside the White House during the Cuban Missile Crisis*. Cambridge, MA: Harvard University Press.

Mayall, J. (ed.) (1996) *The New Interventionism, 1991–1994: United Nations Experience in Cambodia, Yugoslavia and Somalia*. Cambridge: Cambridge University Press.

Mazarr, M. J. (1995) 'Virtual nuclear arsenals', *Survival*, 37(3): 7–26.

Mazower, M. (1999) *Dark Continent: Europe's Twentieth Century*. London: Penguin.

Meadows, D. A., Meadows, D. L., and Randers J. (1992) *Beyond the Limits: Confronting Global Collapse, Envisioning a Sustainable Future*. Post Mills, VT: Chelsea Green.

Meadows, D. A., Meadows, D. L., Randers, J., and Behrens, W. H. (1972) *The Limits to Growth*. New York: Universe Books.

Mearsheimer, J. J. (1990) 'Back to the future: instability in Europe after the end of the Cold War', *International Security*, 15(1): 5–56.

Mearsheimer, J. J. (1993) 'The case for a Ukrainian nuclear deterrent', *Foreign Affairs*, 72(3): 50–66.

Mearsheimer, J. J. (1994–5) 'The false promise of international institutions', *International Security*, 19(3): 5–49.

Mearsheimer, J. J. (2001) *The Tragedy of Great Power Politics*. New York: W. W. Norton.

Mearsheimer, J. J., and Walt, S. M. (2003) 'An unnecessary war', *Foreign Policy*, 134: 50–9.

Medeiros, E. S. (2009) *China's International Behaviour: Activism, Opportunism and Diversification*. Santa Monica, CA: RAND.

Medetsky, A. (2004) 'KGB veteran denies CIA caused '82 blast', *Moscow Times*, 18 March, at www.themoscowtimes.com/news/article/kgb-veteran-denies-cia-caused-82-blast/232261.html (accessed 10 April 2012).

Merom, G. (2003) *How Democracies Lose Small Wars*. Cambridge: Cambridge University Press.

Metz, S., and Kievit, J. (1995) *Strategy and the Revolution in Military Affairs*. Carlisle, PA: Strategic Studies Institute.

Migdal, J. S. (1988) *Strong Societies and Weak States: State–Society Relations and State Capabilities in the Third World*. Princeton, NJ: Princeton University Press.

Migdal, J. S., Kohli, A., and Shue, V. (eds) (1994) *State Power and Social Forces: Domination and Transformation in the Third World*. Cambridge: Cambridge University Press.

Miller, D. (1995) *On Nationality*. Oxford: Clarendon Press.

Milliken, J. (ed.) (2003) *State Failure, Collapse and Reconstruction*. Princeton, NJ: Princeton University Press.

Mills, K. (1998) *Human Rights in the Emerging Global Order: A New Sovereignty?*. New York: St Martin's Press.

Milward, A. S. (2000) *The European Rescue of the Nation State*. London: Routledge.

Ministry of Defence (1995) *Wider Peacekeeping*. London: HMSO.

Minnear, L. (2002) *The Humanitarian Enterprise: Dilemmas and Discoveries*. Bloomfield, CT: Kumarian Press.

Mitchell, J. V. (2002) 'A new political economy of oil', *Quarterly Review of Economics and Finance*, 42(2): 251–72.

Mitchell. T. (2011) *Carbon Democracy: Political Power in the Age of Oil*. London: Verso.

Monbiot, G. (2011) 'The need to protect the internet from "astroturfing" grows ever more urgent', *The Guardian*, 23 February, at www.guardian.co.uk/environment/georgemonbiot/2011/feb/23/need-to-protect-internet-from-astroturfing (accessed 10 April 2012).

Monnet, J. (1978) *Memoirs*. London: Collins.

Montgomery, A. H. (2005) 'Ringing in proliferation: how to dismantle an atomic bomb network', *International Security*, 30(2): 153–87.

Morgenthau, H. J. (1975) 'The failings of foreign policy', *New Republic*, 11 October, pp. 16–21.

Morgenthau, H. J. (1993 [1948]) *Politics among Nations*. New York: Alfred A. Knopf.

Morozov, E. (2011) 'Picking a fight with Clay Shirky', *Net Effect (Foreign Policy)*, 15 January, at http://neteffect.foreignpolicy.com/posts/2011/01/15/picking_a_fight_with_clay_shirky (accessed 10 April 2012).

Morozov, E. (2012) *The Net Delusion: the Dark Side of Internet Freedom*, London: Penguin.

Morse, E. L. (1999) 'The new political economy of oil?', *Journal of International Affairs*, 53(1): 1–29.

Morse, E. L. (2003) 'Personal commentary', *Oxford Energy Forum*, 54: 17–19.

Mortimer, E. (2004) 'International administration of war-torn territories', *Global Governance*, 10(1): 7–14.

Mueller, J. (1989) *Retreat from Doomsday: The Obsolescence of Major War*. New York: Basic Books.

Mueller, J. (2004) *The Remnants of War*. Ithaca, NY: Cornell University Press.

Münkler, H. (2005) *The New Wars*. Cambridge: Polity.

Munro, R. H. (1997) 'The coming conflict with China', *Foreign Affairs*, 76(2): 12–22.

Mutimer, D. (2000) *The Weapons State: Proliferation and the Framing of Security*. Boulder, CO: Lynne Rienner.

Myers, N. (1993) *Ultimate Security: The Environmental Basis of Political Stability*. New York: W. W. Norton.

Myers, N., and Simon, J. (1994) *Scarcity or Abundance? A Debate on the Environment*. New York: W. W. Norton.

Nacos, B. L. (2000) 'Accomplice or witness: the media's role in terrorism', *Current History*, 99: 174–8.

Nagel, T. (1986) *The View from Nowhere*. Oxford: Oxford University Press.

Naim, M. (2003) 'The five wars of globalization', *Foreign Policy*, 134: 28–37.

Narine, S. (2008) 'Forty years of ASEAN: a historical review', *Pacific Review* 21(4): 411–29.

NATO (1999) *Environment and Security in an International Context*. Brussels: North Atlantic Treaty Organization.

Neal, A. (2008) 'Goodbye war on terror? Foucault and Butler on discourses of law, war and exceptionalism', in M. Dillon and A. Neal (eds), *Foucault on Politics, Security and War*. London: Palgrave Macmillan.

Neal, A. (2009) 'Securitization and risk at the EU border: the origins of Frontex', *Journal of Common Market Studies*, 47(2): 333–56.

Newman, E., and Richmond, O. (2001) *The United Nations and Human Security*. London: Palgrave.

Newman, P. R. (2009) *Old and New Terrorism*. Cambridge: Polity.

Nickum, J. E. (2010) 'Hydraulic pressures', *International Security*, 89(5): 130–7.

Niebuhr, R. (1932) *Moral Man and Immoral Society: A Study in Ethics and Politics*. Louisville, KY: Westminster John Knox Press.

Noetzel, T., and Schreer, B. (2009) 'Does a multi-tier NATO matter? The Atlantic alliance and the process of strategic change', *International Affairs*, 85(2): 211–26.

Northedge, F. S. (1986) *The League of Nations: Its Life and Times, 1920–1946*. New York: Holmes & Meier.

Northrup, D. (2005) 'Globalization and the great convergence: rethinking world history in the long term', *Journal of World History*, 16(3): 249–67.

Nye, J. S. (1991) *Bound to Lead: The Changing Nature of American Power*. New York: Basic Books.

Nye, J. S. (2002) *The Paradox of American Power: Why the World's Superpower Can't Go it Alone*. New York: Oxford University Press.

Nye, J. S. (2004) *Soft Power: The Means to Success in World Politics*. New York: PublicAffairs.

Nye, J. S. (2011) *The Future of Power*. New York: PublicAffairs.

O'Hanlon, M. E. (2003) *Expanding Military Capacity for Humanitarian Intervention*. Washington, DC: Brookings Institution.

O'Hanlon, M. E. (2010) *A Skeptic's Case for Nuclear Disarmament*. Washington, DC: Brookings Institution.

O'Neill, O. (1996) *Towards Justice and Virtue*. Cambridge: Cambridge University Press.

Ó Tuathail, G., Dalby, S., and Routledge, P. (eds) (2006) *The Geopolitics Reader*. 2nd edn, London: Routledge.

Obershall, A. (2000) 'The manipulation of ethnicity: from ethnic cooperation to violence and war in Yugoslavia', *Ethnic and Racial Studies*, 23(6): 982–1001.

Oksenberg, M., and Economy, E. (eds) (1999) *China Joins the World: Progress and Prospects*. New York: Council on Foreign Relations.

Olson, M. and Zeckhauser, R. (1966) 'An economic theory of alliances', *Review of Economics and Statistics*, 48(3): 266–79.

Owen, T. (2004) 'Human security: conflict, critique and consensus: colloquium remarks and a proposal for a threshold-based definition', *Security Dialogue*, 35(3): 273–387.

Oye, K. A. (ed.) (1986) *Cooperation under Anarchy*. Princeton, NJ: Princeton University Press.

Pant, H. V. (2012) *Handbook of Nuclear Proliferation*. London: Routledge.

Pape, R. A. (2005a) *Dying to Win: The Strategic Logic of Suicide Terrorism*. New York: Random House.

Pape, R. A. (2005b) 'Soft balancing against the United States', *International Security*, 30(1): 7–45.

Pape, R. A., and Feldman, J. K. (2010) *Cutting the Fuse: the Explosion of Global Suicide Terrorism and How to Stop it*. Chicago: University of Chicago Press.

Parachini, J. (2003) 'Putting WMD terrorism into perspective', *Washington Quarterly*, 26(4): 37–50.

Parachini J. (ed.) (2005) *Motives, Means and Mayhem: Assessing Terrorist Use of Chemical and Biological Weapons*. Santa Monica, CA: RAND.

Paris, R. (2001) 'Human security: paradigm shift or hot air?', *International Security*, 26(2): 87–102.

Paris, R. (2004) *At War's End: Building Peace after Civil Conflict*. Cambridge: Cambridge University Press.

Parker, G. (1988) *The Military Revolution: Military Innovation and the Rise of the West, 1500–1800*. Cambridge: Cambridge University Press.

Paul, T. V. (1999) 'Great equalizers or agents of chaos? Weapons of mass destruction and the emerging international order', in J. A. Hall and T. V. Paul (eds), *International Order and the Future of World Politics*. Cambridge: Cambridge University Press.

Paul, T. V. (2000) *Power versus Prudence: Why Nations Forego Nuclear Weapons*. Montreal: McGill–Queen's University Press.

Paul, T. V. (2009) *The Tradition of Non-Use of Nuclear Weapons*. Stanford, CA: Stanford University Press.

Payne, K. B. (1996) *Deterrence in the Second Nuclear Age*. Lexington: University Press of Kentucky.

Payne, K. B. (2005) 'The nuclear posture review: setting the record straight', *Washington Quarterly*, 28(3): 131–51.

Peluso, N. L., and Watts, M. (2001) *Violent Environments*. Ithaca, NY: Cornell University Press.

Peoples, C. (2011) 'Security after emancipation? Critical theory, violence and resistance', *Review of International Studies*, 37(3): 1113–35.

Perkovich, G., and Acton, J. M. (2008) *Abolishing Nuclear Weapons*, Adelphi Paper 396. London: Routledge for the International Institute for Strategic Studies.

Perkovich, G., Mathews, J. T., Cirincione, J., Gottemoeller, R., and Wolfstahl, J. B. (2005) *Universal Compliance: A Strategy for Nuclear Security*. Washington, DC: Carnegie Endowment for Peace.

Perry, W. J. (2001) 'Preparing for the next attack', *Foreign Affairs*, 80(6): 31–47.

Phillips, D. L. (2005) *Losing Iraq: Inside the Postwar Reconstruction Fiasco*. New York: Basic Books.

Picard, E. (1988) 'Arab military in politics: from revolutionary plot to authoritarian state', in A. Dawisha and W. Zartman (eds), *Beyond Coercion: The Durability of the Arab State*. London: Croom Helm, pp. 116–46.

Pilger, J. (1999) 'Under the influence: the real reason for the United Nations' peacekeeping role in East Timor is to maintain Indonesian control', *The Guardian*, 21 September, at www.guardian.co.uk/politics/1999/sep/21/ethicalforeignpolicy.indonesia (accessed 10 October 2012).

Pipes, D. (2002) *Militant Islam Reaches America*. New York: W. W. Norton.

Pogge, T. W. (1992) 'Cosmopolitanism and sovereignty', *Ethics*, 103(1): 41–57.

Poggi, G. (1978) *The Development of the Modern State*. Stanford, CA: Stanford University Press.

Polanyi, K. (1944) *The Great Transformation*. New York: Octagon.

Politkovskaia, A. (2003) *A Small Corner of Hell: Dispatches from Chechnya*. Chicago: University of Chicago Press.

Posen, B. (1984) *The Sources of Military Doctrine: France, Britain and Germany between the World Wars*. Ithaca, NY: Cornell University Press.

Posen, B. (1993) 'The security dilemma and ethnic conflict', *Survival*, 35(1): 27–47.

Postel, S. (1999) *Pillar of Sand: Can the Irrigation Miracle Last?*. New York: W. W. Norton.

Potter, W. C. (2005) 'India and the new look of US nonproliferation policy', *Nonproliferation Review*, 12(2): 343–54.

Potter, W. E., and Mukhatzhanova, G. (eds) (2010) *Forecasting Nuclear Proliferation in the 21st Century*, 2 vols. Stanford, CA: Stanford University Press.

Powell, R. (1990) *Nuclear Deterrence Theory: The Search for Credibility*. Cambridge: Cambridge University Press.

Powell, R. (1991) 'Absolute and relative gains in international relations theory', *American Political Science Review*, 85(4): 1303–20.

Powell, R. (1999) *In the Shadow of Power: State and Strategies in International Politics*. Princeton, NJ: Princeton University Press.

Pozo-Martin, G. (2007) 'Autonomist or materialist geopolitics', *Cambridge Review of International Affairs*, 20(4): 551–63.

Price, R. M. (1995) 'A genealogy of the chemical weapons taboo', *International Organization*, 49(1): 73–103.

Price, R. M. (1998) 'Reversing the gun sights: transnational civil society targets land mines', *International Organization*, 52(3): 613–44.

Price, R. M., and Tannenwald, N. (1996) 'Norms and deterrence: the nuclear and chemical weapons taboos', in P. Katzenstein (ed.), *The Culture of National Security: Norms and Identity in World Politics*. New York: Columbia University Press, pp. 114–51.

Prins, G. (1990) 'Politics and the environment', *International Affairs*, 66(4): 711–30.

Quester, G. (1977) *Offense and Defense in the International System*. New York: John Wiley.

Quinlan, M. (1993) 'The future of nuclear weapons: policy for Western possessors', *International Affairs*, 69(3): 485–96.

Ramsbotham, O., and Woodhouse, T. (1996) *Humanitarian Intervention in Contemporary Conflict: A Reconceptualization*. Cambridge: Polity.

Ravenhill, J. (2009) 'East Asian regionalism: much ado about nothing?' *Review of International Studies*, 35(1): 215–35.

Rawls, J. (1993) 'The law of peoples', in S. Shute and S. Hurley (eds), *On Human Rights: The Oxford Amnesty Lectures 1993*. New York: Basic Books.

Ray, D. L. (1993) *Environmental Overkill: Whatever Happened to Common Sense?*. Washington, DC: Regnery Gateway.

Ray, J. L. (1995) *Democracy and International Politics: An Evaluation of the Democratic Peace Proposition*. Columbia: University of South Carolina Press.

Reed, P. L. (1996) 'The politics of reconciliation: the United Nations operation in Mozambique', in W. J. Durch (ed.), *UN Peacekeeping, American Politics, and Uncivil Wars of the 1990s*. New York: St Martin's Press, pp. 275–310.

Rees, W. E., and Wackernagel, M. (1994) *Ecological Footprints and Appropriated Carrying Capacity: Measuring the Natural Capital Requirements of the Human Economy*. Washington, DC: Island Press.

Reid, J. (2006) *The Biopolitics of the War on Terror*. Manchester: Manchester University Press.

Reiter, D., and Stamm, A. (1998) 'Democracy, war initiation and victory', *American Political Science Review*, 92(2): 377–90.

Rengger, N., and Jeffery, R. (2005) 'Moral evil and international relations', *SAIS Review*, 25(1): 3–16.

Renner, M. (1996) *Fighting for Survival: Environmental Decline, Social Conflict, and the New Age of Insecurity*. New York: W. W. Norton.

Renner, M. (2002) *The Anatomy of Resource Wars*. Washington, DC: Worldwatch Institute.

Reno, W. (1998) *Warlord Politics and African States*. Boulder, CO: Lynne Rienner.

Rieff, D. (2002) *A Bed for the Night: Humanitarianism in Crisis*. New York: Simon & Schuster.

Risse-Kappen, T. (1995) 'Democratic peace – warlike democracies? A social constructivist interpretation of the liberal argument', *European Journal of International Relations*, 1(4): 491–517.

Roberts, A. (1993) 'The UN and international security', *Survival*, 37(4): 7–28.

Roberts, A. (1999) 'NATO's "humanitarian war" over Kosovo', *Survival*, 41(3): 102–23.

Roberts, A. (2005) 'The "war on terror" in historical perspective', *Survival*, 17(2): 101–30.

Roberts, B. (1993) 'From nonproliferation to counterproliferation', *International Security*, 18(1): 139–79.

Roberts, P. (2004) *The End of Oil*. London: Bloomsbury.

Rosecrance, R. (1986) *The Rise of the Trading State*. New York: Basic Books.

Ross, M. L. (1999) 'The political economy of the resource curse', *World Politics*, 51(2): 297–322.

Ross, M. L. (2001) 'Does oil hinder democracy?', *World Politics*, 53(3): 325–61.

Ross, M. L. (2012) *The Oil Curse: How Petroleum Wealth Shapes the Development of Nations*. Princeton, NJ: Princeton University Press.

Rowthorn, B. (2003) 'Migration limits', *Prospect*, 83: 24–31.

Roy, D. (1996) 'The "China threat" issue: major arguments', *Asian Survey*, 37(8): 758–81.

Roy, O. (1994) *The Failure of Political Islam*. Cambridge, MA: Harvard University Press.

Roy, O. (1999) 'Changing patterns among radical Islamic movements', *Brown Journal of World Affairs*, 6(1): 109–20.

Roy, O. (2004) *Globalised Islam: The Search for a New Ummah*. London: Hurst.

Rubin, B. (2002) *The Tragedy of the Middle East*. Cambridge: Cambridge University Press.

Rudolph, C. (2003) 'Security and the political economy of international migration', *American Political Science Review*, 97(4): 603–20.

Rushing, J. (2011) 'Robot wars', *Al Jazeera English*, at www.aljazeera.com/programmes/faultlines/2011/12/2011122512243829505.html (accessed 10 April 2012).

Russett, B. (1993) *Grasping the Democratic Peace: Principles for a Post-Cold War World*. Princeton, NJ: Princeton University Press.

Russett, B., and Oneal, J. R. (2001) *Triangulating Peace: Democracy, Interdependence and International Organizations*. New York: W. W. Norton.

Sachs, J. D. (1999) 'Twentieth century political economy: a brief history of global capitalism', *Oxford Review of Economic Policy*, 15(4): 90–101.

Sachs, J. D., and Warner, A. M. (2000) 'Natural resource abundance and economic growth', in G. M. Meier and J. E. Rauch (eds), *Leading Issues in Economic Development*. Oxford: Oxford University Press.

Safire, W. (2004) 'The farewell dossier', *New York Times*, 2 February, at www.nytimes.com/2004/02/02/opinion/the-farewell-dossier.html (accessed 10 April 2012).

Sagan, C. (1983–4) 'Nuclear war and climate change', *Foreign Affairs*, 62(2): 257–92.

Sagan, S. D. (1993) *The Limits of Safety: Organizations, Accidents, and Nuclear Weapons*. Princeton, NJ: Princeton University Press.

Sagan, S. D., and Waltz, K. N. (2003) *The Spread of Nuclear Weapons: A Debate Renewed*. New York: W. W. Norton.

Sageman, M. (2004) *Understanding Terror Networks*. Philadelphia: University of Pennsylvania Press.

Sageman, M. (2008) *Leaderless Jihad: Terror Networks in the Twenty-First Century*. Philadelphia: University of Pennsylvania Press.

Saideman, S. M. (2001) *The Ties that Divide: Ethnic Politics, Foreign Policy and International Conflict*. New York: Columbia University Press.

Salameh, M. G. (2003) 'Quest for Middle East oil: the US versus the Asia-Pacific region', *Energy Policy*, 31(11): 1085–91.

Sangiovanni, M. E. (2003) 'Why a common security and defence policy is bad for Europe', *Survival*, 45(3): 193–206.

Santamaria, K. (2011) 'War by remote control? Counting the cost', *Al Jazeera English*, 24 December, at www.aljazeera.com/programmes/countingthecost/2011/12/2011121785524212676.html (accessed 10 April 2012).

Sarotte, M. E. (2011) *1989: The Struggle to Create Post-Cold War Europe*. Princeton, NJ: Princeton University Press.

Sarrazin, T. (2010) *Deutschland schafft sich ab* [Germany does away with itself]. Munich: Deutsche Verlags-Anstalt.

Schell, J. (1982) *The Fate of the Earth*. London: Jonathan Cape.

Schelling, T. (1960) *The Strategy of Conflict*. Oxford: Oxford University Press.

Schelling, T., and Halperin, M. (1961) *Strategy and Arms Control*. New York: Twentieth Century Fund.

Schmitt, C. (1976) *The Concept of the Political*. New Brunswick, NJ: Rutgers University Press.

Schweller, R. L. (1994) 'Bandwagoning for profit: bringing the revisionist state back in', *International Security*, 19(1): 72–107.

Searle, J. R. (1995) *The Construction of Social Reality*. New York: Free Press.

Sen, G. (1984). *The Military Origins of Industrialisation and International Trade Rivalry*. London: Pinter.

Shaffer, B. (2009) *Energy Politics*. Philadelphia: University of Pennsylvania Press.

Shaker, M. (1980) *The Nuclear Non-Proliferation Treaty: Origins and Implementation, 1959–1979*. New York: Oceana.

Shambaugh, D. (2011) 'Coping with a conflicted China', *Washington Quarterly*, 34(1): 7–27.

Shawcross, W. (2000) *Deliver Us from Evil: Warlords and Peacekeepers in a World of Endless Conflict*. London: Bloomsbury.

Shaxson, N. (2009) *Nigeria's Extractive Industry Transparency Initiative: Just a Glorious Audit?*, Chatham House Programme Paper, at www.chathamhouse.org/publications/papers/view/109174 (accessed 10 April 2012).

Shirk, S. L. (2007) *China: Fragile Superpower*. Oxford: Oxford University Press.

Shirky, C. (2008) *Here Comes Everybody: The Power of Organizing without Organizations*. London: Allen Lane.

Shirky, C. (2011) 'The political power of social media', *Foreign Affairs*, 90(1): 28–41.

Simmons, S. (2005) *Twilight in the Desert: The Coming Saudi Oil Shock and the World Economy*. Hoboken, NJ: John Wiley.

Simon, J. (1981) *The Ultimate Resource*. Princeton, NJ: Princeton University Press.

Simon, J. (1989) *The Economic Consequences of Immigration*. Oxford: Blackwell.

Simon, J., and Kahn, H. (eds) (1984) *The Resourceful Earth: A Response to Global 2000*. Oxford: Blackwell.

Singer, M., and Wildavsky, A. (1993) *The Real World Order: Zones of Peace/Zones of Turmoil*. Chatham, NJ: Chatham House.

Singer, P. (2009) *Wired for War: The Robotics Revolution and Conflict in the Twenty-First Century*. London: Penguin.

Sjoberg, L. (2010) *Gender and International Security: Feminist Perspectives*. London: Routledge.

Skeldon, R. (1997) *Migration and Development*. Harlow: Longman.

Sloan, S. S. (2010) *Permanent Allliance? NATO and the Transatlantic Bargain from Truman to Obama*. New York: Continuum.

Smil, V. (1994) 'Some contrarian notes on environmental threats to national security', *Canadian Foreign Policy*, 2(2): 85–7.

Smil, V. (1997) 'China's environment and security: simple myths and complex realities', *SAIS Review*, 17(1): 107–26.

Smil, V. (2002) *The Earth's Biosphere: Evolution, Dynamics and Change*. Cambridge, MA: MIT Press.

Smith, A. D. (1995) *Nations and Nationalism in a Global Era*. Cambridge: Polity.

Smith, B. (2004) 'Oil wealth and regime survival in the developing world, 1960–1999', *American Journal of Political Science*, 48(2): 232–46.

Snidal, D. (1991) 'Relative gains and the pattern of international cooperation', *American Political Science Review*, 85(3): 387–402.

Snyder, G. (1984) 'The security dilemma in alliance politics', *World Politics*, 36(4): 461–95.

Snyder, G. (1997) *Alliance Politics*. Ithaca, NY: Cornell University Press.

Snyder, J. L. (1984) *The Ideology of the Offensive*. Ithaca, NY: Cornell University Press.

Snyder, J. L. (1991) *Myths of Empire: Domestic Politics and International Ambition*. Ithaca, NY: Cornell University Press.

Snyder, J. L. (2000) *From Voting to Violence: Democratization and Nationalist Conflict*. New York: W. W. Norton.

Snyder, J. L. (2004) 'One world, rival theories', *Foreign Policy*, 145: 53–62.

So, A. Y. (1990) *Social Change and Development: Modernization, Dependency and World Systems Theory*. London: Sage.

Solignen, E. (2007) *Nuclear Logics: Contrasting Patterns in East Asia and the Middle East*. Princeton, NJ: Princeton University Press.

Solomon, S. (2010) *Water: the Epic Struggle for Wealth, Power and Civilization*. New York: HarperCollins.

Souaidia, F. (2001) *La Sale Guerre*. Paris: La Découverte.

al-Sowayegh, A. (1984) *Arab Petropolitics*. London: Croom Helm.

Soysal, Y. N. (1994) *Limits of Citizenship: Migrants and Postnational Membership in Europe*. Chicago: University of Chicago Press.

Spiers, E. M. (2010) *A History of Chemical and Biological Weapons*. London: Reaktion Books.

Spruyt, H. (1994) *The Sovereign State and its Competitors*. Princeton, NJ: Princeton University Press.

Steans, J. (1998) *Gender and International Relations: An Introduction*. Cambridge: Polity.

Steffen, W., Crutzen, P., and McNeill, J. R. (2007) 'The anthropecene: are humans now overwhelming the great forces of nature?', *Ambio*, 36(8): 614–21.

Stern, J. (1999) *The Ultimate Terrorists*. Cambridge, MA: Harvard University Press.

Stevens, P. J. (2003) 'Resource impact – curse or blessing: a literature survey', *CEPMLP Internet Journal*, 13(14), at www.dundee.ac.uk/cepmlp/journal/html/Vol13/article13-14.pdf.

Stevenson, J. (2004) *Counter-Terrorism: Containment and Beyond*, Adelphi Paper 367. Oxford: Oxford University Press.

Stiglitz, J. E. (2002) *Globalization and its Discontents*. London: Penguin.

Stokes, D., and Raphael S. (2010) *Global Energy Security and American Hegemony*. Baltimore: John Hopkins University Press.

Straubhaar, T. (2000) 'Why do we need a general agreement on movements of people (GAMP)?', in B. Ghosh (ed.), *Managing Migration: Time for a New International Regime?*. Oxford: Oxford University Press.

Stubbs, R. (2008) 'The ASEAN alternative? Ideas, institutions and the challenge to "global" governance', *Pacific Review*, 21(4): 451–68.

Suhrke, A. (1999) 'Human security and the interest of states', *Security Dialogue*, 30(3): 256–76.

Swaine M. D., and Tellis, A. J. (2000) *Interpreting China's Grand Strategy: Past, Present and Future*. Santa Monica, CA: RAND.

Sylvester, C. (1994) *Feminist Theory and International Relations in a Postmodern Era*. Cambridge: Cambridge University Press.

Sylvester, C. (2002) *Feminist International Relations: An Unfinished Journey*. Cambridge: Cambridge University Press.

Takeyh, R. (2004–5) 'Iran builds the bomb', *Survival*, 46(4): 51–63.

Talbot, S. (1995) 'Why NATO should grow', *New York Review of Books*, 10 August.

Tannenwald, N. (1999) 'The nuclear taboo: the United States and the normative basis of nuclear non-use', *International Organization*, 53(3): 433–68.

Tehranien, M. (ed.) (1999) *Worlds Apart: Human Security and Global Governance*. London: I. B. Tauris.

Terry, F. (2002) *Condemned to Repeat? The Paradox of Humanitarian Action*. Ithaca, NY: Cornell University Press.

Teson, F. (1997) *Humanitarian Intervention: An Enquiry into Law and Morality*. Dobbs Ferry, NY: Transnational.

Tharoor, S. (1996) 'The changing face of peacekeeping', in B. Benton (ed.), *Soldiers for Peace: Fifty Years of United Nations Peacekeeping*. New York: Facts on File, pp. 208–23.

Thies, W. J. (2009) *Why NATO Endures*. Cambridge: Cambridge University Press.

Thomas, N., and Tow, W. T. (2002) 'The utility of human security: sovereignty and humanitarian intervention', *Security Dialogue*, 33(2): 177–92.

Thyagaraj, M., and Thomas, R. G. C. (2006) 'The US–Indian nuclear agreement: balancing energy needs and nonproliferation goals', *Orbis*, 50(2): 355–69.

Tickner, J. A. (1992) *Gender in International Relations: Feminist Perspectives on Achieving Global Security*. New York: Columbia University Press.

Tilly, C. (1975) *The Formation of National States in Western Europe*. Princeton, NJ: Princeton University Press.

Tilly, C. (1985) 'War-making and state-making as organised crime', in P. Evans, D. Rueschemeyer and T. Skocpol (eds), *Bringing the State Back In*. Cambridge: Cambridge University Press.

Tilly, C. (1990) *Coercion, Capital and European States, AD 990–1990*. Oxford: Blackwell.

Tishkov, V. (2004) *Chechnya: Life in a War-Torn Society*. Berkeley: University of California Press.

Toset, H. P., Gleditsch, N. P., and Hegre, H. (2000) 'Shared rivers and interstate conflict', *Political Geography*, 19(8): 971–96.

Trager, R. F., and Zagorcheva, D. P. (2005–6) 'Deterring terrorism: it can be done', *International Security*, 30(3): 87–123.

Tripp, C. (2000a) *A History of Iraq*. Cambridge: Cambridge University Press.

Tripp, C. (2000b) 'States, elites and the "management of change" ', in H. Hakimian and Z. Moshaver (eds), *The State and Global Change: The Political Economy of Transition in the Middle East and North Africa*. London: Curzon Press.

Tripp, C. (2002–3) 'After Saddam', *Survival*, 44(4): 22–36.

Tucker, J. B. (2000a) 'Chemical and biological terrorism: how real a threat?', *Current History*, 99: 147–53.

Tucker, J. B. (ed.) (2000b) *Toxic Terror: Assessing the Terrorist Use of Chemical and Biological Weapons*. Cambridge, MA: MIT Press.

Turse, N. (2011) 'Inside our drone base empire', *CBS News*, 17 October, at www.cbsnews.com/stories/2011/10/17/opinion/main20121271.shtml (accessed 10 April 2012).

UKERC (2009) *The Global Oil Depletion Report*. London: UK Energy Research Centre, at www.ukerc.ac.uk/support/Global%20oil%20depletion (accessed 10 April 2012).

Ullmann, R. H. (1983) 'Redefining security', *International Security*, 8(1): 129–53.

UN Commission on Global Governance (1995) *Our Global Neighbourhood*. Oxford: Oxford University Press.

UN World Water Assessment Programme (2012) *Managing Water under Uncertainty and Risk*. Paris: UNESCO.

UNDP (1994) *Human Development Report 1994*. Oxford: Oxford University Press.

UNDP (1999) *Human Development Report 1999*. Oxford: Oxford University Press.

UNEP (2007) *GEO4 Global Environmental Outlook: Environment for Development*. Nairobi: United Nations Environment Programme.

UNESCO (2003) *Water for People: Water for Life*. Barcelona: UNESCO.

UNESCO (2012) *Managing Water under Uncertainty and Risk*. Paris: UNESCO.

UNHCR (2000) *The State of the World's Refugees: Fifty Years of Humanitarian Action*. Oxford: Oxford University Press.

United Nations (2004) *A More Secure World: Our Shared Responsibility. Report of the Secretary-General's High-Level Panel on Threats, Challenges and Change*, at www.un.org/secureworld/report3.pdf (accessed October 2006).

UNPD (2000) *Replacement Migration: Is it a Solution to Declining and Ageing Populations?*. New York: United Nations Population Division.

US House of Representatives (2010) *Rise of the Drones: Unmanned Systems and the Future of War*, at www.fas.org/irp/congress/2010_hr/drones1.pdf (accessed 12 April 2012).

US State Department (2004) *Patterns of Global Terrorism 2003*. Washington, DC: State Department.

Vakil, S. (2004) 'Iran: the gridlock between demography and democracy', *SAIS Review*, 24(2): 45–53.

Valencia, M. A. (2005) *The Proliferation Security Initiative: Making Waves in Asia*, Adelphi Paper 376. London: Routledge for the International Institute for Strategic Studies.

Van Creveld, M. (1991a) *On Future War*. London: Free Press.

Van Creveld, M. (1991b) *The Transformation of War*. London: Free Press.

Van Creveld, M. (1993) *Nuclear Proliferation and the Future of Conflict*. New York: Free Press.

Van Evera, S. (1990–1) 'Primed for peace: Europe after the Cold War', *International Security*, 15(3): 7–57.

Van Evera, S. (1994) 'Hypotheses on nationalism and war', *International Security*, 18(4): 26–33.

Van Evera, S. (1999) *Causes of War: Power and the Roots of Conflict*. Ithaca: Cornell University Press.

Vasquez, J. A. (1993) *The War Puzzle*. Cambridge: Cambridge University Press.

Vincent, R. J. (1974) *Nonintervention and International Order*. Princeton, NJ: Princeton University Press.

Vincent, R. J. (1986) *Human Rights and International Relations*. Cambridge: Cambridge University Press.

Wade, R. (1992) 'East Asia's economic success: conflicting perspectives, partial insights, shaky evidence', *World Politics*, 44(2): 270–320.

Waever, O. (1989) *Security, the Speech Act: Analyzing the Politics of a Word*. Copenhagen: Centre for Peace and Conflict Research.

Waever, O. (1995) 'Securitization and desecuritization', in R. Lipschutz (ed.), *On Security*. New York: Columbia University Press, pp. 46–86.

Waever, O. (2004) 'Aberystwyth, Paris, Copenhagen: new "schools" in security theory and their origins between core and periphery', paper presented at the International Studies Association, 17–20 March.

Waever, O. (2006) 'Insecurity, security and asecurity in the West European non-war community', in J. Zielonka (ed.), *Europe as Empire: The Nature of the Enlarged Union*. Oxford: Oxford University Press.

Waever, O., Buzan, B., Kelstrup, M., and Lemaitre, P. (1993) *Identity, Migration and the New Security Agenda in Europe*. London: Pinter.

Walker, R. B. K. (1993) *Inside/Outside: International Relations as Political Theory*. Cambridge: Cambridge University Press.

Walker, W. (1998) 'International nuclear relations after the Indian and Pakistani test explosions', *International Affairs*, 74(3): 505–28.

Walker, W. (2004) *Weapons of Mass Destruction and International Order*, Adelphi Paper 370. Oxford: Oxford University Press.

Wallander, C. (2000) 'Institutional assets and adaptability: NATO after the Cold War', *International Security*, 54(4): 705–35.

Wallerstein, I. (1974a) 'The rise and future demise of the world capitalist system: concepts for comparative analysis', *Comparative Studies in Society and History*, 16(4): 387–415.

Wallerstein, I. (1974b) *The Modern World System: Capitalist Agriculture and the Origins of the European World-Economy in the Sixteenth Century*. New York: Academic Press.

Walt, S. M. (1987) *The Origins of Alliances*. Ithaca, NY: Cornell University Press.

Walt, S. M. (1991) 'The renaissance of security studies', *International Studies Quarterly*, 35(2): 211–39.

Walt, S. M. (1997) 'Why alliances endure or collapse', *Survival*, 39(1): 156–79.

Walt, S. M. (1998) 'International relations: one world, many theories', *Foreign Policy*, 110: 29–46.

Waltz, K. N. (1979) *Theory of International Politics*. New York: Random House.

Waltz, K. N. (1981) *The Spread of Nuclear Weapons: More May Be Better*, Adelphi Paper 171. London: International Institute for Strategic Studies.

Waltz, K. N. (1988) 'The origins of war in neorealist theory', *Journal of Interdisciplinary History*, 18(4): 615–28.

Waltz, K. N. (1990) 'Nuclear myths and political realities', *American Political Science Review*, 84(3): 731–45.

Waltz, K. N. (1993) 'The emerging structure of the international system', *International Security*, 18(2): 44–79.

Waltz, K. N. (1998) 'Interview with Ken Waltz', *Review of International Studies*, 24(3): 371–86.

Waltz, K. N. (2000) 'Structural realism after the Cold War', *International Security*, 25: 5–41.

Walzer, M. (1983) *Spheres of Justice: A Defence of Pluralism and Equality*. Oxford: Martin Robertson.

Weber, E. (1972) *Peasants into Frenchmen: The Modernization of Rural France*. London: Chatto & Windus.

Weber, M. (1947) *The Theory of Social and Economic Organization*. New York: Free Press.

Weiner, M. (1992) 'Security, stability, and international migration', *International Security*, 17(3): 91–126.

Weiner, M. (1995) *The Global Migration Crisis: Challenge to States and to Human Rights*. New York: HarperCollins.

Weiner, M. (1996) 'Bad neighbours, bad neighbourhoods', *International Security*, 21(1): 5–42.

Weiss, T. G. (2004) 'The sunset of humanitarian intervention? The responsibility to protect in a unipolar era', *Security Dialogue*, 35(2): 135–53.

Weiss, T. G. (2007) *Humanitarian Intervention*. Cambridge: Polity.

Weiss, T. G., and Collins, C. (2000) *Humanitarian Challenges and Intervention*. Boulder, CO: Westview Press.

Welzer, H. (2012) *Climate Wars: What People Will be Killed for in the 21st Century*. Cambridge: Polity.

Wendt, A. (1992) 'Anarchy is what states make of it: the social construction of power politics', *International Organization*, 42(2): 391–425.

Wendt, A. (1999) *Social Theory of International Politics*. Cambridge: Cambridge University Press.

Wendt, A., and Barnett, M. (1993) 'Dependent state formation and Third World militarization', *Review of International Studies*, 19(4): 321–48.

Wheeler, N. (2000) *Saving Strangers: Humanitarian Intervention in International Security*. Oxford: Oxford University Press.

Whetten, L. L. (ed.) (1976) *The Future of Soviet Military Power*. New York: Crane Rusack.

White House (2002) *The National Security Strategy of the United States of America*. Washington, DC: White House.

Whitworth, S. (2004) *Men, Militarism and UN Peacekeeping: A Gendered Analysis*. Boulder, CO: Lynne Rienner.

WHO/UNICEF (2000) *Global Water Supply and Sanitation Assessment 2000 Report*. Geneva: World Health Organization and UN Children's Fund.

Wilkinson, P. (2001) *Terrorism versus Democracy: The Liberal State Response*. London: Frank Cass.

Wilkinson, P. (2003) 'Why modern terrorism? Differentiating types and distinguishing ideological motivations', in C. W. Kegley (ed.), *The New Global Terrorism: Characteristics, Causes, Controls*. Upper Saddle River, NJ: Prentice-Hall, pp. 106–38.

Williams, C. (2012) 'Anonymous attacks FBI website over megaupload raids', *Daily Telegraph*, 20 January, at www.telegraph.co.uk/technology/news/9027246/Anonymous-attacks-FBI-website-over-Megaupload-raids.html (accessed 10 April 2012).

Williams, M. C. (2004) 'Why ideas matter in international relations: Hans Morgenthau, classical realism, and the moral construction of power politics', *International Organization*, 58(4): 633–65.

Williams, P. (1997) 'Transnational criminal organizations and international security', in J. Arquilla and D. Ronfeldt (eds), *Athena's Camp: Preparing for Conflict in the Information Age*. Santa Monica, CA: RAND.

Wittgenstein, L. (1953) *Philosophical Investigations*. Oxford: Blackwell.

Wohlforth, W. C. (1999) 'The stability of a unipolar world', *International Security*, 24(1): 5–41.

Wohlforth, W. C., and Brooks, S. G. (2000–1) 'Power, globalization and the end of the Cold War: reevaluating a landmark case for ideas', *International Security*, 25(3): 5–53.

Wohlstetter, A. (1959) 'The delicate balance of terror', *Foreign Affairs*, 37: 211–34.

Wolf, A. T. (1998) 'Conflict and cooperation along international waterways', *Water Policy*, 1(2): 251–65.

Wolf, A. T. (ed.) (2001) *Conflict Prevention and Resolution in Water Systems*. Cheltenham: Edward Elgar.

Wolf, A. T., Yoffe, S., and Giordano, M. (2003) 'International waters: identifying basins at risk', *Water Policy*, 5: 31–62.

Wolfers, A. (1952) ' "National security" as an ambiguous symbol', *Political Science Quarterly*, 67(4): 481–502.

Wolfers, A. (1959) 'Collective defence versus collective security', in A. Wolfers (ed.), *Alliance Policy During the Cold War*. Baltimore: Johns Hopkins University Press.

Wolff, G. H., and Gleick, P. (2002) 'The soft path for water', in P. H. Gleick et al. (eds), *The World's Water: The Biennial Report on Freshwater Resources, 2002–2003*. Washington, DC: Island Press.

Woodward, B. (2003) *Bush at War*. London: Pocket.

World Commission on Dams (2000) *Dams and Development: A New Framework for Decision-Making*. London: Earthscan.

World Economic Forum (2011) *Water Security: The Water–Food–Energy–Climate Nexus*. Washington DC: Island Press.

World Resources Institute (1998) *World Resources 1998–99: A Guide to the Global Environment*. Oxford: Oxford University Press.

Wucker, M. (2004) 'Remittances: the perpetual migration machine', *World Policy Journal*, 21(2): 37–46.

Wyn Jones, R. (1999) *Security, Strategy and Critical Theory*. Boulder, CO: Lynne Rienner.

Wyn Jones, R. (2001) 'Introduction: locating critical international relations theory', in R. Wyn Jones (ed.), *Critical Theory and World Politics*. Boulder, CO: Lynne Reiner.

Yates, D. A. (1996) *The Rentier State in Africa: Oil Rent Dependency and Neocolonialism in the Republic of Gabon*. Trenton, NJ: Africa World Press.

Yergin, D. H. (1991) *The Prize: The Epic Quest for Oil, Money and Power*. New York: Simon & Schuster.

Yergin, D. H. (2011) *The Quest: Energy, Security and the Remaking of the Modern World*. London: Allen Lane.

Yost, D. S. (2005) 'France's evolving nuclear strategy', *Survival*, 47(3): 117–46.

Yunling, Z. (2000) 'China: whither the world order after Kosovo?', in A. Schnabel and R. Thakur (eds), *Kosovo and the Challenge of Humanitarian Intervention*. Tokyo: United Nations University Press, pp. 117–27.

Zacher, M. W. (2001) 'The territorial integrity norm: international boundaries and the use of force', *International Organisation*, 55(2): 215–50.

Zakaria, F. (1998) *From Wealth to Power: The Unusual Origins of America's World Role*. Princeton, NJ: Princeton University Press.

Zakaria, F. (2002) *The Future of Freedom: Illiberal Democracy at Home and Abroad*. New York: W. W. Norton.

Zakaria, F. (2008) *The Post-American World*. New York: W. W. Norton.

Zartman, I. W. (ed.) (1995) *Collapsed States: The Disintegration and Restoration of Legitimate Authority*. Boulder, CO: Lynne Rienner.

Zeitun, M. (2011) *Power and Water in the Middle East: The Hidden Politics of the Palestinian–Israeli Conflict*. London: I. B. Tauris.

Zielonka, J. (2001) 'How new enlarged borders will reshape the European Union', *Journal of Common Market Studies*, 39(3): 507–36.

Žižek, S. (2008) *Violence: Six Sideways Reflections*. London: Profile Books.

Zolberg, A. R., Suhrke, A., and Aguayo, S. (1989) *Escape from Violence: Conflict and Refugee Crisis in the Developing World*. New York: Oxford University Press.

Zubaida, S. (1993) *Islam, the People and the State*. London: I. B. Tauris.

Zubaida, S. (1997) 'Is Iran an Islamic state?', in J. Beinin and J. Stork (eds), *Political Islam*. London: I. B. Tauris.

Index